THE ELIXIR AND THE STONE

MICHAEL BAIGENT AND RICHARD LEIGH

The Elixir and the Stone

A HISTORY OF MAGIC AND ALCHEMY

arrow books

Published by Arrow in 2005

1 3 5 7 9 10 8 6 4 2

First published in 1997

The Random House Group Limited
20 Vauxhall Bridge Road, London SW1V 2SA

Random House Australia (Pty) Limited
20 Alfred Street, Milsons Point, Sydney,
New South Wales 2061, Australia

Random House New Zealand Limited
18 Poland Road, Glenfield
Auckland 10, New Zealand

Random House South Africa (Pty) Limited
Endulini, 5a Jubilee Road, Parktown 2193, South Africa

The Random House Group Limited Reg. No. 954009

www.randomhouse.co.uk

A CIP catalogue record for this book is available
from the British Library

Papers used by Random House are
natural, recyclable products made from wood grown in
sustainable forests. The manufacturing processes conform to
the environmental regulations of the country of origin

IBSN 0 0994 9002 1

Typeset by Palimpsest Book Production Ltd, Polmont, Stirlingshire
Printed and bound in Great Britain by Bookmarque Ltd, Croydon, Surrey

Une forêt des symboles est la nature
Où le meute cherche la mandagore.

Fouilles-toi, et tu percevras
L'alisier, cormier et alchemilla.

Ave, regina elementorum.

Le riche art de la chimie noire
Vient du sortilège du gros bois.

La cithare saumâtre lave l'hermine
Et la genêt l'ensachant.

Ave, mundi rosa.

Mais sois sans crainte. et tu verras
Le Normand vainc le capétien.

JEHAN L'ASCUIZ

CONTENTS

CONTENTS

LIST OF PLATES

Hermes Trismegistus (copyright: Scala, Florence (Cathedral, Siena))

Thoth standing before Ra (copyright: British Museum, London)

Thoth and Anubis in the Halls of Justice (copyright: British Museum, London)

Dr John Dee, the Elizabethan magus, anon., British School, 1594 (copyright: Ashmolean Museum, Oxford)

A magical seal, designed in wax by Dr John Dee (copyright: British Museum, London)

The Hermetic philosopher (copyright: British Library, London)

The 'Monochord' of Hermetic philosopher Robert Fludd (copyright: British Library, London)

The Hermetic philosopher following the footprints of nature (copyright: British Library, London)

Geometry and divine proportion (copyright: British Library, London)

The College of the Rosicrucian Brotherhood (copyright: British Library, London)

Primavera by Sandro Botticelli (copyright: Scala, Florence (Uffizi, Florence))

Dr Faustus involving the devil (copyright: British Library, London)

Jimi Hendrix in concert (copyright: Petra Niemeier/
Redferns, London)

The Grateful Dead playing at the Great Pyramid, Egypt
(copyright: Adrian Boot/London Features International)

The pyramid form of the stage at the first Glastonbury
festival (copyright: Mick Huston/Redferns, London)

Mysterious blues guitarist Robert Johnson (copyright:
Redferns, London)

Voodoo: ritual dancing in the temple (copyright: Guido
Mangold/Camera Press, London)

Voodoo: the drawing of the *vever* to the god Agwé (copyright: Images Colour Library, London)

Voodoo: the beginning of the ritual (copyright: Guido
Mangold/Camera Press, London)

LIST OF MAPS

ACKNOWLEDGEMENTS

Once again, we gratefully acknowledge the pastoral skills of Ann Evans and Jonathan Clowes, who, displaying a Cistercian virtuosity with loaves, if not fishes, have shepherded us and this book through the traditional writer's wasteland of illiquidity.

We wish also to thank the staff of Arrow, and especially Robin Waterfield, our editor, for his help and support. And we are grateful as well to Sacha Abercorn, Jane Baigent, Ann Baring, Brie Burkman, Lindsay Clarke, Leonidas Goulandris, Belinda Hunt, Sonia Kanikova, Peter Kingsley, Beverly Kleiman, Francis Kyle, David Milne-Watson, Andrew Newmark, Andrew Nurnberg, Isobel Pilsworth, Peter Phillips, John Saul, Esther Sidwell, Lucas Siorvanes, Yuri Stoyanov, Geoff Vanderplank, Jan de Villeneuve, Tatiana Wolff, as well as the staff of the British Library Reading Room, Bloomsbury, and the Warburg Institute, University of London.

INTRODUCTION

Through whom does our civilization seek to define its identity? The answer would at first appear obvious enough. People still speak of 'Christian civilization', 'Christian culture', the 'Christian world'. Although not quite as frequently as in the past, people still speak of 'Christendom'. From such phrases as these, it is clear that Western society flatters itself by regarding Jesus Christ as the defining figure of the reality it has created. In fact, however, the figure who most accurately personifies Western culture is not the lamb-like 'saviour' nailed to a cross. On the contrary, it is a very different figure – the magus, the magician, the sorcerer who, in Renaissance folklore, signed a pact of blood with 'the Devil'. The defining figure for our civilization is not Christ, but Faust.

Faust, or Faustus, endures today primarily, though not exclusively, through two monumental works of literature – Marlowe's play and Goethe's dramatic poem. Both of these works confront Western civilization with an embodiment of its collective identity. Both revolve around a man who, when one first encounters him, has already mastered all spheres of established knowledge, has traversed the entire spectrum of human experience and wonders compulsively where to venture next – wonders what new worlds there are to conquer, what new disciplines there are to investigate, what new domains of knowledge there are to explore. Unlike Jesus

Christ, this figure does not seek to lead others to God, nor even to attain his own personal oneness with God. On the contrary, he seeks nothing less than to become God himself. In pursuit of this quest, he employs the technical apparatus of his age to conjure to his bidding the repository of an immense and untapped power – a power which, by the standards of traditional Christian morality, is labelled 'infernal', 'demonic', 'diabolic', 'satanic'. With the repository of this power, Faustus makes his pact. He will be granted the resources and capacity to achieve everything he wishes to achieve, to obtain dominion over new realms of knowledge, to scale the heights and plumb the depths of human experience, to probe and chart the hitherto uncharted and unknown. And in exchange, at the termination of his allotted span, he will forfeit his soul.

There is an important distinction, however, between Marlowe's sixteenth-century treatment of the story and Goethe's, composed during the last decades of the eighteenth century and the first decades of the nineteenth. At the end of Marlowe's play, Faustus' forfeiture of his soul is permanent, irretrievable, irrevocable and irredeemable. At the end of Goethe's poem, the forfeiture – thanks to the intervention of '*das Ewigweibliche*', the 'Eternal Feminine' or 'Feminine Principle' – is cancelled, and Faust is enabled to attain redemption and salvation.

Today, civilization has an opportunity to write its own collective Faust script. It remains to be seen whether we do so in accord with Marlowe or with Goethe.

PART ONE

I

HERMES, THE THRICE GREATEST

From the very beginning of the human experiment, there have undoubtedly been magicians, shamans, seers, wonder-workers and healers. Long before any historical record, such figures were already performing the sometimes disparate, sometimes overlapping functions of priest, prophet, sage, sorcerer, soothsayer, dream interpreter, diviner, astrologer, bard and physician. Their activities are among the first to appear in recorded history.

In the Middle East, at the dawn of the Christian era, such figures abounded. Indeed, it has sometimes been asserted that Jesus himself was but one of a plethora of wonder-workers or miracle-workers of his time, whose subsequent influence and impact on civilization was merely a fluke. Thus, for instance, according to the late Professor Morton Smith of Columbia University, Christianity was no more than a chance occurrence, which, like so many other histor-ical phenomena, could easily have evolved differently, or not at all. Save for a haphazard concatenation of circumstances, we could have had, instead of two thousand years of Christendom, two thousand years of a religion based on the teachings of, say, Apollonius of Tyana. And certainly Jesus, as he appears in Christian tradition, has much in common with Apollonius.

A native of Tyana, now in Turkey, Apollonius was born early in the first century and died between AD 96 and 98.

An account of his life was composed by the writer Philostratus around AD 220. According to traditions collected and reported by Philostratus, Apollonius healed the sick, raised at least one individual from the dead and, on his own death, ascended bodily to heaven, accompanied by the singing of temple maidens. At an early age, he reputedly embraced Pythagorean thought. A devout vegetarian, he wore his hair conspicuously long. His opposition to blood sacrifice prompted him to adopt garb of linen, rather than of leather, fur or any other animal product. His passionate propensity for philosophical inquiry impelled him to travel extensively – in Italy, Greece, Egypt, Syria and Babylon. He refused to visit Palestine because he believed the Judaic cult of temple sacrifice defiled both the people and the country. Between AD 41 and 54, he resided in India, studying Hindu thought and what remained of Buddhism. Among his devotees was the Roman Emperor Vespasian, who adopted him as a spiritual adviser. Apollonius believed the only valid philosophy pertained to what he called the soul, 'because it is the soul, subject neither to death nor to birth, that is the source of being'.[1]

It would not be difficult to imagine far worse things than two thousand years of a religion based on Apollonius – although, like any other religion, it would doubtless have been warped by time, by social and political pressures, by dogmatism or fanaticism on the part of its adherents. As circumstances fell out, however, Apollonius was, to all intents and purposes, elbowed out of the picture by the so-called course of history; and it is only through the biography of Philostratus – a document of often dubious reliability – that we now know of him at all. Other wonder-workers of the period have been consigned to an even more complete oblivion.

One, however, whether real or fictitious, has survived in

Christian tradition, to be handed down as the prototype of the magician – and thus, by definition, the 'black' or evil magician, the 'first fully developed legend of . . . the black magician' in Western history.[2] This is the figure who appears in the Acts of the Apostles viii, 9–24, as well as in the writings of Church fathers and later commentators, as Simon Magus. It *is* in the guise of Simon that Faust, or Faustus, makes his début.

There is a body of evidence to suggest that the original Simon – or the individual or individuals on whom he is based – was probably an adherent of the 'heresy' known as Gnosticism. One fourth-century Church father, Epiphanius, actually condemns him as being the founder of Gnosticism – a rather implausible assertion.[3] Other ecclesiastical writers depict him as claiming to be the Messiah, the Son of God and even a personification of God the Father. He is described as travelling in the company of a prostitute from Tyre known as Helen, or Helena – implying an intended identification with, if not reincarnation of, Helen of Troy. One of the other names conferred upon her is said to be Sophia, the Gnostic term for the embodiment of Divine Wisdom. According to one commentator: 'Her representation as a harlot is intended to show the depth to which the divine principle has sunk by becoming involved in the creation.'[4]

In scripture and in later Church tradition, Simon functions as a kind of arch-adversary – an avatar of the forces of darkness, of the unholy and unclean powers to which the newly formulated Christian message is diametrically opposed. Thus, in Acts, he appears as a self-proclaimed wonder-worker and would-be Messiah. A charismatic individual with a fervent following of his own, he is – like Peter, but in his more sinister way – a 'fisher of men', or 'fisher of souls'. And when he and Peter meet, he offers the apostle money for the gift of healing by the laying on of hands. In other words, he attempts to purchase the curative power of the Holy Spirit for selfish and venal purposes, whence the sin known as 'simony' derives. He also casts doubts on Jesus' status and questions Peter's authority as apostle.

In later accounts, the encounter culminates with Simon casting down a symbolic gauntlet and challenging Peter to a species of spiritual or magical duel, each having to match the other miracle for miracle.[5] At first, Simon actually does 'outperform' Peter, the wonders he works being more superficially dazzling. Unlike Peter's, however, they stem not from any divine power or mandate, but – by means of mere sorcery – from a more questionable and (according to Christian commentators) demonic source. To that extent, they are sullied, tainted, impure. Flashy though they may be, they are only the products of trumpery, of legerdemain, of hoax or fraud, appealing to the surface of consciousness but having no more profound validity. And, needless to say, Simon, in the traditional accounts, receives his obligatory comeuppance – tumbling from the height to which he has levitated himself, breaking his leg and being discredited.

On the basis of his appearance in Acts, Simon is a minor and inconsequential figure – a venal showman and charlatan, a petty obstacle to be got out of the way as Peter proceeds on his triumphant evangelical mission to the Samaritans. For later commentators, however, he becomes much more than just Peter's paltry rival with God's cards stacked against him. He becomes conflated with no less a figure than the Antichrist – not merely a human adversary, but an embodiment or emissary of the supreme spiritual adversary. For devout Christians, the original arch-magician came to be perceived, by definition, as a 'black' magician, an ambassador of the forces of cosmic evil. The powers he exercised were seen as emanating, by definition, from the ultimate source of iniquity, the Antichrist or the Devil. And all subsequent magicians, to the extent that they practised 'magical' arts, were stigmatized as walking in Simon's footsteps. Given Church teaching, they could not be seen as anything else. They could not, obviously, be regarded as having access to divine power, could not be regarded as latter-day apostles, for that would have challenged the Church's monopoly of such power. And any exercise of power which did not stem from officially sanctioned ecclesiastical sources could only, by definition, be demonic.

Thus Simon Magus paved the way for Faust, the magician who contracts a pact with the Devil. Nor was the relationship between them confined to thematic parallels and a shared association with the shade of Helen of Troy. In German, the word *Faust* means 'fist' – which might perhaps, albeit with some strain, be deemed metaphorically appropriate. In Latin, however, *faustus* means 'the favoured one'; and it is precisely this sobriquet that Simon Magus adopts. According to Professor Hans Jonas:

> It is of interest . . . that in Latin surroundings Simon used the cognomen *Faustus* ('the favoured one'): this in connection with his permanent cognomen 'the Magician' and the fact that he was accompanied by a Helena whom he claimed to be the reborn Helen of Troy shows clearly that we have here one of the sources of the Faust legend . . . Surely few admirers of Marlowe's and Goethe's plays have an inkling that their hero is the descendant of a gnostic sectary, and that the beautiful Helen called up by his art was once the fallen Thought of God through whose raising mankind was to be saved.[6]

In the Acts of the Apostles, Simon Magus does not see himself as genuinely evil, as an emissary of infernal powers. But even at the time – the mid to late first century – such a figure would have been castigated by most Jews, as well as by the adherents of what would coalesce into Christianity. For Jews, he would have been a religious outlaw, operating beyond the pale of the officially sanctioned Temple priesthood, the fiercely nationalistic messianic sects and the devotees of the embryonic rabbinical Judaism. For the adherents of the new religion – whether promulgated by the faction of the early Church under James or by the converts of the maverick Paul – he would have been even worse.[7] He would have been perceived as a rival Messiah, whose claims and activities encroached on and usurped the prerogatives of the only 'true' one. To that extent, he would indeed have been a certifiable 'anti-Christ'.

But if the figure of the magician, embodied by Simon Magus, was a pariah in the Palestine of the New Testament, there were other milieux in which he was altogether more welcome. During the first century, the most important of these milieux was Egypt, and especially the city of Alexandria.

Alexandria: the Heart of Greek Egypt

During the first century of the Christian era, Alexandria was the wealthiest, most urbane, most cosmopolitan, cultured and civilized city of the Graeco-Roman world, and the 'unrivalled centre of world trade'. The population has been estimated at 500,000, far exceeding that of any other Mediterranean metropolis. The city was renowned for its architecture. Among its chief attractions was the famous lighthouse of Pharos, numbered among the seven wonders of the ancient world. Built on the island of Pharos, the lighthouse was connected to the city proper by a causeway 1,300 m in length. The edifice stood 120 m high, the equivalent of a modern forty-storey building. It was constructed of glittering white stone and surmounted by a massive statue of Zeus. At the apex of the structure, a fire was kept permanently burning, its light being reflected far out to sea by an arrangement of magnifying mirrors.

According to one account, the city itself encompassed more than 800 taverns, more than 1,500 bathhouses, more than 2,400 temples and more than 24,000 houses. There were also theatres, a stadium for games, a forum, a large market, an immense gymnasium, numerous public parks and sacred groves. There were lawcourts. There were military barracks. There were innumerable monuments. At the entrance to the Temple of Augustus stood two columns subsequently known as 'Cleopatra's Needles', one of which now stands on the Embankment in London, the other in New York's Central Park. In all these constructions, there was so prolific a use of white marble that the eyes, in sunlight, were said to be dazzled.

Among the city's primary attractions at the time was the embalmed and linen-swathed body of Alexander, brought back from Babylon to the metropolis he had founded. The great commander's body rested in a gold sarcophagus, housed in an immense tomb which became a pilgrimage centre. The sarcophagus is believed to have been stolen around 89 BC by one of the Prolemaic kings who needed money. The tomb survived somewhat longer. Its last appearance in the historical record dates from AD 215, when it was visited by the Roman Emperor Caracalla.

For many people at the time, however, and certainly for posterity, Alexandria's crowning glory was the famous 'Great Library'. By dint of its bibliographical collections, the city had outstripped other centres of study, such as Athens and Corinth, and emerged as the supreme seat of learning for the classical world. In fact, there were two major libraries in Alexandria. One, the larger, was built of white marble and connected with the 'Museum' – originally the

'Mouseion', or 'Shrine to the Muses'. A smaller library, a a daughter, so to speak, of the first house of the temple dedicated to the god Serapis.[8]

The 'Mouseion' was originally a cult centre, a sacred site dedicated to the Muses. Under the Roman regime that replaced the Ptolemys, it acquired a more secular character, evolving into the ancient equivalent of a modern university. Situated adjacent to the sea, it boasted a roofed walkway, an arcade with seats, a communal dining hall for scholars, rooms for private study, residential quarters and probably lecture halls and theatres. Members of its staff and scholars were subsidized by the institution itself. They paid no taxes. They received free meals and accommodation, good salaries and a host of other amenities, including servants.

The 'Mouseion' had been founded between 300 and 290 BC by Ptolemy I, an educated man who enjoyed the company of artists, philosophers, poets and other writers. Ptolemy decreed that all books found on ships in Alexandria's ports were to be seized and copied. The copies were given to the books' owners. The originals were entrusted to the 'Mouseion'. Ptolemy also commissioned copies to be made of books in other libraries, such as that of Athens; and private collections from all over the known world were bought up as well.

Ptolemy's bibliographical zeal was perpetuated by his successors. The library eventually came to consist of ten halls, each dedicated to a different sphere of learning. Like the Pharos lighthouse, it was considered one of the wonders of the ancient world. Texts were preserved in the form of papyrus manuscript rolls, most of them containing two or more separate works. In the days of its greatest glory, the 'Mouseion' held some 500,000 such rolls, while the smaller library, attached to the Temple of Serapis, held another 40,000. Everything was meticulously labelled and

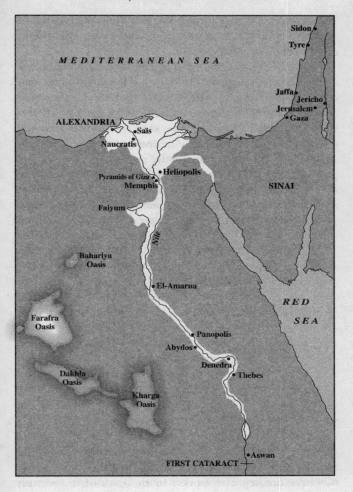

Ancient Egypt under Greek Rule, 332–30 BC

catalogued. And everything was accessible not just to an educated élite, but, freely, to the public at large – to anyone with a desire to learn.

Much of the material held by the city's libraries was in Greek. After the Roman conquest, of course, this material was supplemented by texts in Latin. But there were works in numerous other languages as well, and from much farther afield. There were, for example, commentaries on Zoroastrian sacred writings. And there were also, in all likelihood, copies of ancient Egyptian works.

Like any other library, those of Alexandria were tragically vulnerable to the vicissitudes of war and the excesses of doctrinal fanaticism. In 48 BC, for example, Julius Caesar laid siege to the city. Flames spread from the defeated Egyptian fleet to the buildings on shore, and 70,000 rolls were reportedly destroyed in the 'Mouseion'. Many of these were replaced; but from the end of the third century AD on, the libraries of Alexandria were subject to repeated depredations – from a new wave of Persian invaders, from the Roman Emperor Diocletian, from zealously dogmatic Christians. By the fourth century, the main library, that of the 'Mouseion', seems to have been destroyed – or so reduced as not to warrant any further mention in the historical record. At last, in AD 391, a rabid Christian mob, led by the Patriarch of Alexandria, destroyed the smaller library at the Temple of Serapis, as well as the temple itself. This loss – of the wealth of Alexandria's learning – must be reckoned one of the greatest catastrophes in the history of Western civilization. It constitutes a transgression for which Christianity has never been called properly to account. Christian fundamentalists, even today, are still only too ready to burn books.

The magnitude of the loss can best be illustrated by some of the distinguished names associated with Alexandria and its libraries. Among these 'alumni', so to speak, there was Euclid, the mathematician, whose geometry is still studied today. There was Eratosthenes, who concluded the earth was a sphere and actually worked out its circumference. There was the astronomer and astrologer known as Ptolemy. There was the physician Galen, whose teachings were to influence the next millennium and a half of medical thinking. There was the Egyptian priest and historian Manetho, whose compilation of Egyptian rulers and dynasties is even today, in many quarters, regarded as definitive. There were Church fathers and theologians, such as Origen and Bishop Clement. There were prominent Gnostic teachers, such as Valentinus and Basilides. And there were numerous philosophers, whose work has influenced thinkers ever since – Plotinus, for instance, Proclus and the hellenized Jew Philo.

As the diversity of these figures indicates, Alexandria, at the dawn of the Christian era, was a proverbial melting-pot. The city's population was composed of people from every quarter, every race, every culture, every creed of the known world; and this made for a cosmopolitan metropolis whose modern equivalents can only be found in such centres as London and New York. There were, of course, the native Egyptians. There were representatives from every corner of the Greek-speaking Mediterranean – not just from the Greek mainland and islands, but also from Sicily, Syria, Turkey and Asia Minor. There were Babylonians, Arabs, Persians, Carthaginians, Italians, Spaniards, Gauls from France. And there was the largest concentration of Jews in the world outside Judaea.

Like other ethnic communities in Alexandria, the city's Jews occupied a quarter of their own. Although they looked to Jerusalem for spiritual leadership and paid their annual tax to the Temple there, they had, in their habits, their lifestyle and most other respects, become hellenized. Many had married Greek wives. Many could no longer speak Hebrew; and services in their one large and numerous smaller synagogues were conducted in Greek. There were Greek translations of the Torah. Among the Dead Sea Scrolls found at Qumran, some are in Greek and written on papyrus – which suggests the possibility that they may have originated in Alexandria.[9]

The Jews enjoyed the highest status of any non-Greeks in Alexandria and possessed considerable autonomy. They had their own lawcourts, for example, and their own community leaders. Some rose to exalted positions. One of the Ptolemaic monarchs is said to have entrusted the administration of his entire kingdom, as well as control of the armed forces, to two Jews. Two of the generals in the army of Cleopatra III were Jewish.

When the Ptolemaic dynasty fell, friction inevitably arose between the Jewish community and the new Roman regime, which fostered an increasing and unprecedented anti-Semitism. Palestine, at the time, was in a state of incessant insurgency against Roman occupation, and repercussions of this turmoil radiated across the desert to Alexandria. In AD 66, Judaea erupted in a full-scale rebellion which was to last for the next eight years. As Rome's armies gradually re-established imperial control over the country, many messianic Jewish rebels – Zealots or, as some of them were known, 'Sicarii' – sought refuge in Alexandria, where they endeavoured to foment fresh uprisings.[10] The ensuing riots provoked a dismally predictable backlash. Subsequent insurrections in Judaea intensified the anti-Semitic reaction. By the middle of the second century AD, Alexandria's once populous Jewish community had been decimated.

By that time, Alexandria's own halcyon days were all but over. Yet as late as the fourth century AD, the Roman historian Ammianus Marcellinus could write of Egypt: 'Here, first, far earlier than in any other country, men arrived at the various cradles (if I may say so) of different religions. Here they still carefully preserve the elements of sacred rites as handed down in their secret volumes.'[11] Both Pythagoras and Plato, Ammianus Marcellinus stresses, obtained much of their wisdom from Egypt. And even in the fourth century, he adds, fountains of such wisdom survive in Alexandria:

> . . . yet even now there is much learning in the same city; for teachers of various sects flourish, and many kinds of secret knowledge are explained by geometrical science. Nor is music dead among them, nor harmony. And by a few, observations of the motion of the world and of the stars are still cultivated; while of learned arithmeticians the number is considerable; and besides them there are many skilled in divination.[12]

Ammianus Marcellinus concludes: 'But if anyone in the earnestness of his intellect wishes to apply himself to the various branches of divine knowledge, or to the examination of metaphysics, he will find that the whole world owes this kind of learning to Egypt.'[13]

If Alexandria at its peak was a centre for trade in commodities, it was also a centre for trade in ideas. If it was a melting-pot for diverse peoples, it was also a melting-pot for cults, creeds, beliefs and philosophical systems. The city was, in effect, a nexus, a junction and clearing-house for the learning and knowledge of the entire known world. Within its precincts, virtually every religion and mode of thought was accommodated.

As a kind of sub-stratum, there were the cults deriving from, and often still associated with, the religion of ancient Egypt, extending back to the times of the pharaohs and perhaps before. Superimposed on this sub-stratum, and frequently suffused by it, there were cults to a variety of

Greek deities – as well as to Alexander the Great, the city's founder, and to the Ptolemaic dynasty, whose members had no compunction about deifying themselves. Of particular consequence was the cult of the god Serapis. Serapis can best be described as a deliberately fabricated divinity, calculated and synthesized to appeal to Greeks and Egyptians alike. According to one commentator, Serapis 'was virtually the result of the investigations of a body of philosophers and priests, who collected from all sources and fused together whatever ideas or attributes would be of service'.[14] The cult of Serapis was particularly encouraged by the Ptolemaic dynasty because it transcended religious differences and could be used to maintain civic order. It derived in part from the ancient cult of the sacred bull, Apis, formerly based in the old Egyptian capital of Memphis. This, in turn, had subsumed elements of the even more ancient cult of Osiris. Thus Serapis was often depicted as husband and consort of Isis, the archaic Egyptian mother goddess. Thus inscriptions in Greek addressed to Serapis were, when transliterated into demotic hieroglyphics, addressed to Osiris. For Greek consumption, however, Serapis was amalgamated with Zeus, and the compound name of Zeus-Serapis occurred frequently. Serapis was also associated with other Egyptian deities, such as Amon, and with other Greek gods, such as Poseidon. In every district of Egypt, there was a temple to Serapis. His temple in Alexandria was one of the major architectural features of the day.

Subsequent to the Roman conquest, cults to Roman deities appeared, as well as to Romanized variations of Greek deities; and, as a self-appointed god, the Roman emperor enjoyed his own official cult. There was also a vigorous cult of the eastern Mediterranean goddess Cybele, whose self-castrated priests were, apparently, a common sight in Alexandria's thoroughfares. There was a cult to Ahura-Mazda, the central figure of Persian Zoroastrianism. There were teachers, exponents and practitioners of so-called 'gymnosophy' – of Hinduism, that is, Buddhism and their attendant philosophies, yogic disciplines and methodologies imported from India. And, as previously noted, there were – second only to the Greeks – the Jews.[15]

By the middle of the first century AD, the new creed subsequently known as Christianity had also begun to establish itself in Alexandria. In order to survive and hold its own amid the maelstrom of the city's other beliefs and traditions, it had to adapt. It had to shed certain of the specifically messianic, specifically Judaic, aspects which had characterized it in Palestine. And it had to become more sophisticated, transcending the message preached by Paul to his largely untutored flocks. According to one commentator, 'if Christianity was to be more than a religion for the uneducated it must come to terms with Greek philosophy and Greek science'.[16] As a result, Christianity in Alexandria assumed a radically new direction. Under the auspices first of Bishop Clement, then of Origen, his successor, Christian theologians began to acquaint themselves with Greek thought – with the teachings of the Stoics, for example, and with those of Aristotle and Plato. Thus intellectually equipped, they proceeded to engage in a 'dialogue with paganism' – a dialogue which was to become increasingly 'a dialogue between intellectual equals'. There was often much common ground. Origen, for instance, one of the most influential of the Church Fathers, was a pupil of the same Alexandrian teacher as Plotinus, the founder of the school of pagan philosophy generally known as Neoplatonism. The Christian conception of the Logos was derived from the interpretation of the hellenized Jew, Philo.

The modern mind habitually makes a distinction between theology and philosophy. Theology is perceived as the intellectual formulation, or perhaps rationalization, of a faith, a creed, a system of beliefs pertaining to the divine or the numinous. To this extent, theology is seen as an attempt to address, or account for, the sacred. Philosophy, in contrast, is perceived as something more 'profane', in the traditional sense of that word. Philosophy may be purely secular. It may also, however, be as metaphysical as any theology; but even then it will not be invested with quite the same dimension of the sacred. In most faiths, theology is regarded as divine in origin. Philosophy is essentially human.

In Alexandria during the first centuries of the Christian era – and, indeed, for most of the two subsequent millennia – such fine distinctions did not exist. Theology and philosophy were more or less interchangeable – or overlapped to such a degree that the lines of demarcation between them were indistinguishable. And thus the intellectual ambience of Alexandria was alive not only with diverse faiths and creeds and their attendant theologies, but also with what we today would call philosophical systems; and these enjoyed a comparable respect, a comparable exalted status. Cults, sects, mystery schools and religions in Alexandria were complemented by philosophical teachings. Aristotle, the one-time mentor of Alexander the Great, possessed a considerable following; and Aristotelian thought was subsequently to leave a permanent imprint on Christian doctrine. But Plato was equally revered, and perceived initially as an even more valid link between Christianity and paganism. In mystical philosophers such as Plotinus, Platonic thought was to undergo a major resurgence in the form of what was later called Neoplatonism. Other philosophers were also much in vogue, especially certain of the so-called 'pre-Socratic' teachers with a more or less mystical orientation – Pythagoras, for example, and Heraclitus.

In Alexandria, then, cults, sects, religions, philosophical

schools and systems jostled against each other, contended with each other, cross-fertilized each other, nourished each other in a dynamic and constantly mutating intellectual bouillabaisse. The modes of thought resulting from this interaction are today referred to collectively as 'syncretism'. Alexandrian syncretism was to exercise a determining influence on the evolution and development of Western consciousness, Western attitudes, Western values. And among the most important products of Alexandrian syncretism was the amalgam that would subsequently coalesce into Western magical tradition – the tradition in which Faust, as we have known him since the Renaissance, was steeped. This tradition can most conveniently be called Hermeticism, or Hermetic thought.

The Hermetic Mysteries

And for ages men had gazed upward as he was gazing at birds in flight. The colonnade above him made him think vaguely of an ancient temple and the ashplant on which he leaned wearily of the curved stick of an augur. A sense of fear of the unknown moved in the heart of his weariness, a fear of symbols and portents, of the hawk-like man whose name he bore, soaring out of his captivity on osierwoven wings, of Thoth, the god of writers, writing with a reed upon a tablet and bearing on his narrow ibis head the cuspèd moon.

He smiled as he thought of the god's image for it made him think of a bottlenosed judge in a wig, putting commas into a document which he held at arm's length and he knew that he would not have remembered the god's name but that it was like an Irish oath.[17]

Thus, in *A Portrait of the Artist as a Young Man*, does Stephen Dedalus, Joyce's protagonist, evoke a vision of the tutelary deity presiding over Hermetic thought. Hermeticism derives its name from a figure known as Thoth, or Thoth-Hermes, or Thrice-Great Hermes, or Hermes Trismegistus. Prior to the period of Alexandrian syncretism, Thoth-Hermes was believed to have existed in reality. Plato, for example, had speculated about whether 'Thoth was a god or just a divine man'.[18] For Alexandrian syncretism, he was often (though not always) 'a mortal who receives revelations from the divine world and eventually himself achieves immortality through self-purification, but remains among men in order to unveil to them the secrets of the divine world'.[19] Later – as late, indeed, as the seventeenth century – the figure by then known as Hermes Trismegistus was still believed to have enjoyed an actual historical existence. He was regarded by then as one of the ancient sages and often ranked with Moses, Zoroaster and Pythagoras. According to some commentators, he was believed to have preceded these three, and to have been Moses' mentor.

It is generally accepted today that no single prototype for Thoth-Hermes ever existed in reality. The numerous texts ascribed to him are now acknowledged to be the products of many different authors, whose works were composed over a considerable period of time. But these authors attributed their works to the ibis-headed man-god. They presented their teaching as having been written by him, dictated by him or, at very least, bearing the stamp of his authority.

In earlier Egyptian mythology, the ibis-headed figure was known as Djeuti – pronounced 'Joe-tee'. How his name evolved into Thoth – reminiscent, as Joyce says, of an Irish oath – remains unclear. Perhaps that was how it sounded to Greek ears, or on Greek lips. Neither is it altogether clear why precisely Thoth was 'thrice great'. Some Hermetic texts seem to suggest his triple greatness was a consequence of three incarnations. But his triple greatness was apparently recognized long before these texts were composed. An inscription dating from 172 BC mentions 'Thoth, the three times great'.[20] An even earlier inscription, from the third century BC, alludes to 'Thoth Thrice Greatest'.[21] In ancient Egyptian art, he generally appears as he does in the passage quoted from Joyce – a human figure with an ibis head. At times, however, he is portrayed as wholly ibis. The ibis, at any rate, was his sacred symbol. Cults to him revolved around the ibis, and anyone who killed an ibis was subject to the death penalty. But Thoth was not always confined solely to this manifestation. He was also frequently depicted as a white ape, or white baboon.

As an Egyptian deity, Thoth performed a number of functions. He was a moon god, symbolized by the cusped or horned moon, and silver was sacred to him. He acted as psychopomp – that is, as initiator – into the most arcane mysteries. He served as sentinel or guardian of the gates to the underworld; and in this capacity he weighed the souls of the newly dead in order to determine their posthumous destinies. He was credited with the invention of writing and was often portrayed as he is in Joyce's evocation, inscribing a tablet with a reed. And because writing was perceived as a magical operation – as the 'words of the god' or 'divine words' – Thoth was also regarded as the god of magic, the supreme master magician who confided the secrets of his art to his initiates among mankind.

In certain peripheral respects, Thoth's activities overlapped or coincided with those of the Greek Hermes. Under the Ptolemaic dynasty, therefore, he was conflated with the Greek deity, whose name was compounded with his. But Thoth-Hermes was an even more august figure than his sometime Greek counterpart. Papyrus texts from Alexandria present the new syncretistic Hermes as a cosmic power, creator of heaven and earth and almighty world-ruler. Presiding over fate and justice, he is also lord of the night and of death and its mysterious aftermath – hence his frequent association with the moon (Selene) and Hecate. He knows 'all that is hidden under the heavenly vault, and beneath the earth', and is accordingly much revered as a sender of oracles – many of the magical spells that are addressed to Hermes aim to elicit arcane information, frequently by inducing the god to appear in a dream.[22]

The works attributed or pertaining to Thoth-Hermes are numerous, often opaque, often diffuse. Many of them are suffused with material from diverse sources. Many of them overlap or coincide with certain of the other religions, cults, philosophical traditions and schools of thought that characterized Alexandrian syncretism. There are, for example, the seventeen major dialogues known collectively as *Corpus Hermeticum*. There are some forty excerpts and fragments assembled around AD 500 and included in John of Stobi's *Anthologium*. There are three texts written in Coptic on papyrus and included among the works found at Nag Hammadi, in Egypt, in 1945. There are other fragments which have survived only through selective quotations from early Christian theologians. There are numerous practical works pertaining to astrology, such as the *Liber Hermetis*, and to alchemy. Finally, there are two somewhat later works of particular importance. One is the magical and astrological *Picatrix*. The other, and perhaps most famous, is the so-called *Tabula smaragdina* or *Emerald Tablet*. This last has generally been regarded as the most succinct and, at the same time, definitive summation of Hermetic thought.

Hermeticism reflects a tradition diametrically opposed to that of Aristotle's Athenian rationalism. It sometimes, indeed, declares itself explicitly to be incompatible with the prevailing Greek mentality, invoking instead the mysteries of ancient Egypt. In the sixteenth dialogue of the *Corpus Hermeticum*, for example, Thoth-Hermes declares that the meaning of his work

> will be entirely unclear when the Greeks eventually desire to translate our language to their own and thus produce in writing the greatest distortion . . . But this discourse, expressed in our paternal language, keeps clear the meaning of its words. The very quality of the speech and the sound of Egyptian words have in themselves the energy of the objects they speak of.[23]

In Hermeticism, as in Hebrew and in the later Judaic Kabbala, sounds, words, even individual letters, can be the equivalent of storage cells, repositories charged with a form of divine or magical power as a battery is charged with electrical energy.

In general, Hermeticism is a mystical tradition, a mystical body of teachings, a mystical mode of thought. Like other such traditions, bodies of teaching and modes of thought, it repudiates simplistic belief and blind faith. It repudiates codified dogma and the interpretative necessity and authority of priests. It also refuses to accept the rational intellect as the supreme means of cognition, the supreme arbiter of reality. Instead, it emphasizes and extols the mystical or numinous *experience* – direct and first-hand apprehension of the sacred, direct knowledge of the absolute.

Hermetic and Gnostic

In the vocabulary of Alexandrian syncretism, the word used to denote such direct knowledge was 'gnosis'. That word has led to an unfortunate muddle of terminology which has been perpetuated through the centuries and obtains even today. By dint of this muddle, Hermeticism has often been confused with what is generally called 'Gnosticism', or 'Gnostic thought'. The word *gnosis* simply means direct knowledge. To that extent, Hermeticism is indeed 'gnostic' in orientation. But so, too, were many of the other cults, sects, bodies of teaching and schools of thought in Alexandria at the time. For that matter, many forms of Hinduism, Buddhism and especially Taoism could be considered 'gnostic'. So could certain forms of Christianity, Judaism and later Islam.

As it happened, however, the term 'gnostic', in the world of Alexandrian syncretism, was most frequently employed by schools of thought which were specifically *dualist*. Dualism, as the word itself suggests, presupposes an opposition, often a conflict, between two antithetical principles, two antithetical hierarchies of value, two antithetical realities. In dualism, certain aspects or orders of reality are extolled over others. Certain aspects of reality are repudiated as unreal, or inferior, or evil. In its distinction between soul and body, between spirit and 'unregenerate nature', Christianity is, in effect, dualist.

In the world of Alexandrian syncretism, the word 'gnosis' was most frequently employed by dualist sects who drew a distinction between spirit and matter. Matter was rejected as intrinsically evil. Material creation, the phenomenal world, was deemed to be the handiwork of a lesser and malevolent god. In consequence, matter and material creation had to be transcended in order to attain union with a greater and truer god, whose domain was pure spirit; and it was this union that the term 'gnosis' signified. Such was the orientation of Alexandria's dualist sects. Their thinking had probably originated in the similar dualism of Persian Zoroastrianism. It was subsequently to surface again in

Persia, under a teacher known as Mani, and to be called Manicheism. It was to surface yet again, later, in Europe, with the medieval heresies of the Bogomils and the Cathars.[24]

Simply by virtue of their emphasis on the word, 'gnosticism' became inextricably associated with Alexandria's dualist sects. The identification, erroneous though it was, proceeded to stick; and for many people today, 'gnosticism' and 'dualism' are synonymous. The dualist sects, in effect, divided reality. They labelled a portion of reality evil and repudiated it. 'Gnosis' for them constituted a transcendence of material creation and an apprehension of, or union with, pure spirit. In this process, everything that makes humanity most deeply human was left behind as well.

For Hermeticism, in contrast, there was ultimately only one everything. Reality in all its aspects was embraced as a single all-pervasive, all-encompassing totality, a single whole in which all dichotomies, all distinctions between body and soul, spirit and matter, were accommodated and harmoniously integrated. Everything, in its own way, was valid. Everything was incorporated in the comprehensive design. Even evil, while being confronted and acknowledged as such, had its place in the overall plan. In Goethe's *Faust*, Mephistopheles introduces himself, with rueful self-directed irony, as a principle which constantly intends wickedness, but inadvertently achieves goodness by performing its required role in the moral and cosmic drama of reality. This attitude is characteristically Hermetic. And for the Hermeticist, as opposed to the dualist, 'gnosis' entailed direct apprehension of, and integration with, the all-inclusive harmony.

Within this harmony, everything was interconnected with everything else through a mesh of interlocking relationships. Such relationships rested on the principle of analogy. Things echoed other things, reflected other things, mirrored other things, paralleled other things, corresponded to other things. Reality comprised an intricate, incessantly vibrating and *living* web of correspondences. These correspondences were like notes or chords of music, recurring in ever new combinations and permutations, and thus contributing to a single grand symphony. Or they could be compared to a multitude of different coloured threads, interwoven with each other to create a single seamless fabric or tapestry. According to the *Emerald Tablet*, 'the above comes from below, and the below from above – the work of the miracle of the One'.[25] In a more widely circulated translation, 'that which is above is like that which is below, and that which is below is like that which is above'.[26] This premise has often been abridged to the simple formula 'As above, so below'.

The Way of Hermes

The *Emerald Tablet* elaborates further: 'The structure of the microcosm is in accordance with the structure of the macrocosm.'[27] In other words, the lesser mirrors the greater and the greater the lesser. The structure of the atom mirrors that of the solar system, while the structure of the solar system mirrors that of the atom. Man mirrors the cosmos, and vice versa. And the same principle, by extension, applies, so to speak, horizontally. The world within and the world without mirror each other. The universe contained within the human psyche mirrors the external universe, which can be conceived of as the 'psyche' of the living and sentient totality – or, if one wishes to employ the term, of God, who, in the Judaeo-Christian tradition, 'creates man as his mirror image'.

For the Hermeticist, the analogies or correspondences connecting the diverse skeins of reality were best expressed by symbols. Thus, for example, the interrelationship between microcosm and macrocosm was traditionally denoted by the famous 'Seal of Solomon' – a six-pointed star composed of two interlocking triangles, the apex of one facing upwards, the apex of the other downwards. Such symbols were not, however, merely a convenient shorthand. On the contrary, they were like sounds, letters and words in Egyptian and Hebrew – repositories or storage cells of power, batteries holding a latent charge of energy. These symbols, often called 'seals' or 'signatures', were like cross-stitches in the fabric of reality, the interlacing holding the mesh together. Reality thus comprised, as Baudelaire was to assert nearly two millennia later, a 'forest of symbols'. And what was more, these symbols could be 'activated' in a practical manner. Symbols could be manipulated, like elements or molecules in chemistry, to form new compounds, new amalgams of possibility. By virtue of such manipulation, change could be effected. The process whereby it was, constituted a form of magic: 'Recent research has done much to show how important a place the practice as well as the theory of Theurgy – that is, the "performing of divine actions", chiefly with the aid of magical "symbols" or *symbola* – occupied . . .'[28]

Hermeticism was thus more than just a theory, more than just another philosophical system. It also offered a concrete methodology whereby its tenets could be translated into practice. This methodology encompassed mental disciplines, such as meditation, memory training and breath control, as well as even more practical applications, such as alchemy. To that extent, Hermeticism had much in common with Chinese Taoism, which originated much earlier but was still flourishing around the same time. And indeed, adherents of Hermeticism would often speak of the 'Way of Hermes', implying not just a corpus of teachings, but their practical application. The word 'Tao' also means 'Way', and Taoism incorporated a similar practical dimension. There is no evidence of any cross-fertilization between Taoism and Hermeticism. China is a considerable distance from Alexandria; and the distance was even more considerable in the first centuries of the Christian era. But it is, at very least, striking that Taoist alchemy should appear in China at the same period that Hermetic alchemy appeared in Alexandria.

Hermetic thought was profoundly influential in the tenets it explicitly enunciated. It was profoundly influential in the methodology it proffered for applying those tenets and translating them into practice. But it was, if anything, even more important in the implications, the ramifications, the repercussions to which it opened a door. These implications, ramifications and repercussions were never expressly stated – and certainly not in the kind of language used here. In pursuing them, however, Hermetic practitioners were to effect nothing less than a revolution in the history of Western consciousness, in man's orientation towards the cosmos he inhabited and towards his own life and destiny.

In the past, man's orientation towards the cosmos had been essentially passive. He could observe the natural world. He could monitor its workings and try to predict such phenomena as occurred around him. But he did not believe himself capable of bringing about any significant change beyond his immediate circumstances and environment. He did not believe himself capable, through his own agency, of effecting the kind of change we associate today with, say, physics or chemistry. In order to produce such change, man had to beseech his gods to act on his behalf, and pray for them to aid him by their intervention, their intercession. The gods were the agency through which things happened, and man was entirely at their mercy. Man might treat with them, might try to persuade them, might try to placate them with sacrifices and rituals. Independent of them, however, he himself exercised no power that enabled him to shape reality to his will.

Hermetic thought provided the basis for a new orientation, which enabled man to abandon his passivity, transcend his helplessness and assume a more active role. For if everything were indeed interconnected, man himself, by acting effectively in the sphere accessible to him, could make things happen to other spheres. If one pulled a particular string or thread in the tapestry of reality, something else, in some other quarter of the tapestry, would ensue. With Hermeticism, an entirely new concept entered human thinking – the concept that one could 'press a button', metaphorically or even literally, and cause something to occur. Instead of remaining helplessly passive, therefore, man could himself become an active agent. He could embark energetically on a quest for the means whereby change could be produced in the world around him, as well as in himself. For good or ill, he could proceed to manipulate circumstance.

As a result of this new orientation, man ceased to be merely a victim of reality. He ceased, likewise, to be merely an observer of the world around him. He could now become a determining force – provided he could discover the requisite keys, the requisite 'pressure points', so to speak, whereby reality could be manipulated and made to respond to his will. There was thus inaugurated a radically new and vigorously dynamic investigation of the cosmos and its workings. This investigation was to establish the foundation for Western magical tradition. It was also to establish the foundation for a great deal more – including, not least, scientific exploration. For the Alexandrian Hermeticist, indeed, the distinction between magic and science was, to all intents and purposes, non-existent. It continued to be non-existent for the Renaissance figure of Faust. One could reasonably argue that it remains non-existent today.

Alchemy

If Simon Magus, the original Faustus, had been misplaced amid the Jews and early Christians of the Holy Land, he would have found a congenial ambience in the bosom of Alexandrian syncretism. His chief problem would have been the risk of getting lost among too many others like him, too many rival magicians, too many Hermetic adepts and practitioners. Alexandria, towards the beginning of the Christian era, was virtually awash with prototype Faust figures. Among the earliest, dating from Ptolemaic times, one might cite Bolus of Mendes, who promulgated a fusion of Egyptian and Pythagorean thought. Bolus has been described as 'a crucial figure in shaping the subsequent development of Graeco-Egyptian alchemy, and it is no doubt largely as a result of his influence that we find Pythagoreanism and alchemy starting to overlap. He also shows the closest of affinities with the world of the magical papyri . . .'[29]

And there were women alchemists as well, female Faust figures. One practitioner, for example, was known as Cleopatra, and is credited with a statement strikingly similar to the opening of the *Emerald Tablet*: 'Tell us how the highest descends to the lowest, and how the lowest rises to the highest.'[30] And there was a shadowy personage known only as Maria the Jew, who is tentatively believed to have lived during the early second century AD and survives solely through quotations ascribed to her by later Hermeticists.[31] Some evidence exists to suggest that she invented the technique of alchemical distillation, as well as the equipment needed to perform it.

But if any one individual stands out conspicuously among Alexandria's Hermeticists, it would probably be that of the alchemist known as Zosimus of Panopolis, who lived in the late third century AD. In Zosimus, one finds clearly enunciated a premise that was to become central to the Faustian figures of the Renaissance – that alchemy was essentially a spiritual discipline, a species of 'objective correlative', a reflection in the external world of an ultimately internal process. As one commentator observes, spiritual experiences for Zosimus 'may be explained by material metaphor'.[32] Alchemy, in other words, serves as a vehicle for spiritual purification, and the 'procedures of conventional alchemy are strictly preparatory to the purification and perfection of the soul'.[33]

2

HERMETIC MAGIC, ALCHEMY AND ISLAM

At the heart of Asia Minor, in the desert of southern Turkey, lies the modern town of Urfa, formerly the ancient city of Edessa. Twenty-five miles to the south-east, on a tributary of the Euphrates, stands a village too small to figure on most maps and, near by, a forlorn cluster of crumbling ruins. On this site, guarding the caravan road which linked the Persian Gulf to the Mediterranean, there once stood the mystic city of Harran, as shrouded by legend in its day as centres like Lhasa in Tibet were later to be.[1] Harran is still revered in Judaic, Christian and Islamic tradition. Here, according to the Old Testament, the patriarch Abraham sojourned on his journey from Ur to Canaan. At the presumed time of Abraham's journey, and for centuries both before and after, Harran was dedicated to the Babylonian moon god Sin. By the eighth century AD, however, another moon god had come, in effect, to preside as the city's tutelary deity – Thoth-Hermes, or Hermes Trismegistus.

With the burning of its libraries, Alexandria had gone into decline as a centre of learning. Christian orthodoxy had increasingly stifled the dynamic interchange of thought and traditions that had characterized the period of syncretism; and the thinkers, philosophers and teachers who had once imparted such vitality to the city were scattered to the winds. Edessa, near Harran, had offered a haven for some of them.

Here, during the late second and early third centuries, Hermetic thought had been promulgated by the religious teacher Bardaisan, whose skill in debate had won praise even from such orthodox Church authorities as Eusebius. Bardaisan has traditionally been regarded as the mentor of Mani, the prophet around whom the dualist creed – or heresy – of Manicheism coalesced. And in Manicheism, Hermes Trismegistus was ranked along with Zarathustra, Plato, Buddha and Jesus as one of the 'Heralds of the Good One to the World'.[2]

Edessa, however, never approximated Alexandria as a centre of learning. Insofar as any place could, it was the older intellectual centre of Athens. Here, for example, the Neoplatonic philosopher Proclus presided over the Academy in the fifth century.[3] But here, too, the new faith of Christianity imposed itself, offering its customary bounty – salvation in the next world as recompense for intolerance in this one. In AD 529, the Emperor Justinian – whose predecessor, Constantine, had presided over the Roman Empire's embrace of Christianity two centuries before – closed the Academy of Athens. Hounded by zealous Christians, the last teachers decamped eastwards. They found a temporary refuge at the court of the king of Persia, and then apparently disappeared from the stage of history. It now appears, however, that they, or their disciples, found a new refuge at Harran, where an academy was established that lasted at least until the tenth century.[4] In any case, Hermetic thought, when it re-emerged, did so at Harran, which seems to have become the new centre of Hermetic studies.

Baghdad and Harran

By this time, the religious and political character of the Mediterranean world had changed dramatically. The once mighty Roman imperium had fragmented into two halves, each boasting its own emperor and promulgating its own form of Christianity. The western half of the old imperium, centred in Rome, had then collapsed, being overrun by 'barbarian' invaders migrating from the north and east. The eastern half – the Byzantine Empire, with its capital of Constantinople – still maintained an ostensibly stable existence, but its foundations were brittle, vulnerable and precarious. Nevertheless, Constantinople had supplanted Alexandria as the greatest city of the Greek-speaking east.

In addition to these traumatic changes, there was another, of even greater consequence. Its agent was a travelling merchant known to the world today as Muhammad. According to some accounts, Muhammad was descended from a family of heterodox, perhaps even heretical, Christians. In any case, he was subject to increasingly compelling spiritual calls, and would often retreat to meditate in desert caves. In one, he underwent a numinous experience that transformed him. He emerged to begin preaching against idolatry and extolling the supremacy of a single God, or Allah, for whom Jesus was but one in a sequence of prophets. To this single supreme God, Muhammad taught, everyone owed humble 'submission', the Arabic word for which is *Islam*. Muhammad's sermons on 'submission', or Islam, were collected into the book known today as the Koran. For Muslims, Muhammad is deemed to be but a vehicle, a conduit. The Koran is deemed to have issued directly from God himself.

Muhammad embarked on a campaign to disseminate his faith – if necessary, by holy war and the sword. In AD 622 – the year with which the Muslim calendar officially begins – he moved to the small town of Yathrib, which changed its name to Medinat al-Nabi, 'the City of the Prophet', now known as Medina. In 630, he and his followers captured the

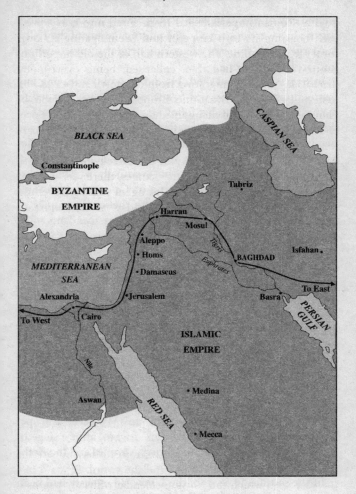

The Arab World in the Middle East, eighth century AD

sacred city of Mecca in what is now Saudi Arabia. The city's pagan idols were destroyed. The pilgrimage site of the Ka'ba – a large black stone of meteoritic origin – was converted into an Islamic shrine.

In 632, Muhammad died. He did so without leaving any instructions about who was to succeed him, and this led to factional strife among his followers. There ensued years of dispute, intrigue and assassination, from which emerged the two main rival branches of Islam that exist today, the Shi'ite and the Sunni. Although the former were never extirpated, it was the latter, the Sunni, who eventually wrested political control and assumed the title of *Caliph*, which means 'successor'. From 661 until 750, the theocratic empire of Islam was ruled by the Umayyad dynasty, descendants of an aristocratic family from Mecca. Their domains came to extend from the Straits of Gibraltar in the west to Samarkand and the Punjab in the east. In 711, they invaded Spain. By 714, they had conquered the whole of the Iberian peninsula except for a Christian enclave in Galicia. Shortly thereafter, an Arab army crossed the Pyrenees into France and, in 719, captured Narbonne, which became a regional capital. From Narbonne, Islam advanced up the valley of the Rhône into the French heartland. Its progress was eventually halted at the battle of Poitiers in 732, by Christian forces under the Frankish ruler Charles Martel, grandfather of the figure subsequently known as Charlemagne. Poitiers constituted the high-water mark of Islam in Western Europe. Thereafter, the tide was rolled back. In 759, after a siege of seven years, Narbonne fell to Christian armies and the Arabs withdrew beyond the Pyrenees.

In the meantime, in 750, the Umayyad dynasty had been overthrown by a rival family, the Abbasids. One of the last Umayyad princes escaped to Spain, where his successors were to continue in power for another three centuries, ruling from their capital of Cordoba. The rest of the Islamic world, however, passed into Abbasid hands. They abandoned their predecessors' capital of Damascus and proceeded to build a new capital city for themselves. This city – officially founded in 762 at a moment calculated as propitious by astrologers – was Baghdad.[5] For the next five hundred years, while Europe floundered through the so-called Dark Ages, Baghdad was to be the most cultured and civilized centre west of the Indian subcontinent.

In AD 830, the Caliph of Baghdad, while campaigning against the Christian armies of the Byzantine Empire, passed through Harran. Among the crowds thronging to receive him, he observed a number of curiously dressed individuals who he guessed were not Muslims. He accordingly asked them who they were and to which 'people of a book' they belonged.[6] By Koranic law, Islam extended protection and tolerance to any 'people of a book'. This was the term for adherents of other religions founded on sacred texts pertaining or attributed to figures whom Islamic teaching recognized as prophets – Moses, for example, Zoroaster, Jesus or the Buddha. Jews, Zoroastrians, Christians and Buddhists were all, therefore, 'peoples of a book'.

In response to the caliph's query, the curiously dressed individuals replied, reportedly, that they were simply Harranians. Dissatisfied with this vagueness, the caliph demanded a more precise answer. Were his interlocutors Jews, Christians or Zoroastrian magi? When they remained evasive, the potentate grew petulant and pronounced them infidels, subject to execution. They were given an ultimatum. By the time he returned from his campaign, the caliph said, the so-called 'Harranians' would have to declare themselves – as Muslims, or as some other recognized 'people of a book'. If they failed to do so, they would be punished under Islamic law.

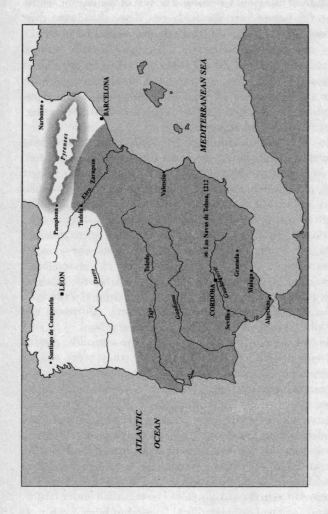

Islamic Spain: the emirate of Cordoba

Some of those under threat did indeed convert, to Islam or to Christianity. Others, however, consulted an expert on Islamic law, who advised them to call themselves 'Sabians', since the Sabians – a people from Saba (or, in the Old Testament, Sheba), the region of southern Arabia now comprising Yemen – were officially recognized in the Koran. This appellation was accordingly adopted, even though the caliph died before he could return to act on his ultimatum. His successors, and subsequent Islamic authorities, proceeded to accord to the self-styled 'Sabians' a formally acknowledged recognition and protection. But to ratify their status, they were required to name the book or books which constituted their sacred scripture. In compliance with this obligation, they cited certain of the texts ascribed to Hermes Trismegistus. Thus Hermeticism became, in effect, the official religion of the 'Sabians', acknowledged and recognized as such by Islamic authority; and thus the 'Sabians' of Harran became the custodians of Hermeticism, preserving it intact while other schools of thought were subsumed by Islam, Judaism or Christianity.

In Harran, Hermeticism thrived. And from Harran, it is believed, there issued a new Hermetic text, and one of the most important of all for later magical tradition. It was to become notorious among devout Christian scholars, a supreme specimen of the 'forbidden book'. As late as the end of the last century, for example, one commentator so loathed and feared it that he 'hoped it may never be translated into any modern language'.[7]

In Arabic, the book in question is called the *Ghayat al-hakim*, or *Goal of the Wise*. Through a mistranslation of the name of the Arab author to whom it was erroneously attributed, it is known to Western scholars as the *Picatrix*. The *Picatrix* is, in effect, a guide, a textbook and manual for the practice of astrological magic.

Astrology had originated in the oldest of human cultures,

the Mesopotamia of the ancient Sumerians and Babylonians. From there, it had filtered down through the centuries and across the civilized world. It had flourished during the period of syncretism in Alexandria, and figured prominently in Hermetic thought. In positing a planetary influence on terrestrial phenomena, it had been regarded as a supreme illustration and manifestation of the Hermetic premise which linked macrocosm and microcosm, 'above' and 'below'.

The *Picatrix* further consolidated the position of astrology in the overall context of Hermetic thought. 'All things in this world,' it asserted, 'obey the celestial forms.' And: 'All sages agree that the planets exercise influence and power over this world . . . from this it follows that the roots of magic are the movements of the planets.'[8] The *Picatrix* then went a step further by making astrology as practical, in magical terms, as alchemy. It offered the aspiring magician meticulously detailed instructions for invoking, manipulating and deploying on earth the celestial influence of the planets. It focused in particular on what it called 'talismans', which it compared explicitly to the alchemical elixir. Through the proper design and construction of a 'talisman', and through proper performance of the rituals associated with it, the magician could control the energy emanating from heavenly spheres. In the form of angelic entities or spirits, he could, for instance, command the powers of Mars in matters of war, of Venus in matters of love. The Hermetic practitioner thus learned how 'to draw these celestial spirits down to the earth and to induce them to enter into a material object (a talisman), which thereupon possesses well-defined magical powers'.[9]

From such procedures, there emerged, in the *Picatrix*, a portrait of 'Hermetic man', who is described as 'the magus, the sage, the master of Heaven and Earth'.[10] In this way,

'Hermetic man' became the nexus, the junction, the point of intersection between macrocosm and microcosm, the greater world and the lesser: 'I tell you that man is called a world, and this is by comparison to the greater one, just as one says that whatever is contained in the greater world, is contained naturally in the lesser one.'[11]

In Harran, the *Picatrix* was integrated with the corpus of earlier Hermetic texts, from Alexandria, from elsewhere in the Greek world, from Syria, from Edessa, from pre-Islamic Arab sources. And it was in large part from Harran that Hermeticism filtered out into the mainstream of Islamic culture, exercising an influence on, among other things, Islamic science and mathematics. Harran, in effect, served as a repository and clearing-house through which the Hermetic traditions of Alexandria found their way into the very heart of Islamic civilization. According to one commentator, 'In the Muslim world, Hermeticism must be considered as one of the most important factors which aided in the construction of the Muslim world view.'[12]

To cite an example, one Arab writer mentions his knowledge of twenty-two works of Hermes Trismegistus – four on magic, five on astrology and thirteen on alchemy.[13] There were numerous Arabic translations of earlier Hermetic texts, and numerous original Arabic works ascribed to Hermes. Needless to say, there was also considerable latitude for confusion. Certain Islamic scholars, for instance, mistakenly identified Hermes Trismegistus with a figure named 'Idris', who is mentioned in the Koran. The sobriquet of 'Trismegistus' was sometimes misconstrued as referring to three separate figures bearing the name of Hermes. One was equated with 'Idris' and believed to have lived prior to the Flood. The second was believed to have resided in Babylon and served as mentor to Pythagoras. The third was placed in Egypt during the period of Alexandrian syncretism. But whether perceived as a single or as a tripartite figure, Hermes was extolled as the original fount of prophetic wisdom, the first teacher of science and philosophy. He was associated with magic, alchemy, astrology, 'everything that had to do with miraculous powers and wisdom'.[14] And 'through him it became possible for Muslims to integrate Greek science and philosophy into their world view without feeling that they were going in any way outside the prophetic tradition'.[15]

Hermeticism, and especially alchemy, was embraced with particular enthusiasm by Sufi circles. Masters of the Sufi school in Baghdad produced treatises on alchemy and were subsequently associated with alchemical legends. Alchemical terminology was often used in expounding Sufi teachings: 'The Sufi master . . . operates upon the base metal of the soul of the disciple and with the help of the spiritual methods of Sufism transforms this base metal into gold.'[16] According to the founder of one Sufi order: 'It is we who through our glance turn the dust of the path into gold.'[17] In Sufism, 'the world is a fashioning instrument which polishes mankind'.[18] The 'Great Work' of the alchemist meant for Sufis what it had meant for Zosimus, the spiritual transmutation of the man; and the elixir, or the Philosophers' Stone, became a symbol of this inner integration and completion. Sufi masters also incorporated the Hermetic doctrine of correspondence, of the interrelationship of macrocosm and microcosm, into their teachings. Many Sufi texts run perfectly parallel to those of the Hermetic corpus.

The most famous, important and influential of Arab alchemists, Jabir ibn Hayyam (c. 721–c. 815), was also a Sufi. In his work, Jabir laid the foundations for all subsequent Islamic alchemy. He promulgated a comprehensive cosmology which closely echoed Alexandrian Hermeticism in its orientation. He drew an analogy, to become immensely significant later, between the alchemist and the Creator, whereby 'man is described as a microcosm and, at the same time, as the image of God, insofar as he is able to know everything and to perform miracles'.[19]

As far as is known, Jabir was the first to introduce animal and vegetable products – blood, urine and bone marrow, for example – into alchemy. He was also instrumental in disseminating to the Islamic world the Pythagorean principle of number. He displayed in his work an enormous erudition, which included a familiarity with alchemy and philosophy as far afield as China. It was in Jabir's books that the earliest extant text of the *Emerald Tablet* appeared, though it is ascribed to much older sources. At the same time, Jabir and his circle wrote on a multitude of other subjects – on mathematics, on magic, on astrology and astronomy, on medicine, on mirrors, on military ordnance such as siege machinery, on mechanical statues or automata. For many years, he lived in Baghdad as court alchemist to the caliph Harun al-Raschid, famous today through *The Thousand and One Nights*. Something of that book's magic, mystery and power of enchantment undoubtedly derives from Jabir and his circle.

By the tenth century, Baghdad had become a centre of learning for the entire Islamic world, with a bustling community of philosophers, teachers, writers and translators. There was even a substantial Jewish community, estimated at some 40,000, members of whom pursued studies in the works and disciplines subsequently known as Kabbala. Hermeticism had always had close links and parallels with esoteric Judaic thought; and it is not, therefore, surprising to find references to schools of Judaic alchemy. Indeed, Hermeticism can now be seen as having emphasized, if not established, many key points of contact between Islam and Judaism, such as a shared view of Old Testament prophets. By the end of the first millennium, it was poised to make its début in

Christian Europe. Before it could do so, however, Christian Europe had to acquire the intellectual sophistication and open-mindedness necessary to receive it.

3

DARK AGE MAGIC

During the first millennium, Hermetic thought did not, of course, exercise an exclusive monopoly over the development of magic. India and China, for example, had their own magical and alchemical traditions, which spread to Tibet, Burma, Korea and Japan. In many aspects, these traditions long pre-dated Alexandrian Hermeticism. But they would not have found Hermeticism – or, at any rate, its basic premises – uncongenial. Taoist alchemy, to cite but one instance, worked with elements other than, or in addition to, the Western quaternity of earth, air, fire and water. For the Taoist alchemist, wood was sometimes also regarded as an element. But in their underlying principles – the correspondence of above and below and of inner and outer, the interrelationship of all things, the capacity to effect transformation by 'pressing the right buttons' – the alchemical traditions of the East harmonized with their Western equivalent. And through the gymnosophists of Alexandria, Indian thought, both Vedic and Buddhist, had contributed something uniquely its own to the coalescence of Hermeticism.

In Western Europe, during the so-called Dark Ages, there was also a magical tradition; but it had little in common with Hermeticism. Among the Slavic and Teutonic peoples, there was the conventional shaman – the tribal soothsayer or 'witch doctor'. In the Celtic world, there were rather more sophisticated figures – the druids, whose roles and activities overlapped those of the bard or, as he was known in ancient Ireland, the 'ollave'. In the absence of a written language, the shaman, the druid, the bard or ollave exercised a species of priestly function. The absence of a written language rendered him heavily dependent on memory; and training of the memory (which was also taught in Mediterranean cultures) became one of the 'tricks of his trade'. His feats of memorization were often prodigious. And eventually, the 'art of memory' from both Mediterranean and Celtic sources, was to fuse with Hermeticism and become an integral component of Western esoteric tradition.

Because of the absence of writing, the druid, the bard or the ollave was, in effect, a living and walking book – if not, indeed, a living and walking library. In his memory reposed the history, the legends, the customs, the legal codes, the entire heritage and self-definition of the tribe or people. To this extent, he was an august and powerful personage, who enjoyed a status at least as sacred as that of any later Christian priest. According to a tradition regrettably not preserved today, the bard of ancient Ireland was authorized to appear on a battlefield and, by a simple command, impose a truce between warring factions. Anyone who defied his edict was deemed accursed.

Pronouncing a curse constituted an act of magic – primitive magic by Hermetic standards, but magic none the less. It often produced an electrifying effect even on those unfamiliar with the traditions in which it was rooted. The Roman historian Tacitus describes a confrontation in AD 61 between imperial soldiery and Celtic warriors: 'The enemy lined the shore in a dense armed mass. Among them were black-robed women with dishevelled hair like Furies, brandishing torches. Close by were Druids, raising their hands to heaven and screaming dreadful curses.'[1] The effect was more than a little unnerving. 'This weird spectacle awed the Roman soldiers into a sort of paralysis. They stood still – and presented themselves as a target.'[2]

If magic of this kind could cow well-trained and disciplined Roman troops, it was all the more intimidating for the people among whom it was an enshrined practice. The Celtic bard was often profligate with his magical curses; and for him, as for the Hermeticist, words and names were intrinsically powerful. By 'naming' a man – by invoking him specifically in a poem, a so-called 'satire' or an imprecation – the bard could bring affliction down upon him, and upon his descendants as well, usually 'unto the seventh generation'. Not surprisingly, this capacity invested the bard with considerable latitude for inspiring terror. According to an ancient Irish proverb, 'Cursed be the man who lifts his hand against a poet.' Such a malediction involved more than petty personal vindictiveness. If the poet was the incarnate legacy and heritage of the people as a whole, any harm visited upon him was, if only symbolically, a harm visited upon the people as a whole. The culprit who perpetrated such harm was accordingly an outcast, an outlaw and duly accursed – the pagan equivalent of excommunicate.

If only as faint echoes, vestiges of such attitudes have persisted in Ireland to the present day. They are reflected, albeit wanly, in the esteem with which the poet is regarded. He is still mantled in a faint aura of magic, a faint nimbus of sacred awe; and his words are accorded more weight and significance than they would be anywhere else in Western Europe. In England, for example, poetry is deemed merely a triumphant adornment of the national culture, and plays a meagre role in most people's daily lives. In France, poetry is cherished, even brandished, as an essential expression of the culture, but only in a secular context. In Ireland, poetry is not just integral to the culture, but imbued, as well, with a quality verging on the spiritual, the orphic, the oracular; poetry is still invested with something that approximates the sphere of organized religion. Language – especially poetic language – still retains a residue of magic, with a power, for good or ill, to enchant. Poetry, in other words, is puissant. And whatever the opprobrium merited by terrorists of all factions in Northern Ireland, they must be granted one point in their favour. Unlike other fanatics – who issue death sentences against men producing works of the creative imagination – those in Ulster have always displayed a virtually sacerdotal respect for the magic of the word in serious literature.

But the magic of the ancient Celts, like that of the ancient Teutons and Slavs, cannot be regarded as in any sense Hermetic. It may perhaps have contained elements similar to those from which Hermeticism evolved. The druids of Celtic France and the British Isles, for example, are thought to have subscribed to such principles as reincarnation and the immortality of the soul; and this caused certain classical writers to fancy they were influenced by Pythagorean thought. That would seem unlikely – although, given Greek commerce with Celtic Europe, it cannot altogether be discounted. Yet despite such parallels, the magic of the European Dark Ages remained fairly primitive. It might express itself in curses, in petty witchcraft, in soothsaying, healing and divination, in purely localized phenomena, at most in such things as rain-making. It lacked, however, the all-encompassing cosmological, metaphysical, epistemological and psychological framework that characterized Hermeticism. It could not be utilized 'to make things happen' on any scale other than the parochial and immediate. And unlike Hermeticism, it could not provide the foundations for what would evolve into scientific investigation – and, eventually, scientific manipulation of reality. According to the delineations established by the Faustian magi of the Renaissance, it remained confined to the realm of 'low magic', or 'conjuration'.

If one thinks of magic during Europe's Dark Ages, the figure who springs most immediately to mind is, of course, Merlin. For many people, Merlin is indeed the archetypal magician, the archetypal sorcerer, the archetypal wizard. But the Merlin who enjoys such status is not, in fact, a product of the Dark Ages. On the contrary, he is a literary creation of the High Middle Ages, of medieval culture at its peak. He is the magician as perceived during the thirteenth and four-teenth centuries, projected backwards into the sixth – just as the knights and the chivalric code of a later epoch were projected back into a legendary Arthurian Britain.

If there was an historical prototype for Merlin, he would have existed towards the middle or the end of the sixth century – the period generally ascribed to Arthur, assuming *he* actually existed. Vague and shadowy images of this earlier Merlin survive in Welsh legend and literature through the figure known as Myrddin. But Myrddin is a very different personage from the imposing, august and majestic mage of later Arthurian romance. He may possibly have been a druid, or a seer influenced by druidic thought.[3] On the whole, however, he emerges as not essentially different from a tradi-tional tribal shaman and soothsayer. And so far from being endowed with a supernatural, almost godlike, authority, he is more victim and martyr than anything else – a persecuted visionary, hounded by his own people, repudiated and outcast. He might have advocated, displayed or been cred-ited with a pantheistic relationship to nature and the natural world. His gifts, such as they were, might have consisted of a typical shamanistic ability to communicate with animals, to change shape, to induce trance in himself and others, to read the meaning of dreams, to perform acts of divination. He might have been deemed capable of interpreting things, of foreseeing things, but not of orchestrating things, engineering things, or causing them to happen. His magic, again, would have been petty, parochial and materialistic compared to the lofty, highly spiritualized magic of the Hermeticist.

The Church absorbs Pagan Magic

In Hermeticism, magic was embedded in a complex and sophisticated psychological, theological and cosmological framework. Measured by such standards, the magic of Europe's Dark Ages was a primitive affair. To say that, however, is not to minimize its influence, or the tenacious resilience and durability which enabled it to survive. Every European community, from large urban centres down to remote hamlets, had its own witches and wizards. In a simplistic, yet often no doubt quite effective manner, they ministered to local people's bodies and souls – as physicians and midwives, as herbalists and weather forecasters, as interpreters of omens and dreams, as dispensers of advice, as the equivalent in their time of the modern psychological counsellor or psychotherapist. The efficacy of some of their herbal and homoeopathic remedies has recently begun to receive renewed, if grudging, recognition from the medical establishment.

In the Europe of the Dark Ages, such magic was widely feared and condemned by ecclesiastical authorities and their secular representatives. Writing in the sixth century, Gregory, Bishop of Tours, recounted how the death of a prince was ascribed to a magical incantation and provoked a witch-hunt culminating in the execution of 'a number of Parisian housewives'.[4] In the early ninth century, Charlemagne passed stringent laws against magic, designed primarily to Christianize – or, at least, tame – the pagan tribes of northern Germany. These laws provided a precedent for much of the persecution which followed. That persecution, instigated sometimes by hysteria, sometimes by cynical calculation, continued into the early eighteenth century and eventually extended across the Atlantic – to Salem, Massachusetts, for example, and to much of Latin America. It is a sorry chapter in the history of Western civilization and of Christendom, but one familiar enough not to require recapitulation here. Suffice it to say that tens, perhaps hundreds of thousands of hapless victims were tortured, hanged, drowned, burned at the stake or subjected to some other gruesome form of death, often on no more valid a basis than a knowledge of herbal lore, an envious neighbour's vindictive denunciation or an inquisitor's sanctimonious and self-righteous zeal.

Despite the persecution visited upon it, pagan magic survived. Well into the twentieth century, there were isolated rural communities which subscribed to it, and some are alleged to survive even today. During the last quarter of a century, moreover, numbers of people, alienated by the perceived hollowness of organized religion, have begun to embrace pagan magic anew. In modern Britain, there are estimated to be upwards of twenty thousand adherents of Wicca, the so-called 'Old Religion', or witchcraft. This, contrary to popular assumption, has nothing to do with conventional concepts of Satanism. On the contrary, Wicca and Satanism are radically different systems of belief and practice, more likely to be hostile to each other than sympathetic. Wicca, or witchcraft, is a survival of ancient pre-Christian paganism. At first, it probably had no theology, no conceptual framework, being more an accumulation of empirical practices and techniques than a system of belief. Only later, as it was forced to explain and justify itself to a nominally Christianized world, did a conceptual framework evolve. This framework can loosely be described as a species of mystical pantheism, a rapport with and respect for the natural world that many people today would find eminently laudable. It would also anthropomorphize natural forces as pagan gods and goddesses; and through this process, a confusion arose – deliberately fostered on the Church's part – with Satanism.

According to a long recognized truism, the gods of any given religion become the demons of the religion that supplants it. Thus, for example, Astarte – the mother goddess of the ancient Phoenicians, the so-called 'Queen of Heaven' and 'Star of the Sea' – had her titles hijacked, was subjected to a forcible sex-change operation and transformed into the demon Astaroth. In classical Rome, Pan, the god of nature, was depicted as horned, bearded, with cloven hoofs and a goat's tail. In the context of the time, Pan was certainly not 'evil'. He simply embodied the forces of the natural world, not least of which was sexual energy and its manifestation in fertility. To Christianity, however, nature was, by definition, 'unregenerate', 'fallen', still in need of redemption; and sexuality was not only regarded with mistrust, fear and loathing, but was also – except in the circumscribed institution of marriage – stigmatized as 'sin'. In consequence, the god of 'unredeemed' nature and of sexual energy became axiomatically wicked, an embodiment of 'evil'. And thus the horned, cloven-hoofed and goat-tailed god of nature was transformed by Christian doctrine into the Devil.

A similar process was imposed on the nature gods of northern Europe, many of them also horned – the figure known as Herne the Hunter, for example, or the Celtic deity Cernunnos. They, too, lent themselves to deliberate conflation and confusion with the Christian Devil. But for most practitioners of the 'Old Religion', Christian theology simply did not exist, was not recognized. 'Sin', in the Christian sense, had no more meaning for them than it might today for a Hindu or a Buddhist. And their devotions to their horned god did not reflect any exaltation of evil, but a simple reverence for nature and the forces of the natural world.

In many places, the Church tacitly admitted defeat in the attempt to extirpate the 'Old Religion', and endeavoured, instead, to co-opt or subsume it. Throughout much of supposedly Christian Europe, Christianity was in reality only a façade, an artificial superstructure imposed from without, which left the strata beneath it more or less intact. Peasants would attend the requisite services on Sundays, would observe the holy days designated by the Church, would make the requisite obeisance to the ecclesiastical hierarchy, would pay their tithes – and, while the priesthood turned a blind eye, would continue to practise the rites of the 'Old Religion'. In this manner, rituals such as the *Walpurgisnacht* – the 'Witches' Sabbath' – survived, with its orgiastic sexual frenzy and its initiatory drug ergot, a potent hallucinogen which produced the sensation of flying. There is some evidence to suggest that the 'voices' supposedly heard by Jeanne d'Arc, and ascribed to Sts Michael, Catherine and Margaret, were in fact a superficial Christianization of figures originally invoked in a Wicca ritual. Thus does the novelist Thomas Keneally, author of *Schindler's Ark* (or *Schindler's List*), depict Jeanne in one of his earlier narratives, *Blood Red, Sister Rose*. Keneally's depiction is as plausible as any other, and more plausible than many.

If the 'saints' whose voices Jeanne heard could ultimately be traced to pagan figures in Christian guise, it would hardly have been unusual. Many pagan deities were suborned in this fashion. So, too, were their shrines and sacred sites. At first, the Church was coy about such procedures, feeling obliged to prevaricate and rationalize them. In AD 398, for example, St Augustine wrote:

> And when temples, idols, groves, etc., are thrown down by permission from the authorities, although our taking part in this work is a clear proof of our not honouring, but rather abhorring, these things, we must nevertheless forbear from appropriating any of them to our own personal and private use; so that it may be manifest that in overthrowing these we are influenced, not by greed, but by piety. When, however, the spoils of these places are applied to the benefit of the community or devoted to the service of God, they are dealt with in the same manner as the men themselves when they are turned from impiety and sacrilege to the true religion.[5]

A mere two centuries later, however, Church policy on such matters had become flagrantly unabashed. In 601, Pope Gregory I wrote that he had

> come to the conclusion that the temples of the idols among that people [of England] should on no account be destroyed. The idols are to be destroyed, but the temples themselves are to be aspersed with holy water, altars set up in them and relics deposited there. For if these temples are well-built they must be purified from the worship of demons and dedicated to the service of the true God. In this way, we hope that the people, seeing that their temples are not destroyed, may abandon their error and, flocking more rapidly to their accustomed resorts, may come to know and adore the true God. And since they have a custom of sacrificing many oxen to demons, let some other solemnity be substituted in its place, such as a day of Dedication or the Festivals of the Holy Martyrs whose relics are enshrined there.[6]

In accordance with this policy, Christian churches, abbeys and cathedrals were generally built on sites of pagan worship. The pagan cults dedicated to deities and heroes were transformed through relics into Christian cults dedicated to saints and martyrs. The pagan mother goddess revered at numerous sacred sites was simply Christianized, baptized, so to speak, and subjected to a forcible conversion. Most of the Notre Dame churches scattered across France were originally consecrated to very different ladies – to Isis, for example, like the Virgin of Le Puy, to Rosmerta, patroness of the river Meuse, or to Arduina, tutelary deity of the Ardennes.[7] By re-dedicating them, the Church 'purified' and 'sanctified' the shrines devoted to such figures and adapted them to its own mother goddess, the Virgin Mary – who was often conflated or confused with the Magdalene.

For the peasantry who worshipped at the place, however, the change in nomenclature made little difference, one mother goddess being quite as good as another. They continued to pay homage to the same deity, regardless of what the Christian ecclesiastical hierarchy chose to call her. Much the same situation obtained elsewhere in Europe. In Ireland, for example, the pagan mother goddess Brigit, patroness of fire, was simply conflated with the alleged daughter of a druid, a woman said to have converted to Christianity and founded a religious community. Canonized as St Brigid, the pagan deity was thus rendered spiritually hygienic, and worship of her became legitimized.

If pagan magic survived through the nominal Christianization of deities and sacred sites, it survived through other forms as well. There were, for example, the romances revolving around the so-called Holy Grail. One thinks of these romances as being distinctly Christian. The Grail, after all, is generally depicted as a specifically Christian relic. By the twelfth century, it had certainly become that. But the Grail romances of the twelfth century are products of the Crusades and reflect a process of hybridization – a sometimes strained grafting of Judaeo-Christian material on to much older narratives of pagan Celtic origin. These older narratives have nothing in any way Christian about them. They are sometimes called the 'pagan Grail' stories. And the Grail which figures in them has nothing whatever to do with Jesus. It is, on the contrary, a magical cauldron in which the wounded can be healed, the dead restored to life. And the protagonist of the 'pagan Grail' stories is not Percival or Parzival, still less the later Lancelot or Galahad, but Gawain, whose quest entails restoring the land to fruitfulness.

The same hero serves as protagonist in another work drawing on material contemporary with that of the 'pagan Grail' narratives, *Gawain and the Green Knight*. This work, emerging from the heart of supposedly Christian Europe, is an unabashed portrayal of pre-Christian pagan magic. The Green Knight is a depiction, in medieval chivalric terms, of the ancient Celtic vegetation deity – the northern equivalent of Pan, who presides over the cycle of the seasons, the sowing and reaping of the harvest, the birth, death and rebirth of the year. The poem reflects the quixotic futility of man's attempts to interfere with these natural processes – the puniness of his efforts, however pious, to meddle with the course of nature.

The vegetation deity of *Gawain and the Green Knight* surfaces in a multitude of other guises as well. In England, to cite but one example, he appears repeatedly as the so-called Green Man, carved unobtrusively in church embellishments amidst more standard and orthodox Christian iconography. The Green Man is often conflated with Herne the Hunter, Cernunnos and other similar horned deities. If there is any difference between them at all, it might be that the Green Man presides over the vegetable kingdom, Herne and his cognates over the animal. All of them, however, are manifestations of the natural order.

Perhaps the most flagrant and popular manifestation of the Green Man is in the medieval figure of Robin of the Greenwood – the Robin Goodfellow, or Puck, of *A Midsummer Night's Dream*. By Elizabethan times, the former vegetation deity of fertility has dwindled to the physical stature of a fairy; but his powers remain undiminished. Even in Shakespeare's play, he functions as a tutelary genius of the mating process. By extension, he is associated – like the bird of the same name – with the advent of spring and the world's renewal into fertility.

In a letter to *The Times* in 1994, an eminent politician complained about alleged plans to abolish the May Day bank holiday. May Day, the author of the letter argued, was a day long enshrined in the traditions of the labour movement and, as such, deeply rooted in the popular psyche – a day of special importance to all 'working people'. In making this assertion, the author of the letter would appear to be displaying the woeful ignorance of history that character- izes only too many politicians today. Given the honourable gentleman's known erudition, however, he is more likely to have been displaying another trait notoriously afflicting politicians – an edited, slanted and selectively partisan version of history.

Long before May Day became sacred to the working class and the traditions of international socialism, it had a special and very different significance in European popular culture. In medieval England, as well as elsewhere, May Day was a fertility festival, celebrating the return of spring, the renewal of the year and the fecundity of the earth. To sow the earth was perceived as a sexual act, a form of pagan sexual magic. For the peasantry of the time, therefore, May Day was a day of sexual licence, of unbridled orgy. The traditional maypole was endowed with explicit phallic implications. The chosen 'Queen of the May' was a thinly disguised avatar of the pagan mother goddesses who had figured saliently in Wicca and other pre-Christian creeds. She and other village virgins would troop off to the adjacent forest, where they would be received by 'Robin of the Greenwood' and his 'merry men' -- or, to be more accurate, by an individual, a local youth or perhaps a seigneur, clad in apparel designed to evoke spring's harbinger. In the frolics that followed, 'Robin' would confer on the girls their sexual initiation. Or he might, in some cases, confer his blessing on the mating of already plighted couples. And nine months later, the village would spawn a winter crop of bastards, who would be known as 'sons of Robin'. It was often from these rituals that such surnames as 'Robinson' derived.

According to a somewhat affronted Elizabethan commentator, 'all the young men and maids, old men and wives, run gadding over night to the woods, groves, hills and mountains, where they spend all night in pleasant pastimes'.[8] The same commentator concludes, on a note of outrage, 'I have heard it credibly reported . . . that of forty . . . or a hundred maids going to the wood over night, there have scarcely the third part of them returned home again undefiled.'[9]

As 'Robin of the Greenwood', the ancient pagan fertility god or Green Man also became conflated with Robin Hood -- and may even, to some degree, constitute the core of the Robin Hood legend. Thus, for example, in 1555, the dour Presbyterian Parliament of Scotland banned a play which had regularly been performed, every May, at Rosslyn Castle by itinerant mummers. The play was known as *Robin Hood and Little John*, and so popular was it that two towers of the castle had come to be known as 'Robin Hood' and 'Little John'. 'No one,' the Parliament primly pronounced, 'should act as Robin Hood, Little John, Abbot of Unreason or Queen of May.'[10] The phraseology of the edict is revealing. The 'Abbot of Unreason' is, of course, Friar Tuck – who, in his original pagan form, presided over the forces of 'unregenerate nature' and anarchy, and conferred his blasphemous parody of a Christian blessing on the May Day fertility rites. The 'Queen of May' was the figure preserved in legend as Maid Marian, with whom every village girl became identified in her sexual initiation by 'Robin'.

In all of these pagan vestiges and residues, an element of magic figured prominently – as it did in such ostensibly innocent things as Morris dancing, mummers' plays, even in many so-called nursery rhymes. Again, however, it was a purely localized magic, often a specifically sexual magic, vested in the mysteries of procreation and reproduction. By analogy, it could sometimes be extended to aspects of the natural world, in such activities as, say, rain-making. But it posited, in man's relation to everything beyond himself, a premise of passivity. Man, in other words, could beseech, could appeal, could *attempt* to placate the unknown forces around him, but could not presume to control or command them. Myrddin may have been a magician of sorts. He had not yet, however, evolved into Merlin, still less into Faust.

Nevertheless, the Church feared him and the powers he represented. As early as the beginning of the fourth century, the Ecclesiastical Council of Elvira pronounced an excommunication on anyone who caused a death through magic – an admission, in effect, that death by magic was indeed a possibility, even a threat. In 667, the Council of Toledo 'deplored the saying of masses for the deaths of enemies'.[11] At the same time, Welsh clergy believed that a requiem mass said ten times over a man's waxen image would cause the man's death within ten days. The gods and goddesses of the 'Old Religion' were certainly not dismissed as facile superstition.

On the contrary, they were regarded as demons who represented a constant peril, even to true believers. And their spokesmen, their emissaries, their ambassadors were dangerous individuals, who could not be ignored, but had to be overcome and neutralized.

Thus, for example, in Irish legend, St Patrick often engages in wonder-working contests with druids. In one such contest, a druid placed in a hut made of green wood is burned alive, while Patrick, in a hut of dry wood, remains unharmed by the flames around him. In another contest, Patrick levitates a druid high into the air, and then lets his adversary drop and be dashed to death on the rocks.[12] The echoes of Peter's exploits in the Acts of the Apostles are obvious. If druidic figures such as Myrddin had not yet attained full-fledged Fausthood, they could still be equated with Simon Magus.

In response to the threat posed by such figures, the Church began to evolve a magic of its own – or, in certain instances, a species of counter-magic. This was exemplified by, among other things, the cult of relics. Saints were invoked as protectors against pagan magic, and devotions to saints 'rapidly came to involve the digging up, the moving, the dismemberment – quite apart from much avid touching and kissing – of the bones of the dead . . .'[13] To establish the site of a saint's cult, it was necessary at first to have at least a small part of his or her body – a finger, for instance, a lock of hair, even a prepuce. This fragment of flesh, however small, established that the saint was actually present at the site in question, and could be addressed personally in worship. Subsequently, it became sufficient to use objects which had merely come into contact with the saint's body, or which the saint had blessed. By some process of spiritual osmosis, such objects were deemed to contain something of the saint's intrinsic virtue. The traffic – and often theft – of relics played an important role in the spread of the Church across Europe. And there were also, of course, portable relics for personal use, relics which could be carried by the individual from place to place – such as splinters of the True Cross. These things functioned, in effect, as magical amulets or talismans, which neutralized, or 'disinfected', the magic of pre-Christian paganism.

A somewhat more sophisticated form of Christian magic – which might even be said to incorporate rudimentary elements of Hermeticism – involved the use of sound. Sound, of course, had always had a magical significance, from the chant and drum beat of primitive shamanism to the complex correspondences of Hermetic thought – which established linkages between the *pneuma* (the Greek word for both 'spirit' and 'breath'), the Logos, or Word, as creative principle, and the Pythagorean harmonies, or 'music of the spheres'. Christianity had adopted a quasi-Hermetic conception of the Logos as creative agent and also linked it with the *pneuma* in the form of the Holy Spirit.

Christian magic in the Europe of the Dark and Middle Ages rested frequently on a simplified adaptation of such premises. The human voice, for example, when performing a ritual religious function, became a vehicle for the spirit. Prayer thus became a species of magical act – a divinely inspired invocation or evocation. And thus, too, did Gregorian chant evolve. It was sung in unison, unaccompanied, and using a sacred text. And it required arduous training, especially in breath control, so as to focus and direct the *pneuma*, or spirit, effectively. Modern research has discovered that Gregorian chant can produce tangible psychological and physiological results.[14] It can often have a healing effect. It can increase stamina by providing a transfusion of invigorating energy. This was particularly necessary for medieval monks, obliged to perform eight ritual offices, day and night, in every twenty-four hours. In recent experiments, monks deprived of the opportunity to chant quickly succumbed to lassitude and fatigue.

Another form of sound-oriented Christian magic involved the employment of the bell. There is some reason to suppose that Christianity's use of the bell also derived from Pythagorean sources by way of Hermeticism. In Pythagorean and Hermetic thought, there are correlations between sound and shape, sound and configuration. Sound can provide a shape and a direction to energy. Thus, for example, the sound of a horn or trumpet can be visualized as a 'blast', a gust or a thrust of force flaring outwards in a fan-shaped configuration from the instrument. In its nature and character, it is essentially aggressive and belligerent, essentially warlike. Thus it could be used to indicate the direction in which soldiers charged. Thus, too, it could be depicted, in almost cartoon fashion, as the explosive impetus enabling Joshua's trumpets to bring down the walls of Jericho.

The sound of a bell, in contrast, would be depicted as something very different – as concentric circles radiating out from a central point, like ripples from a stone dropped into a pool. This quality would be augmented if the bell were ringing from above, so that its peal reverberated downwards and outwards with an ever-widening diameter. The bell, moreover, unlike such instruments as the ram's horn or the reed flute, was man-made. It was not a form of by-product, or detritus, of the natural world. It was deliberately forged for a sacred purpose. It therefore represented the triumph of man, created in God's image, over 'unregenerate nature'. When used in a religious context, it, too, like the human voice, became a vehicle or conduit for the spirit.

One of the earliest references to bells being used in Christian churches is by Gregory of Tours, writing in the late sixth century. The bells he describes, however, are small hand-bells, rung as a call to prayer. They do not appear, at that time, to have been particularly common. Neither would they seem to have been integrated officially with religious ritual and rite. When they became so remains uncertain; but by the tenth century, large bells, hung aloft in belfries, were already in widespread existence, and incorporated as an integral component of Christian observance. Such bells were cast from bronze, with the same skills subsequently deployed for the manufacture of cannon. The manufacture of bells entailed a process of painstaking care and sacerdotal reverence. When finished, they were officially and ritually 'blessed' in a complicated ceremony which amounted to a form of baptism. Each bell was sprinkled with holy water, purified, sanctified, consecrated and anointed repeatedly with oil – 'to make the devil flee at the sound of it'.[15] It was not uncommon for bells to be named, just as swords were, Arthur's Excalibur being perhaps the most famous.

It may be difficult for us today to appreciate the psychological and spiritual significance of the bell throughout the Dark and Middle Ages. One must first understand the chronic and all-pervasive terror in which pious Christians of the time lived. Human settlements – whether towns and villages or simply abbeys and monasteries – were few, isolated and remote from one another. Between them, covering most of the landscape, were vast expanses of uninhabited and ominous forest. In the dark, brooding depths of these tracts of 'unregenerate nature' lurked a plethora of physical and spiritual perils – evil spirits, werewolves, demons in the guise of pagan gods and goddesses, innumerable other 'unclean' or 'unholy' powers, as well, of course, as wild beasts and all too human outlaws, marauders and 'heathen' hostile to the Church. Each Christian settlement was a lonely and vulnerable enclave in the wilderness, surrounded on all sides by a multitude of potential threats, whether real or imagined. Against these threats, the orotund peal of the bell constituted a protective magic circle, a stockade of sound, so to speak, the spiritual equivalent of a defensive perimeter. Such a perimeter comprised a bulwark and rampart against the anarchy encroaching from without. Within the hallowed safety of the perimeter, a divinely ordained and regulated order prevailed.

The bell's peal was a manifestation of this order. Among other things, it marked the hours, dividing the day into methodically fixed units, each consecrated by specific offices and prayers. Thus was God's gift of form and structure imposed on the amorphous fluidity of time. The bell's division of time into measured units was one of a number of devices whereby the forces of chaos, darkness and evil, 'gathered unseen in the air', were held at bay and warded off. According to a provincial Church council in Germany, 'at the sound of bells summoning Christians to prayer, demons are terrified and depart, and the spirits of the storm, the powers of the air are laid low'.[16] A Church service book 'recognizes the virtue of a church bell, wherever its sound is heard, to drive far off the powers of evil, the gibbering and mowing spectres of the dead, and all the spirits of the storm'.[17]

On the occasion of pagan festivals, such as midsummer's eve or *Walpurgisnacht*, bells were rung all night long, so as to confound the hostile magic. Bells were also believed to be capable of fending off plague, often ascribed to the workings of the dark powers. A Cistercian statute forbade the building of an abbey within earshot of any other abbey's bells. In part, this no doubt served a purely practical purpose – to avoid confusion and prevent monks summoned from their work in the fields trooping back to the wrong abbey. But it must also have been intended to prevent the harmonious magic of the bells from being disrupted by discord. And it ensured, as well, a wider dissemination of the faith.

In addition to the magic it evolved to combat paganism, Christianity adopted certain forms of pagan magic for its own use. Exorcism, for example, had been practised since the earliest shamanistic times. Humanity had always been plagued by 'devils' of one sort or another, which required casting out. According to scripture, Jesus himself had performed exorcisms; and this august precedent authorized the Church to adopt the procedure. In the Christian ritual of exorcism, the bell again figured. Apart from the bell, however, Christian exorcism, like many other forms of Christian magic, was virtually indistinguishable from its pagan equivalents. It differed only in the source from which its power was supposed to have issued.

By the end of the first millennium AD, Christianity had developed its own comprehensive system of magic. Like the pagan magic it was intended to counter, however, Christian magic was essentially primitive. It lacked the all-encompassing framework of Hermetic thought, as well as Hermeticism's possibilities for practical application. Unlike Hermeticism, it did not allow man to assume responsibility for his own destiny and, for good or ill, to shape reality to his bidding. Except for such limited phenomena as healing, aiding fertility or protecting against the 'evil eye', it did not endow humanity with the power to 'make things happen' in the world at large.

At last, towards the end of the tenth century, Hermeticism, transmitted along with both Islamic and Judaic teaching, began to seep into Western Europe. Attempts to staunch it proved futile, and the seepage was soon to become a multitude of trickles, then a flood. The flood was to issue from three sources. One was Spain. The second was Sicily. The third, starting with the crusades, was to be the Middle East and the Holy Land. The magic deriving from these sources was to transform Myrddin into the much more imposing personage of Merlin. He would then be only an incarnation away from Faust.

4

THREE ROUTES TO EUROPE

In 711, having overrun north Africa, the armies of Islam swept across the Straits of Gibraltar and into Spain. By 714, a mere three years later, the whole of the Iberian peninsula had been conquered, save for an enclave of Christianized Visigoths and Romanized Spaniards in Galicia, the extreme north-west. In 732, the Arab army crossed the Pyrenees and advanced into France, but, after an engagement lasting six days, were defeated near Poitiers by Charles Martel.

Islamic Spain was ruled, as we have noted, by a refugee prince of the Umayyad dynasty. Not wishing to challenge the new caliphate, soon to establish its capital at Baghdad, the prince took the title of enuir. With its capital at Cordoba, Arab Spain was thus temporarily divorced from the rest of the Islamic world. Under the enuir, Islamic culture in Spain blossomed and flourished. To the north, the Christian enclave of Galicia remained insular, backward and poverty-stricken. Elsewhere, under Muslim auspices, the country prospered. New techniques of irrigation were introduced, as well as other innovations, and agriculture thrived. Many crops now associated with Spain, such as oranges, rice and cotton, were brought there by the Arabs. Lands which today are desolate and barren were then under intensive cultivation, often producing two harvests a year. The virtual deserts of modern-day Andalusia were covered by orchards and vineyards.

Agricultural prosperity was complemented by a new urban commerce and sophistication. Metropolitan centres arose from which trade with the eastern Mediterranean was conducted. Beginning in the ninth century, the ruptured contacts between Spain and the rest of the Islamic world were restored, and the country embarked on a dynamic cultural renaissance. Multitudes of Spanish scholars travelled to Baghdad to study. Books from Baghdad were imported. Schools were founded, writers encouraged and subsidized. Poetry enjoyed a particular vogue, and poets were accorded a status similar to that of the Celtic bard or ollave. Their influence was subsequently to extend across the Pyrenees and inspire the later troubadours and trouvères of medieval France. And during the second half of the tenth century, a library of some 400,000 volumes was built up at Cordoba, which 'became the greatest centre of learning in the whole of the west, Islamic and Christian alike'.[1]

Cordoba itself was an ancient city, founded originally by Phoenician traders. Under the Roman imperium, it had been the birthplace of two future emperors, Trajan and Hadrian. As the capital of Islamic Spain, it rapidly grew into Europe's largest city, with a population of more than a million. At its peak, it accommodated, according to Arab chroniclers, more than 400 mosques, 900 baths, 60,000 mansions, 80,000 shops and 200,000 houses, all within the walled central section. This section was noted for its cleanliness, its paved streets and nocturnal lighting. The wall surrounding it contained 132 towers and thirteen gates. Beyond lay five walled suburbs and another twenty-one unwalled.[2]

More than anything else, Cordoba was a cultural and intellectual centre. The library of 400,000 volumes was considered, along with those of Cairo and Baghdad, as one of the three great libraries of the Islamic world. But there were also another seventy public libraries, and numerous private collections.

By the twelfth century, Cordoba was vying with Baghdad for cultural pre-eminence in the Islamic world. The first university of medieval Europe was, in effect, Cordoba's Great Mosque, to which students flocked in thousands. There were many schools for copyists, most of whom were women. There were 'translation institutes', established to make texts from the East accessible to Western readers. Greek texts, already translated in Harran or Baghdad, thus became available to Spanish scholars. New books were constantly being written – on music, geography, history, astronomy, astrology, botany, mathematics, chemistry, alchemy, philosophy and Hermetic thought.

Except for those engaged in militant opposition to Islam, Christians were treated with tolerance, even benevolence. So, too, were Jews. Churches, monasteries, religious schools and synagogues remained intact and in constant use. Many Christians converted to Islam, finding its regime relaxed and congenial compared to that of Rome. Other Christians from beyond the Pyrenees were drawn to Spain as well, lured by reports of the country's culture, learning and opportunities for wealth. While books in Christian Europe were largely confined to courts and monasteries, in Spain they were available to the populace as a whole. In the mid ninth century, the Christian bishop of Cordoba lamented that his flock had conceived such a love of Arab books that they were 'building up great libraries . . . at enormous cost . . . hardly one can write a passable Latin letter to a friend, but innumerable are those who can express themselves in Arabic and can compose poetry in that language . . .'[3]

The bishop may have grumbled; but there were other nominally Christian potentates who found Islamic Spain altogether more congenial. According to a chronicle composed by a monk of St Albans in 1213, King John of England seriously considered converting to Islam. As is well known, John was an unpopular king – one of the most unpopular of all English monarchs. He resented the public favour enjoyed by his brother, Richard Coeur de Lion, in whose absence he reigned. His own powers were soon to be curbed by the Magna Carta. He was irate with the Pope, who refused to grant him the support he needed to consolidate his position on the throne. In consequence, he cast about for alternatives.

In 1213, a secret embassy was dispatched to the Muslim ruler of Morocco, consisting of two knights and a priest from London, one Master Robert. These ambassadors were authorized to promise the Muslim potentate that King John 'would voluntarily give up himself and his kingdom, and if he pleased would hold it as tributary from him; and that he would also abandon the Christian faith, which he considered false, and would faithfully adhere to the law of Muhammad'.[4] John also offered to help extirpate Christendom from Spain and impose Islam over the whole of the Iberian peninsula.

The Muslim ruler of Morocco responded to John's ambassadors:

> I was just now looking at the book of a wise Greek and a Christian named Paul, which is written in Greek, and his deeds and words please me much; one thing, however, concerning him displeases me, and that is that he did not stand firm in the faith in which he was born, but turned to another like a deserter and a waverer.
> And I say this with regard to your Lord, the king of the English, who abandons the most pious and pure law of the Christians under which he was born, and desires, fickle and unstable that he is, to come over to our faith.[5]

On this basis, he decided that King John 'was a man of no consequence, quite unworthy of any alliance with a Muslim ruler like himself'.[6] And he dismissed the English monarch's three emissaries with an impressively chivalrous peroration:

> I never read or heard that any king possessing such a prosperous kingdom subject and obedient to him, would voluntarily ruin his sovereignty by making tributary a country that is free, by giving to a stranger that which is his own, by turning happiness to misery, and thus giving himself up to the will of another, conquered, as it were, without a word.
>
> I have rather read and heard from many that they would procure liberty for themselves at the expense of streams of blood, which is a praiseworthy action; but now I hear that your wretched lord, a sloth and a coward, who is even worse than nothing, wishes from a free man to become a slave, who is the most wretched of all human beings.[7]

Needless to say, nothing came of John's overtures to Islam. The chief ambassador, the priest known as Master Robert, subsequently travelled to the Holy Land and enrolled in the Knights Templar. He then deserted the Templars, defected to their adversaries and ended his life as an emissary for the Great Khan when the Mongols invaded Austria in 1242.

If John of England was abjectly eager to embrace Islam, there were other Christian princes, closer to hand, who remained adamantly opposed to Muslim Spain. Despite the blossoming of her culture, Muslim Spain existed in a state of virtually incessant war with Christian adversaries to the north; and the country's disunity and political instability usually caused her to get the worst of the conflict. Inexorably, over a period of some five hundred years, Islam was rolled back and eventually driven out of the Iberian peninsula. This process, amounting in effect to a sustained crusade, is known today as the Reconquista.

When Spain had first been overrun by Islam in the early eighth century, the Christian enclave in Galicia, in the extreme north-west, had remained intact and defiant. This bastion was to become the kingdom of the Asturias. Later, in 910, part of it became the kingdom of León – which, by the thirteenth century, was amalgamated with the kingdom of Castille. In the early ninth century, the capture of Barcelona by Charlemagne's son, Louis, was to provide Christendom with a second enclave on the Iberian peninsula. It was from these two strongholds – León and Castille in the north, and Barcelona on the eastern coast – that the Christian counter-offensive was to proceed.

In Galicia, Christian zeal had long drawn inspiration from the shrine of Santiago de Compostela, established during the ninth century. This shrine, subsequently the site of one of Christendom's great cathedrals, quickly became a pilgrimage centre – the most important such centre in Western Europe, apart from Rome. Santiago was to provide the spiritual impetus behind the Reconquista.

From León and subsequently Castille, Christian forces were to push southwards towards the Duero River and eventually into the Islamic heartland of Andalusia. From Barcelona, later incorporated into the kingdom of Aragón, other forces struck across the Ebro plains and down the eastern coast towards Valencia and Murcia. The first decisive event in the Reconquista occurred in 1085, with the Christian capture of Toledo. This city was to become the symbolic capital for the Christian reconquest of Spain.

During the period immediately preceding and following the capture of Toledo, popular consciousness in Spain was dominated by the epic, semi-legendary figure of Roderigo Díaz. Known to history as El Cid – a corruption of the

Arabic *sayyid*, meaning 'lord', 'master' or 'leader' – Roderigo is generally perceived as a Christian hero. In reality, his career was rather more chequered than later idealizations might lead one to believe.[8] On at least one occasion, from 1081 until 1086, he served as a Muslim mercenary, waging war against the Christian sovereigns to whom he technically owed allegiance, as well as against other Christian nobles. By 1093, however, his affiliations had finally become focused. A year later, he captured Valencia and became, in everything but name, a Christian king in his own right. He died five years later, and Valencia was recaptured; but the Reconquista had by then acquired a momentum which was ultimately to prove irresistible.

During the early years of the twelfth century, Christian forces in Spain were augmented by knights and soldiery from elsewhere in Europe, especially from France, who had participated in the First Crusade. It was not difficult to obtain their support, since the conflict in the Iberian peninsula was now officially designated a crusade as well, with all the attendant benefits – indulgences, remission or absolution of sins, the prospect of booty and land to be wrested in God's name from the 'infidel'. Aided by veteran campaigners from the Holy Land, the Christian armies, under the King of Aragón, captured Saragossa in 1118. Like dominoes, other urban centres began to fall in turn. By 1148, Tortosa, at the mouth of the Ebro, was taken.

In the aftermath of the First Crusade, the military religious orders, the Knights Templar and the Knights Hospitaller, appeared in the Holy Land. In 1128, the Templars were extravagantly extolled and given their official rule by St Bernard. Within the year, they had already begun to take in Spanish knights, and to receive donations of money, land and castles from Spanish potentates – who, needless to say, were eager to recruit such professional and experienced soldiery for the Reconquista. By the middle of the twelfth century, Templar and Hospitaller holdings in the Iberian peninsula had become considerable. These included a number of frontier fortresses, bastions on the front line between Christendom and Islam, intended to serve as defensive bulwarks and offensive spearheads. But while both Templars and Hospitallers were ready enough to accept donations, they were rather more diffident, even dilatory, about campaigning and fighting. Both displayed a marked reluctance to take the field and involve themselves in a second front against Islam. Both 'insisted that their real purpose was the defence of Jerusalem and refused to let themselves be deflected towards fighting in Spain beyond the bare minimum needed to avert royal anger'.[9]

This apathy led to the formation of a number of uniquely Iberian orders, modelled on the Temple and the Hospital but devised specifically for military operations in Spain and Portugal. Probably the most important of these was the Order of Calatrava, established initially in 1158 and officially incorporated by the Pope in 1164 with the same Cistercian rule as the Templars. In 1170, the Order of Cáceres was established, evolved into the Order of Santiago and received confirmation from the Pope in 1175. In 1177, a similar confirmation was accorded the Order of Alcántera, which was alamgamated, ten years later, with Santiago. A number of other orders were created during the years that followed. When the Templars were officially suppressed between 1307 and 1314, the Order of Montesa was established as a refuge for knights fleeing persecution.

In the Holy Land, the Templars, the Hospitallers and the various smaller orders that appeared were constantly squabbling. Some of them – the Templars in particular – could also, on many occasions, come to an accommodation with Islam. The Spanish orders seem to have been more uncompromising and fanatical in their zeal; and they tended generally to cooperate closely, not only with each other, but with royal authority as well. They were employed extensively to defend the primary invasion routes between Christian and Muslim-held territory, and their network of castles and fortresses blunted the thrust of attempted enemy advances. At the same time, they provided the medieval equivalent of 'shock troops' for Christian counter-offensives. In the process, they became immensely wealthy and immensely powerful, eventually coming to control vast tracts of Spain and Portugal. Their influence and prerogatives were to continue long after their military role had ceased to be relevant. But without them, it is questionable whether the Reconquista would have succeeded to the extent it did.

Bolstered by the zeal, the discipline, the professionalism and expertise of the military-religious orders, the Christian forces in Spain acquired a new and irresistible impetus. In 1212, a crucial battle was fought at Las Navas de Tolosa, and the tide turned irreversibly against Islam. Cordoba was taken in 1236, the regions of Valencia and Murcia a year later. Seville fell in 1248, Cadiz in 1262. By the last third of the thirteenth century, Muslim Spain had dwindled to the small kingdom of Granada, which was allowed to survive only through a special arrangement with the royal house of Castille.

In 1340, an Arab army from north Africa landed at Gibraltar. With this support, Muslim Granada made a last attempt to regain the territory lost to Christendom. The Arab fleet, however, was defeated in a naval battle off the coast of Algeciras, which choked off all additional, reinforcements and supplies. Shortly thereafter, in June 1340, the Muslim army was decisively defeated at the battle of Salado. Granada was now irrevocably isolated and cut off from the rest of the Islamic world. It tottered on, surrounded by enemies, for another century and a half. Then, in 1479, the rest of Spain was unified when Ferdinand, who was married to Isabelle of Castille, succeeded to the throne of Aragón. In this newly united domain, Muslim Granada was an unwelcome excrescence which had to be eradicated. On 2 January 1492, Granada fell, and 781 years of Islamic presence in Spain came definitively to an end. Its legacy, however, was to continue for centuries, and is apparent in Western civilization even today. An important part of that legacy was Hermetic thought, for which Spain served as the first and the most sustained conduit.

Spanish Mystics and Magi

In fact, elements of Hermetic thought, of magic, alchemy and other so-called 'esoteric' traditions, had found their way to Spain even before Islam did. During the first centuries of the Christian era, Spain had been an integral component of the economic and commercial network which bound the Roman Empire together. Spanish ports had trafficked daily with ships from the whole of the Mediterranean world – from the old Phoenician cities on the Syrian coast, for example, and from Alexandria. These ships carried not only commodities, but ideas as well. Spain thus became a repository for Judaeo-Christian teachings from the eastern Mediterranean, and for Alexandrian syncretism. In Spain, the spiritual descendants of such original Faust figures as Simon Magus and Zosimus were to find a new home.

One such was the prominent heresiarch Priscillian, Bishop of Avila from 381 until his death some five years later. There were elements of Gnostic dualism in Priscillian's teachings. There were also elements of the messianic Judaic tradition which characterizes the Dead Sea Scrolls. But there were elements of Pythagoreanism and Hermeticism as well.

Priscillian was said to have been a disciple of an elusive magus figure from Memphis known only as Mark, and described as 'a most learned expert in the magic art'.[10] Whether Mark actually existed or not remains uncertain; but Priscillian himself, his charisma, his heterodox preaching and his growing number of followers posed a potential threat to the Church, then still endeavouring to consolidate its position as the official religion of the Roman Empire. Priscillianism came to be regarded as a full-fledged heresy. Priscillian himself was accused of practising magic. Among the charges levelled against him was his alleged possession of a magic amulet with the name of God inscribed upon it in Latin, Greek and Hebrew. In 386, accordingly, he was tried, condemned and executed. The adherence he had inspired, however, survived. His grave in Galicia became a shrine and a centre of pilgrimage. One authority, Professor Henry Chadwick of Oxford, has produced evidence to suggest that Santiago de Compostela was built on the site of Priscillian's tomb.[11] Excavations beneath the church there have certainly revealed graves dating from Priscillian's era.

Except for isolated pockets of which scant information survives, Priscillianism – and, with it, such aspects of Hermeticism as it incorporated – would appear to have died out in Spain by the seventh century. In the early eighth century, however, the Muslim invasion of the Iberian peninsula occurred. With Islam came Sufism and its vigorous promulgation of Hermetic thought. And when Islamic Spain's links with Baghdad were re-established in the early ninth century, all the fruits of Eastern learning were imported – Sufi texts and teachings, Arabic translations from Greek and Syriac originals, works from the schools of Edessa and Harran, the entire corpus of Hermeticism, magic, alchemy and astrology. The earliest extant versions of such seminal Hermetic documents as the *Emerald Tablet* and the

Picatrix were to issue, in Arabic translation, from Spain. And Kabbala – the esoteric Judaic discipline which so closely paralleled Hermeticism – began to thrive in Spain as well.

In Cordoba, Islamic magi such as Ibn Masarra (*c.* 883–931) taught what amounted to their own interpretation of Hermetic thought. Having himself visited Baghdad, Ibn Masarra proceeded to disseminate, among other things, a discipline known as the 'Science of Letters', a variant of the system already established in Judaic and Hermetic tradition. He also promulgated the Hermetic premise of the interrelationship between microcosm and macrocosm. Whether Ibn Masarra was himself a Sufi remains uncertain. There is considerable evidence to suggest he was. In any case, his teachings were enthusiastically embraced by later Sufi masters, including the greatest of them, Ibn Arabi.

Ibn Arabi was born in Murcia in 1165. At the age of eight, he moved with his family to Seville, where he began his schooling. At the age of fifteen, he underwent a mystical or numinous experience which was to determine the rest of his life. His subsequent travels took him to Tunis, Fez, Cairo, Jerusalem, Mecca, Baghdad, Anatolia and eventually Damascus, where he died in 1240. In all of these places, he gathered both disciples and further learning. He also wrote prodigiously, being credited with the authorship of more than four hundred works. In these works, he drew extensively on the teachings and symbolism of Hermeticism. Like Zosimus before him, he would often use alchemical images, for example, to convey the process of spiritual purification and refinement. Gold, to cite but one instance, was invoked to denote the soul before it was corrupted by the dross of experience. Ibn Arabi also expounded a characteristically Hermetic interpretation of the Logos as the 'Creative, Animating and Rational Principle of the Cosmos'. Of Jesus, he wrote: 'To say that Christ is God is true in the sense that everything else is God, and to say that Christ is son of Mary is also true, but to say that God is Christ the Son of Mary is false, because this would imply that He is Christ and nothing else. God is you and I and everything else in the Universe.'[12] Here is the typically Hermetic principle that 'there is only one everything' – in contrast to dualism and Christianity, which would dismember reality, and then isolate and repudiate certain aspects of it.

Ibn Arabi's influence was eventually to extend far beyond the Muslim world. It is apparent in the work of such monumental Western figures as Dante. What is more, Ibn Arabi explored, in an extraordinarily modern way, the psychology and phenomenology of the numinous or mystical experience. In this respect, he can be seen as a precursor of such twentieth-century Hermetic (or neo-Hermetic) thinkers as C. G. Jung and Robert Musil.

Ibn Masarra and Ibn Arabi were only two of numerous Hermetically oriented Muslim writers in Spain. Through the commentaries of such writers, and through translations of original Hermetic texts, the corpus of Hermetic teachings began to filter into Christendom. Spain became a veritable paradise for Christians in search of learning, a repository of lost treasures and treasures previously undiscovered. It was from Spain that light first began to radiate northwards and illumine Europe's Dark Ages. The Reconquista brought into Christian Europe land, gold, silk and other material commodities; it also brought manuscripts – by the thousands.

Since most of these were in Arabic or Hebrew, they created a booming industry for translators. Such translators began to flock across the Pyrenees, to accompany the Christian armies and enter each Muslim town as it fell. Here, they would eagerly collaborate with Jewish and Muslim scholars who had chosen to remain in the captured precincts.

During the 1160s, a 'comprehensive programme of translations was planned and undertaken'.[13] But by that time, numerous Hermetic texts had already been translated, including the *Emerald Tablet*. In addition to works on magic and alchemy, there were copious works on astrology – and on the astronomy, mathematics and geometry necessary to compute astrological charts. There were translations of Ptolemy and Euclid. There were translations of Aristotle, Archimedes and other Greek philosophers, from pre-Socratic to Neoplatonic. By 1143, the first Latin translation of the Koran had appeared. And it was from Spain, too, that Western Europe first acquired algebra (from the Arabic *al-jabr*), trigonometry and the Arabic numerals that made higher mathematics possible.

It is not surprising, therefore, that Spain came to be mantled in a kind of luminous aura, a distinctive mystique. For medieval Europeans, it was perceived as a magical domain, harbouring repositories of arcane, abstruse and sometimes forbidden knowledge. If Christians of the time made pilgrimages to the Holy Land out of piety, they made pilgrimages to Spain out of a thirst for learning. In *Parzival*, the most important of the Christian Grail romances, Wolfram von Eschenbach claims to have first heard his version of the Grail story from one Kyot of Provins – who is said to have obtained it in his turn from a 'heathen', named Flegetanis, in Spain. As late as the fourteenth century, European alchemists such as Nicolas Flamel were travelling to Spain in quest of recondite occult wisdom.

Not surprisingly, the prospect of magical knowledge – and, even more significantly, magical power – attracted the interest of Christian princes, and even of Christian ecclesiastics. Given the Church's virtual monopoly of learning, many of the translations were produced by clerics anyway. Many were commissioned and presided over by prelates –

local bishops, for example, seeking knowledge beyond the sanction of Rome. The translators themselves were constantly aware that they were dealing with forbidden and potentially dangerous material. During the mid twelfth century, for instance, two northern European scholars, Hermann of Carinthia and Robert of Ketton, were working with manuscripts from the region of the Ebro. Having produced their Latin translation of the Koran in 1143, they turned their attention to astrological texts. They quote extensively from Hermetic sources but only translate selected items. Although they display an apparent familiarity with the dreaded *Picatrix*, they refrain not only from translating it, but also from quoting it directly. In his own writings, Hermann clearly distinguishes between esoteric and exoteric teachings, between secret schools of wisdom and those more public. He states that he and his colleague have been labouring together on the 'intimate treasures of the Arabs'.[14] He then voices his misgivings about confessing even this much, saying he was prompted to do so by a dream.

Christian potentates had fewer reservations about trespassing on such officially quarantined territory. Certain of them – Jaime I of Aragón, for example – warmly embraced the corpus of new material, including Hermeticism, and established scholarly, intellectually adventurous, worldly and sophisticated courts. The most important of these rulers was Alfonso X of Castille, also known as Alfonso the Wise. Born in Toledo in 1221, he reigned over Castille – which now included León – from 1252 until his death in 1284. He was related to the Frankish royal house of Jerusalem and was a cousin of the Holy Roman Emperor Friedrich II. After the death of Friedrich, Alfonso himself was a candidate for the imperial throne and only narrowly missed being elected.

Alfonso was known as a philosopher king. He was a keen reader, an accomplished poet and musician who would personally compete in contests with celebrated troubadours. He was impressively well versed in history and astronomy, and produced the famous Alfonsine series of astronomical tables. One of his chief passions was astrology:

> King Alfonso always wanted to investigate the heavens in an untiring research about the relations of the stars with man's destiny and in the process of studying astrological charts and horoscopes he encouraged his Arabic and Jewish scientists to experiment and study the skies and heavenly bodies in a more astronomical manner . . . the king's passion was to be able to know destiny . . .[15]

Alfonso also produced a book on chess. He produced a codification of laws so lucid that it is still a standard reference work, and comprises part of the legal code of the United States today. He commissioned numerous translations of Hermetic texts – into Castilian, rather than Latin. And in 1256, underterred by the odour of sulphur pious Christians associated with it, he ordered a Castilian translation of the *Picatrix*.

Crusaders in the Holy Land

By Alfonso's time, however, Spain was no longer the only – nor even the chief – conduit for Hermeticism into Europe. For another two and a half centuries, until 1492, the country was to remain a repository of arcane lore – Hermetic, Kabbalistic, Sufi, sundry other kinds. But the Crusades, commencing at the end of the eleventh century, had begun to offer another, more direct channel of transmission. The Reconquista was more prolonged than the Crusades, lasting over a greater period of time. It began earlier and ended later. It also occurred on European soil – closer to the rest of Western Christendom, separated only by the Pyrenees rather than by the Mediterranean. But the Crusades, paradoxically, were to project Islamic learning, as well as Hermeticism, more quickly and more deeply into the heart of European culture – into Germany and the lands of the Holy Roman Empire, into France, into England and Scotland, even into Scandinavia.

During the last decade of the eleventh century, a ragtag army of knights, pilgrims, religious fanatics, clerics, mercenaries, outcasts, adventurers, freebooters, entrepreneurs and greedy cynics descended *en masse* on the Holy Land – with a mandate and a sanction from the Pope himself, with an *a priori* absolution of sins and with a guaranteed seat in heaven. Their objective was to wrest back to Christendom, from the hands of the Islamic 'infidels', what purported to be the Holy Sepulchre, even though no one knew precisely where the Holy Sepulchre was. The conflict spawned by this folly was to last for two centuries, until May 1291.

In 1099, immediately following the success of the First Crusade and the capture of Jerusalem, the Frankish Kingdom of Jerusalem, or Outremer, was established. The holy city itself was to be recaptured by the Saracens some ninety years later, in 1187, but the putative Frankish kingdom was to survive for another century. In effect, it represented the first great imperialistic enterprise to be undertaken by a still coalescing Western civilization.

Outremer was a species of Western colony, tenuously established in the Middle East. And for two centuries, it was to foster a constant and sustained contact between Christendom and a spectrum of alien cultures – not just those of Islam and Judaism, but those of the ancient world as well. Christians were thus exposed to a multitude of new and bewildering ways of thinking, a multitude of new and bewildering spheres of knowledge. There was one important respect in which the Crusades differed from the colonial enterprises of later epochs. Subsequent enterprises could claim to be – at least materially – an incursion by a more technologically advanced civilization into one more primitive. Whatever the West was later to learn from India or the Far East, for example, may have influenced its philosophy, its attitudes, its manners, its social and commercial life, but did not revolutionize its science and technology. In science and technology, India and the Far East for the most part learned from the West. During the Crusades, however, the invaders had nothing 'superior' on their side except military force. Despite Christian claims to moral supremacy, spiritual supremacy and a monopoly of religious truth, the Western invaders were shockingly backward compared to their supposedly 'benighted' victims – and shamefully less tolerant, less 'civilized'. Western society at the time was still uncouth, largely illiterate, ignorant and technologically crude, while Islam comprised a far more 'advanced', far more refined, sophisticated and humane culture.

There is no need here to recapitulate the history of the Crusades. For present purposes, it will be sufficient to observe that what began as a violent and traumatic culture clash subsided into a two-century-long period of gradual mutual osmosis. Although the Crusades are generally perceived as a chapter of incessant, relentless and uncompromising warfare, the reality was, in fact, quite different. Bouts of fighting were usually short in duration. In the lulls between spasms of combat, uneasy truces and negotiations prevailed, hostages were exchanged, new contacts between adversaries were established. As a result, Christians and Muslims were exposed in sustained fashion to each other's modes of thought, values, customs, practices and technologies. And if Islam had little to learn from such exchanges save certain military techniques, Western Christendom had a great deal to learn. It had much to learn not only from Islam, not only from Judaism, but from other forms of Christendom as well.

Rather than crossing the Mediterranean, many crusaders chose an overland route to the Holy Land, passing through Constantinople or other domains of the enfeebled Byzantine Empire, and then down through Asia Minor. In 1098, as the First Crusade under the co-leadership of Godfroi de Bouillon descended on Jerusalem. Godfroi's younger brother, Baudouin, became ruler and Count of Edessa. Edessa was a nominally Christian principality, but its Christianity was closer to that of Byzantium than to Rome's. The city of Edessa itself was only a few miles from Harran.

On the Fourth Crusade, in 1204, the bulk of the Western army not only passed through Contantinople, but captured the city, sacked it and imposed a Frankish dynasty that ruled the Byzantine Empire for the next fifty-seven years. In cities like Constantinople and Edessa, Roman Catholic knights, scholars and potentates from the West came into sustained contact with the Greek Orthodox Church. They came into contact with nominally Christianized adherents of gnostic dualism, such as the Bogomils – precursors, in many respects, of the Cathar heretics in France. They came into contact, too, with sects of heretical or schismatic Christians such as the Nestorians; and many of these, untouched by the Pauline theology of Rome, embraced a 'purer' form of Christianity, closer to what Jesus himself would have preached. And needless to say, the crusaders were also exposed to the entire corpus of Greek learning, from classical times to the period of Alexandrian syncretism – including, of course, substantial doses of Hermetic thought.

In Jerusalem, the city's Jews were herded into a synagogue by the crusaders and burned alive, along with the building. In case this failed to provide sufficient deterrent, Jews from elsewhere in the Holy Land were forbidden to enter the capital. But throughout Palestine, as well as the territory comprising modern Lebanon and Syria, other Jewish communities survived. With these, certain of the crusaders established a somewhat more amicable contact. In Egypt, too, contact with Jewish communities was established, by captured or renegade Western knights. It is not clear to what extent Kabbalistic material might thus have been transmitted. Undoubtedly, however, some of it was – and would have complemented the aspects of Hermetic thought derived from other sources.

The most important of these sources was, of course, Islam, which had long ago incorporated a substantial corpus of Hermeticism. Despite the official hostility supposed to obtain between them, Christians and Muslims, when not fighting each other, trafficked extensively – in commodities of every conceivable kind and in ideas. Relations between putative adversaries were often cordial, even close. Such relations were assiduously cultivated by potentates like Richard Coeur de Lion of England, by noblemen and soldiers who sometimes converted to Islam, and, in particular, by the Knights Templar. It was accepted procedure, for example, for Templar functionaries and dignitaries to employ Arab secretaries. These secretaries would serve as interpreters, as translators, as emissaries, frequently as friends. Their duties required them to be intelligent men, whose breadth and subtlety of learning could not but influence their employers.

Although detailed documentation is scant, there is substantial evidence to suggest Templar association with Sufism and assimilation of Sufi thought. More exhaustively documented is the Templar relationship with the Hermetically oriented cadre of Ismaili fighters known to history as the Hashishim, or Assassins. For reasons that remain obscure to this day, the Hashishim were known to have paid regular tribute to the Templars through most of the twelfth century. They also served the Templars as translators, interpreters, spies, ambassadors and the medieval equivalent of contract killers.

The Templars are known to have enjoyed an unprecedentedly warm rapport with perhaps the most mysterious and elusive of all sects in the Middle East, the Druse, who still reside in Lebanon today. Druse faith is ultimately rooted in the Koran; but it encompasses so much more that some Muslims dispute its inclusion within Islam at all. Among the texts accepted by the Druse as sacred are the Old and New Testaments, the works of Pythagoras, Plato and Plotinus, and the corpus of teachings ascribed to Hermes Trismegistus.[16]

During the Crusades, the Holy Land itself was something like an alchemical alembic. In this alembic, elements of radically diverse cultures were forced violently together. The result was akin to a chemical reaction which creates altogether new compounds. Through the Crusades, both Islam and Christendom were dramatically transmuted and transformed – Christendom more so, perhaps, because it had more to learn. Among other things, Western concepts of magic were to be significantly altered – and fused increasingly with science and technology. In spheres as diverse as medicine, cartography, mathematics, maritime navigation, drugs, architecture, engineering and psychology, new amalgams were created which blurred old distinctions. In place of the primitive sorcery and shamanism of the Dark Ages, magic acquired an altogether more dynamic and sophisticated dimension. In conjunction with science and technology, it now began to emerge increasingly as 'the art of making things happen' – and Western man, while still paying lip service to Christianity, was set definitively on the path to Fausthood.

The Kingdom of Sicily

The Reconquista and the Crusades were the two primary channels whereby Hermetic thought found its way into Western Europe. There was, however, a third channel, which might perhaps be seen as a tributary of the other two, flowing confluent with them, periodically feeding into them, but retaining an identity and character of its own. If smaller in scale and initially more localized, it was endowed with a concentrated intensity which caused it to exert a profound and ultimately far-reaching influence. This third channel was Sicily.

In the early ninth century, Sicily, formerly a possession of the Byzantine Empire, was overrun by Islam and became a Muslim dominion. The Muslim invaders found on the island a corpus of Greek learning which complemented their own, and which was not to be found elsewhere until later. Sicily thus became a new centre of learning, combining Islamic and Byzantine Greek material. In the eleventh century, Syracuse was the home of Abufalah, one of the greatest of all Muslim exponents of alchemy, astrology and Hermetic magic.

In the meantime, momentous developments had been occurring to the north. Throughout the ninth century, Norse raiders – Vikings from Scandinavia – had plagued France as much as they had Saxon England. In 911, the Treaty of Saint-Clair-sur-Epte had bought them off by ceding to them the north-western peninsula subsequently known as Normandy. But if the Normans were thus accommodated in France, their desire for conquest remained unassuaged. In 1066, they were to turn their attention to England. Before that, however, as early as 1017, they had already advanced into Italy.

The Norman army in Italy was composed largely of

younger sons and adventurers who had meagre opportunities for advancement in their own domains. Southern Italy, still ruled by Byzantine Greeks at the time, offered enticing prospects of land, wealth, nobility and power. By 1038, Norman knights had established a solid foothold there and begun to consolidate their position with land grants and accompanying titles. By the middle of the eleventh century, the whole of southern Italy was under their control.

In 1038, a number of Norman knights had formed a temporary alliance with their Byzantine adversaries and embarked on a joint invasion of Muslim Sicily. This invasion was repelled. Twenty-three years later, a second invasion was launched, by a wholly Norman army, and a beachhead was established at Messina. By 1063, the rest of north-eastern Sicily had been overrun.

The conquest of the island now became an officially pronounced crusade, with the Pope sending a banner under which Norman knights could campaign. For the next eight years, however, the situation was to remain static. During that time, of course, Norman attention was concentrated elsewhere. In 1066, William, Duke of Normandy, proceeded to invade England, and his undertaking siphoned off recruits who might otherwise have reinforced their kinsmen's armies in the Sicilian campaign. But in 1071, that campaign was resumed with an assault on the capital, Palermo. A year later, the city fell. By 1079, the whole of northern Sicily was in Norman hands, while the south remained Muslim. It did not remain so for long. Syracuse fell in 1085, the same year as Toledo in Spain. In 1091, the last Muslim redoubt was captured and the Norman Kingdom of Sicily was established.

In Sicily, as often elsewhere, the Normans were not just tolerant in religious matters, but, by the standards of the age, rather louche. Norman monarchs in Sicily enjoyed an essentially Muslim lifestyle, residing like Arab potentates amidst their palaces and gardens, orange groves and artificial lakes. They maintained harems guarded by eunuchs. They entertained themselves in the evening with music, poetry and dancing girls. Noblewomen who ventured into the streets beyond the court did so in the Muslim manner, hooded and veiled. And under the Norman regime, Palermo came to rival Spanish cities as an intellectual and cultural centre, bringing together the fruits of Christian, Muslim and Judaic learning. Christian, Muslim and Judaic scholars worked side by side, translating texts into Latin, writing commentaries, producing original works of their own. In Sicily, as in Spain, Hermeticism flourished. It was soon to cross the Straits of Messina to the Italian mainland.

Its progress was to be accelerated during the thirteenth century by the single most august and imposing figure of his age, the Hohenstaufen Holy Roman Emperor Friedrich II. In 1194, the Norman regime had ended and the Emperor Heinrich VI had been crowned King of Sicily. He died in 1198, when his son, Friedrich, was four years old. In 1215, Friedrich became King of Germany, in 1220 Holy Roman Emperor. Having scant respect for Christianity, the young sovereign adopted an attitude of cavalier defiance towards the Pope and, in 1227, got himself excommunicated. That did not prevent him from crossing the Mediterranean to the Holy Land, embarking on a putative crusade, manipulating both Christian and Muslim potentates and negotiating complicated deals with the Arabs. In 1229, forty-one years after the holy city had been lost by the crusaders, Friedrich – at no cost whatever in bloodshed – contrived to get himself crowned King of Jerusalem. Rival European rules were outraged because he had achieved this by such un-Christian means as diplomacy, rather than by the sword.

Friedrich's maverick behaviour alienated not just other

European monarchs, but also the Church and the major religious-military orders in the Holy Land, particularly the Templars. His chief support came from the Teutonic Knights, a relatively young order created in 1190 as a Templar derivative. The Grand Master of this order, Hermann von Balke, became one of Friedrich's closest friends and confidants. Friedrich conferred on him a mandate to campaign in the forested wilderness of northeastern Europe and along the Baltic. Out of this territory, the Teutonic Knights were to carve a principality of their own, the so-called Ordensland or Ordenstaadt, which eventually stretched from Brandenburg to the Gulf of Finland and into Russia as far as Pskov. Here lay the future Kingdom of Prussia.

Friedrich himself had little taste for so inhospitable a milieu. Leaving the Teutonic Knights to their own autonomous devices, he proceeded to establish his court in Sicily. This court was to be the most cultured, the most civilized, the most learned and sophisticated of the century, perhaps of the entire Middle Ages in Europe. Like his Norman predecessors, Friedrich maintained an Islamic lifestyle. His harem of Muslim dancing girls was guarded by eunuchs and travelled on camels, veiled and in covered litters. His army incorporated substantial contingents of Muslim light cavalry and archers. When he travelled, he would always transport his library with him. He would also be accompanied by his menagerie, which included lynxes, lions, exotic birds, a pet hunting cheetah and the first giraffe ever seen in Europe. The rear of his entourage would be brought up by an elephant bearing a wooden tower filled with Muslim crossbowmen.

Whatever his sybaritic lifestyle, Friedrich was an impressive scholar. He himself wrote a widely acclaimed and still famous book on falconry. He was deeply interested in and fluently conversant with the sciences, mathematics, medicine, theology and the corpus of Islamic learning which included Hermetic thought. He insisted on the use of Arabic, rather than Roman, numerals. Poetry enjoyed a particularly special status. There were frequent poetry competitions – which were emulated thousands of miles away by the Teutonic Knights in their fortresses on the Baltic. Verse at Friedrich's court was often set to music and composed in Italian, not Latin – which prompted Dante to call the emperor 'the father of Italian poetry'. It was at Friedrich's court, too, that the sonnet form was invented.

Friedrich epitomized the munificent imperial patron. He sponsored an awesome array of scholars, writers and translators in all the arts and sciences, including such illustrious figures as Michael Scot. Scot had previously worked in Toledo, establishing a reputation as an astrologer and translator – of commentators on Aristotle, then of Aristotle's own texts. Around 1220, he became Friedrich's court astrologer, teaching the 'power of words and numbers', supplying the emperor with predictions for military campaigns, political machinations and the building of towns and cities.

In 1224, Friedrich founded the University of Naples, which was one of the first in Europe, pre-dating Salamanca by nineteen years, Oxford by twenty-five, the Sorbonne by thirty-three and Cambridge by sixty. His medical school at Salerno was the most prominent of the Middle Ages, and no physician was permitted to practise in his domains without a degree from it. The programme of studies was exhaustive, with a course in logic followed by five years of medicine, the last spent in practical surgery. Among other things, Salerno pioneered the use of anaesthetics in Europe by introducing the soporific sponge, soaked in a mixture of hashish, opium, belladonna and other compounds. The

knowledge of this device was subsequently lost and not rediscovered until centuries later.

Friedrich took an intense personal interest in the translation, composition and dissemination of medical texts. His
chief intellectual preoccupations, however, were religious in
nature, revolving around such questions as the nature of the
soul and whether or not it was immortal. He made his own
study of Judaism and came to the conclusion that it reflected
influences of Indian philosophy. He also enjoyed confronting
scholars with religious and philosophical conundrums. It was
in this spirit of challenge that, in 1240, he compiled his
'Sicilian Questions' – five queries sent out to scholarly
authorities in Egypt, Syria, Persia, Morocco and elsewhere
in the Islamic world. The questions pertained to the eternity of the world, the limits of theology, the categories of
science, the immortality of the soul and an explanation of
Muhammad's statement that: 'The heart of the believer is
between the two fingers of God.'[17] None of the answers
Friedrich received proved satisfactory to him. His personal
position seems to have combined a sceptical rationalism with
a certain recognition of spirituality – but spirituality in its
broadest Hermetic sense, divorced from the theological
dogma of any established religion. So far as established religions were concerned, he would not 'accept any legend or
theory at its face value'. In 1239, Pope Gregory IX officially
accused him of having denied the Virgin Birth, as well as of
claiming that the world had been deceived by three impos-
tors – Moses, Jesus and Muhammad.[18]

In thirteenth-century Europe, all learning outside the
Church was incipiently suspect, implicitly associated in some
sense with magic. Partly because of his learning, partly because
of his familiarity with Hermeticism, Friedrich was often
perceived as a magus figure. His enemies accused him of
dabbling in forbidden magic, and some of them undoubtedly

believed their own accusations. Undoubtedly, too, their belief was not altogether without justification. In any case, Hermeticism, under Friedrich's auspices, sifted into Europe with the stamp of imperial approval and authority. It sifted, eventually, as far as the Baltic, where the Teutonic Knights were repeatedly charged with the same heretical and magical practices as the Templars – but, unlike the Templars, remained safely beyond the reach of ecclesiastical and temporal persecution. Such was the extent of Friedrich's influence. Had the Faust figure of three centuries later ever aspired to secular power, he would in all likelihood have emerged as an individual similar to the Hohenstaufen emperor.

5

MEDIEVAL MAGI

It must be stressed that our images of the High Middle Ages – images of opulently clad chatelaines, of mail-clad knights errant wandering in search of adventure, of tournaments, courtly love and troubadours, of poets, minstrels and ever more refined manners – all date from after the beginning of the Reconquista and the Crusades. Prior to those movements, Western Europe was as backward, by Islamic or Byzantine standards, as the 'benighted heathen' of Asia and Africa were to seem to the explorers of later centuries – or as the American Indians to the conquistadores and colonists who first established contact with them. Even diplomats, ministers, courtiers and potentates were usually illiterate oafs, with scant awareness of philosophy, history, culture or even geography. The printing press had not yet been invented. Books therefore were limited in number, and the Church sequestered most of them, exercising a monopoly on learning and making it available only, so to speak, by drip-feed. Not until the Reconquista and the Crusades brought contact with Islamic, Judaic and Byzantine thought did Europe begin to become 'civilized' in any conventional sense of that word.

By the beginning of the thirteenth century, however, European society and self-definition – Europeans' own understanding of themselves and their place in the world –

had been transformed virtually beyond recognition. The transformation was as dramatic, in its way, and as rapid, as those with which we credit our own century. Modern media periodically comment on how radically the world of today has changed for that of an individual born in the 1890s, celebrating his or her hundredth birthday. For a European born in 1090, the changes in the world of 1190 would have seemed almost as great. And these changes, again, stemmed directly from sustained exposure to, and assimilation of, Islamic, Judaic and Byzantine thought. In absorbing so many key elements of Islamic, Judaic and Byzantine thought, however, Europe also absorbed key elements of Hermeticism.

Astrology, to take perhaps the most obvious example, was, in itself, nothing new to Europe. It had been widespread throughout the Roman Empire and survived in all that imperium's former domains. In the seventh century, the King of Northumbria employed an astrologer from Spain, who advised him on military matters in his war with the Celtic British.[1] Charlemagne not only employed an astrologer, but became a proficient one himself.[2] But European astrology of the Dark Ages remained a primitive and clumsy affair, relying as much on omens and portents as it did on precise mathematical computation. With the introduction of Arabic numerals, Islamic geometry and Islamic mathematics, European astrology became much more sophisticated, acquiring a new and more comprehensive dimension.

The Church's position on astrology had always been confused and ambiguous. The early Church Fathers had attacked it, citing the Old Testament's condemnation of all forms of divination. Astrology was recognized as being rooted in paganism. It retained, incorporated within it, dangerous elements of pagan thought. Moreover, Christian theologians argued, astrology posited a fatalistic determinism which denied man's freedom of will. If the stars controlled human actions, humanity was effectively absolved of responsibility for good or evil, and salvation became meaningless. Some of the most vociferous fulminations against astrology came from no less a personage than St Augustine. No astrologer could be accurate, Augustine maintained, unless he was aided and guided by evil spirits.[3]

Nevertheless, and despite such pronouncements, astrology was zealously embraced and studied by the Church's own representatives – by monks and friars, by abbots, bishops and cardinals, even by popes. Indeed, it was primarily the Church which, by virtue of her monopoly of learning, preserved astrological methodology. Through the Church, that methodology was kept alive until it could be picked up by later, more secular practitioners. Thus, for example, the Bishop of Lisieux, personal chaplain to William the Conqueror, was also an astrologer. The Archbishop of York, on his death in 1104, was found to have an astrological text under his pillow.[4]

With the introduction of Arabic numerals and Islamic mathematics, astrology was embraced even more energetically and enthusiastically than before. When they began to be founded during the thirteenth century, European universities all proceeded to teach courses in astrology. Theologians engaged in complicated intellectual gymnastics to reconcile astrology with Christian doctrine. It was argued, for example, that astrology could be relevant to the body, but not the soul. An individual's physical maladies, hungers and passions might be governed by the stars, but his soul remained free. Astrological prediction might apply to the former, therefore, but not to the latter. According to St Thomas Aquinas, 'many astrological forecasts were true because so few men resisted their bodily passions'.[5] At the same time, Aquinas worried that the use of astrology to read the future might draw the unwary into transactions with demonic forces.

Aquinas seems to have sensed in astrology something implicitly inimical to Christian doctrine. He did not, however, altogether appreciate the irony of the situation. Pious exponents of Christian teaching had congratulated themselves on banishing the gods of the ancient world. In Rome, centre of the old pagan empire, Mercury, Venus, Mars, Jupiter and Saturn had supposedly been supplanted by the Holy Trinity and the Virgin. Now, however, disguised as the planets in astrology, the antique gods had slipped deviously back into the very heart of Christian culture and begun to reclaim their dominion. Medieval prelates might make formal obeisance to God the Father, God the Son and God the Holy Ghost. But it was in accordance with conjunctions or oppositions between Venus and Mercury, or Mars and Jupiter, that they organized their lives, planned their schedules and made their decisions. In accordance with the same principles, merchants conducted their business, statesmen plotted their machinations, military commanders calculated their strategy. If anything, the gods, in the form of the planets, were coming to exercise an even greater influence than they had in the past. They were deemed to exert a power which was virtually tangible; and by means of the Hermetic principle of analogy, of the intrinsic relationship between microcosm and macrocosm, this power could seemingly be manipulated, regulated, channelled and controlled.

If Aquinas glimpsed something of this phenomenon, others perceived it more clearly. In 1277 the Bishop of Paris issued a new condemnation of astrology, stressing the pagan – that is, the Islamic and Hermetic – sources in which the discipline was rooted.[6] By that time, however, it was already too late, and the process the bishop feared had become irreversible. Hermetically oriented astrology had already established itself too solidly to be extirpated. Contrary to the objections of the early Church fathers, it no longer deprived man of free will. It did the opposite. It conferred on man a greater freedom to assume control of his life, to shape his destiny, to manage his affairs, than Christianity was prepared to sanction. If one could read the stars accurately, and order one's activities in accord with such a reading, the Church and its hierarchy could be rendered redundant and superfluous.

But the more sophisticated astrology that seeped into Europe through the Reconquista and the Crusades was still incomplete. Not having access to the entire corpus of Hermetic teachings, medieval practitioners were necessarily working with fragmented material, and they knew it. They were aware, in short, of something that many self-styled astrologers of today, including most of those who write 'sun-sign columns', tend generally to forget – that astrology must perforce exist in a broader context. For the medieval practitioner, astrology was not a self-contained, isolated and autonomous discipline to be pursued, as it were, in a vacuum. On the contrary, and in accordance with the premise of interconnectedness underlying Hermetic thought, it interacted closely with other spheres of study, other realms of knowledge. It was only one component of an all-encompassing totality; and its validity derived in large part from its inextricable interrelationship with other such components.

The most important of these was, of course, alchemy, sometimes described as 'terrestrial astrology' and, more frequently, as 'the Royal Art' – or even simply as 'the Art', implying a supremacy over all others. Alchemy rested on the same complex network of Hermetic correspondences as did astrology – correspondences or analogies with astrology itself, as well as with numerous other disciplines. Thus, for example, the astrological signs for the seven 'planets' – the sun, the moon, Mercury, Venus, Mars, Jupiter and Saturn – were also used to denote the metals corresponding to each. For the medieval mind, these signs reflected interrelationships and connections that verged on the uncanny, and confirmed the Hermetic premise of macrocosm and microcosm. In astrology, for instance, Mars, named for the classical god of war, was held to preside over the blood and its circulation. Mars was perceived and described as the 'red planet', and red was used to signify it in astrological colour coding. In alchemy, Mars was equated with iron. Iron was generally employed in the alchemical laboratory as ferric oxide – rust – which is reddish in colour. And it is also iron, of course, that imparts redness of colour to the blood.

Alchemy is frequently regarded today as the ancestor of modern chemistry. In many respects, it unquestionably was that. But the medieval alchemist, and his Renaissance successor, would not have seen himself as a chemist at all in the current sense of that word. Had the twentieth-century conception of psychology existed at the time, he might – as C. G. Jung has demonstrated – have seen himself as a spiritually oriented psychologist who was his own client or patient. In other words, he might have seen himself as being engaged in a programme of self-refinement and self-transformation, for which the external alchemical experiment was an 'objective correlative', a mirror image in the exterior world of a state or process occurring within. And as sculptors speak of 'releasing' the latent form from the block in which it lies embedded or concealed, so many alchemists saw themselves as 'releasing' latent potentialities in the world of elements and minerals around them. But the discipline which medieval and Renaissance alchemists most frequently identified as their own was botany.

Botany served to convey for the alchemist an accurate

sense of the work in which he was engaged – work essentially gentle, natural and organic in character, rather than mechanical or artificial. The alchemical laboratory was intended to replicate the processes of nature herself, to aid and abet these processes – not to improve or impose on them, not to distort them by force or coercion. Gold was not to be manufactured or fabricated. On the contrary, it was to be encouraged 'to grow'. Thus the alchemist would repeatedly describe himself as a botanist of metals or minerals, nurturing them, coaxing them, mothering them to an organic fruition. Like botany, the alchemical process required much patience; and, like botany, it was deemed to be generative, and gentle. It had to be – because, as this book will demonstrate, the ultimate subject and object of the alchemical experiment was the alchemist himself.

Nevertheless, and whatever its broader psychological and spiritual implications, alchemy did establish a methodology and a corpus of data which provided the basis for modern chemistry. And its legacy exists in other spheres as well, some of them quite remote from its original objectives. Thus, for example, the intricate and elaborate distillation procedures involved in alchemy led to the dissemination, if not the actual discovery, of distilled alcohol – derived from the Arabic *al-kohl*. Indeed, the very names attached to such alcohol often reflect its alchemical origin – *aqua vitae*, for instance, *eau de vie* and, for that matter, 'spirituous liquors' or 'spirits'. Distilled alcohol was known as 'spirit of wine'. There is a famous story – probably, alas, apocryphal – about the discovery of the liqueur known as Benedictine. According to this account, a medieval monk, defying the strictures of his superiors, was tinkering in his cell one day with his beginner's alchemy kit. In the course of his experiment, he produced a rich jewel-bright amber or topaz-coloured fluid. On sampling it, he found the taste extremely pleasant and conducive to a warm glow of well-being. Not surprisingly, this prompted him to sample a bit more. Before long, he had begun to feel distinctly uplifted, distinctly exhilarated and ebullient. He and his brethren were soon cavorting around the monastery, triumphantly claiming to have discovered the alchemical elixir. With the following morning's hangover, the Church's fulminations against tampering with the forbidden must have seemed profoundly justified.

Alchemy and astrology were the primary manifestations of Hermeticism's seepage into Western Europe. At the same time, however, there were other manifestations as well. Arabic love poetry often employed Hermetic symbolism, for example, and this found its way into the work of European troubadours.[7] Plaints of chaste or courtly love were frequently couched in alchemical images. And there were, of course, the Grail romances as we know them today. In the hands of Chrétien de Troyes, Wolfram von Eschenbach, Robert de Boron and numerous others, culminating with Sir Thomas Malory, a corpus of Judaeo-Christian material was grafted on to the 'primitive' magic of the so-called 'pagan Grail' stories; and this corpus was suffused with Hermetic themes and symbols. Such themes and symbols are particularly apparent in the work known as *Perlesvaus*, re-issued in a recent edition as *The High History of the Holy Grail*. In this work – whose anonymous authorship reinforces internal evidence to suggest it was composed by a Knight Templar – the reader is confronted with a cart drawn by three harts. Inside the cart are the heads of 150 knights, some 'sealed in gold, other some in silver and the third in lead'.[8] There is also the head of a Queen 'sealed in lead and crowned with copper'.[9] Later in the text there is a castle with thirty-three 'Masters', each dressed in white robes with a red cross on his breast. One of these 'Masters' says to the protagonist: 'There are the heads sealed in silver, and the heads sealed in lead, and the bodies whereunto these heads belonged; I tell you that you must make come thither the head both of the King and of the Queen.'[10]

Such symbolism, often associated with Hermetic magic, abounds throughout *Perlesvaus*. It abounds as well in Wolfram von Eschenbach's *Parzival*. The Grail itself in Wolfram's poem is described as

a stone of purest kind. If you do not know it, it shall here be named to you. It is called *lapsit exillis*. By the power of that stone the phoenix burns to ashes, but the ashes give him life again. Thus does the phoenix moult and change its plumage, which afterwards is bright and shining and as lovely as before. There never was a human so ill but that, if he one day sees that stone, he cannot die within the week that follows. And in looks he will not fade. His appearance will stay the same, be it maid or man, as on the day he saw the stone, the same as when the best years of his life began, and though he should see the stone for two hundred years, it will never change, save that his hair might perhaps turn grey. Such power does the stone give a man that flesh and bones are at once made young again. The stone is also called the Grail.[11]

Scholars have suggested numerous interpretations of the phrase '*lapsit exillis*', all of them more or less plausible. It might be a corruption of *lapis ex caelis* – 'stone from the heavens'. It might also be a corruption of *lapsit ex caelis* – 'it fell from the heavens'. It might be a truncation of *lapis lapsus ex caelus* – 'a stone fallen from heaven'. Most obviously, of course, it might be *lapis elixir*, the Philosophers' Stone and elixir of alchemy.[12] Certainly the passage quoted is laden with alchemical symbolism. The phoenix, for example, is a familiar image in alchemical works, and Wolfram invokes it in a familiar alchemical context.

It was through the Hermetic Grail romances, and through the pseudo-histories of the period – through Geoffrey of Monmouth's *History of the Kings of Britain* – that the figure of Merlin emerged in the guise familiar to us today. The Merlin who looms so prominently in the consciousness and literature of the High Middle Ages no longer has anything in common with the primitive shamanistic Myrddin Wyllt of the earlier Celtic accounts. On the contrary, Merlin is now a full-fledged magus, steeped in the spectrum of arcana that comprised the stock-in-trade of the Hermetic initiate and practitioner. For medieval readers who encountered him in Geoffrey of Monmouth, he was deemed relevant not only to their present, but to their future as well. Geoffrey's mythologized history had included a compilation of prophecies supposedly uttered by Merlin. These prophecies were often reproduced as a separate and self-contained text. They are said to have encouraged Owen Glendower in his Welsh rising of 1402. They were also said to have paved the way for Jeanne d'Arc. According to the official version of her legend, as transcribed in the nineteenth century: 'Old Merlin, the ancient seer, had foretold the coming of Joan of Arc, and she came at the time predicted.'[13] Merlin had reputedly prophesied that the 'Kingdom of France, lost by a woman, would be saved by another woman; that a virgin from the marches of Lorraine would come to deliver Orléans . . .'[14]

By the High Middle Ages, then, Merlin had evolved from a primitive tribal shaman into an embryonic Hermetic magician. He was credited with enjoying access to things still at the time inaccessible to any actual historical figure – to aspects of Hermetic thought which existed in Europe only as fragments, more guessed at and suspected than known or understood. He had become, in effect, the connecting link between the biblical figure of Simon Magus and the man who was to imprint himself on Western consciousness in the fifteenth century as Faust.

At the same time, there were some genuine 'Merlin figures' on the European scene, working with such fragments of Hermetic material as were available. They may not have been quite as awesome as the imposing and romanticized mage of Arthurian legend; but some of them made very real contributions to the advancement of learning and scientific discovery, as well as to the history of Western thought.

Probably the most famous, at least in the English-speaking world, is the Franciscan friar Roger Bacon (1214–94). Born in Somerset, Bacon studied mathematics and medicine at Oxford and in Paris. In France, not surprisingly, he fell foul of the ecclesiastical hierarchy and was forbidden to write. When provisionally rehabilitated, he returned to England, where, some years later, he was again in trouble, getting himself imprisoned and his books burned. In addition to Latin, Bacon was fluent in Hebrew, Arabic and Greek, in an age when few European scholars were conversant with even one of these languages. He was also one of the great medieval pioneers of experimental science. His research encompassed alchemy, chemistry, mathematics, astronomy, magnetism and optics – a gauge of the spectrum of knowledge becoming available at the time to men possessed of his hunger for it. He is recognized as having broken significant new ground in the development and use of lenses. His experiments with nitre reputedly contributed to the advent of gunpowder in Europe. In his copious writings, he spoke of ships which would one day proceed without oars or sails, vehicles which would move without horses, machines which would fly through the air.

Inevitably, Bacon's name came to be associated with a corpus of fantastic legend and literature. His alchemical studies were said to have culminated in his forging of an oracular brazen head which could predict the future. He was also credited with possessing a magical scrying glass, or crystal ball, which performed a similar divinatory function. There is, of course, no basis in fact for such stories; but they reflect something of the way in which the medieval magician-scientist was perceived by his contemporaries. In one respect, these perceptions are not altogether inaccurate. Quite apart from the fantasies attached to him, one can discern in Bacon a Faustian thirst for knowledge and power – a determination to comprehend the internal workings of reality, to shape them to his will and 'make things happen'.

In addition to Bacon, there was Michael Scot (1175–c. 1234), who, as already noted, studied in Spain, and then became court astrologer and resident magus to the Emperor Friedrich II in Sicily. Six centuries later, Coleridge contemplated writing a drama based on Scot, whom he pronounced to be a more compelling personality than Faustus; and Scot figured as well (albeit in erroneous anachronism) in Sir Walter Scott's narrative poem, *The Lay of the Last Minstrel*. There was Arnaud de Villanova (1235–1311), born near Valencia, whose career of alchemical and scientific experimentation warrants comparison with Bacon's. There was Ramón Lull of Mallorca (1229–1315), acclaimed as one of the most illustrious Hermetic magi of his age. According to the most recent evidence, Lull never in actual fact practised alchemy at all and never penned a single alchemical treatise. But numerous contemporary and subsequent writers produced a quantity of such treatises to which they appended his name; and this has caused him to figure in virtually every pre-twentieth-century list of prominent medieval alchemists. Yet even though Lull did not himself engage in alchemical experiment, he was impressively versed in Sufi, Kabbalistic and

Hermetic thought, and exerted a considerable influence on later exponents of Hermeticism.

Of all medieval alchemists and Hermetic philosophers, the most important was the Dominican known as Albertus Magnus (*c.* 1193–1280), who became Bishop of Ratisbon before retiring to seclusion near Cologne. More than any other alchemical practitioner of his era, Albertus was hailed as a mentor and model by generations of successors. But he was also an immensely influential theologian and philosopher, who broke significant new ground in the study of Aristotle, as well as in Judaic and Islamic material and the natural sciences. His own writings still warrant inclusion in any syllabus of thirteenth-century Church literature; and during his tenure as an instructor in Paris, his chief disciple and protégé was no less a personage than Thomas Aquinas. It was, indeed, to Albertus that Aquinas owed his immersion in Aristotelian thought.

Albertus is generally recognized as the single most important figure of the thirteenth century in Latin learning and the natural sciences. His books include works on physics, zoology, astronomy, botany, mineralogy, geography and astrology, as well as on magic, alchemy and Hermetic thought. He endeavoured in particular to find some species of accommodation between magic and Christian theology. To this end, he began by distinguishing between different kinds of magic. There was evil magic, or black magic, which entailed trafficking with demonic forces and used incantations and spells. In this category, Albertus also included the sorcery and conjuration involved in such vestiges as survived of the old pagan religion. In contrast, there was so-called 'natural magic', which relied on the inherent principles of nature and the supernal influence of the stars, and which precluded human interference or manipulation. Such, according to Albertus, was the magic of the three 'wise men', or 'magi', who, in scripture, came to honour Jesus on his birth.[15] Such, too, is alchemy, which 'of all arts . . . most closely imitates nature'.[16]

So far, so good. The distinction would appear to be clear enough, even if it does involve a certain sophistry. But in his scientific writings – according to one commentator, 'influenced mainly by Arabian astrology, the pseudo-Aristotelian treatises, the Hermetic literature'[17] – Albertus outlines what amounts to a third kind of magic. It draws extensively on Hermeticism, rests on the Hermetic premise of the interrelationship between microcosm and macrocosm and utilizes the 'occult virtues' of plants, stones, the blood of certain animals, amulets and talismans. Alchemy, of course, could just as readily be classified as this kind of magic as it could 'natural magic'. But Hermetic magic also incorporates elements of what Albertus condemns as evil. In short, Albertus condemns in his theological writings what, in his scientific writings, he condones. One must remember, however, that he was a Dominican, working within the Church, and had necessarily to be cautious. In the preface to one of his alchemical texts, he lists the errors to which alchemists are most frequently prone, and then adumbrates the rules to which they must adhere. The first of these is secrecy.

Among the names most frequently associated with medieval magic and alchemy, one must cite, finally, that of a slightly later figure, Nicolas Flamel. Flamel was born around 1330 and died in 1418. He worked originally as a scrivener, or copyist, in Paris. By dint of his occupation, he obtained access to many rare books and documents, and acquired a familiarity – rare for a layman at the time – with painting, poetry, chemistry, mathematics and architecture. He also began to steep himself in such material as he could find on alchemy, on Kabbalistic and Hermetic thought.

Around 1360, Flamel, according to his own account, happened upon an alchemical text which was to transform his life. He himself supposed it to have issued, and perhaps been stolen, from Judaic sources. The title-page, Flamel reported, was inscribed: 'Abraham the Jew, Prince, Priest, Levite, Astrologer and Philosopher to the nation of the Jewes, by the Wrath of God Dispersed among the Gaules, sendeth health.'[18] Every seventh page of the text contained no writing, only illustrations. There were numerous other illustrations as well, of a specifically alchemical and Hermetic nature. The original of this book is said to have been deposited in the Arsenal Library in Paris. Reproductions of it have been assiduously, religiously and, so far as is known, vainly studied by successive generations of would-be adepts.

According to his own account, Flamel could not himself read the book, which was written in neither Latin nor French. It may well have been written in Hebrew – Flamel became convinced one could not understand it unless one knew Kabbala. He spent more than twenty frustrated years poring over his indecipherable and enigmatic acquisition. At last, on a journey to Santiago de Compostela in Spain, he claimed to have met a converted Jew in León who elucidated the text for him. On returning to Paris, he proceeded to apply what he had learned and reputedly performed – at noon on 17 January 1382 – the first in a series of alchemical transmutations.[19]

The truth of Flamel's account is, of course, open to question. The fact remains, however, that he shortly thereafter acquired the patronage of a woman who herself became known as 'an expert in chemical sciences' – Blanche d'Evreux, also known as Blanche de Navarre, daughter of the King of Navarre and subsequently wife of Philippe VI of France. Reportedly as a result of his alchemical transmutations, Flamel also became phenomenally wealthy. By the end of his life, he owned more than thirty houses and tracts of land in Paris alone. Yet he seems to have been a modest man, who did not revel in power and lavished much of his affluence on good works. By 1413, he had founded and endowed fourteen hospitals, seven churches and three chapels in Paris, and a comparable number in Boulogne. This altruism, perhaps more than his dazzling success, turned him into a legend and endeared him to posterity. As late as the eighteenth century, he was still revered by such men as Sir Isaac Newton, who painstakingly read through his work, copiously annotated it and even copied it out by hand – endeavouring thereby to fulfil his injunction to 'perfect to the glory of God the maistery of Hermes . . .'[20]

It is significant that except for Flamel, all the prominent adherents of medieval magic and Hermeticism were either ecclesiastics or patronized by ecclesiastics. In other words, the Church's monopoly on learning remained intact and virtually unbroken, save for the protégés of one or another court – the authors of some of the Grail romances, for example, who were taken under the wing of secular potentates. With Flamel, however, the latest of the medieval magi, the situation was beginning to change. It was soon to change much more dramatically. A new generation of magi was waiting in the wings of history's stage, and they were to have minimal association with the Church, were often to be opposed to the Church. Faustus was preparing to make his début. And the Church was going to have to produce her own highly heterodox magi simply to keep pace with him.

6

THE RENAISSANCE

By the beginning of the fifteenth century, a secular culture had already taken root in Western Europe. Dante's *Divine Comedy*, for instance, probably begun as early as 1307, may have been 'religious' in its ultimate orientation, but it did not issue from within the Church. It was composed in Italian rather than Latin and its Christianity, in more than a few respects, verged precariously on heterodoxy, if not, indeed, heresy. Subsequent to Dante (1265–1321), there was Francesco Petrarch (1304–74), whose poetry, scholarship and passionate devotion to classical Greece had generated a renewed interest in the world of Hellenic antiquity and caused him to become known as the 'father of Italian humanism'. Contemporary with Petrarch's work, there were the prose narratives of Giovanni Boccaccio (*c.* 1313–75). What was more, the influence of these men travelled. Within a few years of his death, for example, Boccaccio's was to manifest itself as far afield as uncouth and rain-sodden England, where Chaucer's *Canterbury Tales* was to inaugurate the tradition of British secular literature. Petrarch, Boccaccio and Chaucer, like Dante, wrote not in Latin, but in the vernacular of their native languages.

For the most part, however, the Church's monopoly of learning continued more or less intact. Yet it had begun perceptibly to loosen, to show signs of a new flexibility, even audacity. Greek was being taught in Italy and France, and Greek philosophy – insofar as scholars had access to it – was being assiduously studied. For Aquinas and other prominent theologians, Aristotle – whose thought could easily be harmonized and reconciled with Catholic doctrine – remained the supreme classical authority. But Plato was gaining in currency. A thousand years before, he had been given a seal of approval by no less a personage than St Augustine, who found him closer to Christianity than any other pagan thinker. He had been endorsed by other ecclesiastical commentators as well, and Latin translations of his work were to be found in clerical libraries. With the study of Greek, his dialogues became increasingly accessible in the original language and began to exert an increasingly important influence.

Platonism, of course, had much in common with Hermeticism. The promulgation of Platonic thought thus did much to pave the way for the dissemination of Hermeticism across Western Europe. But the chief and most subversive infiltration of Hermeticism into Christendom was to be facilitated by the Church itself. In attempting to extend its authority and hegemony over the Greek Orthodox faith, the Church of Rome was soon unwittingly to admit a mode of thought conducive to its own sedition.

Since the eleventh century – some fifty years before the First Crusade – the Orthodox Church in Byzantium had managed to accommodate itself to Hermeticism. The 'official' *Hermetica* – the corpus of Hermetic works known by that designation today – is believed to date from around 1050, when it was collated and compiled in Constantinople by Michael Psellus, a prominent Byzantine scholar, professor of philosophy, historian, theologian and state functionary. Psellus had initiated a revival of studies in Neoplatonism, and boasted of such fame that pupils as diverse as Arabs and

Celts came to study under his tutelage. It is likely that he obtained his version of the Hermetic texts by way of Harran, where a major temple had been destroyed shortly before. In his editing of these texts, Psellus expurgated many of their purely magical and alchemical aspects, thus making them more acceptable to Greek Orthodox Christianity and ensuring that neither he nor his efforts ended in flames. The philosophical and mystical dimensions of Hermeticism were, however, preserved intact, and, through Psellus, found their way into the mainstream of Byzantine intellectual life.

In the meantime, the long-standing dispute between the Orthodox and Catholic Churches was becoming more acute, and God's will – as manifested, at least, through his temporal institutions – more dramatically schizophrenic. In 1054, just when Michael Psellus was at the peak of his career, any semblance of accord between the two Churches was abandoned. The rupture between them was declared official; each proceeded to excommunicate the other and their mutual antipathy was to continue until 1965. For the next three centuries, Catholic crusaders were to enjoy tacit – and sometimes more than tacit – sanction to wreak havoc on Rome's eastern rival. Thus, in 1204, during the Fourth Crusade, Western armies, supposedly en route to Jerusalem to recapture the Holy Sepulchre, managed to find time to pillage, plunder and sack the Byzantine capital. Having done so, they were unable to find time to proceed to the Holy Land at all.

By the fifteenth century, however, the Byzantine Empire was under increasing pressure from the Turks, and was obliged to seek aid from Western potentates. The price of such aid would necessarily be some sort of accommodation with Rome. In 1438, therefore, the Byzantine Emperor, accompanied by the Patriarch of Constantinople (the Orthodox equivalent of the Pope), came to Italy for an ecclesiastical council intended to explore the possibilities of reuniting Christendom. The council was convened initially in Ferrara; but a sudden outbreak of plague prompted an abrupt transference of proceedings to Florence, the domain of the Pope's banker, Cosimo de' Medici.

The council commenced its work on 8 October 1438, and ended with the departure of the Byzantine Emperor on 26 August 1439. It produced little of consequence. A nominal declaration of nebulous accord was agreed upon by the two Churches, perhaps facilitated by the convenient death of the Patriarch of Constantinople during the course of the negotiations. But the Emperor, on returning to his own domains, was afraid to divulge the supposed accord to his people. It was kept secret until 1452. A year later, Constantinople fell to the Turks and the whole matter was rendered academic.

But if the Council of Florence did little for Christian unity, it sowed seeds of enormous consequence in other spheres. For the Byzantine Emperor had brought with him, to argue the case for the Orthodox Church, an entourage of more than 650 scholars and ecclesiastics; and they, expecting to have to quote from relevant texts, had come equipped with a copious supply of original Greek manuscripts. Not all of these were specifically biblical or Christian. There were others as well, many of which had previously been unknown in the West. Of the greatest interest, perhaps, was Plato, whose work had hitherto been represented to Western scholars mainly by the *Timaeus*.

One of the most prominent scholars in the Byzantine Emperor's retinue was George Gemistus, who, during the council, adopted the *nom de plume* of 'Plethon'. He had previously distinguished himself as a teacher of philosophy in Mistra, the third largest city in the Byzantine Empire at the time, located in the Peloponnesus near the site of ancient Sparta. In everything but name, Plethon was a 'pagan' philosopher. He embraced the syncretism – and especially the Neoplatonism – of Alexandria at the dawn of the Christian era. He was hostile to Christianity. He repudiated Aristotle, philosophical icon to so many Catholic theologians. He dreamed of restoring the vitality and dynamism of pagan tradition and the old Athenian Academy.

In the Byzantine Empire, prevailing law dictated the death penalty for any Christian who reverted to pagan thought or practice. In consequence, Plethon was obliged to keep his true convictions quiet. They were divulged, apparently, only to an exclusive and élite cadre of initiates among his protégés at Mistra. Through this cadre, Plethon promulgated his ideas. He insisted on oral teaching, stressing that both Pythagoras and Plato had preferred the spoken to the written word. The Council of Florence provided him with a unique forum. His sojourn in the city was to produce something like a chemical reaction, radically transforming, through a reciprocal influence, both the man and the place.

In the generation or two preceding the council, Florence had become a hotbed of diverse studies. Secular learning had established a milieu in which it could thrive untrammelled by ecclesiastical constraints. In an environment increasingly unfettered from the guilt fostered by Church doctrine, the dignity and significance of man had come to be accorded a hitherto unprecedented emphasis. A new term, *studia humanitatis*, was regularly invoked. Florence, in short, had become the cradle of humanism, of humanist thought and tradition.

Concurrent with the new humanism, there was also a reaction against Aristotle. The seeds of this reaction had been planted a century before, when Petrarch had learned Greek and extolled Plato. Although little enough of Plato's work was available to a secular audience, it was fervently embraced by Petrarch's protégés and disciples. By the time of the

Council of Florence, Plato – even on the basis of the meagre texts obtainable – had become as well established in the city as humanism. Florence at the time was an independent republic and the fifth largest urban centre in Europe, with a population of 50,000–70,000. With the capture of Pisa in 1406, it had even acquired its own seaport. It was also the home of the continent's largest bank, that of the Medici. From the Medici down, many of its public and municipal figures were not just patrons of humanism, but active humanists themselves.

One can imagine the exhilaration with which Plethon, formerly compelled to keep his interests clandestine, immersed himself in this refreshingly uncensored and unrestricted milieu. He revelled in its intellectual freedom. He did so all the more energetically for not being obliged to attend every session and conference of the ecclesiastical council. Having time and opportunity at his disposal, he was at liberty to fraternize at leisure with Florentine humanists.

By the end of his stay in Florence, Plethon had discarded all pretence to Christian belief. In discreet circles at least, he began to promulgate flagrantly heretical convictions. Repudiating Christian doctrine, he explicitly embraced and advocated something reminiscent of the classical mystery schools. Within a few years, he prophesied, these would have spread across the world, would have supplanted all other faiths (including those of Christendom and Islam) and fostered a new unity for mankind. It was inevitable, he declared, that '. . . Muhammad and Christ would be forgotten and the real truth would shine through on all the shores of the world'.[1] The sheer vehemence of this assertion is striking. Plethon does not suggest that Christianity and Islam are variations of an absolute truth. On the contrary, he implies that they are falsifications of it, and that their extirpation is a precondition for its resurgence.

SWITZERLAND

KINGDOM OF
HUNGARY

DUCHY OF SAVOY

DUCHY OF MILAN

Turin

Po

Parma

Mantua

Padua

Venice

Modena

Genoa

1

2

Bologna

Ravenna

OTTOMAN
EMPIRE

VENETIAN REPUBLIC

Adriatic Sea

Florence

Pisa

3

4

Urbino

Siena

Perugia

Assisi

5

Tiber

6

Rome

CORSICA

MEDITERRANEAN

SEA

Capua

Naples

SARDINIA

KINGDOM

OF THE

TWO SICILIES

SICILY

Palermo

Syracuse

1. REPUBLIC OF GENOA
2. DUCHY OF MODENA
3. REPUBLIC OF FLORENCE
4. DEPENDENT UPON PAPAL STATES
5. REPUBLIC OF SIENA
6. PAPAL STATES

Renaissance Italy, late fifteenth century

While in Florence, Plethon also gave a series of public lectures to audiences of humanist scholars. In these lectures, he compared Plato and Aristotle, scathingly repudiating the latter and endorsing the former. His words carried all the more authority because he was able to quote to his listeners directly from the Greek originals, with none of the distortions in interpretation which characterized Latin and Arabic translations. In his lectures, too, Plethon enunciated his belief in a universal religion, reminiscent of Neoplatonism, which postulated 'one mind, one soul, one sermon'.[2] Such was his erudition, his enthusiasm and his charisma that he inspired in his audience a hunger for more of his vision, and for a more comprehensive knowledge of the sources whence it derived. Among those to feel this hunger most acutely was one man uniquely placed to assuage it – Cosimo de' Medici himself.

Cosimo 'frequently heard a Greek philosopher by the name of Gemistus disputing like another Plato on the Platonic mysteries . . . Cosimo was . . . so inspired, so ensouled, that from that time forth he conceived deep in his mind a kind of Academy, to give birth to it at the first opportune moment.'[3]

Thus, some years later, wrote Marsilio Ficino, a young man who was to become Cosimo's protégé and play a supremely important role in subsequent developments. Exposure to Plethon's lectures had indeed inspired Cosimo, man of the world though he was, with a longing for a higher, more spiritual truth – a truth which the Church, in his opinion, no longer seemed to reflect, but which Plato did. He obtained a complete edition of Plato's works – purchased, the evidence suggests, directly from Plethon. And he embarked on an ambitious project to bring Platonic studies to Florence – to make Florence, in fact, a centre of Platonic studies. The chief component of his dream was to create a full-fledged Platonic Academy in the tradition of those of antiquity. This enterprise was to some extent vitiated by Plethon's return to Byzantium in the summer of 1439. Nevertheless, Cosimo set about recruiting teachers and gathering texts. With the energy that only a sense of mission can confer, he dispatched his agents eastwards in quest of ancient manuscripts for his library of San Marco, which eventually came to comprise some ten thousand items.

Despite his own zest, Cosimo's plans proceeded only gradually at first. In 1453, however, after a prolonged death agony, Constantinople at last fell to the Turks. One result of the débâcle was a massive exodus of fleeing scholars and ecclesiastics, many of whom brought with them in their flight priceless caches of manuscripts. The majority of these refugees found their way across the Adriatic into Italy, where their advent provided a new and dynamic stimulus to Cosimo's dream of a Platonic Academy. In 1459, he summoned a student from the University of Bologna, Marsilio Ficino, to preside over the institution.

Ficino, the son of a doctor, had been born near Florence in 1433. At the time of the Council of Florence, he was only five years old. He had subsequently received a comprehensive education in the humanities, becoming impressively versed not just in the standard subjects of the age, but also in music, in the Greek language and in Greek philosophy. His immersion in Greek thought had dealt a fatal blow to his faith: lectures by Byzantine refugees had so affected him that the Archbishop of Florence had forbidden him to attend them. Undeterred, Ficino had pursued his studies with a zeal that prompted him to be accused of heresy. In any city other than Florence, such an accusation might have been tantamount to a death sentence. Ficino, however, remained unmolested, continuing his work in Bologna until Cosimo summoned him back.

At the age of twenty-six, the precocious young scholar was installed in a Medici villa at Careggi. This became the site of Cosimo's long-planned academy, whose habitués soon included not just scholars, but artists, bankers, lawyers, merchants, politicians and ecclesiastics. Since Cosimo himself knew no Greek, he commissioned Ficino to translate his precious edition of Plato. His passion for this enterprise is obvious in this letter written to his protégé:

> Yesterday I went to my estate at Careggi, but for the sake of cultivating my mind and not the estate. Come to us, Marsilio, as soon as possible. Bring with you Plato's book on *The Highest Good*, which I suppose you have translated from Greek into Latin as you promised. I want nothing more wholeheartedly than to know which way leads most surely to happiness. Farewell. Come, and bring your Orphic lyre with you.[4]

For a year, Ficino proceeded to concentrate on translating Plato. Then, in 1460, Cosimo abruptly ordered him to stop, to interrupt his work, to devote all his energy and resources to something else. The new project consisted of translating something even more exciting. Michael Psellus' own copy of the *Hermetica*, dating from the eleventh century, had just fallen into Cosimo's hands; and Cosimo wanted to read the Hermetic dialogues before he died. Ficino finished this new task in April 1463, and was given a villa at Careggi as a reward. Cosimo died a year later, in 1464.

The Hermetic texts had an electrifying effect on Cosimo – and on Ficino as well, who saw them as the ultimate foundation on which Platonic thought rested. Between 1467 and 1469, Ficino produced a commentary on Plato entitled *The Platonic Theology*. Platonism and Hermeticism had become for him precisely that – a full-fledged theology, which posed a viable and alluring complement, if not indeed an alternative, to the Judaeo-Christian tradition.

By this time, Ficino was actively attempting to revive a form of ancient pagan mystery teaching and had become immersed in attending practices, rituals and ceremonies. He advocated the regular singing of Orphic hymns – the cultic invocations associated with the mystery schools of antiquity. He decorated the villa at Careggi with astrological images, contemplation of which he extolled as spiritually beneficial and conducive to illumination. Around the walls, there was an inscription which he adopted as his maxim: 'All things are directed from goodness to goodness. Rejoice in the present; set no value on property, seek no honours. Avoid excess; avoid activity. Rejoice in the present.'[5]

Modelled on its classical antecedents, the Academy was not a formal school, but a loose, often social association of individuals with an interest in Platonic and Hermetic studies. Lectures were given, symposia and festivals held. Ficino himself offered informal guidance and programmes of study to his disciples and to visiting scholars. Among those who attended were Lorenzo de Medici, Lorenzo the Magnificent, who assumed power in Florence in 1469. There was the architect Leon Battista Alberti, who was instrumental in resurrecting the classical principles of Vitruvius. There was Angelo Poliziano, tutor to Lorenzo's children, translator of Homer and mentor in turn to the Englishmen William Latimer and Thomas Linacre. There was the poet and educator Cristoforo Landino, who, in 1481, published an edition of Dante's *Divine Comedy* with his own commentary and illustrations by Botticelli. Botticelli was only one of a number of great artists to reflect the influence of Ficino's Academy. Others included Leonardo, Michelangelo, Raphael, Titian and Dürer. In the meantime, Ficino maintained a vigorous correspondence with figures as far afield as John Colet in England, Johannes Reuchlin in Germany and the reigning King of Hungary, who invited him to the Hungarian Court.

Drawing specifically on the Hermetic texts, Ficino expounded the principles of a magic new to the West. Through this magic, he explained how man could exploit the relationship between microcosm and macrocosm so as actively to control and manipulate aspects of both. As the authority behind his teaching, he invoked Hermes Trismegistus, the putative author of the Hermetic texts. As in the period of Alexandrian syncretism, 'Thrice-great Hermes' was regarded as a historical personage. Ficino, the Medici and their disciples believed him to have been an ancient Egyptian magus and sage, older and wiser than either Plato or Pythagoras, both of whom had apparently derived their doctrines from him. He was sometimes regarded as contemporary with, and comparable to, Zoroaster and Moses – and sometimes extolled as the source of their inspiration as well. Ancient Egypt once again became perceived as the ultimate and supreme fount of wisdom; and in the writings ascribed to Hermes Trismegistus there shone 'a light of divine illumination'. The Hermetic books were revered as 'revelations of divine truth, not as the products of human reason'.[6]

As in the period of Alexandrian syncretism, Hermes Trismegistus was conflated with the moon god Thoth, inventor of writing, patron of magic, judge of the dead, guardian of the gates to the underworld, whose sacred number was three and sacred metal was silver. Portrayed symbolically as a white ape or baboon, as an ibis or an ibis-headed figure, Thrice-great Hermes, for the next century and a half, was to reign supreme in the pantheon of ancient sages, oracles and religious prophets. Although never explicitly stated as such, his authority came in effect to exceed even that of Jesus. Jesus might still command nominal allegiance in matters of faith. But it was to Hermes that the magi of the time, as well as the princes, the potentates, the military commanders, even the ecclesiastics, began increasingly to turn for aid in practical matters – from organizing their personal lives to planning political activities and martial campaigns. Hermes thus became an active agent through whom things could be made to happen. In other words, he became, through his supposed teachings, a conduit for the practical application of magic.

The magic delineated and extolled by Ficino and those who followed him is generally known as 'talismanic magic'. It differed radically from petty sorcery of the past. It transcended the essentially circumscribed sphere of medieval magic – occult vendettas pursued against personal enemies, cures for sterility, impotence or baldness. Such things, of course, continued to figure; but they did so now in a framework that was ultimately cosmic in scope and scale – a framework which accommodated ambitions and aspirations far beyond the purely personal, the local or parochial. In Ficino's magic, one might draw on cosmic power, cosmic principles, cosmic energy. To avail oneself of the power of the sun, for example, one would wear a mantle of gold, the sun's colour, and conduct a ritual before an altar adorned with the sun's image. At the same time, one would burn an incense made from plants sacred to the sun and, anointed with solar oils, sing an Orphic hymn to the luminary:

Hearken, O blessed one, whose eternal eye sees all . . . Yours the golden lyre and the harmony of cosmic motion, and you command noble deeds and nurture the seasons. Piping lord of the world, a fiery circle of light is your course . . . your light gives light and fruit . . . Eye of justice and light of life . . . Hear my words and show life's sweetness to the initiates.[7]

As Ficino employed it, this was no mere 'hymn of praise' or aesthetic exercise. On the contrary, it was a magical invocation, designed to make the sun actively and literally inhabit and 'possess' its talismanic image – and, through the talismanic image, to inhabit and 'possess' the petitioner, to subsume his personality in a transcendant power. As will become apparent, the talismanic image – the magnet, so to speak, which drew the sun's potency into itself – would often take the form of a work of art. Poems, musical compositions, masques, paintings, sculptures all came to function as talismanic images, or conduits for talismanic magic. So, too, in accordance with Hermetic principles of architecture, did buildings. So, too, did gardens.

Ficino wrote extensively about the techniques whereby planetary powers might be attracted by the principles of Hermetic analogy, and concentrated for the individual's own use: 'If you want your body and spirit to receive power . . . from the Sun, learn which are the Solar things among metals and stones, even more among plants, but among the animal world most of all . . .'[8] To invoke the sun's power, 'you put on Solar things to wear . . . you live in Solar places, look Solar, hear Solar, smell Solar, imagine Solar, think Solar, and even desire Solar'.[9]

Through amulets and talismans, and even more through unguents and elixirs, Ficino sought to devise something akin to a spiritual magnifying glass – something which, like a magnifying glass, would concentrate the sun's energy into a focus of greater intensity than would normally occur in the natural world. Such intensity could theoretically be deployed to accentuate, to illumine, to heal, to warm – or, in certain circumstances, to incinerate. But if the sun exercised the most flagrantly tangible influence, it was by no means the only one. Amulets, talismans, unguents and elixirs could similarly be created to invoke other 'planetary' or stellar influences. Thus, for instance, melancholy was supposed to derive from the effects of Saturn. Because Saturn also presided over the long hours of study necessary to the philosopher, he was particularly prone to melancholy. To neutralize this propensity, he might invoke the counterbalancing effects of Jupiter. By such techniques, Ficino declared, 'one could avoid the malignity of fate'.[10] In other words, one need not remain a passive and helpless victim of circumstance – or, for that matter, of one's birth chart. One could take one's destiny in one's hands and shape it in accordance with one's wishes. In conformity to the traditions of the mystery schools, an individual would submit to a symbolic death and rebirth, and emerge with what was perceived as a new identity, often denoted by a new name. If such a ritual were conducted under astrologically propitious circumstances, one could even, theoretically, correct supposed deficiencies in one's horoscope.

7

THE SPREAD OF HERMETIC WISDOM

With Ficino's translation of the *Hermetica*, in 1463, the incipient and still amorphous phenomenon now known as the Renaissance began to crystallize, to assume a definite orientation, thrust and direction – as well as a potent impetus. This impetus was further stimulated, of course, by technological developments, not least of which was the invention of printing. In 1455, the Gutenberg Bible had been produced, the first book ever to be printed with movable type. In 1476, William Caxton had introduced the first press to use movable type in England. By that time, the initially primitive process had already become more sophisticated and refined.

The two centres of printing in fifteenth-century Europe were Venice, where the first press was licensed in 1469, and Paris, where production commenced shortly thereafter. By the end of the fifteenth century, there were more than 150 Venetian presses in operation, which had published more than 4,000 titles; Paris had published another 2,000. Other cities produced less, but their combined output was enormous. It is estimated that by 1503, some eight million books had been printed in Europe. Printers stood to make substantial profits, anticipating the press barons of today and creating a new moneyed class across the continent. In 1483, it cost three times as much to print Ficino's translation of Plato as it would have done to make a scribal copy. But the scribal copy would have been the only one of its kind. The printed edition put more than 1,000 copies into circulation.

The increasing accessibility of books enabled a body of thought to be much more widely distributed and disseminated than it could possibly have been even a few years earlier. And the sheer proliferation of books acted as a stimulus to literacy. Nobles and potentates who had previously been content to leave learning in the hands of the Church now began to claim it for themselves. So, too, did the burgeoning middle class of burgers, merchants and entrepreneurs. According to the late Dame Frances Yates, printing 'was the one invention which made possible the whole subsequent astonishingly rapid evolution of European culture'.[1] Nor could this evolution be curtailed by the Church's new-found vocation of censorship. 'The Italian Renaissance achieved permanence through being fixed by the print culture.'[2]

The advent of printing enabled Ficino's Academy in Florence to flourish with extraordinary energy. So, too, did the enthusiastic patronage of the Medici – first Cosimo, then, perhaps even more, Lorenzo the Magnificent. The Academy catered not only to scholars, to philosophers and theologians, but also to ecclesiastics, diplomats, doctors, lawyers, wealthy bankers, poets and painters. To these individuals, it seemed that a new age was truly beginning, that the world was about to undergo a momentous change. An unprecedented optimism suffused the air. It was expected, for example, that, within a generation or two, cures would have been discovered for virtually every disease. It was also expected that a new universal religion, reconciling Christianity with Platonism and Hermeticism, would soon be established, and would thereby put a definitive end to the strife that bedevilled human affairs.

From the Academy in Florence, a new *Zeitgeist* began to issue and diffuse itself gradually across Italy. By the end of the 1460s, a second academy had been established in Naples. A third – even more radical, pagan and ritualistic in orientation – had been founded in Rome. Not surprisingly, it was shut down by the Pope and its members were arrested. In 1471, however, a new Pope, Sixtus IV, assumed the throne of St Peter, and the Roman Academy was re-established.

In 1502, an academy of particular subsequent importance was founded in Venice. For the next quarter of a century, conflict in Italy was to preclude the establishment of additional institutions. After 1525, however, they began to appear again, in ever-increasing numbers. Many of them adopted characteristics associated with later Freemasonry; they adopted evocative and often mystical appellations for themselves, like those of subsequent Masonic lodges, as well as ornate symbolic devices, emblems and coats of arms. Elaborate ritualistic rules and ceremonies were instituted. Presiding officers were elected and adopted portentous names – 'The Elevated Ones', for example, or 'The Hidden Ones'.[3]

By the early eighteenth century, there were more than five hundred academies in Italy. Some of them – the Arcadian Academy of Rome, for instance, founded in 1690 – became famous throughout Europe, and welcomed distinguished personages from across the continent. Goethe was to become a member of the Arcadian Academy. For his famous account of his Italian journey, he adopted the motto 'Et in Arcadia Ego'.[4]

That, however, was some three centuries later. Back in late fifteenth-century Florence, Ficino had been increasingly consumed by his own feverish energy. His role as guiding spirit of the original Academy was gradually taken over by an even more audacious, magisterial and charismatic figure,

Hermes Trismegistus – 'Thrice Greatest' – the mystical teacher and magus, as portrayed in the Renaissance. A late fifteenth-century mosaic pavement, Siena Cathedral.

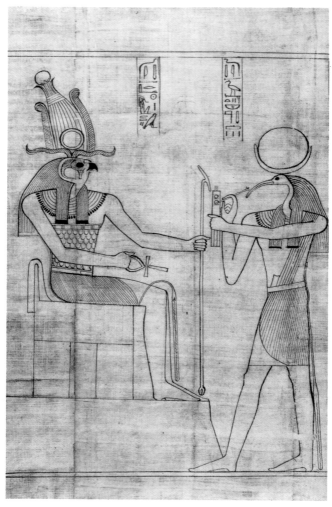

Right: Thoth, the ibis-headed Egyptian god of the moon, of knowledge, divine messenger, inventor of magic and writing, standing before Ra. Thoth was equated with Hermes by the Greeks. The library of his temple at Hermopolis was renowned for its works on magic and Egyptian history. Papyrus from Thebes, around 950 BC.

Bottom left: Thoth recording the result of the weighing of a dead person's heart by Anubis in the Halls of Justice. From *The Book of the Dead*, Thebes, around 1100 BC.

Dr John Dee, the Elizabethan magus, aged sixty-seven, in a portrait dated 1594. He excelled in theology, philosophy, mathematics, geography, science, cryptography and magic.

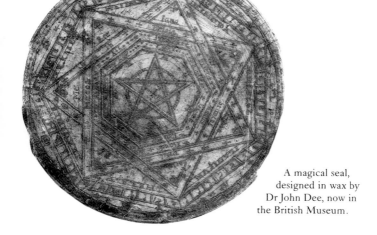

A magical seal, designed in wax by Dr John Dee, now in the British Museum.

The Hermetic philosopher: alchemist, kabbalist, magician and musician.
On the ceiling is written: 'Without divine inspiration, no one is great'.
From Heinrich Khunrath, *Amphitheatrum sapientiae aeternae*, 1609.

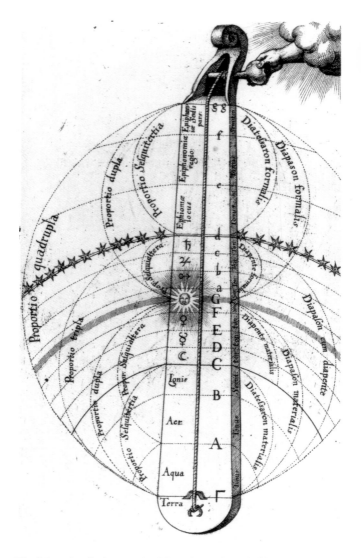

The 'Monochord' of Hermetic philosopher Robert Fludd, symbolizing the musical harmony of the universe. From his *Utriusque cosmi ... historia*, 1617.

The Hermetic philosopher following the footprints of nature: 'Let nature, reason, experience and books be guide, staff, spectacles and lamp for the alchemist'. From the Rosicrucian Michael Maier, *Atalanta Fugiens*, 1617.

Geometry and divine proportion with its associated epigram set to music. From Michael Maier, *Atalanta Fugiens*, 1617.

The College of the Rosicrucian Brotherhood: the rose and the cross appear on either side of the door. It is the invisible brotherhood whose movements are guided by the hand of God. From Theophilus Schweighardt, *Speculum Sophicum Rhodo-Stauroticum*, 1618.

Giovanni Pico della Mirandola (1463–94). If Ficino had been essentially a gentle scholar and a pedagogue, Pico was an altogether different kind of personality. With a boldness Ficino would have found intemperate, even dangerously rash, Pico embarked on the quest which characterized all the most ambitious activity of the Renaissance – to integrate all human knowledge, all human endeavour, in an entirely new and all-encompassing synthesis. And while Ficino was primarily an academic, Pico, though no less skilled academically, was also a practising magician. In Pico della Mirandola, the Faust figure, while not yet having attained his full stature, had at last come of age.

Pico was born into a family of northern Italy's minor nobility. Turning his back in disgust on the privileges attending his rank, he decided, as a precocious youth, to devote himself to scholarship. He studied at the universities of Bologna, Ferrara, Padua, Pavia and Paris. He became versed in canon law, literature, medieval scholasticism and theology, the Greek language and Greek philosophy. He was subsequently to learn Hebrew, Arabic and Aramaic. In the meantime, he employed other scholars in these languages to do translations for him. On a visit to Florence, he became friends with Ficino and a prominent member of Ficino's Academy.

In 1486, he embarked on his boldest project. He drew up a compendium of nine hundred Hermetically oriented theses or propositions, which he published in Rome, announcing his preparedness to defend them against all opponents. In effect, he flung down a gauntlet to the whole of Christendom, challenging the world to debate his philosophy with him. He even offered to pay travel expenses to Rome for any adversaries. In the event, nothing came of his flamboyant gesture. The intended debate was prohibited by the Papacy, and thirteen of Pico's theses were branded heretical. A disingenuous disclaimer purporting to be an apology only got him deeper into trouble, from which he was rescued by the death of the presiding pope and the intervention of Lorenzo de' Medici. Somewhat chastened, he settled in Florence, continuing to write and study, though refraining from subsequent public dispute. He died in 1494, at the age of thirty-one.

Pico's orientation was characteristically Hermetic. Like Ficino, he embraced and extolled the *Hermetica* as a veritable Bible. At the same time, however, he also added something to it. Having discerned the parallels between Hermeticism and the Judaic Kabbala, Pico proceeded to combine them. Through Pico, the Kabbala was adapted to the Christian world and fused with Hermeticism. In effecting this crucial and influential amalgam, Pico drew on the teachings of two mentors.

One of these was a Sicilian, Flavius Mithridates, who had converted from Judaism to Christianity. Mithridates served Pico as a translator, thus making available to him a corpus of Kabbalistic texts. Mithridates' output was enormous. Between May and November of 1486, he translated an entire library for Pico – some forty books, amounting to more than 3,500 manuscript pages.[5] He also taught Pico 'Chaldean' – that is, Aramaic.

Even more important for Pico than Mithridates was the Hermetic Kabbalist Johanan Alemanno. Alemanno drew on a Judaic Hermetic tradition believed to have originated in early twelfth-century Spain, according to which Hermes Trismegistus, in one of his incarnations, was equated with the biblical figure of Enoch. The same tradition outlined a concept of talismanic magic similar to the one subsequently promulgated by Ficino, and maintained the Golden Calf of the Old Testament had not been an object of idolatry, but a magical talisman. Aspects of this tradition are said by some scholars to have been embraced by Wolfram von Eschenbach, thus accounting for some of the Hermetic motifs in *Parzival*.

Such was the tradition on which Alemanno drew. He wrote that the ancient Israelites 'were taught to believe in the possibility of causing spiritual forces and emanations to descend from above by means of preparations made by man for that purpose, such as talismans, garments, and certain objects whose purpose is to cause the descent of a certain spiritual power . . .'[6] Alemanno also maintained that the Temple of Jerusalem was, in effect, 'a gigantic talisman constructed in order to induce the presence of God to descend upon it'.[7] And he argued, too, that if Hermes Trismegistus could be equated with Enoch, both Moses and Solomon were Hermetic adepts and magicians.

Pico eagerly seized on Alemanno's teachings. On Mount Sinai, he asserted, Moses had received not just the Law, but also an esoteric mystical interpretation of it, which was passed down secretly and orally. This 'true and more occult explanation', Pico stated, was the Kabbala – which he then proceeded to draw together with the established corpus of the *Hermetica* as translated by Ficino.[8] The result was a comprehensive and persuasive new synthesis which reconciled the mystical and magical aspects of Christian, Judaic, Islamic and Hermetic thought. To make his synthesis even more complete, Pico added to it Chaldean oracles and Orphic hymns. There thus emerged a species of new world religion – of which magic was an integral component.

When planning the great debate in which he proposed to defend his nine hundred theses, Pico prepared an oration. With this oration, on the dignity of man, he intended to open the proceedings. Because the debate never occurred, the oration was never publicly given. Neither was it published until after Pico's death. It is now regarded, however, as the most succinct and eloquent summation of Pico's thought. In it, he exploits the implications first enunciated by Hermeticism fifteen hundred years before – that man need not be a hapless victim of circumstance or fate, but can acquire the power to shape reality around him and determine, in freedom and responsibility, his own destiny. Pico declares that man was created to sit at the centre of the world, between heaven and earth. From this position, through free will, he may make of himself whatever he wishes. 'Whatever seeds each man cultivates will grow to maturity and bear in him their own fruit.'[9] For Pico, this process is achieved 'by the right use of natural substances in accordance with the principles of sympathetic magic'.[10] And, as he states explicitly, 'so does the magus wed earth to heaven, that is, he weds lower things to the endowments and powers of higher things'.[11]

In assessing Pico, Frances Yates observes:

> We begin to perceive here an extraordinary change in the status of the magician. The necromancer, concocting his filthy mixtures, the conjuror, making his frightening invocations, were both outcasts from society, regarded as dangers to religion and forced into plying their trades in secrecy. These old-fashioned characters are hardly recognizable in the philosophical and pious Magi of the Renaissance.[12]

In contrast to the medieval sorcerer, Pico insists on the 'dignity of Man as Magus . . . having within him the divine creative power, and the magical power of marrying earth and heaven . . .'[13] And it was Pico who, according to Frances Yates, 'first boldly formulated a new position for European man, man as Magus, using both Magia and Kabbala to act upon the world, to control his destiny by science'.[14]

Links with Northern Europe

The energy generated by the Florentine Academy, first through Ficino, then through Pico, could not sustain its pitch indefinitely. As the expectations it had fostered failed to actualize themselves, it was doomed inevitably to flag. In 1492, Lorenzo the Magnificent died. His son proved incompetent – inadequate to the business of banking and fiscal administration which had underpinned the family's power and position. In consequence, the Medici fortunes began to founder and Florentine politics to sink into chaos. In 1494 Pico followed his illustrious patron to the grave. In the same year, a French army under Charles VIII invaded Italy and the Medici family were expelled from Florence.

By that time, however, the movement originating in the Florentine Academy had established firm roots elsewhere. In Italy, the new centre of Hermetic studies was Venice, which had remained independent and unaffected by the convulsions tearing apart the rest of the country. In Venice, there was already a large Greek library and a sizeable community of Greek and Byzantine exiles. There was also a considerable Jewish community, which facilitated the study of Hebrew and furthered Pico's integration of Kabbalistic material with Hermetic thought. And Venice, as already noted, had emerged as the chief centre of European printing, the capital of the continent's publishing industry.

The most important of the Venetian printers was Aldus Manutius, a close friend of Pico's and former tutor to two of Pico's nephews. Around 1489, Manutius had migrated to Venice and established his famous Aldine printing press. By 1500, he had come to dominate the publication of Greek – especially Hermetic and Platonic – texts. Altogether, he published ninety-four classical and post-classical Greek authors. He invented the portable octavo format for books, as well as italic type.

Manutius was dedicated to the furtherance of scholarship and played a crucial role in the dissemination of Hermeticism. His home and bookshop became an established meeting place for writers and thinkers, not only from Venice, but from abroad as well. In 1502, he created a Venetian Academy of his own. By 1505, he was contemplating a move to Germany and the founding of an academy at the court of the Holy Roman Emperor Maximilian I.[15] Nothing was to come of this project; but through the Fuggers, the wealthy banking family of Augsburg, he had numerous connections in Germany and northern Europe. These enabled him to function as a vital 'cultural artery' linking Renaissance Italy with the rest of the continent.

Thus, in 1496, Manutius became close friends with the Englishman Thomas Linacre – who subsequently tutored both Erasmus and Sir Thomas More in Greek, served as court physician to Henry VIII and in 1518 founded the Royal College of Physicians. In 1503, Manutius received a particularly distinguished visitor to Venice, Albrecht Dürer. Five years later, he played host to one of the supreme figures of Renaissance humanism, the Dutch scholar and writer Desiderius Erasmus. Manutius thus provided a bridge between the two most important components and modes of Renaissance thought – the Hermeticism of Ficino and Pico on the one hand and, on the other, the humanism exemplified by such men as Linacre, Erasmus, Sir Thomas More and Martin Luther.

Among the most influential of Manutius' contacts was the German Hermeticist and Kabbalist, Johannes Reuchlin (1455–1522), whom he befriended and published in 1498. Reuchlin embraced Pico's Kabbalistic magic and developed it into his own synthesis of Kabbalism, Hermeticism, Judaic and Greek thought. His first book, published in 1494, is believed to have been the inspiration for Dürer's engravings. His second and more ambitious work, *De arte caballistica*, published in 1517, has been described as the 'first full treatise on Kabbala by a non-Jew' and 'the bible of the Christian Kabbalists'.[16] Reuchlin also created a study group based in Heidelberg which was to evolve into an informal academy of its own, the Academia Platonica. It has been described as making 'a cult of the three ancient languages and of the mystical learning which Reuchlin had imbibed from Pico in Florence'.[17] Among its habitués were another of Manutius' friends, Conrad Celtis, and the prominent exponent of Hermetic alchemy known as Trithemius. Trithemius in turn was to be the mentor of the supreme Renaissance embodiment of the Faust figure, Heinrich Cornelius Agrippa.

The advent of printing, and the emergence of humanist scholars such as Erasmus, had effectively shattered the Church's monopoly of learning. Most of the key protagonists in the propagation of Hermeticism were to be secular writers and teachers. But a number of clerics were also involved, despite the implicit clash with their own orthodoxy. Among the most influential proponents in Hermeticism's new home of Venice was a Franciscan friar, Francesco Giorgi (1466–1540). Giorgi was heavily indebted for his inspiration to Pico. Like Pico, he discerned a multitude of connections between Hermetic thought and the Kabbala. This prompted him to build up an extensive library of Hebrew books, which was to kindle the interest of other Hermetic practitioners. And he incorporated into his system of 'Christian Kabbala' both numerology and sacred geometry, as well as Platonic and Pythagorean concepts of harmony. He also played a crucial role in fostering a preoccupation which would assume increasing importance during the sixteenth century – the extension of Hermetic principles to architecture. Giorgi resurrected philosophical interest in the classical Roman architect Vitruvius, who had presided over the rebuilding of Rome by Augustus Caesar.

In effect, Giorgi saw architecture as a crucial link in the harmonious interrelationship between microcosm and macrocosm – a theme which was subsequently to figure prominently in Freemasonry. Vitruvian theories of architecture, for Giorgi, possessed a religious significance deriving from the Temple of Solomon. His cosmos was based on number, and was constructed by its architect, he believed, 'in accordance with unalterable laws of cosmic geometry'.[18]

Giorgi's views on architecture commanded great respect in Venice. When a dispute arose in 1534 over the proportions of a new Franciscan church, the Doge decreed that the Hermetic friar be consulted as arbiter. Giorgi promptly produced his own design, intended to embody 'the practical application of the harmonies of macrocosm and microcosm'.[19]

By virtue of his patrician background, Giorgi was occasionally commissioned to act as a diplomat for the Venetian Republic. He was also an active intermediary in the negotiations attending the divorce of Henry VIII from Catherine of Aragón. In late 1529, the English monarch secretly dispatched agents to Venice – to obtain advice from rabbis there on the legal status of divorce according to the Old Testament. Giorgi, with his expertise in Judaic studies and his contacts among Venice's Jewish community, played a signal part in the ensuing consultations. He subsequently received personal letters from the English king, thanking him for his aid.[20]

The Church Attacks

In 1527, Italy was again invaded, this time by the armies of the Holy Roman Emperor Charles V, and Rome was sacked. By now, the Protestant 'heresy' was well established and flourishing in Germany. In Italy, however, the 'infection' had not yet become virulent and the Church took advantage of the situation to tighten its grip. In 1542, the Holy Office – the Inquisition – was reformed and given powers comparable to those it already enjoyed in Spain. It now had authority to interrogate, imprison, punish, confiscate and pass death sentences. In 1555, the head of the Holy Office assumed the throne of St Peter as Pope Paul IV, and a vigorous crackdown ensued. Virtually all forms of heterodox thought, including Hermeticism, were driven increasingly underground.

By then, however, the dissemination of Hermeticism elsewhere had acquired an accelerating and irresistible momentum. Indeed, it often derived further impetus from the very measures instituted to curb it. To us today, the year 1492 is significant because of Columbus' first voyage of discovery; but in Europe at the time, it was significant for very different reasons. In 1469, Isabella, heiress to the throne of Castille, had married Ferdinand, heir to the throne of Aragón. In 1474, she had succeeded to her throne. Five years later, he had succeeded to his, and a unified Kingdom of Spain had been established. Then, in 1492, Granada, the last Islamic stronghold in the country, capitulated. Shortly thereafter, Ferdinand and Isabella embarked on an all-encompassing and draconian programme of 'purification' – a kind of precursor of Nazi racial policies and of the more recent 'ethnic cleansing' in what formerly was Yugoslavia. Given a mandate by the two monarchs, the notorious Inquisition was authorized to purge the realm of anything perceived as inimical to the Catholic faith. As Carlos Fuentes has commented, Spain proceeded to outlaw sensuality with the Moors and intelligence with the Jews and thereupon went sterile.

One consequence of the programme of 'purification' was a massive influx of refugees to other parts of Europe – including, needless to say, scholars steeped in Kabbala and Judaic – or Islamic-oriented Hermeticism, who brought with them a fresh corpus of texts. The exodus from Spain was comparable to that which had occurred from Byzantium forty years before. Many of the refugees found their way to Italy, especially to Venice, where they contributed significantly to the burgeoning Renaissance there. Many others found their way to Spain's most remote European dominion, the Netherlands, which proved fertile soil for the teachings they brought with them.

For some years, the Low Countries – Holland and Flanders – had been a hotbed of heterodox and iconoclastic thought. There had been a proliferation of mystical sects, esoteric cults and secret societies – the Brethren of the Free Spirit, for example, who eschewed all organization and hierarchy, embraced a species of spiritual anarchy and are believed to have included Hieronymous Bosch in their membership. More recently, the humanist tradition had been established in Holland by Erasmus and taken tenacious root. The influx of fresh material from Spain was to trigger a full-scale movement comparable to its precursor in Italy – the so-called Flemish Renaissance. As in Italy, Hermetic and Judaic thought were to commingle with humanist teaching, finding common ground in resistance to the attempted suppression by Rome.

On 31 October 1517, a rebellious Augustinian monk named Martin Luther had embarked single-handedly on a seemingly suicidal revolt – and in a mere four years was to precipitate the protestant Reformation. Impelled to righteous wrath by a Dominican hawker of indulgences, he compiled a catalogue of ninety-five indictments against the Roman Catholic faith, and nailed them to the castle church in Wittenberg. The flamboyant gesture of revolt struck an unexpectedly sympathetic chord throughout Germany. The indictments were embraced enthusiastically by many who had pressed for return within the Church. Protestantism spread across northern Europe and Hermeticism travelled with it, sometimes more or less veiled and dissembled, sometimes quite openly. Among the secular potentates who embraced Protestantism, Hermeticism found powerful protectors and often adherents. Reuchlin's Hermetic Academy at Heidelberg, for example, was soon to disseminate its influence to the courts of the region's rulers. By the end of the sixteenth century, a spate of German princelings had espoused Hermetic teachings. The prevailing climate was conductive to the advent of Faust figures.

Inevitably, given these circumstances, the Hermetic *Zeitgeist* soon crossed the English Channel to the British Isles. In Scotland, it found a haven among a network of noble families who, since the Middle Ages, had been steeped in a diverse spectrum of esoteric thought, some of it Celtic in origin, some of it brought back from the Crusades. In England, as elsewhere, it often overlapped humanism and circulated through the same conduits. Thus, for example, Thomas Linacre, as already noted, attended Manutius' Hermetic circle in Venice, and then returned to become Henry VIII's doctor and founder of the Royal College of Physicians. With Linacre in Venice was another of Manutius' protégés, William Grocyn, who, back in England, became a professor of Greek at Oxford. Both men are generally associated with the humanist tradition; yet both were close friends with the Hermeticist John Colet.

In 1493, Colet had embarked on a twelve-year sojourn abroad. Little is known of his travels, but he is generally assumed to have spent some time in Venice with Manutius. In any case, he was heavily influenced by Ficino, whose work he extolled when he returned to England in 1505 and was made Dean of St Paul's. As dean, he played host to one of the most important of the Renaissance magi, Heinrich Cornelius Agrippa, who will figure prominently later in this book.

Like Linacre and Grocyn, Colet was extremely friendly with Sir Thomas More. More, too, is generally regarded as a humanist and is associated with Erasmus. His rationalism in *Utopia* would seem to be inimical to Hermeticism. Yet More was a fervent admirer of Pico; he was conversant with Hermetic thought, and not at all unsympathetic to aspects of it. His 'earliest biography' took the form of a lengthy letter from Erasmus to Ulrich von Hutten, a rebellious Free Knight of the Empire, poet and literary satirist, whose own position encompassed both humanism and Hermeticism. That Erasmus was in correspondence with such a figure as Hutten attests to the degree of overlap between humanist and Hermetic circles.

Amid this climate of religious upheaval and rejection of Rome's authority, both humanism and Hermeticism were able to thrive. By the end of the sixteenth century, Hermetically oriented circles and societies were solidly established in England. Some of them were more or less clandestine. Some seem to have doubled as espionage networks. Some were gradually to cross-fertilize already existing British institutions and produce the amalgam which eventually evolved into Freemasonry. And by the end of the century, too, as will shortly be seen, Hermetic thought had come to play an integral role in Elizabethan culture – including, of course, the theatre of Marlowe and

Shakespeare. In *Dr Faustus* and *The Tempest*, the Renaissance magus was to attain the epoch's definitive literary manifestation.

The Hermetic Emperor

If Hermeticism prospered under Protestantism, it did so in Catholic domains as well. By the end of the sixteenth century, it had established itself in the most powerful Catholic court of Europe, that of the Habsburg Holy Roman Emperor Rudolf II, who was also King of Austria, Hungary, Bohemia and Moravia. Rudolf's reign (1576–1612) was contemporary with those of Elizabeth and James I of England, and almost as culturally dynamic. From the very beginning, however, he comported himself in a fashion which, in the eyes of orthodoxy, ill became his exalted position. Spurning the traditional Habsburg city of Vienna, for example, he gathered his court in Prague, his Bohemian capital. In an age when Europe was becoming increasingly polarized between Protestanism and Catholicism, Rudolf refused to embrace either, declaring himself to be simply a Christian; and though he supposedly represented the Church's temporal power, he refrained from persecuting Protestants, regarded the Papacy with increasing hostility and refused to be reconciled to Rome even on his deathbed.

Rudolf was steeped in esoterica, passionately embracing all manifestations of Hermeticism, especially magic and alchemy. He devoted much time and vast sums of money to the building of his library, which came to comprise the most comprehensive collection of its sort on the continent. It included not only the standard corpus of Hermetic works, but also that dreaded manual of magic, the *Picatrix*, condemned with horror by the Church. Rudolf himself engaged in alchemical experimentation. And he invited to

Prague Hermetic practitioners from the whole of Europe, offering them generous patronage and court positions. His invitations were accepted by Hermeticists as far afield as Michael Sediwoj (known as Sendivogius) in Poland and Alexander Seton in Scotland. Among the most celebrated visitors was the English magus John Dee, often regarded as the prototype for Prospero in *The Tempest*, and later court astrologer to Elizabeth I.

Another illustrious guest of Rudolf's was Giordano Bruno, perhaps the most wildly ambitious of Renaissance magi, who sought nothing less than to 'transmute the human condition'. Bruno is believed by scholars to have been establishing a network of secret societies across the whole of Europe. Prague offered fertile soil for such an enterprise. While residing in the Bohemian capital, Bruno published a book dedicated to Rudolf – and outlined in his dedication his 'philosophy of a single true universal religion rooted in the occult tradition'.[21] Another of the Emperor's distinguished protégés was the German alchemist and Hermetic philosopher Michael Maier. Maier served Rudolf as court alchemist and private secretary until the Emperor's death in 1612, and then migrated to Hesse, Holland and eventually England, where he was instrumental in the dissemination of Hermetic and so-called Rosicrucian thought.

Through his patronage of such men as Dee, Bruno and Maier, Rudolf came to be regarded as an inspiration for Hermeticists across Europe. Some even hailed him as a new Hermes Trismegistus. At the same time, the Emperor's immersion in Hermeticism was matched by his fascination with Kabbala. He presided over an ambitious project to produce a comprehensive compendium of Kabbalistic texts, 'embracing the best of Hebrew wisdom together with leading commentaries on it by Christian scholars'.[22] And while Jews were being persecuted elsewhere in Europe, they lived in Bohemia, and especially in Prague, under the Emperor's personal protection. Thus safeguarded, Prague's Jewish community prospered. The city's wealthiest individuals were Jews, and maintained close contact with the court. They have sometimes been credited with financing the Emperor's immense collection of paintings and of esoteric books. Certainly there was much traffic, in money and ideas, between what the writer Leo Perutz has called 'the ghetto and the castle'. One beneficiary of these transactions was Prague's chief rabbi, the Kabbalist Judah Loew ben Bezalel. In subsequent years, Rabbi Judah was to pass into legend as the creator of the 'Golem', a man-made, mechanical and humanoid automaton, imbued with the spark of life by Kabbalistic and Hermetic magic.

In 1614, there appeared in Germany the first in a series of anonymously written manifestos, purporting to have issued from a mysterious, elusive, Hermetically oriented Rosicrucian brotherhood. These manifestos circulated as rapidly as had Luther's ninety-five theses, and polarized opinions across Europe, eliciting fervent support on the one hand, and a hysterical frenzy of panic, paranoia and hostility on the other. In their general philosophical character, the Rosicrucian manifestos were typically Hermetic, alchemical and Kabbalistic, claiming to herald the advent of a new world religion, a new world order of freedom, harmony and universal fraternity. But they also displayed a marked sympathy for Protestantism and a vehement antipathy towards the Church of Rome. Paradoxically, however, they endorsed the Holy Roman Emperor, supposed defender of the Catholic faith: 'In *Politia* we acknowledge the *Roman* Empire and *Quartam Monarchiam* for our Christian head.'[23]

In 1614, two years after the death of Rudolf II, there appeared in print in Germany the first of a series of anonymous manifestos which incorporated this sentence. It is generally accepted, however, that the tracts were in circulation in manuscript form well before they were made public; the earliest mention of the first is December 1611.[24] Given the context in which it is embedded, the quoted sentence can only be referring to Rudolf, and bears further testimony to the esteem he commanded from European Hermeticists, and from the self-styled Rosicrucians in particular. But it also reflects an aspiration, on the part of European Hermeticism, to a specifically political dimension. According to such scholars as Frances Yates, that aspiration was to be a contributing factor in precipitating the cataclysm of the Thirty Years War. On a scale that encompassed the whole of Europe, Faust was to conjure up forces over which he lost control.

8

FAUSTUS

Mere mention of the Renaissance today evokes a roll-call of illustrious names. Perhaps pre-eminently, it evokes artists of monumental stature: Giotto, Botticelli, Leonardo, Michelangelo, Dürer, Brunelleschi, Donatello, Palladio, Rabelais, Ronsard, Marlowe, Shakespeare. But it also evokes patrons of the arts, such as Lorenzo de' Medici, Ludovico Sforza, the Gonzaga of Mantua. It evokes dynasties such as the Borgias, steeped in intrigue and power politics. It also evokes the names of seafarers, explorers and conquistadores – Vasco da Gama, Henry the Navigator, Columbus, Vespucci, Magellan, Drake, Ralegh, Cortés and Pizarro; evokes theologians like Luther, Zwingli, Calvin and John Knox and humanist writers like Erasmus and Sir Thomas More. He evokes monarchs of seemingly larger-than-life proportions – François I of France, Charles V and Rudolf II of the Holy Roman Empire, Philip II of Spain, Henry VIII and Elizabeth I of England.

Behind all of these individuals, however, there looms the archetypal figure of Faustus, the Renaissance magus, in both his positive and negative aspects. In this figure one finds embodied the governing mentality of the Renaissance – its guiding inspiration, its spiritual and moral (or amoral) context and mandate, the promise, expectation and optimism underlying and justifying its activities. The artists and their patrons, the explorers and conquistadores, the theologians, the humanists, the potentates all pursued their respective endeavours with the unshakeably self-confident conviction that they were creating a better, more spiritualized world – a world in which, as never before, knowledge and power were yoked together on behalf of a new dawn for humanity. It is this specific linkage of knowledge and power that the Faust figure, or the Renaissance magus, most potently reflects. With the Renaissance, Faust was to become the supreme archetype and paradigm of modern Western man, the supreme self-defining myth of Western culture and civilization.

As we have already seen, in German, 'Faust' means 'fist'; and most modern commentators, finding that suggestive, if not particularly relevant, do not bother to look beyond it. In Latin, however, 'Faustus' means 'the fortunate one' or 'the favoured one'. This, it may be recalled, was precisely the appellation arrogated to himself by Simon Magus, who engaged in a duel of miracles with St Peter. Faustus, then, is a latter-day sixteenth-century incarnation or avatar of Simon Magus; and the identification is reinforced by a number of details. Simon Magus, for example, was supposed to have travelled in the company of a prostitute whom he alleged to be the reincarnation of Helen of Troy. In most versions of the Faust story, including Marlowe's and Goethe's, the protagonist utilizes his infernal powers to conjure up and mate with Helen's shade. One could argue that at this point, in Marlowe's play at least, he becomes irrevocably damned, for his union with Helen entails union with a succubus, an incorporeal demonic entity. According to such later commentators as Joris-Karl Huysmans, sexual union with such an entity – with a male incubus or a female succubus – constituted the mysterious, unmentionable and notorious 'sin against the Holy Ghost', the one sin which could never supposedly be forgiven.

Although he was soon to be eclipsed by the legends, folklore and literature pertaining to him, there does appear to have been an historical individual known as Faustus. The earliest recorded mention of him is in a letter of 1507, written by the alchemist and Hermetic philosopher Trithemius and now held in the library of the Vatican. In a missive addressed to Johannes Virdung von Hassfurt, an astrologer and Hermeticist at the court of the Elector Palatine of the Rhine at Heidelberg, Trithemius reports that

that man, about whom you wrote me [*sic*], Georgius Sabellicus, who dared to call himself the foremost of the necromancers, is an unstable character, a babbler and a vagabond . . . continuously asserting in public things that are abominable and contrary to the teachings of the Holy Church . . . Magister Georgius Sabellicus, Faustus junior, the inspiration of necromancers, astrologer, the second magus, palmist, practitioner of divination with the use of high places and fire, and second in the art of divination with the use of water . . . is reported to have said . . . that the miracles of Christ were not so amazing; he himself could do all the things Christ had done . . . he came to Kreuznach, and . . . promised even more remarkable things, contending that in alchemy he surpassed all previous masters and that he understood and could accomplish whatever people wished. In the meantime, a teaching position became vacant . . . and he was appointed to it on the recommendation of Franz von Sickingen, an official of your prince and a man very fond of the occult. With the most criminal kind of design he soon began to seduce the boys, and when this behaviour was suddenly brought to light, he eluded certain punishment by fleeing . . .[1]

Trithemius' comments are interesting in a number of respects. Quite incidentally to Faustus, they bear testimony to Franz von Sickingen's Hermetic preoccupations. Sickingen, a close friend of Ulrich von Hutten, was one of the most powerful Free Knights of the Empire and one of the leaders of the so-called Knights' Revolt against imperial authority. Like Faustus, he was later to fascinate Goethe, and plays a pivotal role in Goethe's drama depicting the Knights' Revolt, *Götz von Berlichingen*.

So far as Faustus himself is concerned, Trithemius' portrait paints a squalid and sorry picture. Instead of an august master magician, there emerges only a petty charlatan and pederast. But it is clear that Trithemius has discerned the connection between Georgius Sabellicus and the biblical figure of Simon Magus. One is even tempted to wonder whether the very appellation of 'Faustus' might not perhaps have originated in Trithemius' contemptuous and derisive dismissal of Sabellicus as 'Faustus junior . . . the second magus . . .' – as a pallid imitation and travesty, in other words, of the scriptural sorcerer.

In any case, and whether it derived from Trithemius or was arrogated by Georgius Sabellicus himself, the name stuck. So, apparently – in many cases, at least – did Trithemius' opinion of him. Of the few subsequent references to a historical Faustus, none is very flattering. In a letter of 3 October 1513, one Conrad Mutianus Rufus claims to have met Faustus, having 'heard him babbling at an inn' and found him 'a mere braggart and fool . . .'[2] On 12 February 1520 Faustus was apparently in Bamberg and cast an astrological chart for the city's bishop, an associate of Ulrich von Hutten. The bishop's account book for the day records payment for the horoscope to 'Doctor Faustus philosoph'.[3] On 17 June 1528, a scribe in Ingolstadt recorded the presence of 'Doctor Jörg Faustus von Haidleberg' – who, shortly thereafter, was ordered out of the town.[4]

Before being thus ejected, Faustus is reported to have said

he was a knight of the Order of St John, and a commander of one of the order's houses on the border of Austrian Carinthia. He is also reported to have delivered himself of astrological pronouncements – to the effect, for example, that the Sun and Jupiter in the same constellation are conducive to the birth of prophets. Faustus is referred to as 'Georgius Faustus Helmstet(ensis)'.[5] Helmstet, a village near Heidelberg, provided a modern researcher, Frank Baron, with a possible lead. Baron searched Heidelberg University's records for students from Helmstet and found one 'Georgius Helmstetter', who had been enrolled at Heidelberg from 1483 until 1487. Of sixty-seven scholars registering at the same time, he was one of two who refused to record any family name. He graduated with a BA on 12 July 1484, and attained the degree of Magister on 1 March 1487.[6] Here, then, is the only information about the historical Faustus' background thus far to have come to light. It does not, however, tell us very much.

In May 1532, four years after being thrown out of Ingolstadt, Faustus is reported to have turned up in Nuremberg. The town records contain a statement signed by the deputy burgomeister: 'Safe conduct to Doctor Faustus, the great sodomite and practitioner of black magic . . . refused.'[7]

In 1534, Ulrich von Hutten's cousin, Philipp von Hutten, also known as Felipe de Urre, embarked with a Spanish expedition to the New World. He was subsequently to disappear in the wilds of the Orinoco on a futile quest for the legendary lost city of Manoa. In one of his last letters, written from what is now Venezuela in early 1540, he reported that 'the philosopher Faustus hit the nail on the head, for we struck a bad year'.[8] This would suggest that Philipp, or someone known to him, had consulted Faustus for a prediction at some point prior to the expedition's departure.

The last recorded reference to the historical Faustus is one of the briefest, and also one of the most tantalizingly provocative. During the course of 1534, a messianic sect of Dutch Anabaptists seized control of the city of Munster. Proclaiming the place a new Jerusalem and their leader the 'King of Sion', they proceeded to anticipate the supposedly imminent Apocalypse by embarking on a reign of unbridled sexual orgy and wholesale murder. Threatened with Anabaptist uprisings elsewhere in northern Germany and the Low Countries, an alliance of local potentates mustered an army and, early in 1535, laid siege to Munster. On 25 June, the besieging forces finally captured the city. On the same day, Faustus is reported to have been present.[9] There is no indication whatever of what he was doing there, nor even whether he was among the defenders or with the attacking army. Neither is there any indication of what subsequently befell him – or of how, if he was with the defenders, he escaped. He is believed to have died at some time prior to 1539, but the precise date is unknown.

Such is the extent of the reliable information pertaining to the historical Faustus. According to Frank Baron, his alleged association, or pact, with the Devil derives primarily from Martin Luther:

> The influence of Martin Luther is the most important single factor in the development of the Faustus legend. At a very early point, within the lifetime of the historical Faustus, Luther made the first known pronouncements in which Faustus the magician was identified as a close associated of the devil, an association made in almost all of the anecdotes written after Faustus' death.[10]

Luther seems to have accepted the distinction – first enunciated during the Middle Ages and subsequently retained by

Hermeticists like Ficino, Pico and Reuchlin – between divine or natural magic on the one hand and, on the other, petty sorcery, necromancy and conjuration. He is not known, for example, to have attacked such prominent contemporaries as Agrippa. But the figure of Faustus, as he emerges from the historical record, would undoubtedly have been fair game. For Luther, whatever magic such a figure commanded could only have been satanic in character. Thus, by the 1540s, Faustus was frequently being invoked as a minatory example in Lutheran sermons. One of these compares him explicitly to Simon Magus: 'Simon Magus tried to fly to heaven, but Peter prayed that he might fall . . . Faust also tried this in Venice. But he was sorely dashed to the ground.'[11]

By the 1560s, the legend of Faustus as 'the devil's brother-in-law' had become widespread. By that time, too, his given name of Georgius, or Georg, had been supplanted, for reasons that remain unknown, by Johannes; and it is as John, the English variant of Johannes, that he appears in Marlowe's play of 1593. In 1562, an alleged biography of 'Johannes Faustus' had been written and published by Philipp Melanchthon, one of Luther's most assiduous protégés. It struck a resonant chord in popular culture and went through nine editions in the next forty years. If one counts excerpts, more than fourteen editions of the Faust story were in print by the end of the sixteenth century. Certain features of the story introduced by Melanchthon soon became standardized. Thus, for example, Faustus was described as being regularly attended by a demonic familiar, Mephistopheles, in the guise of a black dog. From this, as will be seen, there arose in the popular mind a posthumous conflation of Faustus with Agrippa.

In all early – that is, sixteenth- and seventeenth-century – versions of the Faust story, Faust himself comes to an inevitably sticky end. Even Marlowe, a self-proclaimed atheist, felt obliged to placate the religious sentiments of his audience and depict his protagonist as irrevocably damned. The ostensible moral is clear – that a pact with the so-called 'unclean powers' leads ineluctably to perdition. Underlying this ostensible moral, however, there is a much more pernicious subtext, which reflects the Church's – and Christendom's – implacable hostility to learning. For it is not the pact with the Devil that leads Faustus to damnation. Neither is it a lust for power. In every version of the Faust story, including Marlowe's and later Goethe's, the protagonist's governing impetus and motivation is simply a desire for knowledge. It is this desire that stigmatizes him as 'evil' in Christian eyes. It is from this desire that the pact with the Devil ensues; and power is more a by-product of the pact than anything else. From a Christian standpoint, all knowledge, unless filtered through the authorized auspices of the Church, *is intrinsically evil* – intrinsically the province of the infernal 'Tempter' who, in the Garden of Eden, first seduced Eve into tasting the fruit of the Tree. In Judaeo-Christian tradition, the fall of Adam and Eve from original purity results directly from tasting the fruit of the Tree of Knowledge. The Faust story, at least in its Christian variants, thus demonstrates the antipathy with which knowledge was regarded by clerical orthodoxy. Nothing else so eloquently demonstrates the extent to which Christianity not only demanded a monopoly over learning, but also exercised its power by keeping its adherents in a state of terrified ignorance.

Whatever the venal transgressions of the historical Faustus, the Faustus of legend and myth is guilty of something altogether different. In the Church's eyes, he is guilty of hungering after knowledge, and presuming to seek means of assuaging his hunger. Such means necessarily lay beyond the purlieus of Christian teaching. To that extent, they had necessarily to be condemned as infernal.

In later treatments of the Faust story – notably, of course, in Goethe's – the seeker after knowledge does not always meet with so dire a fate. Neither is he altogether morally or theologically culpable. Indeed, Goethe's Faust, by the end of the poem, has not only been redeemed, but has also assumed the status of a Prometheus figure. He is engaged in the rather mundane and prosaic business of reclaiming land from the sea – a process intended, according to Goethe, to symbolize emerging consciousness. And in historical actuality, too, not all the prototypes of the Faust figure were damned. Those who suffered for their quests, moreover, did so at the hands of specifically human, not divine, agencies.

Trithemius

There were, in fact, a number of prototypes for the Faust figure – individuals who, in historical actuality, conformed more accurately than the sixteenth-century charlatan to the Faust of myth and legend. Leaving aside his Italian birth and milieu, for example, there were aspects of Faust in Pico della Mirandola. There were even more such aspects in the individual known as Trithemius (1462–1516), through whose letter, quoted above, the name of Faustus first enters the historical record.

Born to a family of vine-growers named Heidenberg, Trithemius adopted as his *nom de plume* a Latinized variant of his birthplace, the village of Trittenheim on the Moselle. Hungry for learning, the precocious young man embarked on an arduous programme of self-education, which earned him a place at the University of Trèves and, by the age of twenty, a reputation for scholarship. He also studied at Heidelberg, and was a member of Reuchlin's Hermetic

Academy there. In 1482, while on a journey, he sought refuge for a night at a monastery near Sponheim, and found the milieu so congenial that he took monastic vows and stayed. He appears to have been motivated less by piety than by other considerations – the isolation and insulation from an increasingly turbulent secular world, the access to books and materials for his alchemical and scientific experiments, the privacy and idyllic solitude. A year later, however, he was elected abbot, and presided in that capacity for another twenty-one years. During that time, he devoted much time and energy to restoration and improvements of the monastery; he built up a library, large for its time and place, of more than 2,000 volumes. But he also made enemies and in 1506, was induced to resign. Later in the same year, he was elected abbot of a monastery in Würzburg, where he died in 1516.

By 1499, Trithemius had come under suspicion, as he himself said, of being a 'boastful liar' or of dealing with demons. In part, this accusation stemmed from his Hermetic preoccupations, which would, inevitably, have raised clerical eyebrows and hackles. But it stemmed, too, from his references to the book on which he had embarked, eventually published in 1506 under the title of *Stenographia*. The book derived in part from Trithemius' belief that a truly pure and learned man could transfer thoughts, by telepathy, to like-minded fellows across considerable distances. In speaking of his work in progress, Trithemius stated his intention of discussing telepathic communication, secret writing, a revolutionary method for learning languages easily and 'many other things which are not to be divulged publicly'.[12] In fact, the most important aspect of his book was its contribution to cryptography. In effect Trithemius seems to have devised what was subsequently to become a standard technique in espionage – two agents communicating with each other by coded references to passages in the same text. Even at the time, the political application of Trithemius' system would have been recognized and appreciated. It is not surprising, therefore, that his book was enthusiastically embraced half a century later by John Dee – who was not only an Hermeticist, but a spy for Elizabeth I as well.

It is not surprising either that certain of Trithemius' contemporaries, on seeing his work in manuscript or print, mistook his shorthand and cryptography for Kabbalistic or necromantic script concealing forbidden secrets. Trithemius himself did nothing to discourage such fools in their misapprehension. He did indeed produce other works, on precisely those subjects he was suspected of embracing. He wrote, for example, on magic and alchemy. He would quote from that most central of Hermetic texts, the *Emerald Tablet*. He displayed a characteristically Hermetic and Kabbalistic preoccupation with the occult properties of number. And he endeavoured to establish a methodology for invoking unknown and supernatural forces or powers, by means of which reality could be manipulated. Trithemius himself regarded the forces or powers in question as angelic, if only by virtue of the state of mind and moral context in which he invoked them. In other words, he was practising what would come to be called 'white magic'. Others have called it 'angel magic', or 'angelic magic'. Frances Yates describes it as 'applied magic, or power magic'.[13]

Trithemius endeavours actively to exploit the interrelationship between microcosm and macrocosm. He does so within a framework which he regards as angelic. But his methodology is not significantly different from that whereby other, less pure-minded magicians might invoke demonic forces or powers. And to an outsider, or to a pious Christian, the distinction would not necessarily have been immediately apparent – except insofar as the names recited in Trithemius' invocations would be those of angels rather than of demons. It is thus easy to see how Trithemius could come to be regarded as a magician, and conflated by later legend with the Faust figure.

As previously noted, it is through one of Trithemius' letters that Faustus enters the historical record. But while Trithemius, in this letter, castigated Faustus, he allowed himself, in his own behaviour and comportment, to be identified with the target of his abuse. Indeed, a number of the details later associated with Faustus were originally associated with Trithemius. Thus, for example, he described himself as a more knowledgeable and competent magician than Faustus. He also described the sufferings he had incurred at the hands of a demonic spirit he conjured up. And the legends that attached themselves to Trithemius were soon to become interchangeable with aspects of the Faust legend. Like Marlowe's Faustus, for instance, Trithemius is said to have performed miracles at the court of the Holy Roman Emperor – and, through necromancy, is said to have gratified the Habsburg ruler with a vision of his dead wife. Like Faustus, too, Trithemius was popularly perceived as an alchemical adept – and welcomed this perception. The money he spent on restoring his monastery was believed – again, with his own encouragement – to derive from his successful alchemical transmutation of the Philosophers' Stone.

Agrippa and His Occult Philosophy

If there were points of resemblance, even identification, between the Faust figure and Trithemius, there were far more such points between the Faust figure and Trithemius' most illustrious protégé – Heinrich Cornelius Agrippa von Nettesheim. Marlowe's Faustus explicitly models himself on

Agrippa, and Goethe is reputed to have said it was Agrippa, more than anyone else, whose background, personality, demeanour, adventures and impact on his contemporaries provided him with a prototype for his dramatic poem's protagonist. Agrippa also contributes substantially to Marguerite Yourcenar's definitive fictional portrait of the Renaissance magus Zeno in her acclaimed 1968 novel *L'Oeuvre au noir* (published in English as *The Abyss*).

Agrippa was born in 1486 to a family of Cologne's minor nobility. He was educated at the university of his native city and graduated precociously in 1502 with a Master's degree. While still in his teens, he embarked on a military career and served as a soldier under the Holy Roman Emperor Maximilian I, being knighted in the field for valour. By 1507, he appears to have met Trithemius and was temporarily resident in Paris, where he conducted alchemical experiments and was reputed to have founded a secret society – the first of many, according to reliable commentators, across Europe. By 1509, at the age of twenty-three, he was lecturing on the Kabbalistic work of Reuchlin at the University of Dôle, and pursuing further alchemical research; but a charge of heresy levelled against him obliged him to resume his military career, which also included a diplomatic mission to England and probably espionage as well. While in England, he was friendly with John Colet, whose house he regularly frequented. By 1510, he had completed the first version of his major work, *De occulta philosophia*. He showed the text to Trithemius, who warned him against publication. For the next twenty-three years, it was to circulate in manuscript, gaining prestige and a mystique of its own by virtue of its clandestine character. Not until 1533 did it appear, substantially augmented, in print.

Between 1511 and 1517, Agrippa was in Italy, serving the Emperor again, as well as a number of other noble patrons, lecturing in Pavia on Hermeticism and immersing himself in Kabbala. In 1518, he wrote a tract on antidotes for plague which he had discovered through his alchemical experiments; and this was reissued in a revised and expanded edition in 1529. Between 1518 and 1522, he worked as a municipal official for the city of Metz, where he continued his alchemical investigations. On one occasion during this tenure, he risked his life by 'courageously defending a woman who had been hounded down by the mob and inquisitor as a witch'.[14] He then gravitated to his native Cologne, to Geneva and to Fribourg, where, despite his lack of medical accreditation, he became municipal physician, while privately tutoring prominent citizens in Hermetic thought. In 1525, he was reported to be in possession of works by Martin Luther. By that time, he was established as physician, astrologer and alchemist to Louise of Savoy, mother of François I of France, at her court in Lyon. Soon after, however, a rupture with his patroness set him wandering again – to the Low Countries (where he worked as a physician), back to Cologne (where he obtained the protection of the archbishop), to Bonn, eventually back to France, where he died, poverty-stricken, at Grenoble around 1535.

In 1530, some five years before his death, Agrippa published a singularly improbable work, *De vanitate scientiarus*. In this text, he expatiated on 'the uncertainty and vanity of the sciences'. He attacked alchemy, Hermeticism, Kabbala, the entire spectrum of disciplines to which he had devoted his life – as well as his own arguments in his earlier and more ambitious work, *De occulta philosophia*, which was still circulating in manuscript. It is now generally accepted that Agrippa's apparent recantation in *De vanitate scientiarus* was spurious, a mere ploy calculated to lull the inquisitorial vigilance of the clerical authorities and deflect their attention from him. Having thus appeased his potential persecutors with a book of ostensibly orthodox piety, he then proceeded, a year later, to issue the first printed version of *De occulta philosophia* – which, in expanded and augmented form, implicitly refuted the arguments in *De vanitate scientiarus*. It proved to be only the first volume of a much more ambitious project. A second volume followed in 1532. In 1533, the complete text of *De occulta philosophia*, now running to three volumes, finally appeared in print.

By any standard, Agrippa was an extraordinary individual – the epitome and embodiment of what, today, we call the 'Renaissance Man'. He had proved himself an audacious soldier and man of action on the battlefield. Although self-taught in medicine, he was generally recognized as one of the most skilled physicians of his age – and one of the most astute theologians. But it was as an exponent of Hermeticism, an adept in astrology, alchemy, Kabbala and magic, that he earned his greatest reputation, as well as the aura of mystery and occult power that came to surround him. He could obviously display considerable charisma and charm, which gained him access to some of the most puissant and illustrious figures in the Europe of his day. At the same time, he could also be aloof, arrogant, haughty, forbidding and intimidating; and – not being disposed to compromise or suffer fools – he proved as dextrous at making enemies as at making friends. Adopting a cavalier attitude towards money, he was often in financial difficulties, and incurred a brief imprisonment in Brussels for debt. His antipathy towards the Church, and especially the monastic orders, brought down upon him incessant suspicion and frequent harassment. He further antagonized his clerical contemporaries with his startlingly modern attitudes towards marriage, women and sexuality. In an endorsement of marriage, published in a collection of essays, Agrippa states: 'Thou therefore, whosoever thou art, that wilt take a wife, let love be the cause, not substance or goods, choose a wife, not a garment, let thy wife be married unto thee, not her dowry . . . And let not her be subject unto thee, but let her be with thee in all trust and counsel . . .'[15] In another essay, extolling women, Agrippa castigates the men of his epoch and emerges as either (depending on one's own perspective) a romantic or a precocious precursor of feminism: 'Is this a point of manhood, or any ornament of your valour, to busy yourselves for disgrace of women? Is this the thankful tribute you return to the authors of your Being?'[16] He condemns the fact that 'custom spreading like some epidemic contagion, hath made it common to undervalue this sex, and bespatter their reputation with all kind of opprobrious language, and slanderous epithets'.[17] And he concludes: 'Let us no longer dis-esteem this noble sex, or abuse its goodness . . . Let us re-enthrone them in their seats of honour and pre-eminence . . . and treat them with all that respect and veneration which belongs to such terrestrial angels.'[18] To his further credit, it is worth noting that these statements were issued by a man who was married at least three times.

Astute though Agrippa may be in such spheres as this, however, his chief literary achievement remains the massive *De occulta philosophia*, a definitive three-volume opus which comprises an encyclopedic compendium and exegesis of esoteric, and especially Hermetic, thought. In his daunting tripartite summation, Agrippa endeavours to encompass all that was known at the time of Hermeticism and magic. Or, to be more accurate, he endeavours to encompass all he considered it safe to say in print. In a letter of 1527, he stresses that there is a secret interpretation and understanding which cannot be conveyed through the printed word alone, but must be transmitted personally from master to disciple. In this respect, Agrippa conforms to the tradition dating back to Pythagoras, to the ancient mystery schools and to the world of Alexandrian syncretism.

Like Zosimus and other such Hermetic alchemists of ancient Alexandria, Agrippa regards the alchemist as ultimately constituting the only real subject and object of his own experiment. All alchemy, for Agrippa, and all magic as well, must entail a process of personal transmutation: 'Whosoever therefore shall know himself, shall know all things in himself; especially he shall know God . . . and how all things may be fitted for all things in their time, place, order, measure, proportion and harmony . . .'[19] And like Zosimus and other such Hermetic alchemists of ancient Alexandria, Agrippa regards the phenomenal world, the material creation, as a living and sentient entity. For Agrippa, 'the world is a certain whole body, the parts whereof are the bodies of all living creatures . . .'[20]

Like his Hermetic predecessors of Alexandria, Agrippa regards faith as suspect, insisting instead on direct knowledge of the sacred, the numinous of 'Gnostic' experience. And he is thus, not surprisingly, reluctant to accord Christianity a monopoly over truth: 'But the rites and Ceremonies of Religion, in respect of the diversity of times and places, are diverse. Every Religion hath something of good, because it is dedicated to God . . . there is no religion so erroneous, which hath not somewhat of wisdom in it.'[21]

In the course of his *magnum opus*, Agrippa cites a number of scientific inventions or discoveries which he regards as falling within the remit of the aspiring magus. He mentions, for example, the camera obscura. He mentions techniques for reading, hearing or communicating at a distance, in a context which suggests, perhaps, a parabolic reflector. He mentions methods of insulation against heat – which, among other things, might enable a person to carry hot coals without incurring either pain or harm. And he mentions experiments with drugs which may be opium, cocaine or cannabis derivatives.

At the beginning of the first volume of *De occulta philosophia*, Agrippa offers a definition of magic. 'This is the most perfect and chief science, that sacred and sublime kind of Philosophy, and . . . the most absolute perfection of . . . Philosophy.'[22] He then goes on to state that 'all inferior things are subjected to superior bodies', whose power can be drawn down by the magician and applied in practice.[23] The magician, or magus, is, according to Agrippa, 'expert in natural philosophy, and mathematics, and knowing the middle sciences consisting of both these, Arithmetic, Music, Geometry, Optics, Astronomy, and such sciences that are of weights, measures, proportions, articles and joints, knowing also Mechanical Arts resulting from these . . .'[24]

Book I of *De occulta philosophia* addresses itself to what Agrippa calls 'Natural Magic'. Book II is devoted to 'Celestial Magic'. Book III concentrates on 'Ceremonial or Divine Magic'. From these subdivisions, one might assume the work to reflect some species of moral progression – an ascent up the rungs of a ladder, so to speak, which constitutes a more or less Christian hierarchy of values. A glance at the contents of each of the three volumes would, however, quickly dispel any such assumption. Under the classification of 'Natural Magic' Agrippa discusses the four elements (earth, air, fire and water), divination in general, astrology in particular, the planets and their Hermetic correspondences. Under 'Celestial Magic', he includes 'Gematria, Numbers, Kabbala, Pentagrams, Geomantic Figures, Angel Writing, Astrology [again], Talismans, Magic Squares, Planetary Seals'. 'Ceremonial or Divine Magic' encompasses 'Platonism, Kabbalism, Evil Spirits and Demons, Divine Names, Seals of the Spirits'.

The progression, then, is not essentially moral in any conventional sense of the word. It is a progression from the passive to the increasingly active – from interpretation to participation and dynamic invocation. It is also a progression in power, in puissance, in potency. Under such categories as 'Seals of the Spirits', Agrippa hints at forces of apocalyptic potential – the kind of thing we might associate today with, say, the splitting of the atom, or with the energy released at the climax of the fantasy adventure *Raiders of the Lost Ark*. In speaking of Agrippa, one distinguished modern scholar observes that 'by treating magic, pagan religion and Christianity's activities and beliefs of exactly the same kind, he demonstrates strikingly how dangerous . . . magic was from a Christian point of view'.[25] According to Frances Yates:

> The Renaissance ideal of the magus, the 'divine' man with powers of operating on the cosmos and achieving universal knowledge and power – adumbrated in Pico's famous Oration on the Dignity of Man – found its theorist in Agrippa, who wrote a textbook on how to become a magus. His *De occulta philosophia* was the best-known manual of Renaissance magic, incorporating both the Ficinian magic . . . and the Cabalistic magic indicated by Pico and further developed by Reuchlin and the hosts of Renaissance Cabalists.[26]

And Frances Yates concludes:

> Ficino's gentle, artistic, subjective . . . magic, Pico's intensely pious and contemplative Cabalistic magic, are quite innocent of the terrible power implications of Agrippa's magic.[27]

As if all of this were not sufficient to establish Agrippa's reputation, he was also something of an accomplished showman, exercising a rigorous and skilful control over the image he projected. In an age only too eager to believe in master magicians, he deployed a number of tricks to assure his status as one of them. Thus, for example, he would correspond, copiously but secretly, with thinkers and colleagues abroad, often in exotic places – and then ascribe what they told him to the confidences of demons or familiars. He made a point, too, of accompanying himself habitually with a black dog, which he encouraged the credulous to believe was his personal familiar. The historical Faustus was also supposedly accompanied by such a dog, and this further conduced to Agrippa's conflation with the Faust figure. The dog, of course, would reappear some three centuries later, in Goethe's dramatic poem, as one of the guises of Mephistopheles.

By such devices as these, Agrippa contrived to mantle himself in an aura of mystification, and transformed himself, quite literally, into 'a legend in his own lifetime'. Fabulous stories about him abounded. At inns in which he stayed, he was said to pay his bills in coins which appeared genuine enough, but turned into worthless shell or horn after his departure. He was alleged to possess a magic glass, in which he was able to see things temporally and spatially distant. In this glass, the Earl of Surrey, separated from his mistress, supposedly saw her pining for him. On another occasion, Agrippa, in the presence of the Earl of Surrey, the Elector of Saxony, Erasmus and other illustrious personages, allegedly conjured up the shade of Cicero, who (or which) regaled them with a famous oration.

One additional legendary anecdote, dating from the late sixteenth century, serves to demonstrate further the awe with which Agrippa was regarded. On a particular occasion, when the magus himself was absent, a student lodging in his house in Louvain reputedly extorted from his wife the key to his study or laboratory. On gaining access to the master's sanctum, the student stumbled across a book of spells, a grimoire, and – in confirmation that a little knowledge can be a dangerous thing – summoned up a demon he was unable to control. According to one account, the student promptly died of fright. According to another, the demon – reverting rather undemonically to clumsy physical force – strangled the hapless youth. When Agrippa returned and discovered what had happened, he was understandably reluctant to risk being accused of murder. He is said, therefore, to have summoned up the demon himself and commanded it to re-animate, temporarily, the dead youth's body. Infernally zombified, the body reputedly marched out of the house and strode flagrantly about the marketplace, allowing witnesses to see it apparently alive and healthy. Thereupon the demon departed and the youth's corpse collapsed, ostensibly having suffered a natural demise.

Fabrications of this sort were typical of the mystique surrounding Agrippa, typical of the public relations in which he trafficked. But behind the tricks and self-promotional techniques of the charlatan, there was one of the most audacious, original and powerful intelligences of the era. Agrippa's exegesis on magic and Hermetic thought remains a primary sourcebook to this day, and has exerted an influence that extends to the present. One cannot read Joyce, for example, or Thomas Mann, or Jorge Luis Borges, or Robertson Davies, or many other major literary figures of our own century without at some point finding quotes from, or allusions to, Agrippa. And as an individual, Agrippa's personality was sufficiently charismatic to have stamped itself not only on his own age, but also, in the form of Faust, on centuries of posterity.

Alchemy and Medicine

If Agrippa displays one guise of the Renaissance magus, another is displayed by a figure perhaps even more flagrantly larger than life – Aureolus Philippus Theophrastus Paracelsus Bombastus von Hohenheim, generally known simply as Paracelsus. He and Agrippa shared essentially the same *Weltanschauung*, the same values, the same Hermetic vision; but it would be difficult to imagine two more radically different personalities. If Agrippa was cold, haughty, aloof and enigmatic, Paracelsus was boisterous, jovial, extroverted, temperamental, prone equally to exuberance or Homeric wrath, with a demeanour reminiscent of Rabelais or of Shakespeare's Falstaff.

Paracelsus was born around 1493, some seven years after Agrippa, in the foothills of the Alps to the south of Zurich. His father was the illegitimate offspring of a disgraced Swabian nobleman, a former commander of the Teutonic Knights, who had lost both estates and reputation. Trained as a physician, the elder Hohenheim desired his son to follow in his footsteps, and Paracelsus thus embarked on the study of medicine. Around 1509, at the age of sixteen, he entered the University of Basle. Around 1513, he left and set off on the peregrinations that would characterize the rest of his life. At Erfurt, he met and apprenticed himself to one Rufus Mutianus, a friend of Pico della Mirandola. And at some point prior to Trithemius' death in 1516, Paracelsus, like Agrippa, studied under the Hermetic abbot.

Being an outspoken and combative personality, Paracelsus quickly found himself at odds with the medical establishment of his age; and the rest of his career was to be devoted as much to iconoclastic combat with that establishment as to the promulgation of his own views. 'I considered with myself that if there were no teacher of medicine in the world, how would I set about to learn the art? No otherwise than in the great open book of nature, written with the finger of God.'[28]

In his written work, Agrippa was measured, magisterial,

detached, often self-effacing; Paracelsus, in contrast, was arrogant, orotund, dogmatic and oracular, with an ego that cast a shadow the size of a blimp. With no pretence to modesty or decorum, he castigated the medical tradition of Aristotle, Galen and Avicenna, and had no compunction about asserting his own supremacy to it:

> I . . . Paracelsus, say that by Divine grace, many ways have been sought to the Tincture of the Philosophers, which finally all come to the same scope and end. Hermes Trismegistus . . . approached this task in his own method . . . Each one of these advanced in proportion to his own method; nevertheless, they all arrived at one and the same end . . . Now at this time I . . . am endowed by God with special gifts for this end, that every searcher after this supreme philosophic work may be forced to imitate and to follow me . . . through the agency of fire, the true is separated from the false. The light of Nature indeed is created in this way, that by means thereof the proof or trial of everything may appear, but only to those who walk in this light.[29]

So far as the medical establishment of the time is concerned, 'the ancient Emerald Tablet shews more art and experience in Philosophy, Alchemy, Magic and the like . . .'[30]

Having dissociated himself from the medical authorities of the age, Paracelsus set about teaching himself the business of healing – undertaking, in the process, to evolve an entirely new system of medicine. It is only today, really, that this system is beginning to be taken seriously. Starting with the basic and typically Hermetic premise that man is not separate from nature, but intrinsically a part of nature, Paracelsus undertook to address the human organism in its natural context – an approach which today would be called 'holistic'. If everything, in accordance with Hermetic principles, was interconnected, man was a microcosm of the cosmos; and every aspect of humanity was in turn a microcosm of the whole. In consequence, man had to be regarded as a totality within a larger totality – a living organism rather than a mechanism composed of isolated parts. To understand the human organism and its ills, Paracelsus felt that one had to understand the entire corpus of human knowledge, the entire cosmic context in which that organism was embedded. To be a competent physician, therefore, one could not specialize. One had also to be a psychotherapist (or the Renaissance equivalent thereof), a herbalist, a botanist, a chemist, a physicist, an astronomer, an astrologer, an alchemist, a mineralogist, a metallurgist and virtually everything else as well. In all these capacities, the most critical factor was nature – attention to nature, observation of nature, experimentation with nature, respect for nature. For Paracelsus, as for Agrippa, the natural world was a living organism, which had to be recognized and treated as such. Traditional medical practitioners had failed to appreciate this. Ignoring nature, they had relied too exclusively on reason and logic, on mere speculation. As Paracelsus told his students in Basle: 'What a doctor needs is not eloquence or knowledge of language and of books . . . but profound knowledge of Nature and her works . . . If I want to prove anything, I shall not do so by quoting authorities, but by experiment and by reasoning thereupon . . .'[31]

For Paracelsus, the path to nature's secrets had been signposted by Hermes Trismegistus, and the most efficacious vehicle for exploring this path was alchemy. 'The Alchemist,' he wrote, invoking the old parallel between the alchemist and the botanist, 'brings forth what is latent in Nature.'[32] Medicine was ultimately a form of alchemical magic which exploited the interrelationship between microcosm and macrocosm: 'As the physician infuses herbal virtues into the sick man, and so heals his disease, so the magus infuses into man the heavenly virtues just as he has extracted them.'[33] And 'the magus can draw down virtues from heaven and infuse them into a subject . . . why should we be unable to make images conducive to health or disease?'[34]

According to one modern commentator, Allen Debus, Paracelsus and those who followed him were motivated

> by a reaction against the ancient authorities and a belief that fresh observations of nature should form the basis of a new science; by a reliance on Hermetic, neo-Platonic and neo-Pythagorean philosophy; and above all, by a special interest in the application of chemistry or alchemy as the key . . . to the wider problems of the universe . . .[35]

Dr Debus concludes:

> This plea for a new investigation of nature was closely associated with the natural magic of the Renaissance. Vital or magical forces were seen at work everywhere in the universe, and man, as part of the vast encompassing chain of life, was able to participate in the great world about him. The term 'magic' thus came to mean an observational and experimental study of the unexplained or occult forces of nature.[36]

In order to study the great book of nature, Paracelsus, between 1513 and 1524, embarked on prolonged peregrinations across the whole of what was then the known European world. He travelled from Spain to eastern Europe. In Russia, he appears to have become the confidant of a Tartar prince, whom he accompanied to Constantinople. He visited Palestine, Arabia and Alexandria, where he met and conversed with fellow magi. He is even said to have reached India. In many of his wanderings, he worked as a military surgeon for one or another army, and was thus present at the siege of Rhodes in 1522.

In 1525 and 1526, he served as a physician in Salzburg. In 1527, he settled in Basle. Here, supported by Erasmus, he obtained the post of town physician, which included the chair of medicine at the university. As usual, his extravagant and self-promotional rhetoric, his continuing attacks on the medical establishment, his eccentric and erratic behaviour, his gregarious and combative personality, quickly polarized everyone around him, eliciting fervent loyalty or virulent antipathy, and nothing in between. In a climactic gesture of iconoclasm, which caused him to be called 'the Luther of medicine', he publicly incinerated the works of hallowed authorities in a brazen vase, casting into it a compound of nitre and sulphur. This effectively ended his tenure at Basle. Shortly thereafter, a squabble with a magistrate drove him from Zurich and set him wandering again. On his renewed odyssey, he adopted the demeanour of an Old Testament prophet, directing at his enemies an increasingly vituperative biblical wrath. During all this time, he continued to write prolifically. In his attempts to publish, however, he encountered constant opposition, often being thwarted by the machinations of his adversaries. It was not until the 1560s that his numerous tracts and pamphlets began to issue in quantity from the presses. By that time, Paracelsus himself was dead. His death in 1541 is surrounded by an aura of mystery. There is certainly some evidence that he was poisoned at the behest of the medical 'experts' he had so repeatedly and remorselessly attacked and embarrassed.

In his emphasis on observation and empirical experimentation, Paracelsus inaugurated a medical and scientific revolution. He can legitimately be regarded as one of the fathers of modern medicine, and not just of 'holistic' practitioners. True, he insisted, like a modern holistic practitioner, on treating the whole human being, and on addressing himself not solely to symptoms, but to underlying causes as well. Yet at the same time, he also paved the way for many developments in conventional allotropic healing. He recognized, for example, that bodily functions could often, if not always, be reduced to chemical reactions. If that were so, he argued, chemically prepared medicines could correct any imbalance or disruption in those functions.

By experimenting with the active ingredients of the poppy, he developed techniques for the production of laudanum, which became a routinely prescribed palliative for four centuries and survives even today in the form of morphine. He explored the effects of other opium derivatives as well. He investigated the properties of drugs and other medicinal substances imported from the New World. He recognized the therapeutic value of sulphur, which was adopted as the standard antidote to infection until the advent of antibiotics.[37] He became one of Europe's first experts on the clinical understanding of syphilis. And, a century before Harvey 'officially' discovered it in the 1620s, Paracelsus spoke of the circulation of the blood.[38]

Paracelsus was also the first physician to make use of the magnet and to explore the phenomenon of magnetism in relation to the human organism. His conclusions in this respect may have been erroneous, but they paved the way for the work of Mesmer and subsequently Freud. And there were other dimensions, too, in which Paracelsus contributed to the evolution of modern psychology. Insisting always on the Hermetic principle of interrelationship, he recognized the connection between the psyche and the physical organism. Repudiating popular notions of 'demonic possession', he pioneered the investigation of hysteria and psychosomatic disorders. He stressed the importance and potency of willpower in the healing process, and of the positive influence of the imagination. One of the primary definitions of magic for Paracelsus was the practical application of Hermetic principles to the business of healing. And: 'Resolute imagination is the beginning of all magical operations.'[39] In other words, one had to believe fervently in the efficacy of the treatment and use the resources of the psyche to restore health.

At the same time, of course, the same principles, if applied differently, could produce quite different effects: 'It is possible that my spirit, without the help of my body, and through the ardent will alone, and without a sword, can stab and wound others. It is also possible that I can bring the spirit of my adversary into an image and then fold him up or lame him at my pleasure.'[40]

Such claims may well sound portentous or extravagant. They are rooted, however, in principles now universally recognized – the interrelationship of mind and body, the psyche's capacity to redress imbalances and the sheer power of suggestion or suggestibility to reinforce or sap morale. Paracelsus was thus a pioneer in one of the spheres which later magicians, for good or ill, would make uniquely their own – the sphere of psychology.

John Dee: An Elizabethan Magus

Pico della Mirandola epitomized the first generation of Renaissance magi, attaining his prime during the last quarter of the fifteenth century. During the first third of the sixteenth century, the second generation was represented pre-eminently by Agrippa and Paracelsus. The third generation, coming to prominence from the mid sixteenth century onwards, was represented by increasingly divergent figures. So far as the English-speaking world is concerned, the most influential was John Dee.

Of Welsh ancestry, Dee was born in 1527. Between 1542 and 1545, he studied at Cambridge, reading Greek and mathematics. He also immersed himself in the sciences, especially mechanics. And he developed an interest in cartography and navigation which would last for the duration of his life and bring him into regular contact or correspondence with cartographers across the whole of Europe. In 1546, he was made a fellow of the newly founded Trinity College, where he taught Greek. After a trip to the Netherlands to study navigation, he returned to Cambridge and obtained his MA in 1548. For the next two years, he pursued his studies at Louvain. Among his closest associates there was Gerardus Mercator, the greatest cartographer, geographer and globe-maker of the age. It was Mercator, of course, who devised the familiar 'Mercator Projection', which governs most map-making to the present day.

In 1551, after sojourns in Antwerp, Brussels and Paris, Dee returned to England and became associated with Sir William Cecil, later Lord Burghley, the founder of the Elizabethan spy network. Between 1552 and 1555, he served in the households of the Earl of Pembroke and the Duke of Northumberland. Among his closest friends during this period were the duke's son, John, Earl of Warwick, and Robert Dudley, later Earl of Leicester. In the summer of 1555, he was briefly imprisoned for treason against Queen Mary. Not surprisingly, this earned him the favour of the future Queen Elizabeth. When Elizabeth ascended the throne in 1558, it was Dee who selected the most astrologically propitious day for the coronation. He was welcomed at court and, after the death of Robert Recorde, became recognized as the most influential exponent of the sciences in England. In 1561, he augmented and expanded on Recorde's *Grounde of Artes*, the famous text on mathematics using Arabic numerals. Dee's book was the first book of its sort and during the next century was to go through twenty-six editions.

By 1563, Dee had made a number of vociferous enemies and was being attacked in print as 'the Great Conjuror'. A year later, he effectively ratified this status by publishing his most ambitious and celebrated book, the work on Hermetic and Kabbalistic magic entitled *Monas hieroglyphica* – the sign, or hieroglyph, of the One. In this text, dedicated to the Holy Roman Emperor Maximilian I, Dee drew extensively on the Kabbalism of the Venetian friar Francesco Giorgi and on Agrippa's comprehensive summation in *De occulta philosophia*. At risk of oversimplifying Dee's objectives, one might describe the *Monas* as an attempt to distil Agrippa's massive three-volume synthesis down into a single magico-mathematical formula, a single symbol or symbolic equation which embodied within itself the totality of universal wisdom – a species of Hermetic equivalent, so to speak, of Einstein's $E = mc^2$. The *Monas* was subsequently to exert a profound influence on the mysterious Rosicrucian manifestos – in one of which Dee's central symbol, the glyph representing the 'Monas' itself, figures explicitly.[41]

In 1566, Dee made the acquaintance of Edward Dyer, who was later knighted and made Chancellor of the Order of the Garter. In 1570, he wrote a preface to the English translation of Euclid. In the same year, he established his home at Mortlake, near Richmond. His residence here was to become, in effect, an informal Italian-style academy for Elizabethan students of Hermeticism. At Mortlake, Dee had scholars to stay; rooms were set aside for scientific instruments and used as laboratories; and an immense library was accumulated, which filled four or five rooms of the house. In addition to ancient texts, the library included the works of medieval magi such as Ramón Lull and Roger Bacon, as well, of course, as the books of Ficino, Pico, Giorgi, Agrippa and Paracelsus. According to Frances Yates, the 'whole Renaissance' was encompassed by Dee's library, which comprised 'the greatest scientific library in England'.[42] And Dee augmented it by seeking out manuscripts and books from clerical collections, which had become available through Henry VIII's dissolution of the monasteries.

Among the regular habitués at Mortlake was Dee's old friend, Sir Edward Dyer. There was the spymaster, Sir Francis Walsingham. There was Robert Dudley, Earl of Leicester. There was Leicester's nephew, Sir Philip Sidney, who studied Hermeticism in general under Dee and alchemy in particular. There was Adrian Gilbert, half-brother of Sir Walter Ralegh and alchemist to Sidney's sister, Mary, Countess of Pembroke, dedicatee of the poet's *magnum opus*, *Arcadia*. It is likely that the countess herself – renowned as an adept 'chemist' in her own right, with her own alchemical laboratory – also studied under Dee. And while no record survives of Ralegh having personally visited Mortlake, it is probable that he did so. Certainly he was one of Dee's closest friends and most fervent supporters at court.

Through Ralegh and the mathematician Thomas Hariot, Dee's circle overlapped another, with similar interests. This flourished near by, at Syon House, under the auspices of Henry Percy, Earl of Northumberland. At his residence in west Sussex, the earl had built up an impressive library of his own. In addition to Ralegh and Hariot, his entourage at Syon House included Christopher Marlowe and, later, the young John Donne. Thus, through his own circle and through the earl's, 'Dee was exposing some of the most influential figures in Elizabethan England to his philosophy.'[43]

They were not the only figures he exposed to it. Dee had an adventurous spirit, for whom the comfortable demesne of Mortlake did not always provide sufficient scope. He had never relinquished his early passion for cartography and navigation, and had already invested money in maritime exploration. In 1576, he sailed across the Atlantic with Martin Frobisher in a quest for the fabled northwest passage to the orient. In the event, he saw little of the New World save the ice floes of Hudson Bay; but the voyage inspired a book, *General and Rare Memorials pertayning to the Perfect Arte of Navigation*, published in 1577. Among other things in this work, Dee advocated the creation of a permanent British navy. And his interest in maritime exploration intensified. There is considerable evidence to suggest he was one of the sponsors of Drake's circumnavigation of the globe. Certainly the other sponsors – who included Walsingham, Leicester and Dyer – were among his closest friends and most assiduous protégés. And Drake's immediate subordinate, Sir John Hawkins, was also a regular visitor to Mortlake.

So, too, was another explorer, Sir Humphrey Gilbert – half-brother of Sir Walter Ralegh and brother of Adrian Gilbert. In 1580, Sir Humphrey granted to Dee exclusive rights to all land discovered in the New World above thirty degrees north latitude – a tract which would have included most of modern Canada.[44] To the Gilberts and to other associates, Dee promulgated a grandiose vision of a new imperium, a hitherto unheard of 'British Empire', with Elizabeth I as its first ruler.[45] He mustered a quantity of somewhat dubious evidence to prove that England had a mystical, if not a mundane political, right to most of the New World, and adumbrated a comprehensive programme for its colonization. In 1583, the Gilberts set sail across the Atlantic, with the objective of implementing Dee's plans. At Newfoundland, they established the first British colony in North America. On their return, however, their ship foundered and both brothers were lost. But if nothing came of this particular project, it was to pave the way for others.

As Frances Yates says, Dee can legitimately be regarded as 'the architect of the idea of the British Empire'.[46]

In 1582, a year before the Gilberts' disastrous voyage, Dee had made the acquaintance of a man known generally as Edward Kelley. Kelley was a clever and unscrupulous charlatan. He was also a criminal, having had both ears lopped off for counterfeiting. Concealing his disfigurement under a black skull cap, he had contrived to establish a reputation for himself as an alchemist, a necromancer and a medium. Dee, so wise and far-sighted in other respects, allowed himself to be outrageously duped. Perhaps he was simply a victim of his own urgent desire to believe. In any case, he became convinced that Kelley was indeed an occult adept, who could function as a conduit for angelic powers, for the forces associated by Agrippa with so-called 'angel magic'. There ensued a six-year-long partnership with Kelley which does Dee little credit. On more than one occasion, he was gulled into making a sorry fool of himself. There were squalid instances in which Dee's lofty aspirations were subordinated to Kelley's petty greed and venality. In one ignominious episode, Dee was prevailed upon by Kelley's supposedly angelic edicts to engage in some tawdry wife-swapping. The partnership with Kelley lasted only until 1589, but has stigmatized Dee ever since. In the eyes of posterity, his status as a potential peer of Agrippa and Paracelsus was irreparably compromised. Until relatively recently, he was seen less as a true Renaissance magus than as the hapless and gullible pawn of a scurrilous impostor. Indeed, he has often been tarred with the same brush as Kelley and dismissed as a charlatan himself, while his very real achievements and accomplishments have been neglected.

In fact, however, the relationship with Kelley occupied only a small part of Dee's life. And even while it existed, he continued to pursue his own loftier goals. In 1583, for example, he was given the task of reforming the Julian calendar for England. Having done this, he departed (with Kelley) for the continent, where he was to spend the next six years. By 1584, he was in Prague, where he was taken under the wing of Rudolf II, the Hermetically inclined Holy Roman Emperor. A year later, he visited Cracow and expounded Hermetic magic to the King of Poland. By 1586, he was back in Prague again, enjoying the luxury of imperial patronage. To this day, it is unclear who influenced whom more. There is no doubt that Rudolf was impressed by Dee and found the English magus's company both stimulating and illuminating. At the same time, Dee was vouchsafed the opportunity to immerse himself in the Emperor's vast collection of esoterica. As has been noted, the Rosicrucian manifestos of some thirty years later were to reflect aspects of Dee's thought and symbolism, while at the same time extolling and endorsing Rudolf. It is certainly reasonable to assume that the seeds of those manifestos were first sown during Dee's sojourn at the imperial court in Prague.[47]

Not surprisingly, the rapport between a supposedly Catholic Emperor and a magician from Protestant England sent ripples of alarm through the Church. Investigations were hastily instituted by ecclesiastical authorities. In May of 1586, the papal nuncio presented a complaint to Rudolf accusing Dee of conjuring. Shortly thereafter, the Pope demanded that the Emperor arrest both Dee and Kelley, and send them to Rome for interrogation by the Holy Office. Rudolf contrived to dodge this edict by going through the motions of expelling the accused from his domains. With the probable collusion of the Emperor, Dee and Kelley were then taken under the protection of a Bohemian nobleman, Count Rosenberg, who managed to get the expulsion order rescinded. They were to spend the next two years in residence at one of Rosenberg's castles.

Since the 1570s at least, Dee had been involved in espionage. He not only conducted intelligence assessments himself, and did fieldwork as well; he also, according to the testimony of his own diary, ran his own agents. His interest in mathematics had coincided with an interest in ciphers and cryptography. He was acquainted with cryptographers throughout Europe, and was known to extol Trithemius' book on the subject, the *Stenographia*. Certain later commentators have suggested that some of Dee's more impenetrable esoteric writings are, in fact, complex codes. And it must be remembered, too, that one of Dee's closest associates was Sir Francis Walsingham, Elizabeth's chief spymaster and Secretary of State between 1573 and 1590. Walsingham's daughter, Frances, was married to Sir Philip Sidney, who studied under Dee and performed numerous secret missions on his father-in-law's behalf.

In 1587, Philip II of Spain was preparing his army and his supposedly 'Invincible Armada' for the projected invasion of England – an invasion intended, among other things, to extirpate the Protestant 'heresy' definitively. In this undertaking, the Spanish monarch might reasonably have hoped, perhaps, to enlist the aid of his Habsburg cousin, the Holy Roman Emperor. Rudolf, for his part, had no love for the Church, and would probably not have endorsed the enterprise anyway. But it is certainly possible that Dee was commissioned by Walsingham to stiffen the Emperor's resistance to his Spanish relative's design; and the rapport between the Emperor and the English magus may have achieved precisely that objective. In any case, Walsingham drew up a list of measures necessary to obtain information about the proposed invasion. The fourth point on his list was to 'set up an Intelligence post in Cracow for receiving reports on Spanish matters coming from the Vatican'.[48] At the same time, Dee, who had been in Cracow two years before, turned up there again. Given his long-standing friendship with Elizabeth's spymaster, it is more than likely that the business of establishing the intelligence post fell to him.

A year later, in 1588, the Spanish Armada was defeated and the invasion of England thwarted. In 1589, Dee broke definitively with Kelley and returned to England. The remainder of his life was placid enough. In 1595, he was granted the wardenship of Christ's College, Manchester. In 1603, Elizabeth died and James VI of Scotland ascended the throne as James I of England. The new monarch was skittish towards magic and more than a little hostile. By that time, too, most of Dee's former friends and supporters were dead or out of favour. In consequence, his currency at the court suffered. He died in penury at Mortlake in 1608.

Dee's legacy to British history was considerable. As already noted, he advocated the creation of a permanent British navy and was, in effect, 'the architect of the idea of British Empire'. Compared to such figures as Agrippa and Paracelsus, he was a very public-minded, or civic-minded, magus, whose interests extended beyond the esoteric, and encompassed commerce, economics, politics and nationalistic expansion. He was eager for the burgeoning professional and mercantile classes of Elizabethan England to share in the benefits of Hermetic magic. To that end, he cultivated 'contacts with the rising artisan and middle classes'. In order 'to spread knowledge among those not learned in the ancient tongues',[49] and 'specifically for the benefit of the rising middle class of technologists and artisans', he tended to write his scientific works not in Latin, but in English.[50] Thus he endeavoured to implement his 'mystical vision of Britain as the leader in reuniting Christian Europe and re-establishing the new golden age of civilization'.[51]

Another aspect of Dee's legacy can be discerned in his attitude towards architecture. In his preface of 1570 to the first English edition of Euclid, he eulogized the architect as a supreme Hermetic master: 'I think, that none can justly account themselves Architects . . . But they only, who from their childs years, ascending by those degrees of knowledge, being fostered up with the attaining of many languages and arts, have won to the high Tabernacle of Architecture.'[52] And further, 'the name of Architecture is of the principality which this Science has, above all other Arts. And Plato affirms, the Architect to be Master over all . . .'[53]

Architecture, for Dee, was 'an art whose essence is to be found in abstract principles of mathematical proportion and cosmic harmony'.[54] In short, architecture was intrinsically Hermetic, and 'had a magical dimension because ideally structures were patterned after potent celestial harmonies'.[55] Such premises were soon to be embraced by the likes of Inigo Jones and Christopher Wren. Within half a century or so of Dee's death, the same were also to figure prominently in the institution of Freemasonry.

From a Christian – and, more specifically, from a Catholic – point of view, Dee, as a Renaissance magus, would simply have been another Faustus. But it must be remembered that Faustus is damned, in Christian terms, primarily because of his quest for knowledge beyond the limits imposed by the Church. In less dogmatic terms, such a quest for knowledge would be laudable – especially if it were conducted for the sake of the public welfare, and with the objective of integrating the diverse fragments of reality. Dee, in his quest, indisputably conformed to these criteria. He thus emerges not only as Faustus, but also as the obverse of Faustus, the opposite side of the coin. He emerges, in short, as Shakespeare's Prospero in *The Tempest*, the benevolent magus dedicated to service and the protection of those entrusted to his care. Certainly Prospero's character in Shakespeare's last play owes something to Dee. As Frances Yates says, 'Dee is the perfect Elizabethan', in whom 'Prospero and Sir Francis Drake meet and are one'.[56]

Giordano Bruno's Hermetic Mission

Familiarity, as the truism goes, breeds contempt; and Dee was active in England for a long enough time to foster, at least in the public mind, a certain contemptuous familiarity. And while he had his loyal adherents, his vulnerability, his modesty, his benevolence and essential gentleness seem to have elicited from them affection rather than awe, solicitude rather than intimidation. Prospero inspires trust, not fear. At no point does Dee appear to have galvanized or electrified his contemporaries in the way that Agrippa and Paracelsus did theirs. But if he was taken for granted to that extent in his native country, there was one foreigner who exercised a very different kind of influence, produced a very different kind of impact. This most turbulent, tumultuous and ferocious of magi was an Italian, Giordano Bruno.

Bruno, twenty-one years younger than Dee, was born in 1548, in a small town near Naples. At the age of fifteen, he entered a Dominican monastery, where his gregarious, defiant, rebellious and in many respects megalomaniacal temperament was soon to plunge him into conflict with his superiors. In 1576, he divested himself of his habit and absconded, with the authorities – who had officially branded him a heretic – in hot pursuit. For the duration of his life, he was to remain in relentless dispute with the Church, incessantly itinerant, incessantly controversial and provocative, incessantly on the run from ecclesiastical harassment.

In Geneva, he quickly aroused from the presiding Calvinist regime as violent an antipathy as he had from

Catholicism. He was forced to flee to Paris, where he gave public lectures and, in 1582, published his first books. In two of these works, he drew extensively on Agrippa and Paracelsus, and presented himself explicitly as a magician of comparable stature. Perhaps, in the psychological methodology of his magic, he went beyond them. Perhaps he merely divulged openly what they had preferred to keep secret or to pass on personally to chosen initiates. In any case, he adapted the classical techniques of memory training – as practised, for example, by Roman orators – to specifically Hermetic ends. In effect, Bruno endeavoured to outline a practical training programme whereby the magician might transmute his own mind into a conduit for cosmic power – to make his psyche into a kind of force field, to attract celestial energies and then project them outwards again in focused and concentrated form.

The prospect of acquiring such aptitudes earned Bruno the favour and patronage of the French king, Henri III – who, like his mother, Catherine de' Medici, had long been fascinated by magic. But Bruno, for reasons which remain unclear, was eager to get to England. Henri accordingly provided him with letters of introduction to the French ambassador in London. Bruno arrived in London in 1583 and spent the next three years domiciled in the ambassador's residence.

In 1585, Bruno published in London his two most famous and important works, *Cena de le ceneri* (*The Ash Wednesday Supper*) and *Spaccio della bestia trionfante* (*The Expulsion of the Triumphant Beast*). And it was in England that he received his most cordial, indeed enthusiastic, welcome. He is known to have visited Oxford, where his lectures attracted a zealous following. Among those who flocked around him were a number of illustrious literary names, including Fulke Greville and Sir Philip Sidney. There is no record of Bruno ever having met John Dee personally. But after attending one of Bruno's public debates, Sidney is known to have gone directly to Dee's home at Mortlake, presumably to report and debrief. During the debate in question, Bruno had expounded on, and defended, Copernicus' theory that the earth revolved around the sun.

It is difficult to judge what Dee would have made of Bruno. Certainly Bruno was markedly more radical, more potentially subversive. According to Frances Yates:

> Bruno has returned to Ficino's use of talismans with a vengeance, and without any of Ficino's Christian inhibitions, for he believes in Hermetic Egyptianism as better than Christianity ... By his rejection of Christianity, and his enthusiastic adoption of Hermetic Egyptianism, Bruno moves back towards a darker, more medieval necromancy.[57]

More than any other Renaissance magus, Bruno comported himself like a man with a mission. Frances Yates describes it as a specifically 'Hermetic religious mission . . . a mission in which Ficino's magic becomes expanded into a projected full restoration of the magical religion . . .'[58] If one looks closely at Bruno's work, it becomes apparent that he was intent on two quite distinct but overlapping objectives, both of them revolutionary in the extreme. In the first place, he sought to offer a concrete and practical methodology whereby aspiring magicians might turn their minds into receptacles and sources of cosmic power. In the second place, he was bent on nothing less than the establishment of a new world religion – or, to be more accurate, the re-establishment of an ancient religion, the Hermetic syncretism of Alexandria, in updated form.

As Frances Yates says, Bruno 'is taking renaissance magic back to its pagan source'.[59] He repudiates the pious attempts of Ficino and Pico to Christianize Hermeticism or to find some common ground between the two. On the contrary, he condemns Christianity, lamenting its eradication of the classical gods and the magic of ancient Egypt. Invoking the Hermetic corpus, Bruno extols the worship of divinity in all things. In traditional Hermetic fashion, he insists on a single all-encompassing unity in which everything is interconnected, everything interrelated. He stresses that 'one simple divinity which is in all things . . . shines forth in diverse subjects, and takes diverse names . . .'[60] And he prophesies the advent of a new age of reform, to be brought about by 'manipulating the celestial images on which all things below depend . . .'[61] Bruno's vision, in short, posits the creation of a dramatic new world order through magical exploitation of the Hermetic correspondences between microcosm and macrocosm. And by bringing about this new reality, man – man the magus – will, in effect, become god. In Bruno, Faust thus achieves his apotheosis.

Like Agrippa, Bruno is believed to have devoted much time on his travels to creating a network of secret societies.[62] Given his admiration for Agrippa, they may even have been a part, or an extension, of the same network. He was subsequently accused by the Inquisition of attempting to found a new sect.[63]

Frances Yates also sees Bruno's influence, as much as she does Dee's, behind the Rosicrucian manifestos. And she sees Bruno's influence, as much as Dee's, behind Freemasonry as well. Towards the end of the sixteenth century, she observes

men were seeking in religious Hermetism some way of toleration or union between warring sects . . . there were many varieties of Christian Hermetism, Catholic and Protestant, most of them avoiding the magic. And then comes Giordano Bruno, taking full magical Egyptian Hermetism as his basis,

preaching a kind of Egyptian Counter Reformation, prophesying a return to Egyptianism in which the religious difficulties will disappear in some new solution, preaching too, a
moral reform with emphasis on social good works and an ethic
of social utility . . . Where is there such a combination as this
of religious toleration, emotional linkage with the medieval
past, emphasis on good works for others, and imaginative
attachment to the religion and symbolism of the Egyptians?
The only answer to this question that I can think of is – in
Freemasonry . . . Freemasonry does not appear in England
until the early seventeenth century, but it certainly had predecessors, antecedents, traditions of some kind going back much
earlier . . . We are fumbling in the dark here, among strange
mysteries, but one cannot help wondering whether it might
have been among the spiritually dissatisfied in England, who
perhaps heard in Bruno's 'Egyptian' message some hint of
relief, that the strains of the Magic Flute were first breathed
upon the air.[64]

At the same time, the messianic nature of Bruno's
Hermetic mission did not preclude him from becoming
involved, like Dee, in more mundane affairs. Between 1583
and 1586, Sir Francis Walsingham, Dee's friend and
Elizabeth's spymaster, was known to have been receiving
detailed reports from a secret agent operating inside the
French embassy. The reports pertained to Catholic factions
in England and Scotland – those associated with Mary
Queen of Scots, for example, and her son, James VI – and
their links with the pro-Catholic Guise family in France.
The agent who compiled the reports was known to be Italian,
a cleric or ex-cleric, yet implacably hostile to Spain and the
Church. A number of his letters still survive, attesting to his
personal contact with Elizabeth and his loyalty to the English
throne. In a book published in 1991, Professor John Bossy

of the University of York has convincingly identified the spy within the French embassy as Bruno.

Throughout his life, Bruno was impetuous and audacious to the point of reckless foolhardiness. One gets the impression at times that his sense of his own messianic importance fostered a dangerous conviction of invulnerability – and this was to prove his undoing. In 1586 – the year in which the reports from within the French embassy ceased – Bruno returned to Paris. He then embarked on an odyssey through various German cities. For six months in 1588 he was in Prague. There is no record of his having met Dee, who was in Bohemia at the same time, but he did meet the Holy Roman Emperor, Rudolf II. At last, in 1591, Bruno rashly returned to Italy. A year later, in Venice, he was apprehended by the Inquisition. He was brought to Rome, where there ensued eight years of sustained interrogation and torture. In 1600, having refused to recant, retract or repudiate his writings, he was burned at the stake as a heretic.

Unlike other Renaissance magi, Bruno enjoys some modest status as a literary figure, as a poet and a dramatist. His literary oeuvre, in both Latin and Italian, still merits at least some consideration on artistic grounds. But whatever the quality or status of this work, it is eclipsed in scale and consequence by his visionary esoteric treatises. Because of their highly personal, highly idiosyncratic and often chaotic character, however, these have never enjoyed the currency of Agrippa's *De occulta philosophia*, or of some of Paracelsus' texts. It is more as a personality, and as a symbol, that Bruno has survived, to be invoked in our own century by such literary figures as Joyce. The flamboyant nature of his rebellion, his Faustian quest, his defiance and his uncompromising antipathy towards Rome have all served to make him an embodiment of Renaissance values – freedom of thought and imagination, intellectual boldness, mystical intensity and

Promethean aspiration. Through his death, he has become for posterity a martyr to those things, as well as an indictment of ecclesiastical tyranny that shames the Church to this day.

The Theatre of the World

Trithemius, Agrippa, Paracelsus, Dee and Bruno were the most prominent and most influential of the Renaissance magi, and the figures who left the most important legacy for posterity. There were, of course, many lesser Hermeticists, certain of whom made original and lasting contributions of their own. There was, for example, Giulio Camillo, whose magical theatre of talismanic memory images was to influence Bruno's adaptation of memory training to Hermetic ends. There was Tommaso Campanella, who spent much of his life in the prisons of the Inquisition, escaped execution only by feigning madness and, in his most famous work, *Città del sole* ('City of the Sun'), recast the humanistic vision of Thomas More's *Utopia* in specifically Hermetic terms. For the purposes of this book, however, it is worth lingering only with one individual who might be considered the last of the true Renaissance magi, and who brings the continuum of such magi to a close. The individual in question is another Englishman, Robert Fludd.

Fludd (1574–1637) was the son of a knight who enjoyed the patronage of Elizabeth I and had served her as military treasurer in Flanders. Eschewing his father's military career, he studied medicine at Oxford, earning his degrees despite his rejection of conventional doctrine in favour of Paracelsus. Between 1598 and 1604 he led an itinerant life on the continent, visiting France, Spain and Italy, settling for some time in Germany, acting as tutor to various noble houses, including that of the dukes of Guise. By 1605, he was back in England, where his Hermetic orientation, and his repudiation of orthodoxy, delayed his admission to the Royal College of Physicians for four years. In 1606, however, he was granted a licence to practise as a doctor.

He did well, maintaining a 'handsome establishment' which included its own laboratory. Here, Fludd served as his own apothecary, concocting his personal brand of chemical medicines, as well as conducting alchemical experiments. He also began to write prolifically. His work reflects an obvious debt to Agrippa and Paracelsus, but the most important influence upon it is that of John Dee. There is no evidence that Fludd ever knew Dee personally. Indeed, he never even mentions Dee by name – an omission explained perhaps by the fact that Dee was by then out of favour. Yet Fludd's work everywhere bears Dee's unmistakable imprint. He undoubtedly had contact with some of Dee's former protégés and disciples. He may even have had access to certain of Dee's unpublished material – on subjects as diverse as gunnery, surveying and perspective in painting – which he released under his own name.[65]

In 1614, a scholar named Isaac Casaubon performed a textual analysis of the Hermetic corpus. He concluded from this that the corpus was not of the antiquity ascribed to it, but dated from the early centuries of the Christian era. Although the material in the corpus is now recognized to be much older, Casaubon's dating of the texts themselves is generally accepted today as accurate – as is his contention that Hermes Trismegistus was not an historical personage, either man or god, but a fictional composite. Fludd, however, cavalierly ignored Casaubon's findings, not even deigning to contest them. He continued to regard Hermes Trismegistus as historical, and to invoke the Hermetic corpus as an authority of comparable antiquity to the Bible. As Frances Yates observes, virtually every page of every book he wrote contains at least one quote from the Hermetic corpus.

In the same year that Casaubon published his iconoclastic exposé, there appeared in Germany the first of the famous anonymous tracts announcing the existence, and imminent self-disclosure, of the elusive Rosicrucians, or Brotherhood of the Rosy Cross. A second tract followed a year later. In these tracts, Hermeticism acquired a specific religio-political dimension, the overthrow of ecclesiastical tyranny was prophesied and a new world order heralded. A wave of hysterical paranoia swept through Europe, and especially through its Catholic regions.

During his travels on the continent, and particularly in Germany, Fludd had met many of the people subsequently associated with the so-called Rosicrucian movement. He may even have met the author or authors of the anonymous tracts, and been able to identify them as such. If so, he kept his knowledge to himself. But he did rush into print; and at the Frankfurt Book Fair in the spring of 1616, he issued his own defence of Rosicrucianism, *Apologia compendiaria*, described as 'A brief apology washing away and cleansing the stain of suspicion and infamy applied to the Fraternity of the Rosy Cross with, as it were, a Fludd of truth'.[66] In this apology, and in an expanded version published a year later, he hailed the antique wisdom of Hermes Trismegistus and commended the Rosicrucians for their 'admirable knowledge in both divine and natural secrets'.[67] He added a personal letter 'to the Brothers of the Rosy Cross', declaring that he 'would be most willing to do the utmost for the companions of your order' and inviting them to establish contact with him.[68] There is no indication that he ever received a reply. But it is hardly surprising that Fludd quickly came to be regarded as a Rosicrucian himself, and is often seen so today. This perception of him was to be reinforced by his association with other Rosicrucian-oriented figures, such as the alchemist and Hermeticist Michael Maier, physician first to the Holy Roman Emperor Rudolf II, then to Friedrich, Elector Palatine of the Rhine – a potentate who openly embraced Rosicrucianism. Fludd shared with Maier the same publisher, De Bry of Oppenheim. In 1611, he sent a greeting card with explicit Rosicrucian symbolism to James I.[69]

Fludd's major work was the multi-volumed opus *Ultriusque cosmi historia (The History of the Macrocosm and the Microcosm)*. The first volume, published in 1617, was dedicated to King James I – and promptly placed on the Index by the Inquisition. In this encyclopedic text, as everywhere else in his oeuvre, Fludd echoed John Dee; and like the Rosicrucians, he endeavoured to weave the entire spectrum of Hermetic thought and esoterica into a coherent whole, uniting alchemy, astrology, Kabbala, numerology, sacred geometry and much else besides in an all-encompassing totality. He also conducted experiments in magnetism and thus, like Paracelsus, paved the way for Mesmer and the foundations of modern psychology.

Like Dee and other Renaissance magi, Fludd was particularly interested in the application of Hermeticism to architecture. But for Fludd, the supreme manifestation of the Hermetic talisman in architectural form appears to have been the theatre. For Fludd, in other words, the theatre replaced the temple and other such edifices as a magical structure designed to draw down the sidereal energies of the cosmos. Within the microcosm of the theatre, the macrocosm was embodied and reflected, while the drama being enacted became a microcosm for the macrocosm of human life and activity it depicted. The theatre thus became for Fludd 'the theatre of the world', whose most apposite form was that of the globe.

If Frances Yates's interpretation is accurate, Fludd's work contains architectural blueprints for the Globe Theatre, in which many of Shakespeare's plays were performed.[70] A work such as *The Tempest* would thus have been a magically talismanic microcosm, performed in a structure which was also a magically talismanic microcosm. In his opus on the macrocosm and the microcosm, Fludd describes methods of producing theatrical effects – for replicating the sound of thunder or of cannon, for example, for representing 'the burning of Troy' or the 'conflagration of Rome', for depicting 'burning sacrifices on altars with hidden arrangements of lights'.[71] Such techniques, as well as the rationale behind them, were to exert a profound influence on Inigo Jones.[72]

Quite apart from his own writings, Fludd is important because he reflects an important transition in the evolution of Hermeticism and in the orientation of Western philosophical consciousness. This transition was to play a vital – and costly – role in the development of Western culture, and in the coalescence of the world as we know it today.

From Magus to Secret Society

Prior to the mid sixteenth century, the Renaissance magus – Agrippa, for example, or Paracelsus – was ultimately engaged in a solitary quest, a quest for his personal self-perfection, self-refinement and self-transcendence, his personal experience of the sacred or the numinous. True, he sought converts, sympathizers, kindred spirits, but only so that they might understand the nature of his undertaking and pursue similar enterprises of their own. And if Agrippa did indeed go about creating secret societies across Europe, it would not have been for the reform of European society as a whole, but for the preservation and perpetuation of his own arcane discoveries – the most important of which, as he said, could only be communicated personally, from master to disciple, and not by writing. The emphasis, in short, was entirely on the individual, who embodied in himself the mysteries and sacred relationship between microcosm and macrocosm. The numinous, for Agrippa and Paracelsus, could only manifest itself in an intensely private fashion. Society as a whole was left to fend for itself.

Dee and Bruno both echoed something of this. At the same time, however, they also looked outwards, towards society and the world at large. In Fludd, the reorientation inaugurated by Dee and Bruno is virtually complete. By Fludd's time, Hermetic studies had begun to shift away from the individual practitioner perfecting himself in solitude. The new thrust was primarily towards the secret society, the cabal, which was oriented quite precisely towards the perfection of society as a whole. In other words, the Hermeticism of Fludd, of the Rosicrucians and of early Freemasonry was no longer solitary, but increasingly interconnected with the world – and, as an inevitable consequence, with politics.

Many commentators regard this as a simple and straightforward evolutionary development. For such commentators, the secret society, as exemplified by the Rosicrucians and by Freemasonry, was the natural heir to solitary figures like Agrippa and Paracelsus. As will be seen, however, it can also be argued that the secret society was in some sense an aberrant development, a species of mutation, and that the true heirs to Agrippa and Paracelsus are to be found elsewhere.

9

HERMETIC THOUGHT AND THE ARTS:

THE TALISMAN

At the root of culture, as Thomas Mann says, lies cult. Ever since the earliest days of human prehistory, when man first began to weave his primitive pre-Hermetic magic into coherent systems of belief, the arts have been inextricably associated with religion. There may possibly have been some exceptions – the decoration of clay pots, for example, and other such utensils. For the most part, however, the earliest music, the earliest painting and drawing, the earliest sculpture, the earliest dance, the earliest literature were all almost invariably apprenticed to religious principles, all adjuncts of religious doctrine and ritual. Only much later in the development of civilizations did a purely secular art of any significance begin to appear. And even when it did, it drew extensively on the techniques and motifs employed in religious art.

In Western Christendom, isolated instances of secular art had begun to appear as early as the dawn of the Middle Ages. One might cite, for example, *The Song of Roland*, or the poems dealing with El Cid – though these still incorporated a strong, if implicit, religious dimension, extolling Christianity's struggle against the Islamic 'infidel'. One might also cite the somewhat later romances pertaining to the Holy Grail – though these, too, embodied a pervasive spiritual, if not quite religiously orthodox, dimension. Towards the end of the Middle Ages, one might cite some of the more purely, even earthly, secular narratives such as Boccaccio's *Decameron* or Chaucer's *Canterbury Tales*. Such works, however, were still very much exceptions to the rule. Until the Lutheran Reformation, most art, whatever its form, served an essentially Catholic religious purpose, either testifying, or leading its audience, to an apprehension of the sacred as defined by the Church.

Whatever its secular relevance or implications, Hermeticism was essentially spiritual in its orientation. Indeed, as has already been noted, it constituted, at least for some of its adherents, a crucial adjunct to established Christianity. For some, such as Agrippa and Bruno, it actually constituted an alternative, the basis for an entirely new, all-encompassing world religion. Inevitably, therefore, Hermetic thought began increasingly to manifest itself through the arts – and to become, during the Renaissance, a primary and dynamic impetus, to artistic creation. By the end of the sixteenth century, artists in every medium – from music, painting and literature through architecture and landscape gardening – would be drawing upon Hermetic principles to establish the foundation of a new aesthetic, informed by a new governing vision. In certain cases, the work of art would simply express or illustrate key tenets of Hermetic thought, such as the premise of analogy or the relationship between microcosm and macrocosm. In other cases, the act of artistic creation would be seen as nothing less than a magical operation; and the finished work would itself be a magical object, a species of talisman, capable of invoking and concentrating occult or cosmic energies.

The Magical Power of Music

According to recent scientific research, music can directly affect those centres of the brain which govern emotion.[1] This 'revelation' has engendered considerable speculation in the media. Can stimulation of the relevant centres in certain specific ways transform the personality? Can a child's temperament be shaped and moulded by music? Will children raised on the requisite dosage of Mozart subsequently display higher intelligence than children raised on Bach? Or Beethoven? Or Wagner? Or the Beatles? Or the advertising jingles used to market a cola drink?

Such questions may indeed be provocative. But we hardly needed scientific research to tell us that music can act upon us in such a way as to effect changes of mood. We all recognize that music can soothe us or agitate us, can make us dreamy or intensely alert, calm or irascible, peaceful or belligerent and aggressive. Music can lull or stimulate us, can render us quiescent or excited, can anaesthetize us or inspire us. In a fashion which circumvents and neutralizes all rational judgement and critical capacity, music can evoke in us intimations of the spiritual or the bestial, of the supernal or the savage and brutal. Religious music can convey an uplifting sense of the sacred or the numinous. In its pulsating appeal to heart and blood, certain kinds of rock music can stimulate something basic, something elemental, often something sexual. On parade, the massed pipes and drums of a Highland regiment can be deeply stirring, eliciting a *frisson* from the nervous system. On the battlefield, the eerie skirl of bagpipes can produce terror in an enemy, threading itself through the din of combat like the frenzied shrieking of Valkyries swooping down from the heavens to gather up the slain. During the American Civil War, certain Confederate regiments contrived to sound the same shrill cacophonous warlike note with the banjo – an instrument whose capacity to chill the blood will be familiar to anyone who has seen the duelling banjos sequence in the film version of James Dickey's novel *Deliverance*. Music can also, of course, be used to charm. A reed pipe can mesmerize a human being as effectively as it can a snake. In classical times, Pan's pipes were credited with the power to drive an individual insane. And it has long been recognized that a drum beat, initially synchronized with the beat of the human heart, will, if gradually accelerated, cause the heart to accelerate to a comparable tempo.

The magical potency of music was undoubtedly exploited by the shaman in the earliest tribal rituals of mankind's infancy. In the Occident, this potency was first explored, enunciated and formulated by Pythagorean thought, from which it passed to Alexandrian Hermeticism. Pythagorean and Hermetic doctrine rested on certain self-evident premises. If two strings are tuned to the same frequency and one is plucked, the second will vibrate to the same resonance – will vibrate in what appears to be 'sympathy'. In scientific terms, the plucked string causes the air surrounding it to vibrate. The vibrating air will then elicit a similar note from the second string – provided, of course, that both strings have been 'harmonically attuned'.

For the Pythagoreans, and for the Alexandrian Hermeticists who followed them, 'harmonic attunement' was the governing principle. And it applied not just to music, but to the whole of creation. Creation was perceived as a single all-embracing and all-encompassing totality, an all-pervasive whole in which everything was interconnected and interrelated. Harmony was regarded as the binding agent, the adhesive whereby every component of creation was connected and related to every other. The cosmos, in short, comprised a single vast musical instrument in tune with itself, producing its own music, to which it incessantly vibrated and resonated. Humanity and the gods, earth and heaven, microcosm and macrocosm were all linked by harmony and reflected the same harmonious proportions. These proportions could be defined and described in mathematical terms. But numbers corresponded to fixed musical notes or tones; and thus the proportions defined and described by mathematics could be replicated and activated by music. According to Pythagorean teaching, 'both the universe and man, the macrocosm and microcosm, are constructed on the same harmonic proportions'.[2] The powers of the cosmos could therefore be invoked not by beseeching them, as in conventional prayer, but by placing oneself 'in tune' with them, by placing oneself on the same frequency, and manipulating them. 'The use of anything having the same numerical proportions as a certain heavenly body or sphere will make your spirit similarly proportioned and provoke the required influx of heavenly spirit, just as a vibrating string will make another, tuned to the same or a consonant note, vibrate in harmony.'[3] It was by virtue of such attuned proportions that Pythagoras reputedly claimed to hear the harmony of the universe, the 'music of the spheres' – the notes actually 'emitted by the planets in the course of their perfectly ordered circuits'.[4]

For the Pythagoreans, as for the Hermeticists who followed them, it was natural enough that music should be regarded as having a therapeutic function. It could be used as an antidote for various 'afflictions of the soul', such as passion, depression or rage. This concept was later to be embraced by Ficino and other Renaissance magi, and was even to be invoked by Shakespeare (*The Merchant of Venice* v, i):

> nought so stockish, hard, and full of rage,
> But music for the time doth change his nature.

According to Plato, the process of education involved gymnastics for the health of the body and music for the health of the soul. Music, he maintained, fostered 'a certain harmony of spirit', which every child should learn to experience.[5] In classical mystery schools, music, conjoined to dance, was employed to induce one or another altered state of consciousness. In this capacity, it was embraced by Sufism and practised by the so-called 'whirling dervishes'. And singing or chanting in conjunction with rigorous patterns of breath control was subsequently to find its way into the discipline of Christian monasticism.

The texts of the Hermetic corpus were quite explicit in stressing the necessity of tuning the human microcosm to resonate with the macrocosm of the cosmos. The Hermetic practitioner, for example, 'should tune the inward lyre and adjust it to the divine musician'.[6] Music, in the Hermetic corpus, is the key to the numinous: 'And to be instructed in music is precisely to know how all this system of things is ordered, and what divine plan has distributed it. For this order, having brought all individual things into unity by creative reason, will produce as it were a most sweet and true harmony, and a divine melody.'[7] And music was also the conduit linking the powers of the cosmos with their terrestrial representations as anthropomorphic gods, for 'those gods are entertained with constant sacrifices, with hymns, praises and sweet sounds in tune with heaven's harmony: so that the heavenly ingredient enticed into the idol by constant communication with heaven may gladly endure its long stay among humankind. Thus does man fashion his gods.'[8] According to a Roman text dating from imperial times, 'in Egypt the priests, when singing hymns in praise of the gods, employ the seven vowels, which they utter in due succession; and the sound of these letters is so euphonious that men listen to it in place of flute or lyre'.[9]

This latter fragment vouchsafes an important indication of the way in which music was later to be used by the Hermetic magi of the Renaissance. They subscribed, of course, to the principles of harmony enunciated by their Hermetic, Platonic and Pythagorean predecessors. At the same time, they also stressed the importance of harmonious marriage between the musical note or chord and the word. Poems were composed with the explicit intention of setting them to music as songs; and the words or text of such poems comprised as crucial a component of the music as the music itself. At times, indeed, the 'rhythm of the music is completely subjected to the metre of the verse'.[10] Verses and melody were thus fused into a single inseparable whole. From this practice, as extolled, for example, by the Hermetic poets of the Pléiade in sixteenth-century France, arose the genre of musical sacred drama – from which, in turn, opera was to evolve.[11]

The practical application of Hermetic magic during the Renaissance involved the same synthesis. The *sounds* of specific words, as intoned by the human voice at a specific pitch or timbre, and to a specific cadence or rhythm, were conjoined with specific notes and chords in a specific melody. The harmonious integration of all these components had to be perfect, calculated with mathematical precision. When such perfection was achieved, the resulting invocation became activated – charged with the requisite power, the requisite virtue. It could then shatter the barriers between dimensions of reality, just as a note struck on a tuning-fork can shatter a vessel or pane of glass; and thus the invisible and elemental forces of the cosmos, whether celestial or infernal, could move freely and intermingle with the human world.

Through its application in magic and ritual, music, during the Renaissance, came to be perceived in new ways and evolved into new forms. In Italy, for example, there appeared the form of the secular madrigal – an elaborate song for several voices, each of which sang its own part rather than joining, as in a choir, with the others. The madrigal was also to contribute to the development of opera. And as the madrigal gained in popularity, so did the instruments with which it was most frequently accompanied – the lute, the lyre, the viol and the clavichord. As Hermeticism swept across Italy and then the rest of Europe, many nobles took to composing madrigals, as well as other poems set to music. Many became proficient with musical instruments.

Citing the Hermetic corpus, Ficino posited a 'cosmic spirit' flowing like a wind – the *pneuma*, or breath, of the divine – through the whole of creation. This intrinsically harmonious spirit constituted the 'channel of influence' between above and below, heaven and earth, macrocosm and microcosm. The individual's personal spirit, he maintained, was nourished, sustained and purified by 'attracting and absorbing' the cosmic spirit; and music was a paramount agency and medium for the process of attraction and absorption. Through the conduit of music, cosmic energy could infuse the individual. Music, in short, was akin to prayer, but prayer imbued with a dynamic and active potency: 'David and Hermes Trismegistus command that as we are moved by God to sing, of God alone we should sing.'[12]

When speaking of stars, according to one modern commentator, Ficino 'is not speaking of worshipping stars, but rather of imitating them, and by imitation capturing their natural emanations'.[13] And he 'is not content to point out possible analogies between macrocosm and microcosm, between musical and celestial harmonies, but gives practical directions for making music which may usefully exploit these analogies'.[14] Thus Ficino undertook to compose and perform 'magically powerful songs'. He would sing the Orphic Hymns, for example, and accompany himself on the lyre, as an act of magical ritual.

Subsequent magi introduced their own innovations and variations on the foundation established by Ficino. Francesco Giorgi, the Kabbalistic friar, for example, used music as the basis for architectural design. The church built to his plan in Venice was conceived according to musical proportions. Giorgi would often refer to God as the 'arch-musician'. He would speak of the world as God's song, or as God's instrument.

Agrippa echoed Ficino in declaring that 'the virtue of any star, or Deity', could be attracted by music 'according to due harmony', and endorsed the singing of the Orphic Hymns. But whereas Ficino sought merely to elicit the desired influences, Agrippa, in his Faustian fashion, sought to compel planetary and other 'intelligences' to his bidding. The Orphic Hymns, Agrippa maintained, 'do confer a very great power' on the magician and enable him to 'bind and direct' the object of his 'enchantment'.[15] While Ficino was careful not to violate the tenets of Christian orthodoxy, Agrippa had no such qualms. According to one commentator, 'Ficino is anxious to assert that his astrological songs are not incantations used to summon demons and compel them to produce magical effects.'[16] But 'instead of being conditioned by music, as in Ficino's theory, into a suitably receptive state for planetary influence, the spirit of the operator of Agrippa becomes itself an active instrument which is projected into the enchanted thing, so as to constrain or direct it'.[17] Yet even though he introduced an element of magical coercion, Agrippa still insisted on the beneficent effects of music. As he himself asserted: 'The wise ancients . . . did not in vain use Musical sounds and singings, as to confirm the health of the body, and restore it . . . until they make a man suitable to the Celestial Harmony, and make him wholly Celestial. Moreover, there is nothing more efficacious to drive away evil spirits than Musical Harmony.'[18]

In the Islamic world, Muslim Hermeticists had established a correlation between music and alchemy. This correlation was readily embraced by Renaissance magi in the West. In the *Ordinall of Alchimy*, published in 1477, the English alchemist Thomas Norton wrote:

> Join your Elements Musically
> For two causes, one is for Melody:
> Which there accords will make to your mind,
> The true effect when that ye shall find.
>
> With other accords which in Music be,
> With their proportions causing Harmony,
> Much like proportions be in Alchemy . . .[19]

The association between music and alchemy continued to be actively pursued into the seventeenth century. An illustration in a Rosicrucian-oriented work of 1609, for example, depicts an alchemist praying before a pentagram in his laboratory. In the foreground, a collection of stringed musical instruments lies on a table to which a Latin motto is affixed, asserting that 'sacred music disperses sadness and malignant spirits'.[20]

In 1618, the Rosicrucian Hermeticist Michael Maier published a book entitled *Atalanta fugiens*. It contains fifty symbolic engravings intended to reflect phases of the alchemical process. Each illustration is accompanied by a Latin epigram, and each epigram includes a sequence designed to be set to music in the form of a fugue for three voices, the musical score actually being printed with the text.

One suspects that these fugues were composed specifically to be sung in the laboratory, each at the relevant stage of the process of transmutation.

Around the same time, Robert Fludd, Maier's contemporary and friend, was expounding a similarly Hermetic association between music, magic and alchemy. Fludd, according to one commentator, 'sees music in the same light as alchemy'.[21] Fludd condemned the music of his day as being 'only the shadow of the truer and deeper music', the ancient Hermetic music, which has to be rediscovered, for through it man may recognize himself and thus finally attain a mystical knowledge of God'.[22] For Fludd, 'the secret and essential object of music' is described as 'an ascent from imperfection to perfection, from impurity to purity . . . from darkness to light, from earth to heaven . . .'[23] Fludd believed that the divine emanations which connected microcosm with macrocosm should be visualized by means of a musical analogy. A single-stringed instrument, the 'monochord' of two octaves, was said to reflect the correspondence between heaven and earth, and God was the player of this 'monochord'.[24]

Perhaps inevitably, aspects of Hermetic and Kabbalistic mathematical magic found their way into the Church, where they were adapted to Christian music. They were applied most frequently in the cult of the Virgin. The number seven, for example, was deemed especially sacred to Mary, symbolizing the seven joys and seven sorrows ascribed to her by Church tradition.[25] Thus, in 1498, the Dutch composer Matthaeus Pipelare wrote a seven-part song for the Feast of the Seven Sorrows. Another composer, Pierre de la Rue, wrote two masses for the same feast, the dominant motif in each consisting of a seven-note phrase. Marian masses in seven parts became increasingly common.[26] And during the sixteenth century, the English composer Thomas Tallis (*c.* 1510–85) wrote a number of works dedicated to the Virgin which comprised verse texts of seven stanzas.

All of this, of course, was anodyne enough, and could easily be reconciled with official Christian doctrine. But other, more heterodox forms of Hermetic music and magic were also embraced by the ecclesiastical hierarchy – as high up, on occasion, as the Papacy itself. In the early seventeenth century, for example, Pope Urban VIII was a keen astrologer, and often amused himself by computing charts for his cardinals and predicting their deaths. The situation became disconcerting when other astrologers began to predict his death; and in 1628 – a year in which an eclipse of the moon occurred in January and an eclipse of the sun in December – the Pope became seriously alarmed. He solicited the magical aid of the Hermeticist Tommaso Campanella.

Throughout 1628, Campanella and the Pope met regularly in private and conducted rituals to combat adverse astrological influences. The room would be sealed off 'from outside air', then 'sprinkled . . . with . . . aromatic substances'. Laurel, myrtle, rosemary and cypress would be burned. The walls would be hung with white silken cloths and decorated with branches. Two candles and five torches would be lit to represent the seven planets. Stones, plants, colours and odours associated with the beneficent influences of Venus and Jupiter would be deployed. The magician and the Pope would then drink 'astrologically distilled liquors' and play music intended to invoke the energies of Venus and Jupiter.[27]

To the Pope's mind, these rituals must certainly have proved their efficacy. Despite the ominous predictions, he survived for another sixteen years, until 1644. That did not, however, prevent Campanella – who had already spent years in prison – from incurring the wrath of the Inquisition for endorsing Galileo. In 1634, he sought refuge from the ungrateful Church in Paris.

Paintings as Magical Talismans

Hermeticism posited the interrelationship, the intercon-nectedness, the correspondences between all things. It is therefore obvious that the principle of harmonious propor-tion, which linked magic, mathematics and music, should also be applied to painting and sculpture. The Hermetic painters of the Renaissance were all accomplished mathe-maticians, and some of them were musicians as well. In *Lives of the Artists*, Giorgio Vasari describes Leonardo as more than just an accomplished player on the lyre. His perfor-mace for Ludovico Sforza, Duke of Milan, is described by Vasari as 'superior to that of all the other musicians who had come to Ludovico's court'. Leonardo possessed a lyre he had crafted for himself – of silver, in the shape of a horse's head. 'Music,' he is on record as saying, 'is the sister of painting.'[28]

The parallel between harmonic proportion in music and harmonic proportion in spatial measurement was one of the established premises of Renaissance Hermetic art. According to the architect Palladio, 'the proportions of the voices are harmonies for the ears; those of the measurement are harmonies for the eyes'.[29] For men like Palladio, 'both music and painting convey harmonies; music does it by chords and painting by its proportions'.[30] Hermetic painters of the Renaissance employed the principle of harmonic proportion in a variety of ways. One such was the depiction of perspec-tive – 'objects of equal size placed so as to recede at regular intervals, diminish in "harmonic" progression'.[31]

Harmonic proportion in Hermetic paintings of the Renaissance is particularly apparent in the frequent use of the so-called 'Golden Proportion', or 'Golden Mean', or 'Golden Section'. A number with an infinite sequence of decimal places, the Golden Section is usually denoted by the Greek letter phi Ø. It denotes a specific and constant ratio derived from a precise geometric relationship. One must visualize a regular pentagon, a figure of five equal sides. One must then visualize a pentagram, a five-pointed star, inscribed inside it. The length of each line in the internal pentagram will always have a constant relationship to the length of each side of the external pentagon. This ratio is the Golden Section, or Ø. It represents a unique harmonious proportion. It constitutes a means of dividing a given line so that each division has a specific fixed relationship to every other division and to the whole.

Because it was inherent in the immutable principles of mathematics – in the immutable laws governing number, angle and form – the Golden Section was deemed a particularly felicitous manifestation, and confirmation, of the harmonious relationship between microcosm and macrocosm. Its significance was deemed all the greater by virtue of the fact that it could be found, like a divine signature, in nature – in the structure of the conch or nautilus shell, for example, whose spiral expands geometrically in accordance with the Golden Section. And it also bore the stamp of authority conferred by antiquity. It had consistently been used by architects and sculptors of the classical world. The Parthenon, for instance, was built according to the ratio of the Golden Section. In ancient Egypt and Greece, moreover, the Golden Section was thought to be present in the dimensions of the human body, divided by the navel into the ratio of Ø. A building constructed according to the same ratio was therefore held to be more harmoniously suited to those living or working within it.

Hermetic painters of the Renaissance regularly composed their works on the basis of an underlying geometry embodying harmonious proportions. The Golden Section often constituted the governing principle of such geometry.

It was often used, for example, by Leonardo. It is apparent in *The Baptism of Christ* by Piero della Francesca, who, in his lifetime, was actually better known as a mathematician than as a painter. An underlying pentagonal geometry based on the Golden Section is also apparent in Dürer's famous *Melancholia*.[32] A century and a half later, the same geometry was still being employed by Poussin.

Along with other mathematical and geometric formulae, the Golden Section was held to incorporate an inherent metaphysical dimension. Being based on number, it existed 'eternally' and pervaded all things. It could thus be perceived as a manifestation, even as an attribute, of divinity. God the Creator could be seen demonstrably to work through the immutable laws of number and proportion. And it was therefore natural to seek these laws in the microcosm of the human body. The classical Roman architect Vitruvius – whose teachings were revived by Renaissance Hermeticists – had advocated the construction of temples in accordance with proportions derived from the human body. These proportions included not only the Golden Section, but also an extrapolation of circles and squares originating from an upright human figure standing with arms and legs extended. A famous drawing of this figure – often referred to as 'Man the Microcosm' – appears in Leonardo's notebooks. It was subsequently adapted by Agrippa and Fludd, who depicted it in a cosmic context – in a circle corresponding to the zodiac, with astrological signs inscribed in their appropriate places. The eternal harmonious proportions of all creation were thus revealed as inherent in the miracle of the human body, which incarnated in the microcosm the divine perfection of the macrocosm.

But the work of art, in painting or in sculpture, could do more than just exemplify, embody or bear testimony to the Hermetic principle of harmonious proportion. Like a piece

Sandro Botticelli's *Primavera*, now in the Uffizi Gallery, Florence. This painting is a magical talisman designed to directly affect the viewer; to draw down and render accessible the divine spirit of Venus.

Dr Faustus, within a magic circle, invoking the Devil. Frontispiece from Christopher Marlowe's *Doctor Faustus*, 1620.

Beneath the Holy Spirit, God the Father and God the Son sit with their feet on the perfect cube: *La Gloria*, a sixteenth-century fresco by Luca Cambiaso at the Escorial Palace, Spain.

Melancholia, an engraving by Albrecht Dürer, 1514, based on a quote from Agrippa's *De occulta philosophia*, in which Saturn's gift of melancholy was said to lead to wisdom and revelation.

Leonardo da Vinci: scheme of human proportion.

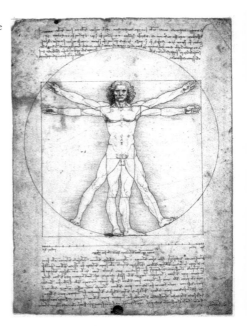

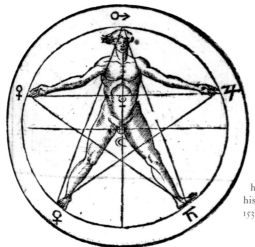

Heinrich Cornelius Agrippa: scheme of human proportion (from his *De occulta philosophia,* 1533).

Robert Fludd: scheme of human proportion (from his *Utriusque cosmi ... historia*, 1617).

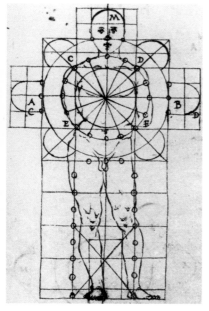

Drawing by Francesco Giorgi: human proportions in harmonic relationship with a design for a church.

The church of S. Maria della Consolazione, Todi, Italy: a centrally planned church, based on the circle, rather than the cross, as a symbol of the Divine.

Interior view of the cupola of S. Eligio degli Orefici, Rome, showing the central circular geometry.

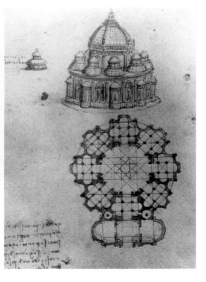

Leonardo da Vinci: church design based on a circular geometry.

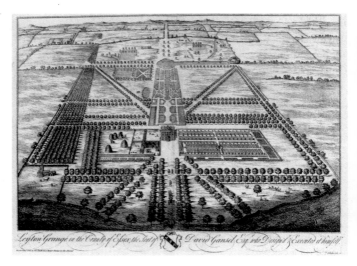

Leyton Grange, Essex in 1740: a centrally planned geometric garden forming a magical unity with the house; both are united by harmonious proportions.

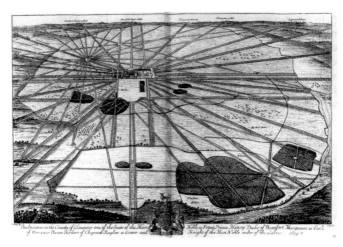

Taming wild nature: at Badminton the geometry radiates from a central focus into the countryside in a magical attempt at domination. Engraving dated 1720.

of music, it could also function as a talisman, a species of invocation. In other words, it could be an active agency, a dynamic element, in the magical operation – could indeed constitute in itself a magical act. Through harmonious proportion, the work of art could act as a magnet, a receptacle and a conducting medium for transcendent or numinous energies. And these energies emanating from the macrocosm, when concentrated and focused by the work of art, could exert an occult influence on the microcosm of man. That influence might only be subliminal, but it was none the less potent. In the terminology of twentieth-century psychology, the work of art could use certain universally resonant symbols to stir recesses of the psyche – and particularly of the unconscious – inaccessible to rational discourse or to logic.

In classical mythology, Venus (Aphrodite), goddess of love, had, through an adulterous relationship with him, 'tamed' Mars (Ares), the god of war. By later astrologers, this was taken as an allegorical representation of the way in which the gentle and beneficent influence of the planet Venus could neutralize the belligerence, aggressiveness and impulsive energies emanating from Mars. That Venus could 'tame' Mars and demonstrate the supremacy of love over strife became an accepted astrological assumption of Renaissance Hermeticists. It was asserted, for example, by both Ficino and Pico. Embracing this assertion, a number of Renaissance artists, including Botticelli, produced paintings on the theme – depicting Mars, for example, sleeping tranquilly at Venus' side. Such pictures were not mere exercises of technique, or quaintly charming renderings of mythic fancy and conceit. Still less were they intended to be works of erotic titillation. On the contrary, they were designed to be magically potent talismans which, by invoking cosmic energies in specifically 'Venusian' form, might restore a measure of peace to strife-torn Italy.

As an illustration of how a talismanic painting operated magically, it is worth looking closely at one of the greatest of them, Botticelli's famous *Primavera*, executed for a cousin of Lorenzo de' Medici and disciple of Ficino. Before doing so, however, one must recognize that Botticelli subscribed to the concept of a 'Cosmic Spirit' enunciated by Ficino and promulgated by Pico. This 'Cosmic Spirit' can be conceived as analogous to light, which, when filtered through a prism, produces colour. When filtered through the effluence, or force field, of a particular planet, the 'Cosmic Spirit' was believed to conduct and convey the planet's energies. In the *Primavera*, Botticelli endeavours to invoke the vernal energies of Venus, in order to disseminate them through the terrestrial world and foster an atmosphere of perpetual spring – an atmosphere of rebirth and renewal, of awakening sexuality and of love.[33]

At the geometric centre of the painting stands the patroness of the process, Venus herself, embowered in vernal greenery and fertile vegetative growth. To her right, in the foreground, are her earthly avatars, the Three Graces, Beauty, Chastity and Passion. According to Pico, 'the unity of Venus is unfolded in the trinity of the Graces',[34] and it is through them that her influence will be transmitted to the domain of humanity.

The 'Cosmic Spirit' is conjured into the painting at the extreme right. It is exhaled into the scene by the wind god Zephyr, whose breeze is also the Hermetic *pneuma*, denoting both breath and spirit. Zephyr's exhalation of *pneuma* is to be conceived as actively *circulating* through the painting, moving dynamically from right to left, like a Kabbalistic text in Hebrew. It first touches the flimsily clad earth nymph Chloris, who reflects the denuded world of winter. At Zephyr's touch, Chloris makes way for – or perhaps metamorphoses into – Flora, nymph of spring, whose luxurious apparel reflects the springtide earth, sumptuously clad in vestments of lush vegetation. Continuing on its path, as if through a carefully constructed pipeline, the *pneuma* will then animate the dance of the Three Graces; and one of them, Chastity, her hair still modestly braided and bound up rather than loosely flowing, will be initiated into love by the prick of Cupid's arrow, aimed at her from above. Her love, like her gaze, will be directed at Mercury, or Hermes, who stands calmly at the painting's extreme left, in symmetrical balance and counterpoint to Zephyr. And he, with his upraised hand and eyes, will redirect it back into the cosmos again.

The painting thus depicts, and simultaneously seeks to induce, a dynamic process. By means of this process, the 'Cosmic Spirit' is conjured down to earth in specifically 'Venusian' form. It is channelled through the terrestrial world according to a precise itinerary or trajectory. Having produced its effects, it is then guided back into the firmament again. Through its circulation, below is linked with above, earth with heaven, microcosm with macrocosm. And the process will repeat itself eternally, in an ever-recurring cycle. 'The 'Cosmic Spirit' will eternally enter the world through Zephyr's impetuous vernal breath. Having renewed and revitalized dormant nature, it will then return to the sublime serenity of the numinous, whence it will reappear again with the spring of the following year.

Magical Architecture

In the world of Renaissance Hermeticism, architecture possessed a sacred pedigree long pre-dating that of painting or sculpture. Like music, this pedigree extended back to Pythagorean thought, if not, indeed, before. But it had also been accorded recognition by ancient Judaism, and subsequently by Islam during the centuries when Hermeticism flourished primarily under Islamic auspices.

Judaism had traditionally forbidden the making of graven images. Islam had inherited and perpetuated this taboo. Under both Judaism and Islam, a cultural heritage had evolved which was inimical to representational art – to any depiction of organic forms, including, of course, that of man himself. The kind of decoration one associates with Christian cathedrals is not to be found in the synagogue or the mosque.

In part, the interdict derived from the fact that any attempt to depict the natural world, including the human form, was deemed to be blasphemous – an attempt by man to compete with God as creator, even to usurp and displace God as creator. God alone was held to possess the prerogative of creating forms out of nothingness, creating life out of clay. For man to create a replica of such forms, or a replica of life, out of wood, stone, pigment or any other substance, was a trespass on the divine prerogative – and, of necessity, a parody or travesty of it.

But there was also a deeper theological justification behind this apparently over-literal dogma – a justification which overlapped, and may in fact have been influenced by, Pythagorean thought. Like the cosmos in Pythagoreanism, God, in both Judaism and Islam, was One. God was a unity. God was everything. The forms of the phenomenal world, on the other hand, were numerous, manifold, multifarious and diverse. In Judaism and Islam, such forms could be perceived as bearing witness not to the divine unity, but to the fragmentation of the temporal world. If God was to be discerned in the creation at all, it was not in the multiplicity of forms, but in the unifying principles running through those forms and underlying them. In other words, God was to be discerned in the principles of shape – determined ultimately by the degrees in an angle – and by number. It was through shape and number, not by the representation of diverse forms, that God's glory could be regarded as manifest. And it was in edifices based on shape and number, rather than in representational embellishment, that the divine presence was to be housed.

The synthesis of shape and number is, of course, geometry. Through geometry, and the regular recurrence of geometric patterns, the synthesis of shape and number is actualized. Through the study of geometry, therefore, certain absolute laws appeared to become legible – laws which attested to an underlying order, an underlying design, an underlying coherence. This master plan was apparently infallible, immutable, omnipresent; and by virtue of those very qualities, it could be construed as something of divine origin – a visible manifestation of the divine power, the divine will. Thus geometry came to assume sacred characteristics, becoming invested with a status of transcendent and immanent mystery.

Towards the end of the first century BC, the Roman architect Vitruvius had enunciated what were to become some of the basic premises for later builders. He had recommended, for example, that builders be organized into mutually beneficial societies, or *collegia*. He had insisted on altars looking towards the east – as, of course, they do in Christian churches. More important still, he had established the architect as something considerably more than a mere technician. The architect, he said, 'should be . . . a skilful draughtsman, a mathematician, familiar with historical studies, a diligent student of philosophy, acquainted with music . . . familiar with astronomy . . .'[35] For Vitruvius, in effect, the architect was a species of magus, conversant with the sum of human knowledge and privy to the creation's underlying laws. Paramount among these laws was geometry, on which the architect was obliged to draw in order to construct temples 'by the help of proportion and symmetry'.

In Vitruvian precepts, Judaism and Islam converged with classical and Hermetic thought. For was not architecture the supreme actualization and application of geometry – an actualization and application which went further than painting possibly could and rendered geometry three-dimensional? Was it not in architecture that geometry, in fact, became incarnate?

During the Reformation, the taboo against representational art was to be adopted by some of the more austere forms of Protestantism. Prior to that, however, under the hegemony of the Catholic Church, medieval Christianity had had no such inhibitions or prohibitions. Yet Christendom was still quick to seize upon the principles of sacred geometry, and utilized them in its own attempts to embody and do homage to the divine. From the period of the Gothic cathedrals on, sacred geometry in architecture and in architectural adornment went hand in hand with representational art as an integral component of the Christian house of worship.

With Renaissance Hermeticism, sacred geometry in architecture assumed a new dimension, which, at the same time, harked back to ancient antecedents – to Kabbala, to Vitruvius, to Platonic and Pythagorean thought. It was accepted as a given that 'music and geometry are fundamentally one and the same; that music is geometry translated into sound, and that in music the same harmonies are audible which inform the geometry of the building'.[36] Hermetic architects invoked Vitruvius' principles of symmetry – the 'correspondence of each given detail among the separate details to the form of the design as a whole'.[37] They also invoked Vitruvius' dictum that architectural edifices 'should mirror the proportions of the human body' –

and that the square and the circle should be extrapolated from the figure of a man standing with arms and legs outspread.[38] The laws of 'cosmic order' were to be embodied in 'mathematical ratios that determine the harmony in macrocosm and microcosm'; and 'it is not the actual numbers but their ratios that are of importance'.[39]

During the Middle Ages, churches had been laid out in a cruciform pattern, in the configuration of a cross – a symbolic representation of Christ crucified. Around 1450, however, Leon Battista Alberti (1404–72) wrote the Renaissance's first book on architecture. Alberti cited Pythagoras to link architecture and music: 'the numbers by means of which the agreement of sounds affects our ears with delight, are the very same which please our eyes and our minds . . . We shall therefore borrow all our rules for harmonic relations from the musicians to whom this sort of number is extremely well known.'[40] And he argued that the perfect design for a church was based not on a cross, but on a circle. The circle, he explained, was the highest form found in nature – the form of the stars, the form of the terrestrial globe. In the *Timaeus* Plato had said the Creator made the cosmos a living unity in the shape of a sphere, 'which of all shapes is the most perfect'.[41] For Alberti himself, it was necessary to establish an 'integration of the proportions of all the parts of a building' so that they conformed to each other in a mutual and general harmony; and the best geometric form to satisfy this criterion was the circle. According to a modern commentator, 'for Alberti – as for other Renaissance artists – this man-created harmony was a visible echo of a celestial and universally valid harmony'.[42]

The implications of Alberti's pronouncements were profound and incipiently subversive. 'What had changed,' according to one authority, 'was the conception of the godhead.' The Christ 'who had suffered on the Cross for humanity' had, in effect, been supplanted by 'Christ as essence of perfection and harmony'.[43] Emphasis had subtly shifted from God the Son to God the Father, the Creator, who, as Plato said, had made the cosmos one, alive and in the shape of a sphere. The house of worship was no longer a commemoration of sacrifice and death, but a celebration of the creation and its architect. Like Botticelli's painting, the house of worship had become a work of talismanic magic, invoking and facilitating the circulation of the *pneuma*, or divine breath, linking above and below, macrocosm and microcosm, in Hermetic unity.

The Church of Rome was not unaware of such implications. There were a number of ecclesiastical grumbles. In 1572, the Archbishop of Milan, who was later canonized, explicitly condemned the circular church as 'pagan' and urged a return to the pattern of the Latin cross.[44] By that time, however, it was already too late. Italy already abounded with centrally planned churches based upon the circle. Among them, it is worth noting S. Maria degli Angeli at Florence, designed by the architect Brunelleschi, and S. Maria delle Carceri in Prato, near Pisa, by Giuliano de Sangallo. The latter is based entirely on the geometry of the circle and the square – a high circular dome surmounting a perfect cube.

In 1534, a squabble arose in Venice over the proportions of S. Francesco della Vigna, a new church under construction. To act as arbiter, the Doge called upon Francesco Giorgi, the Kabbalistic friar, whose advice had been solicited in the divorce of Henry VIII of England. Giorgi redesigned the church in accordance with his own Hermetic and Kabbalistic principles, using harmonic ratios or proportions which could be expressed in musical terms. Among the experts Giorgi consulted in his task was the painter Titian.[45]

In 1560, Andrea Palladio (1508–80) produced his own

monumental book on architecture, the greatest such work of the entire Renaissance. Palladio drew on both Vitruvius and Alberti, and echoed Giorgi as well. For Palladio, beauty 'will result from the beautiful form and from the correspondence of the whole to the parts, of the parts amongst themselves, and of these again to the whole'.[46]

Underlying Palladio's thinking, there was, again, the harmonious relationship between microcosm and macrocosm: 'we cannot doubt, that the little temples we make, ought to resemble this very great one, which, by his immense goodness, was perfectly completed with one word of his'.[47] And Palladio, too, advocated churches based on a circular pattern. In the shape of a circle, the church 'is enclosed by one circumference only, in which is to be found neither beginning nor end . . . every part being equally distant from the centre such a building demonstrates extremely well the unity, the infinite essence, the uniformity and the justice of God'.[48]

In the mid sixteenth century, Palladio co-founded an architectural academy, the Accademia Olimpica, in Vicenza. The interests of this academy soon extended beyond religious architecture and came to focus particularly on theatrical performances. In 1562, it was closely involved in the construction of a purpose-built theatre. Half a century later, Palladio's theatrical concerns were to exert an enormous influence on Inigo Jones – who, during a trip to Italy during 1614 and 1615, purchased many of the Italian architect's original designs and drawings. Among Jones's acknowledged achievements, of course, is the introduction of Palladian architecture to England.

In architecture, as in so many other spheres, Hermeticism often prospered most vigorously amid milieux that might appear most inimical to it. One such milieu was that of Spain during the second half of the sixteenth century, a fanatically

Catholic country, dominated by the Inquisition and ruled by the grimmest of monarchs, Philip II, self-proclaimed defender of the faith. In his fervent devotion to the Church, Philip had vowed to extirpate the Protestant 'heresy' – not only in his own domains of the Spanish Netherlands, but in England as well. It was Philip who, in his determination to re-establish Rome's authority over England, launched the Armada of 1588.

Yet Philip, despite his Catholicism, was fascinated by Hermetic thought. He was impressively versed in alchemy. When he visited London during his brief marriage to Mary Tudor, he became personally acquainted with John Dee, who cast horoscopes for him and his wife. Despite his subsequent hatred for all things English, the Spanish king retained his admiration for Dee and kept a copy of the *Monas hiero-glyphica* among the other esoteric volumes in his library. And Dee's Hermetic orientation towards architecture undoubt-edly contributed something to one of Philip's most grandiose enterprises – to build a magical edifice comparable to the Temple in the Old Testament, with himself cast in the role of Solomon. This edifice was to become the Escorial – a palace, a monastery and a church all in one.

The Escorial was built by Philip's architect, friend and personal magus, Juan de Herrera, a kind of Spanish equiv-alent of John Dee. It is even possible that Herrera and Dee knew each other, both men having been in Flanders between 1548 and 1550. In any case, Herrera was the most promi-nent Spanish Hermeticist of the age, who regularly 'performed certain occult services for his master' – services presumably of a medical, astrological and alchemical char-acter.[49] In addition to the entire Hermetic corpus and other works of antiquity, his immense library included texts by his immediate predecessors and contemporaries – including Ficino, Pico, Trithemius, Agrippa, Reuchlin, Paracelsus,

Bruno and John Dee. He possessed two copies, in fact, of the *Monas hieroglyphica*.

Having accepted Herrera's design for the structure, Philip supervised the construction and embellishment of the Escorial in every detail. The edifice was devised and built in rigorous conformity to principles of geometric harmony and proportion. Various phases of the construction were computed and inaugurated in accordance with astrologically propitious dates. Much use was made of the cube, a sacred symbol in Hermetic texts and in the work of the medieval Mallorcan Hermeticist, Ramón Lull; and the library of the Escorial today contains a treatise by Herrera on Lull's interpretation of 'the Cubic Figure'. In a vault over the church's raised choir, there is an enigmatic fresco painted by Luca Cambiaso – *La Gloria*, or *The Vision of Paradise*. In the centre of this fresco, God the Father and God the Son are depicted, surrounded by an effulgence of light, seated on a rainbow. Their feet rest on a cube of stone, painted so that it seems to project outwards, three-dimensionally, towards the viewer.[50]

The Escorial was, in fact, perceived as a latter-day Temple of Solomon, a deliberate re-creation of that edifice; and Philip – whose titles included the kingship of Jerusalem – welcomed his identification with the Hebrew King of the Old Testament. When a Spanish edition of Vitruvius was published in 1582, it was dedicated to Philip II as 'second Solomon and prince of Architects'.[51]

Until the last quarter of the twentieth century, Spain was to remain the sternest daughter of the Church, the staunchest bulwark and bastion of European Catholicism. Yet as Carlos Fuentes demonstrates in his monumental novel *Terra Nostra*, there stood, at the spiritual centre of this ecclesiastical orthodoxy, perhaps the supreme architectural achievement of pagan Renaissance Hermeticism.

Magical Landscapes

As an extension of their application to architecture, Hermetic principles were also, as a matter of course, applied to gardens. The garden, indeed, was often conceived as an adjunct, if not an integral component, of the architectural structure. Both were deemed to constitute a talismanic or magical whole, united by harmonious proportions. According to Alberti, for example, the garden was as much the architect's domain as the house itself. But the garden could also be a magical talisman in its own right. It might be divided into quarters, for instance, representing the four elements – earth, air, fire and water. It might be divided into twelve, reflecting the signs of the zodiac. And at the appropriate points, it might contain grottoes, shrines, herb gardens, mazes, arrangements or juxtapositions of shape, scent or colour calculated to invoke cosmic energies.

Concurrent with the garden as a component of the overall architectural structure, there also arose the concept of the botanical garden – a harmoniously proportioned arrangement of space which brought together an assembly of all possible plants. In this capacity, the garden became, symbolically, a new Garden of Eden, a microcosm in which the entire spectrum of the macrocosm was reflected. Such gardens also meshed with Paracelsian concepts of natural, medicine. They functioned, in effect, as 'physic' gardens, from whose array of plants and herbs a diverse range of medicines and remedies could be produced. In this respect, the garden reinforced the traditional association between alchemy and botany. It became, in effect, an extension of the alchemical laboratory.

Both the talismanic garden and the botanical or 'physic' garden were held to be imbued with a potent symbolic significance. They reflected an ideal harmonious rapport between man and the natural world. In the garden, man and nature collaborated to produce a harmonious ordering of space. Through the garden, man quite literally 'husbanded' the earth, espousing or uniting with the earth in a species of symbolic matrimony.

The earliest Hermetic gardens of the Renaissance were created by the Medici. Their villa at Careggi, for example, conferred on Ficino as the site for his Academy, was endowed with just such a garden. It conformed meticulously to 'the classical tradition of pastoral retirement' and the concurrent 'search for the soul's homeland'.[52] Ficino often wrote and spoke of walking in his garden and, at a quiet spot, playing Orphic Hymns on his lyre. It was from this garden, or from one very like it, that Botticelli was believed to have gathered the flora for his *Primavera*. The magical or talismanic power of such sites was emphasized by Palladio: 'The garden's boundaries no longer fence it from a radically different world outside, but serve instead to localize a potency which is now perceived to be universal.'[53]

In England during the second half of the sixteenth century, a mystical cult grew up around Elizabeth I. The 'Virgin Queen' was identified with Astraea, or the Just Virgin of one of Virgil's *Eclogues*, whose return from the heavens to earth brings again the Golden Age'. It has even, indeed, been suggested that the imagery associated with Elizabeth was deliberately intended to install her, in Protestant England, as a surrogate for the Virgin Mary.

Such imagery would constantly dwell 'upon the almost magical powers of the sovereign over the physical universe'.[54] Thus Elizabeth was often identified with the moon, and with the classical moon goddess of antiquity – the Roman Diana or the Greek Artemis. At Nonsuch Palace, Surrey, grottoes dedicated to the moon goddess were constructed in homage to Elizabeth. The queen was also symbolized by images of the phoenix and the pelican. According to one commentator, these images reflected her status as 'nursing mother' of the Anglican Church. At the same time, however, the phoenix and the pelican were long-established symbols for the process of alchemical transmutation. In alchemical terms, Elizabeth, as goddess and sovereign, presided over the process whereby the world itself was transmuted from its dross and fallen state into a renewed Age of Gold.

Not surprisingly, perhaps, 'the cult of the Virgin Queen' frequently expressed itself in horticultural terms. The Age of Gold which Elizabeth supposedly heralded was conceived as an age of perpetual spring, perpetual rebirth and renewal. Like Botticelli's Venus in the *Primavera*, therefore, the English monarch was habitually associated with spring, with flowers and floral abundance. In this context, she was usually symbolized by the five-petalled eglantine rose.

All of this, naturally enough, fostered a preoccupation in England with Hermetic gardens. One of the most impressive was that of the queen's favourite, Robert Dudley, Earl of Leicester at Kenilworth Castle. Another was created by Sir Robert, younger son of Lord Burghley, the queen's spymaster prior to Walsingham. Cecil's garden typifies the Hermetic gardens of Elizabethan England. In it, the twelve virtues were both symbolized and theoretically invoked by roses, the three Graces by pansies and the nine Muses by flowers of nine different species.

The most famous garden designer of the late Renaissance, whose legacy is still apparent in England, was a French Huguenot hydraulic engineer, Salomon de Caus. Like John Dee and Robert Fludd, de Caus was fascinated by automata and other mechanical devices – moving statues and figures of animals, doors which opened or closed of their own accord, mysteriously operating waterworks, a host of seemingly magical phenomena which were in fact technologically produced and today would be classified as 'special effects'.[55] But while Dee and Fludd were interested in the adaptation of such machinery for the theatre, de Caus devised his inventions for the garden.

During the last decade of the sixteenth century, de Caus travelled extensively throughout Italy, visiting the most famous gardens of the time and studying Vitruvius as well as Alberti and Palladio. By 1601, he was in Brussels, designing gardens for the Habsburg rulers of what was then the Austrian Netherlands. Between 1607 and 1613, he resided in England, where he and Inigo Jones became fast friends and worked closely together. He carried out commissions for the wife of James I, Anne of Denmark, and for the heir to the throne, Henry, Prince of Wales. Among his most impressive achievements was the creation of 'elaborate gardens and water-works in the grounds of Richmond palace in association with Inigo Jones'.[56]

When Prince Henry died unexpectedly in 1612, Caus moved to Heidelberg and the Rosicrucian-oriented court of Friedrich, Elector Palatine of the Rhine, husband of James I's daughter, Elizabeth. Here, he undertook to design the famous gardens adjacent to Heidelberg Castle. At times, he was obliged to blast away whole hillsides in order to create plane surfaces on which to lay out his complicated geometric patterns. Within these patterns, grottoes were constructed to house automata. These automata – mechanical giants, speaking statues, organs which sounded notes in response to air or water pressure – were intended not only to awe spectators, but also to serve a talismanic function. Thus, once again, did magic and science fuse to create the foundations of modern technological development.[57]

The talismanic garden culminated in the ingenious designs and contrivances of Salomon de Caus. The botanic garden, in the meantime, had also evolved. The discovery of the New World had fostered the recognition that there were many lands, peoples, plants and animals of which classical authorities had been ignorant. Europeans began assiduously to observe, collate and classify their often startling new discoveries. The world itself came to be regarded as 'the book of God'. It was even older than the Bible, and was equally worthy of study – if not, indeed, more so. At the time of the Fall, it was now argued, the wonders of the Garden of Eden had been scattered across the four continents then believed to exist; and with the discovery of the New World, those wonders could be reassembled, reintegrated into their original harmony. Thus the botanic garden – the garden as replica of Eden – came to assume an increasingly metaphysical dimension. The garden of Padua, for example, laid out in 1545, was quite deliberately intended to constitute a microcosm of the terrestrial globe. It took the form of a circle, within which there was a square divided into four quarters. Plants from east, west, north and south were cultivated in their appropriate quarters. For the Hermetic adherent of the time,

> the value of a Botanic Garden was that it conveyed a direct knowledge of God. Since each plant was a created thing, and God had revealed a part of himself in each thing that he created, a complete collection of all the things created by God must reveal God completely. Given the supposed relation between the macrocosm and the microcosm, the man who knew nature best knew most about himself.[58]

Magical Ritual and Literature

Hermeticism had found its way to Western Europe, and had them been disseminated in large part through literature –

through the Hermetic corpus and other works of antiquity, through Islamic texts, through the works of medieval magicians and Renaissance magi. Even before the Renaissance, elements of it had, as we have seen, begun to appear in imaginative literature, or in literary art – in the Christianized Grail romances, to cite perhaps the most obvious example, and in Dante's *Divine Comedy*. During the sixteenth century, Hermetic thought began increasingly to suffuse imaginative literature, just as it did the other arts.

The novel, in the sense that we know it today, did not exist as a literary form at the time, although there were prose narratives – often juxtaposed with fragments or passages of verse. Among the first such works to display a patently Hermetic orientation was the anonymously authored *Hypnerotomachia*, also known as *The Dream of Poliphilus*, published in Venice in 1499 by Aldus Manutius. The *Hypnerotomachia* is a work of talismanic literature in the same way that Botticelli's *Primavera*, virtually contemporary with it, is a work of talismanic painting. Drawing in part on Dante's metaphysical theory of allegory, it seeks not only to describe, but also to invoke cosmic energies. On the surface or literal level, it is a romance illustrated by woodcuts, whose sexual explicitness would probably cause it to be classified as erotica, if not unabashed pornography. In reality, however, it both reflects and constitutes a magical operation, a magical act, which draws extensively on astrology and corresponds to the stages of the alchemical process.

Of an essentially similar character is another pastoral romance, *Arcadia*, by Jacopo Sannazaro (*c.* 1456–1530), completed around 1496 but not published until 1501. Like the *Hypnerotomachia*, *Arcadia* revels in a pyrotechnic display of symbolic imagery, beneath which lives a rigorously controlled structure based on numerology and geometry. Both works seek to adapt to literature the principles of harmonious proportion employed in Hermetic painting, music and architecture. Both can be conceived as musical and architectonic compositions. And both were to exert a profound influence on subsequent literary figures – on Ariosto, for example, and on Tasso, Sidney, Spenser and Cervantes. The *Hypnerotomachia* in particular is believed to have provided a prototype for perhaps the most important of the seventeenth-century Rosicrucian manifestos, *The Chemical Wedding of Christian Rosenkreutz* – which contributed, in turn, to the underlying conception of Goethe's *Faust*.

In France, the principles of talismanic magic were adapted to poetry by the seven figures known (after the seven stars of the Pleiades) as the Pléiade. The leader and most important poet of this group was Pierre de Ronsard (1524–85). Among the others were Jean Dorat, Joachim du Bellay and Jean-Antoine de Baïf. The members of the Pléiade experimented extensively with the magical puissance of poetry, especially when set to music. Drawing in part on Dante's theory of allegory, and anticipating the principles of later symbolist writers, Ronsard spoke of his and his colleagues' work in terms that might equally well be applied to alchemical texts. He described 'how one must dissemble and conceal fables . . . and disguise well the truth of things with a fabulous cloak in which they are enclosed . . .'[59] Thus the poet might 'make enter into the minds of ordinary people, by agreeable and colourful fables, the secrets which they could not understand when the truth is too openly disclosed'.[60]

The members of the Pléiade embarked on an extensive reform of the French language, 'purifying' it by excising older and more 'vulgar' words, rendering it more 'lofty' by the incorporation of other words from the vocabulary of Renaissance Italian. Under the patronage of King Charles IX, the Pléiade poets formed an Academy on the Italian model, which further pursued the fusion of poetry and music and, in the process, contributed to the foundations of opera. Their experiments again rested on Hermetic premises. According to Frances Yates:

> The degree of magic behind the incantatory psalms and songs of Baïf's Academy is difficult to assess, but the movement could certainly be related to the Ficinian therapy in which the use of music was advised. David charming away Saul's melancholy with his harp was the obvious image for musical – medical humanism.[61]

The avowed objective of the Academy was to recapture the effect of 'the ancient music' – the magical power, that is, ascribed to such mythic figures of antiquity as Orpheus.

In 1581, a lavish festival was mounted under the auspices of Henry III, to celebrate the marriage of the Duc de Joyeuse to Marie de Lorraine. The affair lasted for the better part of two weeks, with fresh entertainments every day. The poets of the Pléiade and the Academy were largely responsible for devising these entertainments, which included theatrical performances, chivalric jousts dances and recitations of poetry to musical accompaniment, often with exotic costumes and elaborate sets. Here was an opportunity to test, in public and on an ambitious scale, the magical effects of 'the ancient music'. According to eyewitness accounts, the effects – on certain members of the audience, at least – were not inconsiderable. At one point, for example, the music reportedly 'caused a gentleman who was present to take up arms' – and, when the mood changed, 'he became quite tranquil again . . .'[62] Frances Yates observes that at least one of the poems set to music 'certainly sounds like an incantation'.[63]

This poem was performed at a specific and significant

moment in the festivities – when the French king was scheduled to joust in a tourney against his rival and enemy, the Duc de Guise. Both Henri III and his mother, Catherine de' Medici, were steeped in Hermetic thought. They would have recognized and appreciated the magical import of the poem and its accompanying music – would have discerned it as a protective talisman. 'They would have understood it for what it was, a most learned incantation an effort to influence events through the latest magico-scientific techniques, an attempt to avert the influence of dark stars of war and treason, represented by the Guises . . .'[64]

Hermetic Masques of the Stuart Kings

In England, the Hermetic principles of the Pléiade were enthusiastically embraced and implemented by the two greatest non-dramatic figures of the Elizabethan age, Edmund Spenser and Sir Philip Sidney. As has already been noted, Sidney (1554–86) was a disciple of John Dee and a dedicatee of two of Bruno's books. It is hardly surprising, therefore, that he should espouse the adaptation of talismanic magic to literature. His sonnets reflect the influence of the Pléiade's two greatest lyricists, Ronsard and du Bellay. In his *Defense of Poesy*, Sidney again echoes the luminaries of the Pléiade and arrogates to the poet the status of an Orphic or mantic bard. His most ambitious work, *Arcadia*, exists in three versions, none of which was published in his lifetime. It was written for his alchemist sister, the Countess of Pembroke, and is heavily indebted to Jacopo Sannazaro's talismanic work of the same name.

Spenser (1552–99) was one of Sidney's closest friends. Along with Sidney, he dreamed of doing for the English language what the poets of the Pléiade had done for French. In 1578, he joined the household of Robert Dudley, Earl of

Leicester, Sidney's uncle and one of Dee's supporters. Along with Sidney, Sir Edward Dyer and others, he founded a literary circle, the Areopagus, modelled at least in part on Ronsard's Pléiade. He would undoubtedly have been a regular habitué of Dee's circle at Mortlake had he not been posted in 1579 to Ireland as secretary to the lord deputy there. For the next twenty years, until his death in 1599, he was to reside almost exclusively in Ireland. Subsequent to the deaths of Leicester and Sidney, his chief supporter in England was another of Dee's protégés, Sir Walter Ralegh.

Spenser's shorter lyrics, like Sidney's, reflect the influence of Ronsard and du Bellay, as well as that of another French poet loosely associated with the Pléiade, Clément Marot. In his two great marriage odes, *Epithalamion* and *Prothalamion*, Spenser's use of talismanic magic is particularly apparent. Both exemplify the adaptation of poetry to Hermetic invocation, seeking to conjure down cosmic blessing and protection on the nuptial rite. In *The Shepherd's Calendar*, a sequence of eclogues or pastoral poems Spenser echoes not only the Pléiade, but Sannazaro's *Arcadia* as well. His supreme achievement, however, is, of course, *The Faerie Queene*, a massive work intended to run to twelve books, although only seven were actually completed. Frances Yates describes *The Faerie Queene* as 'a great magical Renaissance poem, infused with the whitest of white magic, Christian Kabbalist and Neoplatonic'.[65] It is undoubtedly the single most ambitious work of talismanic magic to have emerged from Elizabethan England.

In his complex romance, Spenser draws heavily on the Kabbalis Kabbalistic teachings of Francesco Giorgi, as well as on the Hermeticism of the other major Renaissance magi. Each of the poem's extant seven books, for example, is oriented towards one of the planets whose energies, qualities and virtues it seeks to invoke. To embody the interrelationship between microcosm and macrocosm Spenser employs super-imposed strata of allegory, radiating outwards from the intensely intimate and personal to the general and collective and ultimately to the cosmic. On the general and collective level, he echoes John Dee's vision of a mystical British imperium ruled by a mystical goddess-queen, whose reign would herald the advent of a new Golden Age.

By Sidney's and Spenser's time, the magical experiments of the Pléiade poets had reverberated back to Italy, the original source of their inspiration. Here, they had been amalgamated with a form of ritualized sacred drama deriving ultimately from Ficino – drama in which 'words have not only semantic meanings, conveyed by grammar and syntax . . . but also, sonorous meanings, conveyed by pitch and rhythm'.[66] The result of this union was opera, the very name of which – deriving from the Latin for 'work' in the alchemical sense of effecting a new and illuminating synthesis – reveals its hermetic origins. The first true opera, Peri's setting of Rinuccini's *Dafne*, was performed in Florence in 1598.

In England, the synthesis of artistic media assumed a different and distinctive form, that of the Elizabethan and Jacobean masque. The masque was a species of private drama, mounted at extravagant expense, by and for a royal (or perhaps aristocratic) court. A story in verse would be enacted on a purpose-designed stage, which accommodated the most advanced technological machinery, special effects and cunning tricks of perspective. Music and dance were integral components of the production, and distinguished members of the audience would often themselves take part in the performance. As the masque ended, it mutated into a ball, the participants descending from the stage and mingling with the assembled spectators. The invisible barrier between illusion and reality was thus breached, and the microcosm of the performance on stage fused with the macrocosm of the greater world surrounding it. The energies talismanically invoked by the former were induced to circulate at large through the latter. Through the masque, the tableau of the *Primavera* came to three-dimensional life and merged with the festive company, drawing them into its magic.

According to Frances Yates,

> the masque is a case in which the connection in the Renaissance mind between magic and mechanics finds expression. The masques were the latest thing in mechanics and stimulated improvements in machinery; and in them mechanics were being used, partially at least, for magical ends, to form a vast moving and changing talisman which should call down divine powers to the assistance of the monarch.[67]

The masque was uniquely suited to the cult of the Virgin Queen and a mystical British imperium. Thus, as early as 1578, Sir Philip Sidney wrote a masque for Elizabeth, *The Lady of May*, which implicitly associated the monarch not only with the Virgin of the Church, but also with the pagan mother goddesses of antiquity and of native folk tradition. A quarter of a century later, the masque form was warmly embraced by the Stuarts. Having designed masque costume for Anne of Denmark, wife of James I, Inigo Jone expressed his intention that the colour, grace and splendour of her apparel, 'shining in the Queen's majesty, may draw us to the contemplation of the beauty of the soul, unto which it hath analogy'.[68]

James I was himself aware of other analogies. 'A king,' he wrote 'is as one set on a stage, whose smallest actions and gestures, all the people gazingly do behold.'[69] In 1609, Inigo Jones and Ben Jonson collaborated for the first time in

The Masque of Blackness, an explicitly Hermetic portrayal of the power of kingship.[70] Jonson subsequently fell out with Jones and proceeded to launch a sequence of attacks on Hermeticism, the most famous of which, of course is *The Alchemist*. But the Hermetic form of the masque remained dear to him.

James I invoked the Hermetic principle of analogy to sanction and justify the divine right of kings. The monarch, he argued, was God's representative on earth, and answerable to God alone. 'Therefore,' he instructed his son, 'you are a little GOD to sit on his throne, and rule over other men.'[71] Under the early Stuarts the masque was used increasingly to reinforce this Hermetic correspondence.

The masques of the time were dauntingly costly. Most involved an expense of around £3,000, the value at the time of a respectable aristocratic estate. One, produced for the monarch by the Inns of Court, cost £20,000. This was rather like commissioning a Steven Spielberg Hollywood spectacular, which would be shown once only, to a restricted private audience, and then destroyed.

Despite such profligacy, the masque continued in vogue until the eve of the English Civil War. A particularly notable late example is *Comus* (1634), written for the Earl of Bridgewater's inauguration as Lord President of Wales by the young John Milton – who was much more steeped in Hermeticism than his self-proclaimed Puritanism led his contemporaries to believe. But the sheer expense of such extravaganzas, their essentially ephemeral nature and their narrowly exclusive audiences rendered them ultimately unsuitable to the needs of the time. As John Dee had recognized, the benefits of the Hermetic vision had to be conveyed not only to the educated court and aristocracy, but also to England's flourishing mercantile and artisan classes. For such a purpose, another, more popular and accessible artistic medium was required. This medium was to be the theatre, the supreme manifestation of English Renaissance culture.

The Magical Power of the Theatre

For more than a century after Henry VIII dissolved the monasteries and broke with the Church of Rome, no churches were built in England. Instead, England built theatres. Alone among European cities, London possessed a multitude of wooden theatres, which inspired wonder in foreign visitors. The English theatre became, in effect, a new species of church, a new species of temple. Within the magical precincts of this structure, the rites and rituals of Hermetic mysteries were performed for an insatiable public.

Vitruvius, the architect of classical Rome so frequently invoked by Renaissance Hermeticists, had advocated the construction of wooden theatres. In stone theatres, he had argued, acoustics had to be augmented by large bronze sounding vessels placed in the stage area, which amplified the actor's voice by allowing it to resonate. In contrast, wood was itself a resonant medium, and did not therefore require such acoustic augmentation. In accordance with Vitruvian principles, the theatres of Elizabethan and Jacobean England were built of wood.

The first Vitruvian-style theatre, called simply the Theatre, was built in London in 1576 by James Burbage, an actor himself as well as a carpenter. At the time, actors were organized into troupes or companies under the protection of one or another wealthy, noble or influential patron. Such protection was necessary, because England was already being plagued by fundamentalist Puritan fanatics – who, under Cromwell some seventy-five years later, would force the closure of all theatres. The acting company for whom Burbage built his theatre enjoyed the protection of Robert

Dudley, Earl of Leicester. Leicester, as has been noted, was the uncle of Sir Philip Sidney and a supporter of John Dee, whose residence at Mortlake he regularly visited.

Dee, of course, was a fervent exponent of Vitruvian architecture as a conduit for Hermetic talismanic magic. He was also fascinated by the theatre and, like Fludd and Inigo Jones after him, by mechanical theatrical effects. While at Cambridge in 1574, he had staged a production of Aristophanes, for which he had devised a mechanical 'flying machine'. According to Vitruvius, such technological expertise was an adjunct of the architect's role as magus.

Frances Yates is convinced that Burbage must have consulted Dee in the building of the Theatre. She even suggests that Dee may have designed the edifice himself. In any case, she points out, the increasing sophistication of Elizabethan drama required increasingly sophisticated stage effects. Where, she asks, could the theatre obtain the requisite aid in producing such effects? Not from the universities, which did not address themselves to applied science and practical matters. It could only have been 'among the Hermetic philosophers . . . that the theatrical producer would look for help, for the Hermetic philosophers were the technicians in an age in which science was emerging from magic'.[72]

Burbage's Theatre of 1576 was swiftly followed by a multitude of others, both public and private. Among the most important public theatres built before the end of the sixteenth century were the Curtain, the Rose, the Swan, the Fortune and the Red Bull. A dispute with the owner of the land on which it stood led to Burbage's original Theatre being dismantled. In 1598, its timbers were carried to the south bank of the Thames and used for the construction of a new edifice, the Globe, which opened in 1600. The Globe was owned by the Lord Chamberlain's theatre company, of which Shakespeare, already established as a playwright, had been a member since at least 1592. In 1603, the Lord Chamberlain's company was taken under the protection of the newly crowned sovereign, James I.

According to Vitruvius, the ground plan of the theatre was to be based on the circle of the zodiac. This circle was divided into four equilateral triangles marking the 'trines', the most harmonious of astrological relationships, or 'aspects'. Each triangle connected the three zodiacal signs corresponding to each of the four elements – earth, air, fire and water. The circular ground plan of the theatre thus constituted a microcosm of creation as a whole. Its status as such was reinforced by an awning over the stage, painted with stars to represent the firmament. The result was a '"Theatre of the World" in which Man . . . was to play his parts'.[73]

Here then, Frances Yates maintains, was the design of the Globe, which denoted by its very name the microcosm it embodied and which resurrected the 'cosmic and therefore religious implications' of the Vitruvian theatre. The theatre itself thus became an integral component and extension of the drama enacted within it, effecting the harmonious integration of play and setting.

A theatre, the plan of which expressed in simple geometrical symbolism the proportions of the cosmos and of man, the world music and the human music, is surely one which would have been a worthy vehicle for the genius of Shakespeare. It is always in terms of music that he thinks of a man's destiny in its cosmic setting.[74]

By virtue of its status as Hermetic microcosm, a theatre such as the Globe became 'a magical theatre, a cosmic theatre, a religious theatre'.[75] And 'the Magus as creator of the theatre and its magic' became analogous to God, the supreme Magus, creator of the theatre of the world.[76]

It was in the Hermetic temple of the theatre, in that microcosm of talismanic magic, that the Renaissance magus attained his literary apotheosis. He did so, for many of his contemporaries as well as for posterity, in the guise of Marlowe's Faustus. Although Marlowe professed to be an atheist, his atheism consisted merely in a rejection of Judaeo-Christian concepts of divinity. And despite this rejection, he retained a pervasive sense of the sacred, of spirituality. As has been noted, he belonged to the Hermetic circle of the Earl of Northumberland, which overlapped the circle of John Dee. And as *Doctor Faustus* reveals, Marlowe was steeped in Hermetic thought. It would seem clear that he admired Agrippa in particular. Indeed his Faustus regards Agrippa as a virtual role model:

> Then, gentle friends, aid me in this attempt,
> And I, that have with concise syllogisms
> Gravell'd the pastors of the German church
> And made the flow'ring pride of Wittenberg
> Swarm to my problems as th'infernal spirits
> On sweet Mesaeus when he came to hell,
> Will be as cunning as Agrippa was,
> Whose shadows made all Europe honour him.[77]

Marlowe admires, indentifies himself with and projects himself into his protagonist. In effect, Faustus is, for Marlowe, a species of romanticized and idealized self-portrait – a mirror image of how he saw, or wished to see, himself. Faustus reflects Marlowe's own 'overvaulting ambition', Marlowe's own antinomian disdain for the restrictions on knowledge imposed by Judaeo-Christian theology and morality.

But the stage for which Marlowe wrote was a popular medium, like the films issuing from Hollywood today. And while Protestant England was eager enough to lampoon Catholicism and the Pope, it was still sufficiently pious in its Christianity to recoil from a pact with 'unclean powers'. This placed Marlowe in a position analogous to that of scriptwriters and directors in the cinema of, say, the 1950s – obliged to observe the prevailing moral codes and taboos, to provide an ethically acceptable ending, to ensure that audiences went away with the approved message of vice punished and virtue rewarded. In consequence, *Dr Faustus* adheres fairly closely to the standard English translation of the Faust story published in 1587. By the tenets of established morality, Faustus must, of necessiry be damned. If the Renaissance magus was to be depicted on stage at all, it would have to be in less controversial, less subversive and more benevolent guise.

Many commentators, including the authors of this book, are prepared to see Prospero, in *The Tempest*, as a portrait of John Dee. Indeed, it is now widely accepted that Dee was Shakespeare's model for Prospero.[78] Given his association with Burbage's theatre and with the Earl of Leicester's company of actors, it would have been virtually impossible for the playwright not at some point to have come into contact with the magus.[79]

Earlier in his career, in *As You Like It*, Shakespeare had enunciated the Hermetic correspondence between the theatre and the world, between the artist and the Creator, as the correspondence between microcosm and macrocosm:

> All the world's a stage,
> And all the men and women merely players:
> They have their exits and their entrances,
> And one man in his time plays many parts.[80]

The same correspondence is enunciated by Prospero in *The Tempest*:

> Our revels now are ended. These our actors,
> As I foretold you, were all spirits, and
> Are melted into air, into thin air;
> And, like the baseless fabric of this vision,
> The cloud-capp'd towers, the gorgeous palaces,
> The solemn temples, the great globe itself,
> Yea, all which it inherit, shall dissolve
> And, like this insubstantial pageant faded,
> Leave not a rack behind. We are such stuff
> As dreams are made on, and our little life
> Is rounded with a sleep.[81]

This correspondence – between the work of art and the creation, between the artist and the Creator – was to become of paramount importance to literary figures of the nineteenth and twentieth centuries. In their hands, poetry and the novel were to serve perhaps the chief conduit and repository for Renaissance Hermeticism. The artists and the magus would coalesce into the same figure; and the true heirs of Agrippa and Paracelsus would prove to be Goethe and Flaubert, Joyce and Thomas Mann.

10

THE RISE OF SECRET SOCIETIES

By the beginning of the seventeenth century, Hermeticism had dramatically transformed the character of Western civilization. It had also, however, conjured up the very forces that would lead to its own marginalization. The solitary magus, exemplified by Agrippa and Paracelsus, had given way to the secret society, or cabal, exemplified by the self-styled Rosicrucians and by early Freemasonry.

By shifting the emphasis from transformation of the individual to transformation of society as a whole, the cabal had begun to politicize Hermeticism. In the England of Elizabeth I and John Dee, politicized Hermeticism was theoretically tenable, at least for a time. It was even tenable in scattered enclaves across the continent – in, for example, the Rosicrucian-oriented court of Friedrich, Elector Palatine of the Rhine, who, in 1613, had married Elizabeth Stuart, daughter of James I. By 1618, however, politicized Hermeticism on the continent would culminate in a Europe-wide catastrophe, the Thirty Years War, comparable in scale to the First World War.

And yet, in the years immediately preceding this débâcle, prospects had seemed so roseate. Seldom before in Western history had the future appeared so promising; seldom, if ever, had the return of a Golden Age appeared so imminent. Through the knowledge fostered by Hermeticism, it had even seemed possible to heal the religious lesions of the age.

Prior to the Renaissance and Reformation, knowledge in Western culture had effectively been held together by Roman Catholicism. Virtually the whole of human creative endeavour – the arts, the sciences, philosophy, the entire machinery of social and civic life – had existed under the all-encompassing umbrella of the Church. To study, as a rule, one needed to be a cleric.

With the Renaissance and the Reformation, Rome's umbrella had grown frayed and had ceased to be all-encompassing, had ceased to cast its shade over the whole spectrum of creative activity. But Hermeticism, during the sixteenth century, had seemed to offer a new binding agent, a new adhesive. Despite the schism between Catholicism and the recently established forms of Protestantism, a more or less unified and integrated approach to knowledge had come to seem possible across religious barriers, held together by Hermetic thought. The basic premise of Hermeticism – the interrelationship of all things – provided the foundation on which an altogether new trans-denominational umbrella might be established.

The earlier Hermeticists – Ficino, Pico, Trithemius and Francesco Giorgi – had, after all, worked within the Church; they had been clerics and had managed to reconcile Hermetic magic with Catholic doctrine. Even that arch-Catholic monarch, Philip II of Spain, had contrived to accommodate Hermeticism to his piety and the Escorial bore monumental testimony to the accommodation he had effected. In France, during the second half of the sixteenth century, under the Hermetic lawyer and writer Jean Bodin, an entire movement was launched which sought to use Hermetic thought as a means of establishing a rapprochement between Protestantism and the Church of Rome. The same principle of rapprochement was enunciated by the Italian Dominican Tommaso Campanella, who, after years in prison, won the support of Pope Urban VIII. Later, in France, Campanella was to win similar support from the effective head of state, Cardinal Richelieu, even if the cardinal's motives were not of the purest. Among Catholic Hermeticists, there was even a prominent Jesuit, Athanasius Kircher – who, among other things, was to teach the painter Nicolas Poussin the techniques of perspective.

Kircher was probably the supreme representative of Hermeticism within the post-Reformation Church. He studied, and then taught, philosophy, mathematics, Greek and Hebrew. Like other Hermetic practitioners, he was proficient in developing mechanical devices, moving scenery and other special effects for the stage. He investigated magnetism. Having purchased a telescope, he took up the study of astronomy and, in 1625, recorded his observation of sunspots. He travelled widely around Europe, zealous to see as much as he could and appease a voracious curiosity about the origins of things – of music, language, religion, plague, volcanic eruptions and lava. On one occasion, he had himself lowered into the crater of Vesuvius during a phase of imminent eruption, hoping thereby to glean a first-hand knowledge of what was occurring.

When his Jesuit superiors rejected his application to conduct missionary work in China, Kircher was bitterly disappointed. He maintained, however, a vigorous correspondence with other Jesuit missionaries, as well as with scholars from the whole of the known world. He harboured a particular interest in what would today be called comparative religion. He regarded Egyptian paganism as the fount of virtually all other beliefs and creeds – Greek, Roman, Hebrew, Chaldean, even Indian, Chinese, Japanese, Aztec and Inca. By studying later and better documented systems of religious thought, he hoped to learn more of the source from which he felt they sprang – that is, ancient Egypt. The Hermetic corpus, he believed, contained the core of an ancient theology once embraced by all peoples. Every religion, he concluded, possessed an exoteric and an esoteric aspect; and in the esoteric aspects of the world's faiths, he sought a common denominator. Quite remarkably for a devout Jesuit, 'Kircher accepted the possibility of inspired truth existing in nearly all the religions of the past, and among non-Christians of his own time whom the Christian message had not yet reached . . .'[1]

Among Kircher's correspondents and most enthusiastic readers was a Scot, Sir Robert Moray, one of the earliest recorded brethren in Freemasonry.[2] In a letter to one of his own correspondents, Moray urgently recommended a particular book of Kircher's, on Egyptian hieroglyphics. One of Kircher's other texts, the *Ars magna sciendi (The Great Art of Knowledge)*, depicts in its frontispiece an eye contained in a triangle, illumined by the effulgent rays of the Deity. This device, of course, was later to find its way into Freemasonry and, from there, on to the dollar bill of the United States.

Perhaps surprisingly, Kircher contrived not to run foul of his superiors or of the ecclesiastical hierarchy. Unlike Campanella, for example, he was left unmolested. But if Kircher's activities were somehow overlooked, Rome had long before become alarmed at the prospect of Hermeticism supplanting the Church as a principle potentially capable of uniting Western Christendom. More alarming still, of course, was the advance of Protestantism, which continued to win converts across the whole of Europe – and often, in the process, provided Hermeticism with a sympathetic haven. Confronted by this crisis, the Church had embarked on the movement now known as the Counter Reformation

– a massive and concerted attempt to regain the ground lost to 'heresy' and to re-establish Catholic supremacy.

The first moves of the Counter Reformation were made by Pope Paul III, who became pope in 1534, a year after the excommunication of Henry VIII of England. In 1538, the Pope issued a Bull against Henry, which served only to alienate further the Anglican Church and stiffen its defiance. In 1540, Paul officially sanctioned the formation of the Society of Jesus – the Jesuits. In 1542, he augmented the powers of the Inquisition, which could now deploy everywhere in Catholic territory the authority it exercised in Spain. In 1545, in order to consolidate the Church's doctrinal position against Protestantism, the Pope convened the Council of Trent, which was to continue in session under his successors until 1563. Among other things, the council created the Index of Prohibited Books, which was not abolished until 1966. The council concluded that religious truth was expressed equally through scripture and through tradition. It established that the sole and exclusive right to interpret scripture resided with the Church and that the sacraments of the Church, which Protestantism had challenged, were obligatory for salvation. At the Diet of Worms in 1521, the Papacy's desire to eliminate Luther and his followers had been inhibited by the Holy Roman Emperor, who sought accord and accommodation. The Council of Trent effectively precluded all possibility of accommodation or accord, and asserted papal supremacy over the Emperor in all doctrinal matters. In short, there was now to be war, whether literally or spiritually, to the death.

The shock troops in this war were the Jesuits. Although they engaged in no literal physical combat, they are believed to have been modelled on the organization, structure and austere discipline of the Knights Templar, established some four centuries earlier. Like the Templars, the Jesuits saw themselves as a military institution, a new '*milice du Christ*' or soldiery of Christ. Armed with the tools of logic, education and rigorous theological training, they embarked on a new species of crusade – to reconquer the lands lost by the Church, as well as to impose Rome's authority in lands newly discovered or rendered accessible. In the years that followed, Jesuit missionaries were to penetrate, and found outposts, as far afield as India, China, Japan and the Americas. In Europe, regions such as Poland, Bohemia and southern Germany, which had briefly turned predominantly Protestant, were reclaimed for the Church, and have remained Catholic ever since. With the defeat of the Spanish Armada in 1588, England had been abandoned, at least temporarily, as a lost cause. But there still seemed to be a prospect of isolating England; and England, if successfully isolated from a continent reunited under Catholicism, could not long survive.

If the Jesuits confined their crusade to the realm of the spirit and the intellect, other adherents of the Church did not. During the sixteenth century, the armies of Catholic Spain had wrought havoc in the largely Protestant Spanish Netherlands and Flanders. In France, Catholics and Protestants had fought incessantly, had engaged in campaigns of conspiracy, intrigue and assassination, and had eventually wiped out the Valois dynasty. Towards the end of the second decade of the seventeenth century, however, the Counter Reformation's crusade on behalf of the Church turned violent on a previously unprecedented scale.

In 1612, Rudolf II – the Hermetically inclined Holy Roman Emperor with his esoteric court in Prague – had died. In 1618, the nobles of Bohemia, in revolt against his successors, offered the country's crown to a Protestant prince, the Rosicrucian-oriented Friedrich, Elector Count Palatine of the Rhine, husband of Elizabeth Stuart and son-in-law of James I of England. Friedrich's rash acceptance provided Ferdinand II – the new Holy Roman Emperor and a staunch supporter of the Church – with an excuse to act. Bohemia was quickly overrun. So was Friedrich's principality, the Palatinate of the Rhine with its court at Heidelberg; and he and his wife, dispossessed, fled into exile at The Hague. Intent on the total extirpation of Protestantism, the imperial armies continued to advance through Germany, devastating the country in their wake.

As one Protestant principality after another fell before the onslaught, Protestant Sweden, under her dynamic and charismatic monarch, Gustavus Adolphus, intervened. Gustavus' 'New Model Army' – on which Cromwell, soon after, was to base his own – temporarily turned the tide. But the beleaguered forces of the Empire were rescued by the appearance of a mysterious aristocratic mercenary and soldier of fortune, Albrecht von Wallenstein, whose Hermetic preoccupations did not prevent him offering his services to the Catholic cause. Wallenstein was steeped in astrology. His seemingly inexhaustible wealth, which enabled him to sustain his troops, was ascribed by rumour to alchemical sources.

There ensued an epic clash between two larger-than-life military adversaries. For five years, the armies of Wallenstein and Gustavus engaged in a bloody contest of combat and manoeuvre, with the whole of Germany as their arena. By 1634, both commanders were dead, the Swedish king slain on the battlefield, Wallenstein mysteriously assassinated by his own subordinates, possibly on the Emperor's orders. Yet the war was scarcely half over, having another fourteen years to run. The forces of Habsburg Spain were thrown into the conflict, aligned with those of Habsburg Austria. Other soldiers – from Italy, from Hungary, from the Balkans, from Denmark, Holland and Scotland – joined those already marching back and forth across an increasingly ruined Germany. At last, Cardinal Richelieu of France intervened. He did so in a paradoxical fashion, setting French nationalism above his own religious affiliations. Catholic troops from a Catholic country were dispatched by a Catholic cardinal to support the Protestant cause. When the Thirty Years War ended in 1648, Spanish martial invincibility had been irreparably shattered and France had emerged as the supreme military power on the continent. Germany was left politically fragmented, and German unification was to be delayed for two and a half centuries. The country had been reduced to a derelict wasteland. Fully one third of her entire population had been exterminated. The Thirty Years War was the most terrible conflict to be conducted on European soil prior to the twentieth century.

Protestantism survived, but largely in an austere, ascetic and intolerant fashion. Hermeticism was driven increasingly underground. A year after the outbreak of the war, Johann Valentin Andreae – probable author of the third of the Rosicrucian manifestos, *The Chemical Wedding of Christian Rosenkreuz* – published his last known work. In this book, entitled *Christianopolis*, Andreae depicted an ideal society, a kind of Hermetic Utopia, situated in a magical city constructed according to Hermetic geometry. Life here was portrayed as revolving around teaching and learning – in the sciences, in mechanics, in medicine, in architecture, in painting and especially in music. Echoing John Dee, Andreae stressed the importance of education and inventiveness in the artisan class. After *Christianopolis*, however, he effectively went silent, devoting his energies primarily to organizing a network of 'Christian Unions'.[3] These may have incorporated elements of the Masonic lodge and the secret society, but their chief objective seems to have consisted of smuggling endangered Hermeticists to safe havens. Andreae himself survived the Thirty Years War unscathed, but kept so low a profile that little is known of his activities after 1620.

Perhaps the sole Renaissance magus of the seventeenth century – the only figure working in the solitary tradition of Agrippa and Paracelsus – was the German Jakob Böhme (1575–1624). Born in Silesia, Böhme was almost wholly self-taught, and passed much of his life as a modest cobbler. Attempts to form a contemplative circle of speculative thinkers in his native town of Görlitz were repeatedly thwarted by charges of heresy from the local hard-line Lutheran pastor. As a result, Böhme published relatively little during his lifetime, most of his major works appearing posthumously. He was heavily steeped in Hermetic thought, especially alchemy, and can be seen as having gone further than his predecessors in regarding alchemy less as a practical discipline than as a symbolic system – a Kabbalistic-style psycho-spiritual methodology for leading the human mind to a direct experience of the numinous. At the same time, Böhme was himself a genuine mystic, who endeavoured to fuse the 'pure' tradition of ecstatic contemplatives like Meister Eckhart with the more applicable aspects of Hermetic thought. But whatever practical application he sought, Böhme remained essentially a philosopher and a contemplative. One sees him today more as a visionary and a thinker than as an active practitioner. Profound, illuminating and important though his work may be, he was not, strictly speaking, a 'magician', and would probably have winced at any description of himself as such. Towards the latter part of the seventeenth century, he was to enjoy a considerable vogue among certain enclaves in England, such as that of Elias Ashmole and the Vaughan brothers. Later, he was to exert a substantial influence on literary figures such as Goethe and Novalis, and on philosophers such as

Schelling, Hegel and Schopenhauer. But until the Thirty Years War and the Counter Reformation had run their course, he was largely consigned to oblivion.

Böhme was dead long before the Thirty Years War ended. Andreae survived the conflict, but his major work either pre-dated it or appeared during its earliest phases. By the end of the seventeenth century, Hermeticism on the continent had all but vanished from the mainstream of religious, polit-ical and cultural thought. Only here and there were scat-tered vestiges of it discernible. As Frances Yates points out, one can detect traces of it in the work of the philosopher Gottfried Wilhelm von Leibniz (1646–1716), who served as adviser to the Elector of Hanover, subsequently George I of England, and tutored the future Queen Caroline, wife of George II. Professor Yates cites 'a persistent rumour' that Leibniz was a member of a clandestine 'Rosicrucian' society,[4] which may originally have been founded by Bruno. And indeed, as Frances Yates says: 'A "Rosicrucian" aura clings to Leibniz.'[5] Certainly his philosophy is suffused with aspects of Rosicrucian-oriented Hermeticism. But it was not for this that Leibniz was known in his lifetime. Neither was it for this that he came to enjoy such status as he does today in the history of Western philosophy. And even that status is equivocal. Within a few years of his death, his thought was subjected to the rationalist scrutiny of Voltaire, and merci-lessly lampooned in *Candide*. In our own century, he is prob-ably better known for the French satirist's savagely scornful depiction of him than for his own achievements.

If Hermeticism was virtually extinguished on the conti-nent, it found a refuge of sorts in England. As the Thirty Years War spread to engulf Europe, many Hermeticists fled to safety in England, some with the aid of Andreae's 'Christian Unions'. Among the more distinguished German refugees were such Rosicrucian-oriented figures as the

Prussian Samuel Hartlib, the Moravian Jan Amos Komensky (known as Comenius) and Michael Maier, formerly physician to James I and then to the soon-to-be-deposed Friedrich, Elector Count Palatine of the Rhine.

In England, the German exiles found a number of like-minded spirits, together with whom they formed a more or less Rosicrucian-oriented 'Invisible College'.[6] Certain members of this institution were later to become founding members of the Royal Society. But the sanctuary offered by England was soon to become less secure than it had at first appeared. By 1642, the country had plunged into its own civil war, which many historians regard as an adjunct of the wider conflict on the continent. The English Civil War culminated, of course, in Cromwell's Protectorate. Under this austere puritanical regime of the self-styled 'elect', the theatres were closed, the witchfinders-general operated and the atmosphere was scarcely more conducive to Hermetic magic than it was on the continent.

Yet despite the prevailing Puritan mentality, Hermeticism survived sufficiently to make at least some notable contributions to English culture. In 1650, the original Hermetic corpus appeared in English translation, and a second edition was issued in 1657. In 1651, Agrippa's *De occulta philosophia* was published in English, followed a year later by two of the Rosicrucian manifestos. Hermetic thought was promulgated by certain of the individuals associated with early Freemasonry, such as Sir Robert Moray and Elias Ashmole. It was promulgated by the so-called 'Cambridge Platonist' Henry More, subsequently an influence on figures as diverse as W. B. Yeats and C. G. Jung. It was promulgated by the poet Henry Vaughan, and by his twin brother, the alchemist Thomas. And there is more than a little Hermeticism in the work of John Milton, who was friendly with a number of English and foreign Hermeticists, including Samuel Hartlib.

Indeed, some of Milton's poetry involves talismanic magic of the sort previously practised by Sidney and Spenser.

As some of the above names suggest, however, Hermeticism was becoming increasingly channelled into the arts and increasingly isolated from the rest of the social, religious, philosophical and – most importantly – scientific mainstream. So far as that mainstream was concerned, Hermeticism was coming under pressure from an entirely new mode of thought – a mode of thought quite as inimical to it as Church dogma after the Council of Trent, or as the Spartan austerity and fundamentalism of puritanical Protestantism. This mode of thought would take the form of sceptical rationalism and scientific materialism. It had originated, ironically, from within Hermeticism. The parent, in short, was about to be disowned and repudiated by an ungrateful child. Science, technology and mechanics, which had emerged out of magic and the old Hermetic unity, were now beginning to assert their independence and autonomy – to break free of their former context and, as fragments, become laws unto themselves. The result was to be the fragmented reality which obtains to the present day.

A key figure in this process was Sir Francis Bacon, Baron Verulam and Viscount St Albans (1561–1626). Bacon's father had been a civil servant in the government of Elizabeth I, his mother an aunt of William Cecil, Lord Burghley. Bacon himself had belonged to the circle of the Earl of Essex. In 1613, under James I, he had become attorney-general of England, in 1618 lord chancellor. In 1621, he was briefly imprisoned for bribery and corruption.

Bacon's thought was originally rooted in Hermeticism, and his orientation, in many respects, remained essentially Hermetic. He was, for example, a fervent advocate of learning and dreamed of compiling an encyclopedic compendium of all knowledge. Some of his assertions patently echo Agrippa. And there are echoes, too, of Rosicrucian Hermeticism in certain of his works. *The New Atlantis*, his allegorical Utopian idyll published posthumously in 1627, reflects the influence of Andreae's *Christianopolis*. It depicts an ideal society on an island in the Pacific, ruled by an order of scholars called the 'Society of Salomon's House'. These initiates wear white turbans bearing a red cross. The rules governing their world are identical to those adumbrated in the Rosicrucian manifestos. Their seal derives from the manifestos as well.

In other respects, however, Bacon parts company with Hermeticism. Although rooted in Hermetic tradition, he made a point of distancing himself from what he deemed its more extreme and subversive manifestations. He deliberately distanced himself from conventional conceptions of the Renaissance magus. He condemned magic and alchemy in general. He criticized Paracelsus in particular. He condemned 'mathematical magicians and their mystical diagrams' – a transparent allusion to John Dee.[7] Instead of the Hermeticist's insistence on the harmonious interrelationship between man and nature, Bacon stressed the need for man's dominance and mastery of nature – thus implying that nature was intrinsically evil, intrinsically 'unregenerate', and therefore demanded to be tamed and controlled. This attitude, not surprisingly, endeared him to the mustering forces of Puritanism in England.

So, too, did his emphasis on utility. Bacon repudiated metaphysical and cosmological speculation, arguing that 'philosophical method must be proven by its utility'.[8] This enshrinement of utility shifted his intellectual focus from the old Hermetic totality to the separate and diverse components of that totality – specifically to such components as could be applied concretely to the 'relief of man's estate'. The connection between macrocosm and microcosm was discarded in favour of concentration on the microcosm alone, and on its constituent parts. Scope and breadth of vision contracted and narrowed to an embrace of methodology for its own sake, which took the form of experimentation – to determine, for example, the laws of cause and effect. Herein lay the seeds of later British empiricism. And, in the process, the thrust of philosophical and scientific inquiry shifted from synthesis to analysis.

The tools of analysis – the methodology – were employed by Isaac Casaubon in his dating of the Hermetic corpus, which was published in 1614. Casaubon (1559–1614) was a Swiss Protestant, the foremost Greek scholar of his age, who migrated to England in 1610 and received encouragement in his endeavours from James I. In the course of a voluminous attack on Catholic scholarship, he applied himself to a detailed textual analysis of the Hermetic books, comparing internal references, authors quoted, fine points of vocabulary and style. His examination led him to conclude that the Hermetic corpus – as it existed, at least – dated from around the end of the first century AD. He did not attempt to deny the existence of an individual known as Hermes Trismegistus, who had been contemporary with, or even pre-dated, Moses. But if Casaubon's dating was accurate, either Hermes Trismegistus would have had to have lived much later, or the books ascribed to him could not have been written by him at all.

Some Hermeticists, such as Robert Fludd, simply ignored Casaubon's conclusions. When the first English translation of the Hermetic corpus appeared in 1650, it was still extolled in some quarters as the oldest compilation of works in the world, pre-dating the Old Testament. On the whole, however, most scholars, from Casaubon's time to the present day, have accepted his dating as more or less accurate. It is acknowledged that the original sources of the Hermetic corpus are lost in the proverbial 'mists of time'. But the corpus itself, as it has been handed down, would indeed appear to date from the first century of the Christian era; and the works attributed to Hermes Trismegistus are now deemed to have been compiled by a number of different authors.

As a result of Casaubon's research, the Hermetic texts were deprived of the prestige which their supposed antiquity had conferred on them'.[9] They were no longer indisputably invested with a credibility and oracular authority as unimpugnable as the Bible, no longer stamped with a divine seal of approval. On the contrary, they could be assessed, accepted or repudiated in the same way as the works of Aristotle or Plato. They were reduced, in short, to the status of one body of teachings among many others.

Bacon advocated a specific methodology which was inherently inimical to Hermeticism, stressing the constituent parts of reality at the expense of the whole, stressing analysis, empiricism and measurable proof. Although he had no conscious or deliberate intention of doing so, Casaubon effectively employed Bacon's methodology against the Hermetic corpus itself. But the intellectual counter-current which would displace Hermeticism in Western thought found its chief exponent in René Descartes (1596–1650), often regarded as the 'principal founding father of modern philosophy'. It is from Descartes, more than from anyone else, that the mentality which has shaped our world today ultimately derives. Cartesian thought was to precipitate a revolution in Western consciousness as profound as that precipitated by the Renaissance. It was to launch Western civilization into the so-called 'Enlightenment', or the 'Age of Reason'.

Like Bacon, Descartes was preoccupied with an empirical methodology; his most important work, indeed, is entitled

Discourse on Method. But like Bacon, too, Descartes was rooted originally in Hermeticism. Despite having received a Jesuit education, Descartes himself admitted that 'not contenting myself merely with the subjects taught, I had gone through all the books I could lay my hands on dealing with the occult and rare sciences'.[10] And Descartes was also strongly attracted to Rosicrucianism, or, at least, to what he knew of it. In 1623, placards appeared in the streets of Paris, announcing the imminent arrival in the city of the 'Brothers of the Rose-Cross' – who would, it was promised, 'teach without books or marks', enable one 'to speak all languages' and 'pull men from error of death'.[11] Among pious Catholics and their institutions, the resulting hysteria could not have been much greater if the advent of the Antichrist himself had been proclaimed, and a predictable witch-hunt ensued – a witch-hunt all the more frenetic in that its objects were supposed to be 'invisible'. Descartes at the time had been campaigning in central Europe with the Catholic armies of the Counter Reformation. He arrived in Paris with the express intention of locating the elusive Rosicrucians and applying for entry to their esoteric fraternity. By his own admission, he never found a living and breathing Rosicrucian, but he himself was soon accused of being one. He whimsically refuted these accusations by exhibiting his 'visibility'. And though rumours of Rosicrucianism have continued occasionally to cling to him, the thrust of Cartesian thought suffices in itself to dispel them.

In his *Discourse on Method*, Descartes declared himself sufficiently knowledgeable 'not to be liable to be misled either by the promises of an alchemist or the predictions of an astrologer, the impostures of a magician or the tricks or boasts of any of those who profess to know more than they do'.[12] Like Bacon, he extolled a form of empirical rationalism. He sought in philosophy the same certainties and demonstrable proofs that could be obtained in geometry or mathematics. Repudiating all manifestations of the irrational, he believed the rational intellect to be the supreme arbiter and judge of reality – not recognizing that belief in the intellect's supremacy was ultimately as irrational as any other form of belief.

'*Cogito ergo sum*', 'I think, therefore I am.' This became the famous, oft-quoted cornerstone of Cartesian thought. Whether deliberately so or not, it was to be taken all too literally. In the centuries that followed, Western man was to identify himself increasingly with his faculty for thought, his capacity for ratiocination. Anything not subject to quantification or analysis by the rational intellect was deemed irrelevant, if not illusory. Anything in man himself that lay beyond his powers of intellection – his emotions, for example, his intuitions, his dreams, his numinous experiences, his altered states of consciousness, his encounters with the domain subsequently known to pyschology as the unconscious – was deemed to be insignificant, subordinate, incidental or non-existent. No knowledge other than that obtained through reason was deemed admissible. No sphere of study other than that of the empirically measurable was deemed valid.

Cartesian thought was soon to dominate the English Royal Society – many of whose early members, like Bacon and Descartes before them, were rooted in Hermeticism but then (at least publicly) repudiated it. During the Civil War and the Protectorate, a number of learned individuals – Rosicrucian-oriented refugees from the continent, Englishmen such as John Wilkins, Robert Boyle and Christopher Wren – had begun to meet more or less regularly in loosely knit, informal and often overlapping organizations. There was, for example, the so-called 'Invisible College'. There was a group which met at Gresham College in London, established some fifty years earlier by Sir Thomas Gresham, a wealthy Elizabethan merchant who had also founded the Royal Exchange. There was an offshoot of the Gresham College circle at Oxford. In the beginning these organizations devoted themselves to exploring the then nebulous frontier between Hermeticism and science. And it was from these organizations that the founders and original members of the Royal Society emerged.[13]

In 1660, Cromwell's Protectorate ended and the monarchy was restored in the person of Charles II, who returned to England from exile abroad. In November of that year, a learned society was officially constituted at Gresham College. In July 1662, it was accorded the king's patronage and incorporated as the Royal Society. Among its founding members were Sir Robert Moray, John Wilkins, John Evelyn, John Aubrey, Robert Boyle and Christopher Wren. The total membership came to 115, a few of whom – Moray for example, Ashmole and, probably later, Wren – were also Freemasons.

Certain of these figures, such as Moray and Ashmole, displayed an Hermetic orientation. As a whole, however, the Royal Society tended to ignore, if not repudiate, Hermeticism, and to embrace the empirical rationalism advocated by Bacon and Descartes. This soon coalesced into a new and increasingly dogmatic orthodoxy of scientific materialism, in which Hermetic thought no longer had any place. So rigid did this orthodoxy become that individuals who retained an interest in Hermeticism were obliged to conceal it. The hypocrisy of such figures was exemplified by Robert Boyle. Throughout his life, Boyle was deeply immersed in alchemy and other Hermetic studies, but the full magnitude of his involvement in these spheres did not become apparent until very recently. He conducted his research in secret and recorded his preoccupation in elaborate codes. In public, and in his dealings with the Royal Society, he championed Bacon, endorsed empirical rationalism, satirically attacked alchemical writings and proclaimed his hostility to 'hermetick doctrine'. It was, of course, his declared public position that characterized him for his contemporaries and for posterity. His clandestine Hermetic inquiries and experiments were, like Hermeticism itself, relegated to the shadows and marginalized as scientifically disreputable. Such was the power of the new orthodoxy, such the pressure to conform.[14]

During the second half of the seventeenth century, there was sporadic fighting on the fringes of Europe – against the Turks on the Austrian Habsburgs' eastern frontiers, in Scandinavia, between France and Spain in the Pyrenees, between England and Holland and then England and France at sea, between the forces of James II and those of William of Orange in Ireland. For the most part, however, Europe, still debilitated by the Thirty Years War, enjoyed a period of relative peace. Except in Ireland, where it was subordinated to dynastic allegiances, even the struggle between Catholicism and Protestantism subsided, each denomination consolidating its position in its own territory. But a philosophical struggle continued, between two opposing modes of thought, two opposing traditions, two opposing orientations. This struggle and its outcome were to be decisive defining influences on the world we know today. Our own modern attitudes to knowledge and reality date, in effect, from the conflict between an essentially Hermetic perspective and the empirical rationalism of the new scientific materialism.

Except in the arts, the struggle was one-sided and Hermeticism increasingly marginalized from the mainstream of Western development. But the dwindling number of Hermetic adherents still clung to the tradition of the

Renaissance magus. For the Cambridge Platonist Henry More, to cite but one example, everything comprising reality remained interconnected, forming a single all-encompassing unity, a seamless tapestry. And to comprehend this unity, knowledge, too, had to be perceived as a seamless whole. All disciplines were as interconnected as the reality to which they addressed themselves; all disciplines were intrinsically linked to each other, flowed into each other, nourished and augmented each other. In order to fathom the mysteries of the human body, one had to fathom the nature of the cosmos in which that body was embedded and of which it was an integral part; and one had also to fathom the nature of the human mind, spirit and soul. Man was regarded and treated as an organism which comprised a single cell so to speak, in a larger organism – the microcosm, in short, wherein the entire macrocosm was implicit. And so-called 'lateral thinking', regarded today as a revolutionary and innovative approach, was in Hermetic tradition, the norm.

In contrast to the Hermetic tradition there was now its own renegade offspring, the rationalism, the empirical methodology, the scientific materialism of Bacon and Descartes. Subordinated to this new approach, the old Hermetic unity was dismembered and dissected into an ever-proliferating multitude of smaller and smaller components, each of which became a separate and autonomous discipline, a separate and autonomous sphere of research and investigation. Domains of knowledge which had previously been puddles now became bottomless wells or pools, wherein a researcher could sink for a lifetime, and often drown. The connection between disparate fields of investigation became progressively more tenuous, progressively more attenuated and frayed, and often snapped completely. The Renaissance concept of encyclopedic knowledge gave way to a plethora of specializations, each of which became ever more divorced and dissociated from all others. Integration was supplanted by fragmentation and the exaltation of fragments. Synthesis was supplanted by analysis – an analysis so intoxicated with its own capacity for dissection that it lost the capacity for reassembling what it had dismantled. And organism was supplanted by mechanism. The cosmos came increasingly to be perceived as a species of machine, a vast clockwork contraption – created by some divine architect or engineer perhaps but now left as an automaton to its own devices. And man began to be perceived in similarly mechanistic terms, as a mere assembly of parts, many of which – like tyres or fan belts – were interchangeable.

At the end of the seventeenth century and the beginning of the eighteenth, one figure – a figure of monumental status – attempted to effect his own reconciliation between Hermetic and Cartesian thought. This individual was Sir Isaac Newton. Today, of course, Newton is regarded as a scientist – indeed, as one of the founding fathers of modern science. Yet Newton himself would have bridled in horror at any such status, and would vehemently have repudiated it. Newton saw himself not just as a 'natural philosopher' – a scientist – but as a 'philosopher' in the broader and traditional sense of that word, a 'lover of wisdom'. And he was a philosopher of specifically Hermetic orientation, for whom science was known and perceived simply as 'natural philosophy'. The scientific achievements with which Newton is associated today in fact constituted only a part – and, for him, a less consequential part – of his life's work. Even in volume, his scientific writings are exceeded by other, more diverse material – alchemical research, prophecy, theological meditation, studies of the possible architecture and dimensions of Solomon's Temple, a genealogy of the kings of Israel in the Old Testament. According to one modern biographer, it is 'a curious anomaly . . . that Newton's studies in astronomy, optics and mathematics only occupied a small portion of his time. In fact most of his great powers were poured out upon church history, theology, "the chronology of ancient kingdoms", prophecy, and alchemy.'[15]

For Newton, as for Agrippa and Paracelsus, philosophy encompassed the entire spectrum of human knowledge and human activity; and the pure science to which he made such a signal contribution was, for him, embedded in a much broader, much more comprehensive context. To excise it from that context and pursue it as an autonomous discipline would have been, in Newton's eyes, folly, error and a morally culpable mutilation of the greater truth he sought.

And yet that, of course, is precisely what happened. If Newton himself was Hermetic in his orientation, stressing an interlocking connection of all things, his followers and disciples were Cartesian, intoxicated by a methodology of analysis which grew ever more rationalistic, ever more circumscribed, ever more dissociated from their mentor's original totality. They even endeavoured to suppress the aspects of his work which failed to conform to the new scientific 'respectability'. When Newton died in 1727, his non-scientific works – including his material on alchemy, amounting to some 650,000 words in his own hand – were marked 'Not fit to be printed' and secreted away.[16]

They did not see the light of day until more than two centuries later. In 1936, Newton's descendants disposed of his unpublished papers by auction at Sotheby's. A total of 121 lots proved to pertain to alchemy and Hermetic thought. The catalogue of the sale lists a comprehensive library of alchemical and Hermetic texts, many of them copiously annotated. It also includes handwritten indices to these texts amounting to 162 pages.[17]

As a result of the 1936 auction, scholars were enabled, for the first time, to assess the magnitude and scale of Newton's

Hermetic interests. It came as a startling revelation. The first commentator to publish the hitherto suppressed work was John Maynard Keynes, later Lord Keynes, who concluded that Newton's 'deepest instincts were occult, esoteric, semantic . . .' According to Keynes: 'Newton was not the first of the age of reason. He was the last of the magicians . . .' And Keynes elaborated:

> Why do I call him a magician? because he looked on the whole universe and all that is in it *as a riddle*, as a secret which could be read by applying pure thought to certain evidence, certain mystic clues which God had laid about the world to allow a sort of philosopher's treasure hunt to the esoteric brotherhood. He believed that these clues were to be found partly in the evidence of the heavens and in the constitution of elements . . . but also partly in certain papers and traditions handed down by the brethren in an unbroken chain back to the original cryptic revelation in Babylonia. He regarded the universe as a cryptogram set by the Almighty . . . By pure thought, by concentration of mind, the riddle, he believed, would be revealed to the initiate.[18]

In the words of a subsequent commentator:

> It may safely be said nevertheless that Newton's alchemical thoughts were so securely established on their basic foundations that he never came to deny their general validity, and in a sense the whole of his career after 1675 may be seen as one long attempt to integrate alchemy and the mechanical philosophy.[19]

And a forthcoming book on Newton by Michael White, appropriately entitled *The Last Sorcerer*, will produce evidence attesting not only to his immersion in alchemy, but to his immersion in Hermetic magic as well.

Such was the side of Newton's character which his immediate followers and disciples sought to suppress as incompatible with their own Cartesian orientation. In the years subsequent to his death, they proceeded to hijack not only his research, but his name as well. Their distorted portrait of their mentor was soon to become generally accepted. Less than a century later, Newton's name had become inextricably associated with those through whom the era came to be called the Age of Reason. Thus he (like Rousseau) was to be unjustly perceived by Blake as an arch-villain, a butcher of higher truth, intoxicated to the point of blindness by a misplaced faith in his own arrogant intellect:

> Mock on, Mock on Voltaire, Rousseau:
> Mock on, Mock on: 'tis all in vain!
> You throw the sand against the wind,
> And the wind blows it back again.
>
> And every sand becomes a Gem
> Reflected in the beams divine;
> Blown back they blind the mocking Eye,
> But still in Israel's paths they shine.
>
> The Atoms of Democritus
> And Newton's Particles of light
> Are sands upon the Red sea shore,
> Where Israel's tents do shine so bright.[20]

Blake's vision, of course, was characteristically Hermetic, presupposing a web or network of correspondences linking microcosm and macrocosm:

> To see a World in a Grain of Sand
> And a Heaven in a Wild Flower,

Hold Infinity in the palm of your hand
And Eternity in an hour.[21]

By Blake's time, Hermeticism had already found a refuge in
the arts. As rationalism, empiricism and scientific materialism consolidated their position in the vanguard of Western
civilization, that refuge was to become one of the few of its
kind. And an increasingly irreconcilable rift was to open
between the arts and the sciences, culminating in what the
twentieth-century commentator C. P. Snow was to describe
as the 'Two Cultures'.

I I

THE FRAGMENTATION OF REALITY

As recently as Newton's time, an essentially Hermetic orientation towards reality – an all-encompassing, all-embracing, unified orientation – was still tenable. Since then, however, the world has changed. The world we inhabit today is a world in which, according to one commentator, reason devises 'moral systems determined by what is useful to society'.[1] This world is a product of the so-called 'Enlightenment' or 'Age of Reason'.

Since the triumph of Cartesian thought at the beginning of the eighteenth century, Western civilization has extolled analysis at the cost of synthesis, mechanism at the cost of organism. One consequence of this has been a proliferation of specializations and a concurrent fragmentation. Instead of a single all-pervasive principle of knowledge which imparts meaning to the totality of human activity, there is a multitude of conflicting principles, each vying with the others, each jostling the others for supremacy – and for our allegiance. Each of these conflicting spheres of knowledge comprises a self-styled 'discipline'. Each such discipline constitutes a species of cult, presided over by its own priesthood and governed by its own 'theology'. Art, science, psychology, sociology, history, economics, politics and religion – as well as the numerous and often divergent 'denominations' within each of these – all have their own high priests promulgating a highly specialized body of dogma. Each such priesthood has its own mysteries, usually couched in obfuscating jargon, which are inaccessible to all save initiates; and each such priesthood, like every priesthood, has its own vested interests to protect, on behalf of which 'heretics' will be 'excommunicated'.

For a hapless humanity seeking meaning, purpose and guidance for its existence, the result is baffling. We are today confronted by a bewildering welter of conflicting absolutes, each of which purports to hold the answers we are seeking, each of which urges upon us its own idiosyncratic interpretation of reality. Chemistry, biology and physics – as well as the various combinations thereof – all assert their claim to a definitive truth. In stark contrast, organized religion – and especially religious fundamentalism – asserts a claim of its own. So does sociology. So does psychology. So does politics. And, of course, there are the numerous 'isms' which have proliferated during the last century and a half – Marxism, Maoism, fascism, capitalism and all the others.

Confronted by the clamour of rival and often mutually exclusive claims to legitimacy, how can the individual make an intelligent choice of allegiance – especially when the validity of each claim is kept inaccessible by its respective priesthood and has to be taken on trust? One result is that we tend to choose the claim which is 'safest', which entails the least commitment and the least risk. Unfortunately, that claim will also tend to be the least relevant. Most people today, for example, are perfectly prepared to accept, on blind faith, that they and the cosmos around them are composed of molecules, and that molecules are composed of atoms, and that atoms are composed of protons, neutrons and electrons, which in turn are composed of a myriad smaller particles. Without fully comprehending the concept of a 'light year', most people are similarly prepared to accept on faith that Sirius, for example, is a precise number of 'light years' away from the earth. But how do such unquestioned 'articles of faith' help us to live our lives, to make decisions, to derive any sort of meaning, purpose or guidance for our existence? How do such 'articles of faith' help us to determine a course of action or provide us with a moral framework, an ethical imperative, a hierarchy of values? So far as those things are concerned, we live with what the Austrian novelist Robert Musil has called 'a relativity of perspective verging on epistemological panic'.

Rational Philosophy

The fragmentation of knowledge that began with Baconian and Cartesian thought gained momentum throughout the eighteenth century. It was promulgated with particular zeal in France, where it found expression in the work of the *philosophes* – Montesquieu, Diderot and, supremely, Voltaire. In Augustan England, it was promulgated by such figures as the philosopher David Hume (1711–76), whose *Treatise of Human Nature* was subtitled 'An Attempt to Introduce the Experimental Method of Reasoning into Moral Subjects'. Literary luminaries such as Pope and Swift, Addison and Steele, made rationalism a governing principle even in the arts, and accepted reason as 'our ultimate guarantee of knowledge'. A formalized scepticism was adopted as the most intellectually respectable stance; and wit, as a purely cerebral exercise, was esteemed more highly than the irrational and therefore suspect faculty of imagination. Towards the latter part of the century, this attitude was perpetuated by the most prestigious belletrist of his age, Samuel Johnson.

If rationalism infiltrated the arts, it was also introduced

into organized religion, where it assumed the form of deism. According to deism, God, having created the cosmos, had effectively withdrawn from it, leaving man to inhabit, interpret and explore the domain of which he was now sole custodian. This domain was not perceived as the all-inclusive living organism in which, according to Agrippa and Paracelsus, everything was interconnected. On the contrary, it was now perceived as a cosmic mechanism, a vast clockwork machine, which could be disassembled by analysis into its component parts; and so exhilarating did the process of analysis become that scant attention was paid to how the contraption might be put together again. For Descartes, even plants and animals were mere mechanisms. 'It is as natural,' he asserted, 'for a watch to indicate the time by means of its wheels, as it is for the trees to bear fruit.'[2] For his followers, it was man's virtual duty to dismantle the tree as if it were a watch in order to fathom its workings. Thus the deist sought to establish man's mastery over nature – and, by virtue of such mastery, a sanction to exploit nature.

Like the pious pre-Renaissance Christian, the deist regarded man not as an inseparable part of nature, but as distinct from nature. For the pious pre-Renaissance Christian, man's dissociation from nature had derived from his spirit, his soul, and nature's unredeemed or 'unregenerate' status. For the deist, man's dissociation from nature derived from the powers of his rational intellect and from nature's ordained subservience to those powers. But like the pious pre-Renaissance Christian, the deist would invoke the Bible as a mandate to exploit the earth's resources: 'Be masters of the fish of the sea, the birds of heaven and all animals on the earth.'[3]

The biblical conception of nature liberated man from the naturalistic bonds of Greek religiosity and philosophy and

gave a religious sanction to the development of technology
. . . to the dominion of nature by human art. Though the mechanistic world picture is not contained in the Bible, yet it shares
in common with the biblical concept the fact that it implies a
de-deification of nature. This took away the obstacles caused
by its deification to the ancients and made it possible to accept
not only that man *could* compete with nature or even surpass
her, but that he *should* do so. No prohibition now existed, and
the numinous holy character of nature had vanished.[4]

During the nineteenth century, the fissures and fractures
in what had formerly been a unified approach to knowledge
became ever more acute, ever more pronounced, ever more
irreparable. Darwinian thought placed science in seemingly
irreversible and irreconcilable opposition to organized religion, and also, in many respects, to humanist tradition; and
in Darwin's wake, agnosticism, as promulgated by Thomas
Huxley and Herbert Spencer, became not only respectable,
but fashionable. Yet Darwin was not the only unwitting
instrument of fragmentation. There were also a number of
social philosophers, including Marx and Engels, whose
rationalism reduced the entire realm of human affairs to a
simplistic mechanism governed by social and economic laws.
And there was Freud, who brought the same rationalism to
bear on psychology, extolled the study of the human mind
as a 'science' and reduced even the intangible dynamics of
the psyche to the status of a machine.

In 1959, the English novelist, scientist and politician
C. P. Snow published a highly influential work entitled *The
Two Cultures*. In this book, Snow argued that Western civilization had become dangerously split and polarized between
two modes of thought, two hierarchies of value, neither of
which could communicate any longer with the other. On
the one hand, he maintained, there was what he called

'literary' tradition, which encompassed the arts, religion, imagination and everything else rooted in the irrational; on the other hand, there was the mentality of science and scientific methodology. But Snow was neither a great artist nor a particularly profound thinker; and the situation, by his time, had become much more complicated than his simple dichotomy could accommodate. There were no longer merely two cultures. There were many. Each, as noted above, had developed its own terminology, its own phraseology, its own jargon. Each had turned what began as a mere vocabulary into a full-fledged theology, complete with attending dogma. Each had evolved words initially to denote a simple convenience, and then proceeded to confuse that convenience with a truth.

Measurement, to take a flagrantly obvious example, is ultimately a convenience. Divisions of space and time – into inches or miles, into minutes, hours or years – are essentially arbitrary. They are inventions of the human intellect, devised to denote much more intangible realities. By virtue of these inventions, a semblance of order is imposed on the proverbial chaos, and human society is enabled to function more efficiently. But all of us know that clock time, to cite but one instance, has precious little to do with other kinds of time. All of us know that 'internal time' – time as directly experienced by the human mind – has little connection with the divisions of the clock. If one is actively involved or interested, an hour can whisk by in what seems a few minutes. If one is bored the same hour can become agonizingly long drawn out. The same relativity applies to time as measured by the calendar. In adolescence and youth, a year can seem to elongate interminably. As one grows older, a decade can flit past with disconcerting rapidity, and the calendar will become a blur.

Measurement, then – the division of time and space into

manageable units – is a convenience, not a truth, and certainly not an Absolute Truth, even though it is often confused with Absolute Truth. 'Light years' and 'nano-seconds' have no meaning other than that assigned to them by the human intellect. Such conveniences, of course, are as old as civilization itself, and are necessary for the efficient conduct of human affairs. Thus we invent money, supposedly to denote the intangible quality of value or worth. Yet we all recognize that a five-pound note or a five-dollar bill will possess a very different value or worth in Africa or Asia from that which it possesses in Europe or North America – and in the wastes of Antarctica, it will have no value whatever. By the same token, we all recognize that a fortune in one quarter of the globe will be a mere pittance in some other.

The ultimate convenience is language itself. Words in themselves are certainly not Absolute Truths. Their meanings can vary even within one language. In other languages, they can mean nothing at all, or something radically different. Thus, according to an oft-told and perhaps apocryphal story, Rolls-Royce proposed to market a 'Silver Mist' in Germany, not realizing that *Mist* in German means 'shit'.

With the proliferation of specializations, whole lexicons of words, whole edifices of concepts, have been introduced – to be regarded as conveniences initially, but then to be accepted as truths, as axiomatic realities in themselves, with an assumed concreteness and quantifiable tangibility. One might cite, for example, the 'Oedipus complex' of Freudian psychology. One might cite the 'class struggle', or the 'prole-tariat', or capitalized 'History' in Marxism. One might cite 'democracy' as it is invoked in modern politics, even though many 'democratic' governments govern with a majority opposed to them. One might cite such absurdities as the currently fashionable 'feel-good factor', extolled by purportedly educated politicians and journalists as if it were some species of social Grail, to be calibrated as precisely as the rise or fall of house prices. All of these terms, in their respective spheres, are perceived not merely as conveniences, but as truths, even as demonstrable facts.

The Hiding of Hermeticism

Amidst the process of fragmentation, what became of Hermeticism, with its vision of an all-pervasive unity – a vision which, during the Renaissance, had seemed on the verge of actualization, of being translated into practice? What became of Hermeticism's chief custodians – the magi or magicians in the tradition of Agrippa and Paracelsus, or of their fictionalized avatar, Faustus? According to orthodox historians, as well as to accepted wisdom, the history of Faust and Hermeticism – for three and a half centuries a mainstream of Western culture – degenerated into a mere tributary, the history of so-called 'esotericism'. And 'esotericism' is regarded as having been left behind by the Enlightenment and the 'Scientific Revolution'.

As has been noted, Hermeticism survived the Renaissance, but became increasingly marginalized, while its custodians came to be perceived as increasingly irrelevant, if not indeed positively suspect. In the eyes of orthodox historians, the true heirs of Agrippa and Paracelsus are not individuals, but the collectives which claimed that legacy for themselves. The secret society is deemed to have replaced the solitary magus and to have inherited his tradition. In the beginning, such secret societies – seventeenth-century Rosicrucianism, for example, or early Freemasonry – are acknowledged to have contributed, albeit obliquely, to the mainstream of history. They are then deemed to have become progressively more peripheral, progressively more divorced from the evolution and development of Western culture. They are deemed to have been relegated to the 'lunatic fringe', and will seldom be accorded more than a footnote in any history books other than those specifically devoted to so-called 'esoterica'. Such is the case, for example, with the eighteenth-century Illuminati of Bavaria, with the Order of the Golden Dawn or the Ordo Templi Orientis in the late nineteenth and early twentieth centuries. Such is the case with the bizarre German sects – the Order of the New Templars, the Thule Gesellschaft and the Germanorden – which contributed to the rise of the Third Reich.[5] Such is the case with some of the cults and covens of today, which claim to teach and practise ritual magic according to explicit or implicit Hermetic principles – the flamboyantly self-destructive Order of the Solar Temple, for instance, whose members' collective suicides commanded international headlines in the mid 1990s.

According to orthodox historians, there has also been the occasional individual figure. As late as the eighteenth century, some of them were still regarded by the gullible as 'high initiates', functioning in a lofty isolation and enigmatic solitude. Such, for instance, is the status accorded the legendary and supposedly ageless Comte de Saint-Germain, who certainly never existed in the guise ascribed to him by wishful thinkers. Such is the status accorded the Sicilian Giuseppe Balsamo, better known as the Conte di Cagliostro – who, in all probability, was as much a charlatan as his detractors alleged.

By the nineteenth century, however, the self-styled magus had been even further marginalized. He had been reduced to a mere propagandist, an eccentric if not certifiably deranged proselytizer, competing with others of his ilk in seeming to harbour the most secrets, trafficking in mystification rather than genuine mystery, often founding his own cult, sect, order or system. One might cite, for example, Eliphas Lévi, the most prominent figure in nineteenth-century French esotericism. One might cite Dr Gérard Encausse, known as 'Papus'. One might cite the notorious Aleister Crowley, as well as Crowley's one-time disciple, Dion Fortune. And one might cite, too, certain individuals who fused Hermetic tradition with other bodies of material and thereby sought, in effect, to establish new religions – H. P. Blavatsky, for instance, founder of Theosophy, or the father of Anthroposophy, Rudolf Steiner.

It is generally, if grudgingly, conceded that such post-Enlightenment manifestations of Hermetic thought occasionally exercised an influence beyond the peripheral and rarefied sphere of 'esoterica' as such. Rosicrucianism and Freemasonry, for example, are admitted to have had repercussions in political and cultural spheres, though these repercussions are seldom accorded more than a simple reluctant acknowledgement. In some cases, the repercussions, glossed over though they may be, are deemed more important than the Hermeticism in which they originated. Few people today, for example, would ever have heard of the Order of the Golden Dawn, had its membership not included William Butler Yeats.

Orthodox historians will ruefully admit – and deplore – the occurrence of several so-called 'occult revivals' during the last three hundred years. They will acknowledge the Hermetic skein running through European Romanticism during the late eighteenth and early nineteenth centuries. They will acknowledge the movement in mid-nineteenth-century France, which culminated in the 'decadence' of the *fin de siècle*. They will acknowledge the dissemination of 'esoteric' interest in Russia on the eve of the Revolution. They will acknowledge the subterranean stream feeding the current which surfaced as National Socialism in Germany.

They will acknowledge 'woolly-minded mysticism' as one of the reprehensible characteristics of the shamelessly 'permissive' 1960s. And they will invoke such mysticism as an alarming barometer of the hunger for meaning, purpose and direction prevailing today.

Such 'occult revivals' will reluctantly be allowed to have exerted some oblique influence on social and political affairs. It is still widely believed, for instance, that the French Revolution was fomented, at least in part, by Freemasonry and other secret societies. Rather more demonstrably, 'occult revivals' will be allowed to have exercised some influence on the arts. But they will still be regarded as essentially peripheral to the mainstream and development of what we call Western history. And when they must perforce be acknowledged, they will be acknowledged as some species of deviation, if not as a positively pernicious and perverse phenomenon. Figures such as Eliphas Lévi and Aleister Crowley will be dismissed (not without justification) as freaks. Theosophy and Anthroposophy will be regarded as derisory, not to be taken seriously by any respectable commentator. The inescapable 'esoteric' preoccupations of W. B. Yeats will be regarded by literary critics and scholars with pained embarrassment, as an awkward aberration – the kind of weirdness held to be the prerogative of a poet, engendering some original inspiration and grist for his aesthetic mill.

Science Discovers Sin

Thus, reduced to a mere adjunct of 'esoterica', has Hermeticism been perceived during the last three centuries. It has been shunted into a siding of cultural history; and its custodian, the magician, has been degraded to the status of an eccentric anomaly whose primary accomplishment consists in corrupting artists. If he is seen to take himself too seriously, he is regarded as a deluded fool and a laughing-stock. If his attitude remains inscrutable, he will be casti-gated as a cynical and manipulative charlatan. The self-styled magi of the modern world have often, of course, been either or both of these things. But that is not the whole of the story. If Faust nowadays deigns sometimes to play the clown, he also operates in a much more serious and influential capacity. He does so, however, incognito.

The integrated and all-encompassing *Weltanschauung* of the Renaissance was, in its orientation, essentially Hermetic. When the unity of that *Weltanschauung* fragmented, Hermeticism, in effect, fragmented with it. Vestiges of Hermetic thought survived and were preserved – but diffused, now, over as many diverse spheres, disciplines and fields of study as was knowledge itself. Each such sphere, discipline or field of study proceeded to engender its own Hermetic adepts, its own magicians, its own Fausts.

If Renaissance magi like Agrippa and Paracelsus could also be regarded as scientists, the modern scientist has come increasingly to be regarded as a magician – a magician in his own right. For many people, indeed, the modern scien-tist would appear to be the true heir to such figures as Agrippa and Paracelsus. One need only adumbrate a list of the distinguished scientific names of the last three centuries – Henry Cavendish, Antoine Lavoisier, André Ampère, Michael Faraday, Pierre and Marie Curie, Ernest Rutherford, Max Planck, Wolfgang Pauli, Albert Einstein. These individuals are generally acknowledged to be the magicians of our own age. And, in addition to such 'adepts' of pure science, there are the practitioners of applied science, the inventors, the engineers and technicians – George and Robert Stephenson, Isambard Brunel, George Westinghouse, Thomas Edison, Nikola Tesla, Guglielmo

Marconi. The supreme scientific magus would be the individual who combines, like such Renaissance predecessors as John Dee, both pure and applied science. The most obvious examples of this would be Robert Oppenheimer and his team of colleagues – including Enrico Fermi, Edward Teller and Niels Bohr – who, at Los Alamos, ushered in the nuclear age. More recently, one might cite the rocket designer Werner von Braun – whose dreams of sending men to the moon seemed, a mere half century or so ago, as far-fetched as any attempted transmutation of lead into gold. Finally, one might cite the 'genetic engineers' of today. Among other things, the Renaissance magus sought to create life, in the form of the so-called 'homunculus'. Through the techniques associated with cloning and with *in vitro* fertilization, the modern scientist has come close to actualizing that ambition.

There are also, of course, the fictional depictions of the scientist. There is the positive stereotype – the high priest of benevolent powers, presiding over august mysteries, advancing progress, revolutionizing the world around us, improving the human condition, discovering cures for disease. And there is the negative variation – the familiar eccentric boffin or demented genius, exemplified by Dr Frankenstein or Dr Strangelove, by the gallery of neo-Faustian experimenters who populate the pages and frames of horror stories and science fiction. All of these figures are essentially magus figures, whether creative or destructive. They represent, for many people, the magicians of our era – one of the guises in which Faust continues to survive and operate. All of them adhere to the basic principles of Hermetic magic – exploiting the web of interrelationships in order 'to make things happen'.

Some scientists, at least, have been well aware of the Faustian character of their endeavours. Alfred Nobel, for example, the nineteenth-century inventor of dynamite, sincerely hoped his explosives would cause war to be outlawed by making it too terrible. Disillusioned and bitterly resentful at the military exploitation of his achievements, he sought to atone. In a gesture akin to Goethe's Faust 'reclaiming land from the sea', Nobel used the fortune he had earned to endow international prizes for benevolent advances in science, as well as for the promotion of literature and peace.

Robert Oppenheimer and his team, as they worked in the New Mexico desert at Los Alamos, believed they were venturing, if not actually trespassing, on religious territory. Some of them compared themselves explicitly to Faust, as well as to Prometheus. Some of them were convinced they were dealing with a mystery of cosmic proportions. More than one of them went on record as wondering whether their efforts might not perhaps disrupt the very fabric of creation, and perhaps bring them face to face with God – if only a god in the form of pure energy. When early (and fortunately erroneous) computations suggested their research might, in an instantaneous chain reaction, touch a match to all the hydrogen and nitrogen on earth, the awesome magnitude of the power they were exercising became terrifyingly apparent – to the point of seeming, indeed, a usurpation of God's prerogatives.[6]

Oppenheimer himself was a complex and deeply moral individual, a reader and writer of poetry, a polymath fluent in a number of languages including Greek and Sanskrit, with an avid interest in comparative religions, especially those of the East. After witnessing the first atomic test in the spring of 1945, he reportedly stated that a verse from the eleventh chapter of the *Bhagavad Gita* sprang spontaneously to mind: 'If the light of a thousand suns suddenly arose in the sky, that splendour might be compared to the radiance of the

Supreme Spirit.'[7] The chapter in question evokes a vision of the numinous, the Absolute, of which the god Krishna is an avatar. Profoundly shaken, 'trembling with awe and wonder', the human protagonist of the *Gita* addresses the majesty he has confronted: 'When I see thy vast form, reaching the sky, burning with many colours . . . my heart shakes in terror: my power is gone and gone is my peace . . .'[8]

Oppenheimer himself appears to have experienced something very similar. Although he assented reluctantly to the bombing of Hiroshima, the second attack, on Nagasaki, left him stricken. He quickly resigned his post as director of the research establishment at Los Alamos. And as the establishment's work, now increasingly under the authority of the military, proceeded from atomic to hydrogen weapons, Oppenheimer became ever more tormented by anguish and guilt. 'In some sort of crude sense,' he wrote, 'which no vulgarity, no humour, no overstatement can quite extinguish, the physicists have known sin.'[9]

Wisdom, or mere Information?

Hermetic thought had posited an interrelationship and interconnectedness of all things – so that pulling a thread at one point in the fabric of reality might cause something to tauten, or to unravel, somewhere else. Nuclear physics, if anything, confirmed the general validity of this premise, and translated the theory behind it into an all-too-actualizable practice. In the analogous structures of the atom and the solar system, nuclear physics also found a species of confirmation for the old Hermetic doctrine of macrocosm and microcosm. There can be few serious-minded science students who did not at some time wonder, even if only idly, whether each atom might not in itself constitute an entire solar system – and whether the solar system we inhabit might not perhaps be a single atom in some immensely vaster creation. Such thinking is, in itself, characteristically Hermetic.

Quite apart from such vertiginous speculation, modern science – without, of course, calling it by its name or acknowledging its source – has, in effect, accepted the Hermetic principle of interconnectedness. The concept of an interconnected microcosm and macrocosm may, in its literal sense, be too metaphysical for scientific empiricism; but the principle of interconnectedness will not be disputed. Every schoolchild learns, for example, of the cycles of evaporation and precipitation, of growth and decay. Few informed people today can be ignorant of the relevance to their own lives of the ostensibly remote Brazilian rain forests. Environmental studies confront us daily with the need to recognize our planet as a living and ultimately threatened organism, the brutalization of which, however distant, will have repercussions on our own existence. It is now generally appreciated that the resources of the earth are not infinite, but limited, and that we have come precariously close to exhausting them. It is also generally appreciated that our smallest acts can have consequences of catastrophic, even apocalyptic, magnitude – an application of chaos theory's 'butterfly effect'. An aerosol with CFC squirted in the privacy of one's bathroom will produce effects radiating out to the ozone layer. A bonfire of autumn leaves in the garden will contribute to global warming. The toxins with which we pollute our surroundings will eventually return to us in the food we eat, the water we drink, the air we breathe. As the Hermeticists of ancient Alexandria insisted, we are interdependent with the natural world and an inseparable part of it.

In many respects, of course, Cartesian methodology,

rationalistic empiricism and scientific analysis have achieved indisputable triumphs. Transplant operations, for example, are commonplace today, and organs *can* be replaced, or even fabricated, like the components of a machine. To that extent, the mentality stemming from the Enlightenment has indeed vindicated and validated itself. All too often, however, its proponents tend to forget the extent to which the alternative orientation – that of Hermetic integration and synthesis – has also justified itself. All too often they fail to recognize the degree to which they themselves embrace it and depend on it.

At the beginning of this century, for example, biology, chemistry and physics had evolved into three separate, distinct and autonomous disciplines, each a specialization, a self-contained world, in itself. Only gradually, and belatedly, were connections established between them, producing such spheres of research as astrophysics, biophysics and biochemistry. When they emerged, these supposedly new spheres of research were hailed as innovative and revolutionary. And yet they reflect what was, ultimately, the reality all along – the reality taken as a given by men like Agrippa and Paracelsus. They reflect a unity which existed long before the process of analysis created an artificial distinction between their constitutents and components. In actuality, biology, chemistry and physics have always been interconnected, and Cartesian science was mistaken in ever having presumed them to be separate.

In such fields as environmental studies, then, science is rediscovering – and finding confirmation for – the Hermetic premise of interconnectedness. Science is also currently engaged in an essentially Hermetic reintegration and synthesis of its own subdivisions. But science remains reluctant to attempt a similar reintegration and synthesis with other realms of learning, other domains of human creative activity – with philosophy, for example, with organized religion, with psychology or with the arts. Indeed, so far as these other domains are concerned, science, as often as not, stands in implicit or explicit opposition to them. And as long as such opposition continues, knowledge will remain fragmented and fragmentary – will partake more of mere information than it will of wisdom.

This situation is reflected – and perpetuated – by the modern educational system. Ideally, and in theory, the educational system is supposed to foster an increasing understanding of more and more spheres of knowledge. This process is supposed to culminate with the university, which, as its very name implies, encompasses a scope and perspective of 'universal' proportions, embracing the totality of human learning. In practice, however, the educational system leads to just the opposite. The modern university is hardly 'universal'. On the contrary, it is an institution dedicated to the proliferation of specializations. Knowledge is rigorously compartmentalized, each field or discipline being insulated and segregated from all others. This compartmentalization is a legacy, and a reflection, of Cartesian science and rationalistic empiricism.

If science remains reluctant to establish connections with other modes of knowledge, it also remains reluctant to establish connections with something even more important – with a moral framework, with a sense of moral responsibility and a hierarchy of moral values. There are, of course, exceptions – Einstein, for example, and, as previously noted, Robert Oppenheimer. And as science today moves into increasingly uncharted territory, an increasing number of scientists are coming to recognize the need for some moral constraint, some moral imperative. On the whole, however, most would agree with Werner von Braun in his assertion that science 'by itself has no moral dimension', and that even the development of weapons of mass destruction is 'morally neutral'. Thus Professor Lewis Wolpert, distinguished pioneer in embryo research and a prominent member of the Royal Society, can write today of the ethics of 'genetic engineering': 'These are not issues for the scientist but for the public at large . . . Even for the introduction of genes into human cells, it is not for the scientist or the doctors to decide on the wisdom or otherwise of such procedures . . .'[10]

Professor Wolpert almost seems surprised that his position should engender ethical misgivings. Sounding increasingly like Dr Frankenstein, he asks, 'What . . . is wrong with the "supermarket" approach in which genes would be available at a price and with suitable warnings about possible side-effects?'[11] And in his defence, the professor offers an extraordinary modern reformulation of the old Cartesian methodology, condemning synthesis and extolling analysis: 'Any philosophy that is at its core holistic must tend to be antiscience, because it precludes studying parts of a system separately – of isolating some parts and examining their behaviour without reference to everything else.'[12] This is the authentic voice of the contemporary Faust. It is not the voice of Faust as Renaissance magus, who merely – and justifiably – defies the narrow precepts and tenets of Judaeo-Christian morality. It is the voice of a uniquely twentieth-century Faust, who, in pursuit of knowledge rather than wisdom, denies the foundation of our humanity.

I2

THE RETURN TO UNITY

Through Hermetic thought, the Renaissance magus had worked 'magic' in the so-called 'objective' or phenomenal world, the world of measurable quantities and concrete facts. In this world, 'magic' was more or less synonymous with science. Subsequent to the Enlightenment, 'magic' was gradually supplanted by science – or, rather, by the sciences, since each became a realm of research in itself – and the scientist became a magician in his own right. Chemistry, biology and physics all produced their own magicians – then new combinations, such as biophysics and biochemistry, produced higher magic and higher magicians of their own. Manipulation and control of the external world became, increasingly, the domain and prerogative of science. Before the advance of science, the mysteries of the external world appeared to reveal their secrets, or to retreat progressively into metaphysics.

But the Hermetic premise of interconnectedness did not only apply to 'above' and 'below', to macrocosm and microcosm. It also applied to 'inner' and 'outer', to that which was external to man and that which was internal. The Hermetic magus of the Renaissance also worked his 'magic' on the world within – the unmeasurable and unquantifiable dimensions inside the human body and, even more elusive, inside the human mind. In these spheres, he attempted to manipulate such entities as the 'humours', the 'magnetic fluids' and the incubi, succubi or demons credited with the state known as 'possession'. At the dawn of the Enlightenment, these spheres were left untouched by science, remaining the province of organized religion and the arts. Only gradually did science begin to address them, only gradually to seek to annex them as its own domain.

Science initially colonized the inner world through research into magnetism and electricity, both of which, it was discovered, produce discernible effects not only on the human body, but on the human mind as well. Out of this research was to come the discovery of hypnotism, then of depth psychology. And through hypnotism and depth psychology, the men of science would rediscover their Hermetic predecessors. Science would thus come full circle, tortuously finding its way back to the Hermetic principles it had arrogantly discarded.

The inner world today is the acknowledged domain of psychology. In this inner world – the intangible realm of the psyche or of 'mind' (as opposed to the more tangible scientific concept of 'brain') – the psychologist has become another type of the modern magus. Like his Renaissance predecessor – and, for that matter, like the priest – he performs the therapeutic function of confessor. Like his predecessor, or like the priest, he attempts to exorcize the 'demonic possessions' of our own era – guilt, anxiety, obsession, compulsion and all the other disorders officially classified as neuroses or psychoses.

Scientists of the Unconscious

But for most of the nineteenth century, psychology, to the extent that it was deemed a legitimate sphere of study at all, existed as a mere peripheral adjunct of neurology; and psychological disorders were generally attributed to disorders of 'the nerves'. Apart from that, psychology, as we know it today, was accorded attention only by religion and by the arts. Religion, of course, subordinated psychology to its own tenets, its own dogma. To all intents and purposes, then, the artist – primarily the literary artist – was the only real psychologist. Until the emergence of psychology as an autonomous discipline, the artist and the psychologist were, in effect, synonymous. And when psychology did emerge as an autonomous discipline, its founders invariably invoked as their precursors such figures as Sophocles, Shakespeare, Goethe, Balzac, Stendhal and Dostoyevsky.

The artists of the early nineteenth century would sometimes attempt to address psychology from the perspective of Enlightenment science and methodology. In the novel *Elective Affinities* (1809), for example, Goethe employed the scientific concepts of his age as a metaphor to explore the psychological dynamics of sexual attraction and adultery. 'Elective affinity', as understood by the world of Goethe's time, was the explanation for the process whereby the elements of two chemical compounds would, when brought into proximity, 'change partners', so to speak, and recombine to form two entirely new compounds. But Goethe used this chemical analogy only as a metaphor, a symbol, not as a literal explanation. Unlike the scientists of his era, Goethe thought in terms of organism, not mechanism. Even in his scientific inquiries, the significance of any object of study resided for him in its 'relationship to the whole'. In other words, his perspective was precisely that of the Renaissance magus – a perspective that rested on synthesis rather than analysis, on the totality rather than on its constituent parts. It has, of course, become a cliché to describe Goethe as 'the last true Renaissance man'. But if he transplanted a characteristically Hermetic Renaissance orientation into the late eighteenth and early nineteenth centuries, he was also – through his influence on the founders of modern psychology – to project that orientation forward into our own epoch.

That was not to happen, however, until some three-quarters of a century after his death in 1832. In the meantime, the uncharted realms of depth psychology remained uncharted, only reconnoitred and, in an unsystematic way, signposted here and there by other literary figures – E. T. A. Hoffmann in Germany, for example, Edgar Allan Poe in the United States, Gogol and Dostoyevsky in Russia. Enlightenment rationalism accorded little serious attention to the man who today, with the wisdom of hindsight, is generally recognized as the founding father of modern depth psychology. Franz Anton Mesmer was born in 1734 (fifteen years before Goethe), in a small Swabian town on the German side of Lake Constance. His father was gamekeeper to the local bishop, Johan Franz Schenk von Stauffenberg. Having studied philosophy and theology at two Jesuit universities, Mesmer decided against entering the Church and, in 1759, embarked on the study of law at the University of Vienna. A year later, his interests shifted to medicine, in which he earned his doctorate in 1766. The subject of his dissertation was the effect of the planets on the human body. It revealed a substantial debt to Paracelsus.

Paracelsus had suggested that healing could be effected by 'subtle fluids' – what we today might call 'electromagnetic force fields' – passed into the body of the patient. Mesmer theorized that the influence of the stars might be exercised by just such 'subtle fluids', which he saw as 'a physical means of transferring force'. Like Newton, Mesmer saw himself as a scientist, investigating the physical laws of the cosmos; and like Newton's science, Mesmer's was embedded in an essentially Hermetic context and framework. All things, he believed, were interconnected by virtue of being immersed in 'subtle fluids' as if 'in a cosmic sea' – a sea whose ebb and flow, whose tides and currents, produced a demonstrable effect on an individual's health.

In 1767, a year after completing his dissertation, Mesmer began to practise as a doctor. In 1768, he married a wealthy aristocratic widow who owned an opulent mansion in Vienna and gained him access to the most prestigious Viennese society. He quickly became wealthy and successful, hosting stylish gatherings and patronizing the arts, especially music. Mesmer was among the earliest sponsors of Mozart, one of whose operas was given a private performance in his house. He and his wife became close friends of the Mozarts, and occupied a prominent place at the centre of the Viennese *haut monde*.

In 1773, Mesmer was treating a woman whose hysteria took the form of convulsive attacks and other symptoms initially suggesting madness. Her affliction, he observed, recurred in a cyclical pattern, at regular intervals, which led him to suspect a 'tidal flow' in the 'subtle fluids' affecting her condition. Seeking some means of regulating the 'tidal flow', he experimented by applying strong magnets to his patient's body. Whatever the explanation, the experiment proved successful, and the woman's condition, if not completely cured, was dramatically improved. Mesmer had, in effect, discovered some indeterminate relationship between magnetism and the human metabolism. That relationship remains, to some extent, indeterminate today. It is, however, more or less recognized. Thus one can purchase, by mail order or from chemists, magnetic bracelets, belts and sticking-plasters – which can indeed prove effective in alleviating arthritic or rheumatic pain, muscular strain and tension.

But Mesmer also appears to have been something of what we today might call a 'natural healer'. There is ample evidence to attest that he could mitigate localized disorders and discomforts by the application, or 'laying on', of his hands. This led him to conclude that magnetic force could flow not only through magnets as such, but also from one human body to another. He formulated his conclusions, couched in the scientific language of the age, as a theory of 'animal magnetism'.

Whatever the name he attached to it, Mesmer's treatment – whether through his natural aptitude for healing or through some still unquantifiable principle of electromagnetic force – did prove impressively successful in practice. To his rationalistic contemporaries, however, his theory smacked of the 'occult', and he was soon being denounced as a conjuror and a charlatan. In 1778, he was impelled to decamp with his wife from Vienna and establish a new clinic in Paris.

In Paris, as in Vienna, he failed to win much sympathy or support from the scientific establishment, but his clinic became – for a time, at least – hugely successful. Many of his patients came from the aristocracy and the court, and eagerly disseminated word of his cures throughout the upper echelons of the city's society. But he did not disdain to treat 'ordinary' Parisians, at substantially reduced fees. He also came to believe increasingly in the old Hermetic principle of the healing power of music, maintaining that 'animal magnetism' could be communicated by sound. His therapy thus came to be accompanied by increasingly ritualistic elements – music, dim or fluctuating lights, special and often elaborate apparel, a supposedly magnetic wand which bore a suspicious resemblance to the wand of a magician. Although he could not have named it, Mesmer was, in reality, working with the psychological principle which we today would call 'the power of suggestion'. And in the process, he had discovered 'mesmerism', or, as it is known to us,

Heidelberg Castle with gardens created by Solomon de Caus, a close friend of Inigo Jones. This castle was the centre of an active Rosicrucian court until its destruction by Habsburg armies in 1620.

One of the automata designed by Solomon de Caus for the gardens at Heidelberg. From his *Les Raisons des Forces Mouvantes*, 1623.

Door to the
amphitheatre
of eternal
knowledge. A
Rosicrucian
engraving in
*Amphitheatrum
sapientiae aeternae*,
published by
Heinrich
Khunrath, 1609.

PORTA
AMPHITHEATRI
SAPIENTIÆ ÆTERNÆ
SOLIVS VERÆ.

IHVHI ALSON
MINEI

IEHOVA ELOHIM universis, omnibus, cunctis ac singulis liberaliter extrudit; Vbi per Cœlum, Astra, Terram,
superficie Terræ, aut sub Cœlo nascuntur, IEHOVÆ mirabili SAPIENTIAM mirificam in libro Naturæ catholico ac
_MENTIÆ æternæ scintillula sapiens, naturaliter—magicè manifestando infesso docet ac profitetur: quod Patres &
_es & Regiones, pro chartis, fructus immeneri pro libris & Linguis; iam olim secundum longum, latum, altum atq;
_sq studiosi Philosophiæ Theosophicæ solius veræ, fideles, etiam irim hodierno die, autoritate Divina & Sapien-
_TERNÆ, solius veræ, in Vniverso Mundano hoc Sapientær manifestata, cognitionem solidam atq; perfectam, etiam
_bis haurient; Physici genuini verèq Philosophi non opinantes, sed scientes, ita sient: quales; plures hic fa-
_æ speculo, CREATOREM, quæ videlicet æterna eius sit suim Potentia, tum Divinitas, Rom 1. v. 20. quem imisi
_eq; possimus; deoq iisdem, Semper & Vbiq orthodoxi ac Sapientes Philosophari; beneq vivere, & beatè mori
_I LIPS. Theosophiæ amatore fideli, & MED. utriusq Doct. Anno à MASCHIACH nato M.DC.II.

Fighting between Hells Angels and spectators during the Rolling Stones concert at Altamont, December 1969.

Jimi Hendrix, rock shaman, in concert, London, 1967.

The Grateful Dead playing at the Great Pyramid, Egypt, in 1978, in an experiment to discover what ancient energies might be invoked.

The pyramid form of the stage at the first Glastonbury festival. The pyramid was a one-tenth scale model of the Great Pyramid. Such structures were popularly credited with the ability to concentrate cosmic energies.

Mysterious blues guitarist Robert Johnson, some of whose songs are apparently voodoo hymns. Reputed to have been initiated into voodoo. Murdered 1938.

Voodoo, grandfather of the blues. Haiti: ritual dancing in the temple, with the sacred diagram, or *vever*, to Legba, god of the crossroads.

Voodoo: the drawing of the *vever* to the god Agwé, ruler of the seas, before beginning the ritual banquet.

Voodoo: the beginning of the ritual. Drawing the *vever* of Legba around the centre post – the sacred axis which marks the crossroads, the connecting point between the sacred and profane worlds.

'hypnotism'. Having put his patient into a hypnotic trance, he could then plant suggestions in the mind which produced dramatic changes in behaviour. 'In modern terminology, Mesmer . . . [was] . . . probing into the unconscious . . . working in depth psychology and dynamic psychiatry.'[1] He was a pioneer 'in the art of mental healing . . . in the trek toward multilevel studies of personality in the nineteenth and twentieth centuries when the magisterial names would be Charcot and Bernheim, Freud and Jung'.[2]

In 1783, Mesmer founded a secret society called the Société de l'Harmonie. At clandestine meetings, training was offered in techniques for controlling and manipulating the mesmeric trance. Among the members, each of whom had to sign a contract with Mesmer personally, were a number of prominent aristocrats, including the Marquis de Lafayette. In 1784, on a visit to the newly established United States, Lafayette enthused about what he had learned to George Washington, who proceeded to embark on a cordial correspondence with Mesmer. In the meantime, Mesmer's Société de l'Harmonie, based in Paris, had begun to spawn associated 'lodges' – five more in France, one in Italy and one in Switzerland. He himself became increasingly associated with certain of the more Hermetically oriented rites of Freemasonry.

Not surprisingly, Mesmer's involvement with secret societies – his own and others – did little to endear him to the scientific establishment of the time. The ritualized and ostensibly 'occult' aspects of his therapy aroused further antipathy. So, too, did his propensity for extravagant showmanship, for comporting himself with the demeanour and accoutrements of a magus. A backlash inevitably ensued. In 1784, the French government created a committee – headed by Benjamin Franklin, a prominent Freemason and traditionally regarded as the 'discoverer' of electricity – to investigate 'animal magnetism'. The committee, needless to say, found no evidence for the existence of any such phenomenon.

Mesmer's star, and his academic reputation, began to wane. On two occasions, he felt compelled to leave Paris, only to return again. Then in 1799, he published a work on what today would be labelled 'parapsychology'. This effectively shredded the last remnants of his prestige. In 1802, he retired to his native region of Lake Constance, where he lived until his death in 1815. Contrary to popular opinion, he did not die in obscurity, a failure, poverty-stricken and embittered. On the contrary, he maintained a comfortable enough existence, practising medicine intermittently, playing music – and declining invitations to return to Paris, as well as to visit the Academy of Science in Berlin.

In the years that followed, however, he acquired a posthumous reputation akin to that of Cagliostro or the Comte de Saint-Germain – the reputation of a charlatan, a species of sophisticated snake-oil salesman who had flashed briefly through a gullible world, then been discredited and vanished. This image of him was subsequently reinforced by the zeal with which his theory of 'animal magnetism' was embraced by such self-styled latter-day Rosicrucians as Edward Bulwer-Lytton, and by the movement subsequently known as spiritualism. In reality, Mesmer had much in common with his acknowledged precursor, Paracelsus. Like Paracelsus, he was a true pioneer, whose unwarranted vilification owed more to professional jealousy and his own aptitude for making enemies than it did to any crankiness. If his theories were sometimes erroneous, they were no more so than many other scientifically respectable theories of the age. And whatever the flaws in his theories, his practice yielded demonstrable results, alleviated the sufferings of a good many people and blazed an important new trail for humanity's evolution towards understanding of itself and its own mysterious psychological processes.

Mesmer is probably the earliest example of the psychologist as magus or magician. For the better part of the nineteenth century, however, the trail he had blazed was not followed by others. Would-be esotericists and spiritualists mistook his maps for dogma, which they then used to support their own contentions. Literary figures such as Dostoyevsky and Rimbaud blazed their own trails, which were not amenable to scientific systemization. At last, in the 1880s, the phenomenon of 'mesmerism', or hypnotism, was seriously embraced by the eminent French neurologist, Jean-Martin Charcot.

Charcot (1825–93) had received his medical degree in 1853. From 1860 until his death, he was a professor at the University of Paris. Addressing himself specifically to the study of neurology, he was credited with having first distinguished and labelled a spectrum of previously unrecognized neurological diseases. In 1882, he established what was soon acknowledged to be Europe's foremost neurological clinic. Seeking the 'physiological roots of psychic behaviour', Charcot became increasingly interested in the phenomenon of hysteria, and adopted hypnotism as a technique for controlling the previously uncontrollable actions of his patients.

Students from all over the world came to apprentice themselves to Charcot. Among them, in 1885, was a young Austrian Jew, Sigmund Freud. Freud quickly became Charcot's star pupil and chief protégé, and the two men embarked on a progressively more profound study of hysteria through the use of hypnotism. For Charcot, this investigation remained essentially neurological and physiological. Freud, however, began to suspect the involvement of something more. His research came increasingly to suggest the existence of an entire world which lay beyond the rational control, and even the conscious knowledge, of the individual. He labelled this world 'the unconscious'.

Today, of course, the unconscious is widely taken for granted. Unless it erupts dramatically into their everyday lives, most people tend to be more or less blasé about it. It is difficult to convey, therefore, the excitement engendered by Freudian thought at the end of the nineteenth century and the dawn of the twentieth. Since the earliest recorded history, and no doubt before, man had, needless to say, been aware of some unknown territory within himself. He would find himself in this territory, often unexpectedly and disconcertingly, through dreams, through onslaughts of 'madness', through inexplicable fluctuations of consciousness. But he had no adequate vocabulary for dealing with such phenomena, no conceptual framework for interpreting or making sense of them. Did dreams, for example, issue from some source within, or were they visited upon one by some external agency, such as the gods? Were dreams to be taken as significant, perhaps even prophetic, or were they incidental and inconsequential? Was madness something which originated within the individual, or was it inflicted on him from without – whether by demonic forces which invaded and possessed him, or by the circumstances responsible for other disorders and diseases, such as plague? And what did it indicate when an apparently 'normal' and well-adjusted person experienced a terrifying nightmare attesting to violent or criminal propensities, or a sudden bout of hysteria, or an hallucination?

By simply naming 'the unconscious', by offering an explanation of its workings and by positing its existence as a universal attribute of humanity, Freud imparted to it – and to the study of it – a semblance of scientific respectability. The irrational impulses, proclivities and dimensions of the human mind were no longer to be regarded as aberrations, but as a part of mankind's shared heritage, an intrinsic and inherent characteristic of *Homo sapiens*. This was simultaneously reassuring and exhilarating.

For the men and women of Freud's time, the discovery of the unconscious was comparable in magnitude to Columbus' discovery of the Americas, or the exploration of space for our own era. Here, within the human mind itself, lay an entire 'lost continent', a veritable sunken Atlantis, a rich and fertile land to be reclaimed from the sea – precisely like the land reclaimed by Faust at the end of Goethe's poem, in the process Goethe himself had described as symbolizing 'emerging consciousness'. Sated by two centuries of increasingly arid rationalism, individuals flocked to the new domain in quest of everything from self-knowledge to mere novelty. Whole artistic movements – surrealism in France, for example, and expressionism in Germany – plunged into it with a zeal comparable to that of Spanish conquistadores four centuries earlier.

Freud effectively and definitively established psychology as an autonomous discipline, and himself – for a time, at least – as its proprietary magus and high priest. Under Freud, psychology proceeded to evolve a vocabulary, and eventually a theology, of its own, which enabled it to compete with Darwinism and Marxism as a species of new – or alternative, if not surrogate – religion. And the psychologist began increasingly to exercise, along with the traditional authority of the magus, the clerical function of the father confessor.

But if Freud was a self-appointed magus, his orientation was certainly not Hermetic. On the contrary, his approach was thoroughly in accord with Cartesian rationalism. In effect, Freudian psychology was another manifestation of the fragmentation of knowledge – and, in consequence, of reality. And the fragmentation was accentuated and exacerbated by

Freud's misguided insistence on establishing psychology as a full-fledged science, employing scientific methodology and purporting to deal with intangible phenomena as if they were no less concrete and measurable than the data of chemistry, biology or physics. Freudian thought rested ultimately on an irresolvable paradox. It aspired to a supposedly 'scientific objectivity'. But man's only apparatus for knowing anything whatever is his mind, and the mind cannot possibly be 'scientifically objective' about itself. Still less can a mere part of the mind – the part comprising rational consciousness – objectively assess its totality, including those aspects of it which are, by definition, unconscious. Freud was, of course, sufficiently intelligent to recognize this paradox. He chose to pretend, however, that it simply did not exist. Instead, he undertook to establish procedures whereby the psychologist might become a kind of psychic surgeon – analysing, dissecting, fragmenting knowledge and reality into smaller and smaller units, each of them becoming progressively more dissociated from the larger context in which they were embedded. In attempting to legitimize psychology as a science, Freud perpetuated the errors of science itself – and became, like the magicians of science, yet another shaman in a rigorously circumscribed domain, a sphere of study hedged in it by its own dogma.

The most important corrective to Freudian psychology was provided by Freud's own one-time friend, colleague and disciple, the Swiss psychologist Carl Gustav Jung (1875–1961). Like Mesmer, Jung was born on the shores of Lake Constance, but subsequently moved with his family to Basle. His father was a pastor clinging doggedly, but ever more hopelessly, to a faith being incessantly eroded by doubt. As a boy, Jung was fascinated, and often haunted, by religious questions. The spectacle of his father's struggle, however, crystallized his antipathy to the Christian Church as an institution, and to the unquestioning faith it demanded of its congregation. As he matured, he inclined increasingly towards the ancient Hermetic insistence on gnosis, direct knowledge or experience, which rendered all matters of a priori belief irrelevant. 'Belief,' he concluded, 'is no adequate substitute for inner experience.'[3] And: 'The arch sin of faith, it seemed to me, was that it forestalled experience.'[4] As for the dogmatism of Christian propagandists: 'They all want to force something to come out by tricks of logic, something they have not been granted and do not really know about. They want to prove a belief to themselves, whereas it is a matter of experience.'[5]

As a youth, Jung developed an impressive spectrum of interests – in science, philosophy, archaeology, literature and the other arts. At various times during his student years, he was influenced by Schopenhauer, Kant and Nietzsche. The most profound and long-lasting influence upon him, however, was that of Goethe. Although he claimed to find it 'annoying', he was secretly flattered and gratified by a family tradition that he himself was descended from one of Goethe's illegitimate offspring. Throughout his life, *Faust* was to remain for him his most sacred book. He perceived it as a work of Hermetic magic, an alchemical transmutation in itself, and Goethe as an alchemical magus:

I regard my work on alchemy as a sign of my inner relationship to Goethe. Goethe's secret was that he was in the grip of that process of archetypal transformation which has gone on through the centuries. He regarded his *Faust* as an *opus magnum* or *divinum*. He called it his 'main business', and his whole life was enacted within the framework of this drama. Thus, what was alive and active within him was a living substance, a super personal process, the great dream of the *mundus archetypus* (archetypal world).[6]

For Jung, Goethe exemplified the premise enunciated by Hermetic magi of the more distant past, from Paracelsus and Agrippa back to Zosimus and the practitioners of ancient Alexandria – that the alchemist must ultimately be the subject and object of his own experiment, an experiment by which he himself is transmuted. And Jung applied the same principle to his own work as a psychotherapist:

> The psychotherapist . . . must understand not only the patient; it is equally important that he should understand himself. For that reason the *sine qua non* is the analysis of the analyst, what is called the training analysis. The patient's treatment begins with the doctor, so to speak. Only if the doctor knows how to cope with himself and his own problems will he be able to teach the patient to do the same. Only then. In the training analysis the doctor must learn to know his own psyche and to take it seriously. If he cannot do that, the patient will not learn either. He will lose a portion of his psyche, just as the doctor has lost that portion of his psyche which he has not learned to understand. It is not enough, therefore, for the training analysis to consist in acquiring a system of concepts. The analysand must realize that it concerns himself, that the training analysis is a bit of real life and is not a method which can be learned by rote.[7]

Method, however, and especially method learned by rote, was just what Jung himself had first to contend with. Having embarked on medical studies, he quickly gravitated to the then fledgling discipline of what was called psychiatry. In 1900, at the age of twenty-five, he graduated with his doctorate and began to work at a mental hospital in Zurich. Freud, at this point, seemed to offer a welcome new depth to a sphere otherwise devoted to statistical compilations, routine by-the-numbers diagnoses and simplistically mechanistic classifications of psychological disorders. Jung enthusiastically embraced Freud's general concept of the unconscious and, like Freud, saw dreams as a primary route of access into that hitherto uncharted territory. During the ensuing decade, he and Freud became close friends and colleagues. Freud, indeed, regarded the young Swiss doctor as his star pupil, his chief protégé and his heir apparent. They were in constant contact with each other and travelled together on a visit to the United States.

By 1909, however, the relationship between the two men had begun to fray. Jung recoiled increasingly from what seemed to him Freud's excessively mechanistic and materialistic approach. He recoiled from Freud's desperate attempts to cling to rationalism in the name of scientific respectability. He recoiled from Freud's insistence on reducing virtually everything, including spirituality and man's quest for meaning and order, to repressed sexuality. Most of all, he recoiled from Freud's dogmatism. When Freud compromised his own integrity by refusing to accept empirical data which might challenge the tenets of his 'theology', Jung rebelled. A rupture occurred between the former master and pupil, and Jung thereafter went his own way.

It would be neither feasible nor desirable to attempt here a detailed presentation of Jungian thought. Suffice to say that Jung, like Freud, was naturally eager to establish a respectability for psychology; and if respectability could only be attained through scientific legitimacy, he endeavoured to claim something of the sort for his work. Ultimately, however, Jung was less interested in such scientific legitimacy than he was in something much more ambitious, something summarized by one of his own favourite and most frequently reiterated words – integration. In his clinical work, he constantly insisted on the need for the psyche's own integration – for a harmonious balance and equilibrium of the mind's various functions and processes, based on the old Hermetic premise of synthesis as opposed to analysis, of organism as opposed to mechanism, of unity as opposed to fragmentation. If man's mind was his only instrument for confronting, assessing and determining reality, a fragmented mind must necessarily apprehend a reality similarly fragmented. Before reality could be reassembled into a coherent and meaningful whole, the mind had to establish its own wholeness.

By reintegrating the psyche's processes of interacting with reality, Jung therefore endeavoured to reintegrate reality itself – to make it a coherent totality again, as it had been during the Renaissance, rather than a multitude of disparate and disconnected principles, each dominated by a separate discipline. In consequence, Jung's work was soon to take him far beyond the narrow confines of clinical psychiatry. His research radiated out into the arts, into comparative religions, into comparative mythology and into what Western rationalism had dismissed as 'esoterica' – astrology, alchemy and the entire corpus of Hermetic thought. In Hermetic and alchemical symbolism, Jung discovered images, motifs and themes which recurred in sources as disparate as dreams, myths, fairy tales, great works of art, religions across the globe and the fantasies of the clinically 'insane'. Such common denominators offered a profoundly illuminating insight into the most basic and universal patterns of human psychological experience, in accordance with which the mind perennially functioned. For Jung, as for the Hermetic magi of the past, the alchemical process came to symbolize an internal or interior dynamic of change, growth, development and maturation. In Hermeticism, as he later wrote, 'I had stumbled upon the historical counterpart of my psychology of the unconscious.' And thus, if Freud invoked

Darwin, Jung – while not neglecting Darwin – also, and simultaneously, invoked such figures as Agrippa and Paracelsus.

To the consternation and mortification of Freud and other contemporaries, Jung's work began to confront them with serious inquiries into aspects of Hermetic thought which Western rationalism had long ago consigned to the realm of outmoded and quaintly archaic superstition. In consequence, Jung, during his lifetime (and even in certain benighted quarters today), was castigated and repudiated as a 'mystic' – implying that this was something necessarily reprehensible. He exercised a dramatic influence on such literary contemporaries as Joyce, Rilke, Thomas Mann, Hermann Broch, Hermann Hesse and Eugene O'Neill. Among later artists, his impact is particularly discernible in the work of Patrick White, Doris Lessing, Robertson Davies, John Fowles and Lindsay Clarke. But so far as the orthodoxy of the still tentative psychological establishment was concerned, he represented an embarrassment. For the burgeoning ranks of those who sought a scientific legitimacy for psychology, Jung was a heretic at best, an aberration at worst.

In his aspiration to integration, Jung, throughout his life, tried to construct bridges or conduits – between psychology and science, between psychology and organized religion, between psychology and the arts, between psychology and philosophy, between psychology and mythology. He also demonstrated the profound underlying relevance of Hermeticism to our lives, both personal and collective, today. He constitutes, undoubtedly, the supreme twentieth-century example of the psychologist as Renaissance magus. The very breadth and sweep of his scope places him squarely in the tradition of men like Agrippa and Paracelsus – as does his insistence on integration, organism, synthesis, balance, equilibrium, harmony.

But his world is no longer theirs. His world, unlike theirs, has already been fragmented, and his voice issues from only one piece of reality's disassembled jigsaw puzzle. Instead of occupying a position at the centre of a unified dominion of knowledge, he commands respect and authority from just one of the petty fiefdoms into which that dominion has been dismembered. In consequence, he can easily be dismissed or ignored by the self-appointed priests and potentates of other such fiefdoms. And even within his own, that of the supposedly self-contained discipline of psychology, there remains a majority who seek a spurious scientific respectability to which Jung's orientation is inimical.

Thus has much modern psychology, especially in the universities, degenerated into superficiality, into statistical studies of conditioned reflexes and behavioural patterns – into a puerile science of the self-evident. Thus do students train for years in order to become nothing more than sadistic ringmasters in circuses of hapless rodents. Thus are vast sums of money expended to prove that if a dog is punished when it barks and fed when it rolls over, it is more likely to roll over than to bark. And thus does our reality reflect the fragmented nature of our own psyches.

13

THE REDISCOVERY OF HERMETIC
THOUGHT

Jung's unexpected and 'heretical' espousal of Hermeticism imparted a new currency and credibility to it. That, however, did not occur until the twentieth century. And while Jungian thought has begun to trickle as if by drip-feed into the main-stream of Western culture, it remains, even today, largely confined to the periphery. In the meantime, Hermeticism, elbowed aside by the advance of scientific rationalism, had, as previously noted, found a refuge primarily in the arts, and especially in literature. There were, of course, Hermetic adherents in other media – Wagner, for example, Debussy and Marcel Duchamp. But it was chiefly poetry and the novel which, during the nineteenth and twentieth centuries, kept Hermetic tradition alive, and perpetuated the Faustian figure of the Hermetic magus.

By the end of the eighteenth century, a number of literary artists, first in Germany, then in England, had begun to grow disillusioned with the arid intellectualism, the spiri-tual and emotional sterility, of Cartesian thought. By 1800, this disillusion had materialized into full-fledged rebellion. The rebellion was instigated initially in Germany by the young Goethe, by his fellow poet and playwright Friedrich von Schiller and by their colleague, Johann Gottfried Herder. The cultural movement they inaugurated was

known as *Sturm und Drang*, 'Storm and Stress', and repudiated scientific rationalism in favour of the more profound
and internal 'truth' of the emotions. Goethe, Schiller and
Herder produced a dramatic influence on Wordsworth and
Coleridge in England, on Byron and Shelley. Within a
generation, *Sturm und Drang* had blossomed into a still
broader movement, which, under the subsequent label of
'Romanticism', was soon to engulf the whole of European
culture. With Romanticism, Western man rediscovered the
inner world of emotional and spiritual significance which
scientific rationalism had repudiated. And with the rediscovery of this inner world came the rediscovery of
Hermeticism.

In his *Biographia Literaria*, for example, Coleridge extolled
'the vital philosophy of the Sabalists and Hermetists, who
assumed the universality of sensation',[1] and launched into
an impassioned defence of Jakob Böhme. There is no record
of Wordsworth (who was not a particularly voracious reader)
having actually studied Hermetic texts, but he certainly
would have learned of Hermeticism through Coleridge; and
poems such as 'Tintern Abbey' and 'Ode: Intimations of
Immortality' are as perfect an expression of Hermetic
thought as anything in English literature. This applies as
well to certain of Shelley's poems, such as 'Mont Blanc' and
'Hymn to Intellectual Beauty'. Shelley was steeped in
Hermeticism and particularly influenced by the work of the
seventeenth-century Cambridge Platonist, Henry More.
Like virtually every other literary figure of the time, he was
also deeply stirred by the first published part of Goethe's
Faust, and embarked for a time on his own version of the
Faust story. So, too, did Byron in *Manfred*. So did Maturin
in *Melmoth*.

In Germany, Hermeticism was embraced by the fabulist
E. T. A. Hoffmann, as well as by the mystical poet and

philosopher Friedrich von Hardenberg, better known under his pen name of Novalis. But the supreme German exponent of Hermeticism remained, of course, Goethe. Goethe is often described as the 'last Renaissance man', and the description is unquestionably apt. Throughout his life, he was aware of, and exasperated by, the fragmentation of knowledge. Single-handedly, single-mindedly, with a titanic effort that earned him the sobriquet of 'Olympian', he undertook to reintegrate the fragmented world around him. To this end, he established himself not just as a poet, a playwright and a novelist, but also as a painter, a composer, a philosopher, an aesthetician and cultural commentator, a scientist, an economist, a sociologist, a courtier and a minister of state – a veritable Napoleonic figure in the domain of the mind and the spirit. Behind the encyclopedic scope and breadth of his activities lay essentially the same impetus that had motivated Agrippa and Paracelsus – the quest for self-perfection, self-refinement, self-transcendence. Much more so than the secret society, Goethe was the true heir of the Hermetic magus of the Renaissance, working primarily in solitude and making himself the real subject and object of his alchemical experiment. Goethe not only depicted a Faust figure. As his contemporaries recognized, he was himself a Faust figure, whose fictional depiction of the magus was but an adjunct of his own personal Hermetic quest. If Shakespeare had implicitly equated himself with Prospero, Goethe explicitly equated himself with Faust.

From Goethe's time on, the Faust figure was to find his way into works of art in all mediums, sometimes under his own name, sometimes in disguise. Byron's *Manfred* and Maturin's *Melmoth* have already been cited. One might cite also the operas of Bizet and Gounod. One might cite such subsequent works as *The Brothers Karamazov*, with the

Faustian figure of Ivan, or, more recently, Patrick White's *Voss*. But from Goethe's time on, the Faustian magus was to become increasingly equated specifically with the creative artist himself. Thus, by the twentieth century, does the artist appear in Thomas Mann's *Doktor Faustus*, or in Patrick White's novel *The Vivisector*.

Nor was it solely in a fictional context that the artist and the magus became conflated. In what we call 'real life', too, the artist began, like Goethe, to identify himself with the magician, and to regard his work as an operation of Hermetic magic. The creative process and the alchemical process – which had never ultimately been so very different – now came increasingly to be perceived as one and the same. Thus, for example, did Wagner see his work. Thus, too, did Flaubert.

Flaubert is generally acknowledged as the father of the modern novel. But in the anchoritic solitude of his Rouen home, he was also, as much as Goethe, an heir to Agrippa and Paracelsus – relentlessly pursuing a sublime ideal of perfection, shuffling synonyms about like alchemical tinctures in quest of *le mot juste*, combining and rearranging words and images as if engaged in an alchemical operation, and, in the process, entering into his experiment. 'I am Madame Bovary,' he famously declared. He did not mean that Emma Bovary was an expression of himself, a species of self-portrait. He meant that in order to create her, to render her effectively, he had to become her – had to cease to exist himself, refine himself out of existence, and infuse the character he was portraying with the breath, the spirit, the *pneuma* of his own imaginative energy.

But there was more to Flaubert's Hermeticism than this. From the 'ivory tower' of his artistic solitude, Flaubert cast a jaundiced eye out over the increasingly fragmented, increasingly materialistic world of the mid nineteenth century. Organized religion, he concluded (and stated in his letters), had abdicated its responsibility for addressing or conveying the sacred, the numinous, the spiritual. Organized religion had effectively shed its hypocritical pretence to 'holiness' and revealed itself for what it had always in fact been – a social and political institution with a more or less arbitrary moral code promulgated primarily for the sake of civic order and control.

This, of course, was hardly an original or a revolutionary insight. But the corollary attending it for Flaubert was indeed new – or, if not altogether so, at least never explicitly enunciated before. Art, Flaubert asserted in his letters, now had an obligation to fill the vacuum created by organized religion's dereliction. Art had to assume the responsibility abdicated by organized religion and become what organized religion was supposed in theory to be – a conduit or a lens into the sacred. Art was again to become what it had been in the beginning – a testimony and repository of the numinous – and culture was to reclaim the lofty prerogatives of cult. To this end, the work of art was to be invested with the same magical properties, based on Hermetic correspondences, that had characterized the talismanic art of the Renaissance:

> In a work whose parts fit precisely, which is composed of rare elements, whose surface is polished, and which is a harmonious whole, is there not an intrinsic virtue, a kind of divine force, something as eternal as a principle? (I speak as a Platonist.) If this were not so, why should the right word be necessarily the musical word? Or why should great compression of thoughts always result in a line of poetry? Feelings and images are thus governed by the law of numbers, and what seems to be outward form is actually essence.[2]

For Flaubert, then, art entailed, as it did during the Renaissance, a magical process, an alchemical operation, resting on essentially Hermetic principles. And the artist had to be, simultaneously, a high priest and a magus. In order to clarify this point, Flaubert invoked the old Hermetic principle of analogy, establishing a correspondence between the creator of the microcosm and the Creator of the macrocosm: 'An artist must be in his work like God in creation, invisible and all-powerful; he should be everywhere felt, but nowhere seen.'[3]

While Flaubert was drawing Hermetic analogies privately, in his letters, his contemporary, the poet Charles Baudelaire, had been doing so publicly. Baudelaire's famous poem 'Correspondances', evoking that most crucial of Hermetic doctrines and positing 'forests of symbols', remains one of the supremely eloquent Hermetic statements in modern culture, and one which has influenced all the arts to the present day.

> Past Nature's vibrant pillared temple where
> Mysterious words at times may sound, man strays
> Through forests of symbols; as he wanders there
> They watch him with their old familiar gaze.
> As long-drawn echoes merge so far beyond
> In unity profound and faint, as night
> Unbounded, vast, immeasurable as light –
> So perfumes, sounds and colours all respond.
>
> Some perfumes are as sweet as infants' flesh,
> Dulcet as oboes, green as meadows lit,
> And others, rank, in triumph rise afresh
>
> To flaunt the increase of things infinite,
> Like musk and amber, benjamin and incense,
> That sing hosannas to the soul and sense.[4]

A veritable Faust-figure himself, Baudelaire pursued his Hermetic vision in his life as well as in his art, using absinthe, hashish and sundry other forms of dissipation to attain a species of psycho-spiritual 'breakthrough' – a glimpse of the numinous at the very heart of human squalor. In this respect, he, too, conformed to the dictum of Renaissance magi such as Agrippa and Paracelsus, who insisted that the alchemist was himself the 'base metal' of his own experiment. And, just as Agrippa and Paracelsus had done, Baudelaire spoke of Hermes Trismegistus:

> Hermes unknown who always assists
> My schemes, though causing me to fear,
> Changes me into Midas' peer,
> The saddest of the alchemists.[5]

A generation later, Baudelaire was to be outdone in the business of self-transmutation by that child prodigy, Arthur Rimbaud. Rimbaud, too, insisted on the artist venturing into territory abdicated by the priest, and daring to confront the sacred. The poet, he maintained, had to be a full-fledged seer, and, in characteristically Faustian fashion, had to pursue his quest beyond the limits of human experience, into 'the Unknown':

One must, I say, be a *seer*, make oneself a *seer*.
The poet makes himself a *seer* through a long, a prodigious and rational disordering of *all* the senses. Every form of love, of suffering, of madness; he searches himself, he consumes all the poisons in him, keeping only their quintessences. Ineffable torture in which he will need all his faith and superhuman strength, the great criminal, the great sickman, the utterly damned, and the supreme Savant! For he arrives at the unknown! Since he has cultivated his soul – richer to begin

with than any other! He arrives at the unknown: and even if, half crazed, in the end, he loses the understanding of his visions, he has seen them! Let him croak in his leap into those unutterable and innumerable things: there will come other horrible workers: they will begin at the horizons where he has succumbed.[6]

Seeking Hermetic correspondences beyond even Baudelaire's, Rimbaud formulated the 'alchemy of the word', and sought correlations between sounds, as expressed through vowels, and colours: 'I invented the colour of vowels – *A* black, *E* white, *I* red, *O* blue, *U* green – I regulated the form and the movement of every consonant, and with instinctive rhythms I prided myself on inventing a poetic language accessible some day to all the senses. I reserved all rights of translation.'[7]

Perhaps inevitably, experiments of this sort, and the quest for new correspondences beyond the frontiers of rational consciousness, were to lead into sometimes bizarre terrain. The Faustian aspirations extolled by Baudelaire and Rimbaud were eventually to culminate in the so-called Decadence, which imparted its own distinctive stamp to the period now known as the *fin de siècle*. In Oscar Wilde's novel, *The Picture of Dorian Gray*, Dorian Gray is 'corrupted' by the influence of a sinister little 'yellow book'. The book in question actually existed. It was a novel entitled *A Rebours*, written by Joris-Karl Huysmans. In search of ever new and undiscovered correspondences, as well as ever new sensations and experiences, Huysmans' protagonist devises a unique apparatus, a species of organ or piano composed of bottles or vials filled with differently coloured and flavoured liqueurs, each of which corresponds to a different note or chord. By sipping liqueurs in specific sequences, the protagonist contrives to play melodies on his palate, on his gullet, through his metabolism – internalizing, so to speak, the music of the spheres.

Quite apart from such drolleries, Baudelaire's 'forests of symbols' and Rimbaud's 'alchemy of the word' were to spawn an entire aesthetic, an entire school of literature, painting and music, now known as French Symbolism, or *le symbolisme*. Its high priest and arch-magician – often referred to as 'Master' or 'Mage' – was the cryptic and enigmatic poet Stéphane Mallarmé. Each of Mallarmé's few, fastidiously honed and dauntingly opaque works of verse is intended to be a magical spell in itself, an alchemical precipitate, which circumvents the rational faculties and projects the reader's mind into a direct apprehension of 'the Infinite', 'the Ideal', the numinous. In Mallarmé's poetry, the work of art as a work of talismanic magic attains a new psychological dimension.

The Hermetic principles underlying French Symbolism quickly spread. They spread to the other arts, being embraced in the theatre by the Belgian playwright Maurice Maeterlinck, in music by Claude Debussy (who composed scores for works by Mallarmé and Maeterlinck), in painting by Odilon Redon and James Whistler. And they spread abroad. In English, they were espoused by Yeats, Joyce, Eliot and Virginia Woolf. In Germany and Austria, they were espoused by poets such as Hugo von Hofmannsthal, Stefan George and Rainer Maria Rilke, as well as novelists like Franz Kafka, Thomas Mann, Robert Musil and Hermann Broch. In Italy, the principles of French Symbolism engendered the self-styled 'hermetic' school of poets, *ermetismo*, exemplified by Giuseppe Ungaretti, Salvatore Quasimodo and Eugenio Montale. Further east, Russian Symbolism became a major movement in its own right, producing such figures as the poet Aleksandr Blok and the novelist Andrey Bely. Through the cultural dissemination of symbolism, Hermetic thought was to become perhaps the single most important influence on the development of early twentieth-century literature.

The work of art as a work of talismanic magic is illustrated by one of Yeats's most famous poems, 'Sailing to Byzantium'. Thus the opening stanza evokes the 'dross' or 'base' matter of the physical world, a domain pullulating and teeming with cycles of burgeoning and decaying life:

> That is no country for old men. The young
> In one another's arms, birds in the trees
> – Those dying generations – at their song,
> The salmon-falls, the mackerel-crowded seas,
> Fish, flesh, or fowl, commend all summer long
> Whatever is begotten, born, and dies.
> Caught in that sensual music all neglect
> Monuments of unageing intellect.[8]

By the third stanza, the poem has become an incantation, an invocation. The ageing poet appeals to be transmuted out of nature, into the permanence, the durability, the immortality of art:

> O sages standing in God's holy fire
> As in the gold mosaic of a wall,
> Come from the holy fire, perne in a gyre,
> And be the singing-masters of my soul.
> Consume my heart away; sick with desire
> And fastened to a dying animal
> It knows not what it is; and gather me
> Into the artifice of eternity.[9]

In the concluding stanza, the transmutation becomes complete:

Once out of nature I shall never take
My bodily form from any natural thing,
But such a form as Grecian goldsmiths make
Of hammered gold and gold enamelling
To keep a drowsy Emperor awake;
Or set upon a golden bough to sing
To lords and ladies of Byzantium
Of what is past, or passing, or to come.[10]

'Sailing to Byzantium' does not just evoke or depict or describe the process of alchemical transmutation. In itself, it constitutes and demonstrates the process of alchemical transmutation. By its final stanza, in which the world 'gold' occurs no less than four times, the poem itself has become 'golden'. In its very sounds, in its resonating and reverberating sonorities, it has itself become the verbal equivalent of 'such a form as Grecian goldsmiths make/Of hammered gold and gold enamelling'. The poem itself, as well as its subject-matter, has been Hermetically transmuted. A similar process occurs in the poem's companion-piece, simply entitled 'Byzantium'.

In the mid nineteenth century, Flaubert had invoked the Hermetic principle of analogy, of correspondence, of microcosm and macrocosm, and compared the relation of the artist to his work with that of God to the creation. Sixty years later, his assertion was to be echoed, almost verbatim, by a figure of comparable, if not even greater, significance in modern literature. In *A Portrait of the Artist as a Young Man*, Stephen Dedalus, Joyce's protagonist, declares himself explicitly to be a 'priest of the imagination', and arrogates to himself all traditional priestly prerogatives. His commitment to art, like a priest's to his faith, is not a choice, but a 'calling', a 'vocation'. In the course of the text, Stephen, functioning at this point as Joyce's mouthpiece, adumbrates a lengthy and complex aesthetic theory. Deriving in large part from Flaubert, the theory appropriates the accepted language of theology and adapts it to specifically aesthetic ends. Art, for Joyce, becomes a repository and a conduit for 'epiphany', a luminous 'showing forth', a moment of illumination or revelation. And he, too, in words flagrantly echoing Flaubert's, invokes the Hermetic analogy of the artist and the Judaeo-Christian conception of God: 'The mystery of esthetic like that of material creation is accomplished. The artist, like the God of the creation, remains within or behind or beyond or above his handiwork, invisible, refined out of existence, indifferent, paring his fingernails.'[11]

For Joyce, as for Flaubert, God is the supreme magician, the supreme conjuror, using the word – analogous to the Word – to conjure out of nothingness an illusion, or artifice, more 'real' than 'reality' itself. The prototype of the artist for Joyce is his protagonist's namesake, the Dedalus of Greek myth – magus, master craftsman, architect, who first endowed man with wings, and devised and built the labyrinth of Crete as a species of Hermetic microcosm. It is to this figure, this 'fabulous artificer', that Stephen appeals in the famous sentence which ends the book: 'Old father, old artificer, stand me now and ever in good stead.' But behind Dedalus, there looms another, even older tutelary figure, evoked for Stephen, as he comes to recognize and understand his 'calling' or 'vocation', through the Hermetic doctrine of correspondences. The figure conjured before his mind's eye is Thoth, Egyptian god of writing and magic, alter ego of Hermes Trismegistus. In a passage already quoted at the beginning of this book, Thoth's image appears as Stephen stands on the steps of the library at Trinity College, Dublin, watching the flight of birds overhead:

Why was he gazing upwards from the steps of the porch, hearing their shrill twofold cry, watching their flight? For an augury of good or evil? A phrase of Cornelius Agrippa flew through his mind and then there flew hither and thither shapeless thoughts from Swedenborg on the correspondences of birds to things of the intellect and of how the creatures of the air have their knowledge and know their times and seasons because they, unlike man, are in the order of their lives and have not perverted that order by reason.

And for ages man had gazed upward as he was gazing at birds in flight. The colonnade above him made him think vaguely of an ancient temple and the ashplant on which he leaned wearily of the curved stick of an augur. A sense of fear of the unknown moved in the heart of his weariness, a fear of symbols and portents, of the hawklike man whose name he bore soaring out of his captivity on osierwoven wings, of Thoth, the god of writers, writing with a reed upon a tablet and bearing on his narrow ibis head the cusped moon.[12]

Ulysses, like 'Sailing to Byzantium', is a work of talismanic magic, a fastidiously constructed microcosm held together by an all-encompassing network of Hermetic correspondences, for which Joyce also adapts the Christian doctrine of consubstantiation. Each chapter corresponds to an organ of the body. The work as a whole becomes a manifestation of 'Adam Kadmon', the primal man of the Kabbala. And the pun, with its multiple levels of meaning, knits the web of Hermetic interconnectedness even tighter. The same applies to *Finnegans Wake*, the last sentence of which flows into the first. In its very form, *Finnegans Wake* replicates in microcosm the alchemical Uroborus, the snake coiled in a circle and swallowing its own tail.

In a similar way, talismanic magic underpins much of the

work of Thomas Mann. At the end of his 1924 novel, appropriately entitled *The Magic Mountain*, the reader is told succinctly that the story just narrated 'has been neither long nor short, but Hermetic'. One can then look back over the preceding seven hundred odd pages and discern in them a sustained tour de force of Hermetically symbolic correspondences, a complex architectonic structure established on the formal foundations of music and mathematics. A comparable structure characterizes *Doktor Faustus*, published in 1947, which explores, at exhaustive length and breadth, the subterranean Hermetic connections between magic, mathematics, music and the arts in general. *Doktor Faustus* not only constitutes the most important treatment of the Faust story since Goethe's. It also constitutes the definitive application of the story to our own century. In the 1950s, towards the end of his life, Mann returned to a 'nouvelle' originally published in 1911, *Felix Krull*. Although only one volume was completed and published before his death, Mann had intended to expand the 'nouvelle' into a multi-volumed summation of his entire literary career. Not surprisingly, Hermes Trismegistus is repeatedly invoked as the book's presiding tutelary spirit. Again and again throughout the text, Mann stresses the Hermetic doctrine of interconectedness, the relationship between microcosm and macrocosm:

> This interdependent whirling and circling, this convolution of gases into heavenly bodies, this burning, flaming, freezing, exploding, pulverizing, this plunging and speeding, bred out of Nothingness and awaking Nothingness – which would perhaps have preferred to remain asleep and was waiting to fall asleep again – all this was Being, known also as Nature, and everywhere in everything it was one. I was not to doubt that all Being, Nature itself, constituted a unitary system from the simplest inorganic element to Life at its liveliest, to the

woman with the shapely arm and to the figure of Hermes. Our human brain, our flesh and bones, these were mosaics made up of the same elementary particles as stars and star dust and the dark clouds hanging in the frigid wastes of interstellar space. Life, which had been called forth from Being, just as Being had been from Nothingness – Life, this fine flower of Being – consisted of the same raw material as inanimate Nature. It had nothing new to show that belonged to it alone. One could not even say it was unambiguously distinguishable from simple Being. The boundary line between it and the inanimate world was indistinct. Plant cells aided by sunlight possessed the power of transforming the raw material of the mineral kingdom so that it came to life in them. Thus the spontaneous generative power of the green leaf provided an example of the emergence of the organic from the inorganic. Nor was the opposite process lacking, as in the formation of stones from silicic acid of animal origin. Future cliffs were composed in the depths of the sea out of the skeletons of tiny creatures. In the crystallization of liquids with the illusory appearance of life, Nature was quite evidently playfully crossing the line from one domain into the other. Always when Nature produced the deceptive appearance of the organic in the inorganic – in sulphur flowers, for instance, or ice ferns – she was trying to teach us that she was one.[13]

In both his essays and his creative literary works, Mann repeatedly echoes the Hermetic analogy enunciated by Flaubert and repeated by Joyce – the 'word', in lower case, is a microcosm corresponding to the capitalized 'Word', the Logos. The 'word' thus becomes an instrument of creation, a means whereby the artist, like the Judaeo-Christian God, conjures up an illusion more apparently 'real' than so-called 'reality' itself. This analogy has been adopted by a number of other literary figures, especially since the Second World

War. One finds it in the work of Vladimir Nabokov. One finds it in Patrick White. One finds it in the French novelist Michel Tournier. One finds it in Jorge Luis Borges and the phalanx of major writers who have subsequently emerged from Latin America.

In Gabriel García Márquez's famous *One Hundred Years of Solitude*, alchemy and the alchemical process constitute a recurring symbolic motif. One of the central characters, a practising alchemist, is named 'Aureliano', deriving from 'gold'; and this name is conferred on successive generations of the family around which the story revolves. At the end of the narrative, Aureliano Babilonia, the last surviving member of the dynasty, skims through a text which he has just decoded. The text proves to be the very text in which he himself and his family are written. The book (lower-case b) thus becomes a Hermetic microcosm for a greater Book – the Book of History, the Book of Reality (or Hyper-reality), the Book of Life itself. And when the smaller book culminates in an apocalypse, so, too, does the greater Book:

> At that point, impatient to know his own origin, Aureliano skipped ahead. Then the wind began, warm, incipient, full of voices from the past, the murmurs of ancient geraniums, sighs of disenchantment that preceded the most tenacious nostalgia. He did not notice it because at that moment he was discovering the first indications of his own being in a lascivious grandfather who let himself be frivolously dragged along across a hallucinated plateau in search of a beautiful woman who would not make him happy. Aureliano recognized him, he pursued the hidden paths of his descent, and he found the instant of his own conception among the scorpions and the yellow butterflies in a sunset bathroom where a mechanic satisfied his lust on a woman who was giving herself out of rebellion. He was so absorbed that he did not feel the second surge of wind either as its cyclonic

strength tore the doors and windows off their hinges . . .
Macondo was already a fearful whirlwind of dust and rubble
being spun about by the wrath of the biblical hurricane when
Aureliano skipped eleven pages so as not to lose time with facts
he knew only too well, and he began to decipher the instant he
was living, deciphering it as he lived it, prophesying himself in
the act of deciphering the last page of the parchments, as if he
were looking into a speaking mirror. Then he skipped again to
anticipate the predictions and ascertain the date and circumstances of his death. Before reaching the final line, however, he
had already understood that he would never leave that room,
for it was foreseen that the city of mirrors (or mirages) would
be wiped out by the wind and exiled from the memory of men
at the precise moment when Aureliano Babilonia would finish
deciphering the parchments, and that everything written on
them was unrepeatable since time immemorial and forever more,
because races condemned to one hundred years of solitude did
not have a second opportunity on earth.[14]

In one of his short stories, 'Blacamán the Good, Vendor
of Miracles', García Márquez offers a species of coda, or
key, to his work as a whole. The narrator-protagonist here
is an itinerant wonder-worker or miracle-worker, a conjuror,
a trickster, a charlatan – and, metaphorically, the artist as
magician-cum-God:

. . . and who dares say that I'm not a philanthropist, ladies and
gentlemen, and now, yes, sir, commandant of the twentieth
fleet, order your boys to take down the barricades and let
suffering humanity pass, lepers to the left, epileptics to the right,
cripples where they won't get in the way, and there in the back
the least urgent cases, only please don't crowd in on me because
then I won't be responsible if the sicknesses get all mixed up
and people are cured of what they don't have, and keep the

music playing until the brass boils, and the rockets firing until the angels burn, and the liquor flowing until ideas are killed, and bring on the wenches and the acrobats, the butchers and the photographers, and all at my expense . . . The only thing I don't do is revive the dead, because as soon as they open their eyes they're murderous with rage at the one who disturbed their state, and when it's all done, those who don't commit suicide die again of disillusionment. At first I was pursued by a group of wise men investigating the legality of my industry, and when they were convinced, they threatened me with the hell of Simon Magus and recommended a life of penitence so that I could get to be a saint, but I answered that it was precisely along those lines that I had started. The truth is that I'd gain nothing by being a saint after being dead, an artist is what I am . . .[15]

Custodians of the Sacred

The arts, as previously noted, had always addressed themselves to the sacred, to material regarded as the domain of organized religion, and had always, in some sense, employed magical techniques. One need only cite Dante's *Divine Comedy* and Milton's *Paradise Lost*, the paintings of Raphael, the music of Bach and Handel. Even amidst the rationalism, secularism and fragmentation of the Age of Reason, there were individuals like Blake who sought the numinous beyond the perimeters of organized religion; and Shelley, a self-proclaimed atheist, could still express a sense of the sacred in 'Mont Blanc' and the 'Hymn to Intellectual Beauty'. After the mid nineteenth century, however, the artist's endeavour to assume the mantle of magus and priest became, increasingly, a conscious and deliberate policy, a governing aesthetic principle. As Flaubert had urged, the artist began to assume for himself the responsibility organized religion had abdicated – the responsibility for confronting and conveying the sacred. And with this responsibility there went another which organized religion, prior to the Renaissance, had attempted to perform – to bind the fragments of reality together into an all-encompassing unity. With organized religion no longer tenable as an effectively adhesive binding agent, Hermetic thought – the Hermetic principle of analogy and correspondence – provided the most viable alternative. By the dawn of the twentieth century, the need for such an alternative had become ever more desperately urgent.

By the dawn of the twentieth century, the fragmentation of knowledge had attained crisis proportions, and humanity found itself confronted by an acute crisis of meaning. This crisis, with what Hermann Broch called its concurrent 'disintegration of values', obsessively engaged the sensibilities of the epoch's cultural figures. Apart from Jung and other isolated individuals in other spheres, the artists alone seem to have appreciated the magnitude of the dilemma with which Western civilization was confronted. And they were also pervasively aware of something even more alarming. They recognized that – as a consequence of the fragmentation of knowledge and the proliferation of specializations – the four central pillars sustaining the edifice of Western rationalism had begun to crumble.

Prior to the twentieth century, Western rationalism – and, by extension, Western civilization – had rested implicitly on four crucial assumptions. Time, space, causality and personality were all deemed to be fixed, immutable, stable, unshakeable -- unimpugnable certainties on which the foundations of 'consensus reality' could safely be established. Time, space, causality and personality had all been accorded a supposedly 'objective' validity – a validity held to be proof against all 'subjective' and irrational vicissitudes.

Since the advent of human measurement, time had seemed to be effectively 'tamed', rendered quantifiable by clock or calendar. Space, or distance, had seemed similarly subordinated to measurement. And the relationship between time and space, the more or less constant ratio, had apparently reinforced the immutability of both. From as far back as prehistory, journeys had taken essentially the same period of time, on foot, on horseback or by horse-drawn conveyance. By oar or by sail, the ratio between time and space had been similarly determined in crossing a body of water, whether the Mediterranean or the Atlantic. The age of steam, which came with the nineteenth century, modified such ratios significantly, but did not disrupt them.

With the twentieth century, however, established notions of time and space came increasingly to be called into question – theoretically, by various specialized disciplines, and empirically, by developments in technology. Psychology, for instance, destabilized external measurement by demonstrating the importance of internal time and internal space. Time was no longer confined exclusively to the calendar and the clock, space no longer to the ruler and the map. Each now had its own internal continuum, which was accorded a validity comparable to the external. In consequence, external measurements began to emerge not as definitive truths, but as what they had in fact always been – mere conveniences, arbitrary inventions of the human intellect. And even the reliability of such conveniences began to be challenged by science and technology. As a matter of scientific consensus, time and space became fluid, mercurial, uncertain, ultimately relative. What was more, one could experience this relativity in practice. By car, one could cover sixty miles in less time than it once took a man on foot to cover five. By Concorde, one could cover three thousand miles in less time than it took a man in a car to cover three hundred. By Concorde, indeed, one could fly across the globe on, say, the twelfth of a given month and arrive on the eleventh. Measurement thus ceased to be 'objective fact' and became, instead, an adjunct of one's inner state, of technology or of both.

If time and space were disrupted by twentieth-century developments, so, too, was the cherished principle of causality. Since earliest antiquity, the supposed 'law' of cause and effect had seemed inexorable and all-determining. Now this supposedly infallible 'law' began to seem precariously fallible. Psychology, for example, demonstrated the impossibility of quantifying or simplifying human motivation, insisting on an ambivalence in behaviour which defied logical equations of cause and effect. Indeterminacy, unpredictability, random elements and unforeseen mutations began increasingly to enter scientific theory. Moreover, causality had previously been regarded as proceeding or unfolding in a linear progression, 'through' time and space. If time and space were relativized, the temporal and spatial basis on which causality rested was effectively neutralized. As a result, Jung was prompted to posit an entirely new concept, 'synchronicity', to serve as what he called 'an a-causal connecting principle'.

The new instability of causality radiated out to other, more practical spheres. Morality, for instance, rested, to some significant degree, on the premise of punishment and reward. Punishment and reward rested, in turn, on cause and effect. With cause and effect compromised, the underlying laws governing punishment and reward became ever more malleable. Punishment no longer followed ineluctably from transgression, nor reward from virtue. On the contrary, one could hope to elude the punishment one 'deserved', and reap rewards one did not.

If time, space and causality had previously constituted three of the most important pillars of Western rationalist thought, personality had constituted a fourth. Since Aristotle's time, 'character' had been regarded as a more or less fixed quality, the individual as a unique entity. In different ages, character was believed to be determined by different factors – by the alignment of the planets at one's birth, by the four elements of earth, air, fire and water, by the so-called 'humours' in the blood, by fluids. Except in cases of disease, derangement or the occasional religious conversion, however, it was deemed to be stable. Now, the individual character or personality found itself suddenly confronted with the unsettling awareness of its own instability – if not, indeed, of its non-existence. Sociology was presenting personality as little more than an accretion, a layering of conditioned reflexes governed almost exclusively by environment and heredity. Science was offering support for these claims and going even further, reducing character or personality to biology and chemistry, to neural impulses and DNA coding. And psychology, by positing the existence of the unconscious, was administering a *coup de grâce* to personality as it had been conceived in the past. Dreams – previously regarded as something issuing from external sources, as something peripheral to one's identity – were now declared to be as much an expression of one's self as waking consciousness. Madness could no longer be perceived as a random occurrence, nor even as a disease in the conventional sense, but rather as a potentiality dormant within every human being. Man was forced increasingly to recognize that he contained many selves, many impulses, many dimensions, many sub-personalities within him, not all of which could necessarily be reconciled with each other. And character or personality could also be altered or transformed with alarming ease – by drugs, by trauma, by sensory deprivation, by conditioning, by the application of electrodes or a surgeon's knife to the brain. If the individual existed at all, he was revealed as both more and less than he had previously thought himself to be. As a consequence of augmented knowledge, man became even more of a mystery to himself – and, to that extent, more self-alienated.

Earlier and more effectively than anyone else, the twentieth-century creative writer diagnosed, identified and confronted the crisis resulting from the fragmentation of knowledge and from the relativization of time, space, causality and personality. T. S. Eliot's poem, *The Waste Land*, published in 1922, can still be invoked as a summation of twentieth-century experience. In *The Waste Land*, the reader is plunged headlong into the abrogation of time and space, the negation of causality, the disintegration of personality; and there is left only a small lost voice desperately mustering 'these fragments I have shored against my ruins'. In order to convey the immediacy of the modern dilemma, Eliot not only quotes directly from the French Symbolists, but also employs the Hermetic techniques inherited from them. And when he finds his way, both personally and professionally, out of the wasteland, it is once again in accord with Hermetic principles. Attracted in large part by its element of ritual, Eliot converted officially to the Church of England. But such later works as *Four Quartets* are hardly conventionally Christian. On the contrary, they contain numerous lines, numerous complete passages, that might have come almost verbatim from the Hermetic corpus. And they contain other passages which employ the techniques of French Symbolism again to express the Hermetic premise of the interrelatedness between microcosm and macrocosm:

> The dance along the artery
> The circulation of the lymph
> Are figured in the drift of stars . . .[16]

Since the beginning of the twentieth century, the underlying thrust of the arts, and particularly of literature, has been largely determined by two objectives, either explicit or implicit. The first has been to confront, and make meaningful in human terms, the relativization of time, space, causality and personality. The second has been to reintegrate, through essentially Hermetic principles, the fragmentation of knowledge into a new and all-encompassing unity – a unity which, again, is meaningful in human terms.

And yet the effort has proved for the most part quixotic because art itself has been shunted out of the mainstream of Western civilization. Art itself has become marginalized, reduced to the status of one fragment among many, and, in the eyes of the majority, more peripheral than most. In the 'ivory towers' of the universities, moreover, art too has been fragmented by rationalist methodologies. Under such names as the 'New Criticism', or 'deconstructionism', the study of a novel or a poem has been twisted into a form of pseudo-science. The work of art will be dissected and analysed as if it were a mere mechanical contraption – a dead construct of words and images, to be dismembered and scrutinized piecemeal, like the organs of a corpse in an autopsy. What the artist is actually trying to communicate will be deemed incidental or superfluous.

In consequence, people hungry for meaning, for purpose and direction in their lives, will turn to Eastern thought, will gravitate to sects or cults, or doggedly and masochistically slog through hundreds of pages of Gurdjieff, Blavatsky or Rudolf Steiner – not realizing that what they are seeking lies in fact under their noses. For such people, the arts are a remote and self-contained domain, a sphere of specialized and rarefied academic study which has no relevance whatever to their lives. It will not occur to such people to see in the arts what Flaubert intended – a repository and conduit for the sacred. Neither will it occur to such people to ask so impertinent yet simple a question as who is more 'spiritual' – Rilke or the Pope? Quite patently, Rilke is more 'spiritual' – just as Nikos Kazantzakis, author of *The Last Temptation*, is more 'spiritual' than the self-proclaimed pious Christians who condemned his book and the film based upon it by Martin Scorsese.

PART TWO

14

THE MAGIC CIRCLE

In its broadest sense, magic is 'the art of making things happen'. In a broad sense, therefore, magic can be seen as a metaphor describing the dynamic relationship between human consciousness or will and everything that lies beyond it – events, circumstances, objects, other people. Magic implies at least some element of control, either through guidance or manipulation. It implies, that is, a technique whereby reality is encouraged, persuaded, induced or coerced to conform to certain specific objectives. Magic, in short, is the process of exploiting the malleability of reality, and of shaping it – or alchemically transmuting it – in accordance with given purposes or goals.

The psychological and moral orientation with which one embarks on the process of shaping or transmuting reality will determine whether the magic one employs is, according to medieval and Renaissance definitions, 'white' or 'black', 'clean' or 'unclean', 'sacred' or 'profane'. At risk of over-simplification, it could almost be said that humanity, in effect, can be divided into three general categories – 'sacred' magicians, 'profane' magicians and victims.

The magician, whether sacred or profane, assumes an active role in relation to the world he inhabits, and transforms it accordingly. The victim, in contrast, remains passive, a powerless slave to circumstance. It should go without saying, of course, that these roles are not immutably fixed, nor are they very necessarily consistent. One can be, so to speak, a profane magician in certain circumstances, a sacred magician or a victim in others. Regrettably, however, most human beings, throughout most of their lives, are, in fact, victims. They do not shape, still less create, their realities. On the contrary, they accept their realities at second-hand – and, by so doing, become slaves to their realities.

This apparently controversial assertion can be clarified by a simple analogy, to that of the alchemist in his laboratory. Metaphorically speaking, the alchemist in his laboratory can also be the scientist conducting experiments with nuclear fission or fusion. He can be each of us, individually or collectively, experimenting with the elements in the laboratory of our individual or collective lives. He can be Western civilization as a whole, in the laboratory of the elaborate human experiment more generally known as 'history' or 'culture'.

The alchemist in his laboratory, performing his experiments with elements and compounds, with animals, vegetables and minerals, can employ the techniques of either sacred or profane magic. When viewed externally, the process may appear the same. Seen from within, however, the dynamics of each will differ significantly.

The profane magician or alchemist endeavours to keep himself aloof and immune from his experiment. He endeavours to manipulate it as though with tongs, from without. He endeavours to exercise an absolute control, while remaining himself untouched and unchanged. From his detached position, he can presume to coerce the components of his experiment, even to employ 'unnatural' procedures to bend them as he wishes. Disregarding the strain he imposes on reality, he will bend it forcibly to his will, often having recourse to procedures which run counter to those of nature. He will ignore, perhaps even disrupt, the underlying

Hermetic principle of harmonious interconnectedness. And because he keeps himself at an apparent distance from his experiment, he can cherish the illusion that whatever energies and powers he employs or unleashes will not affect him personally.

Thus do we invent machines – not so much to save time as to save 'dignity', to keep our hands clean, to insulate ourselves from what Yeats called the 'mire and blood' of the human condition. Thus do we employ technology – to hold a potentially threatening reality at bay, and, at the same time, to insulate ourselves from it. And we tend to lose sight of the fact that the very devices we design to protect us also serve to isolate us. We become like magicians conjuring up powers from within the protective precincts of a magic circle. As long as it remains intact, the circle may indeed keep the powers invoked at bay. But the circle also imprisons us, restricts our capacity to interact with the world beyond it. In seeking to avoid risk, we incur the greatest risk of all – that of relinquishing our humanity.

The sacred magician or alchemist endeavours, in contrast, to become what the Renaissance magus maintained he must – the subject and object of his own experiment. He endeavours to immerse himself in it, to experience it, so to speak, from within – to let his experiment become a mirror for his own transformation, and his own transformation a mirror for his experiment. Instead of dominating things from without, he attempts to guide them from within – to become so deeply a part of his own experiment that when he moves, it moves with him. He submits himself to change, with all the risk that may entail. Yet because he is himself the subject and object of his own experiment, he will avoid coercion, avoid violence, avoid the unnatural. Thus, as has been noted, the Renaissance magus would compare his activity to that of the botanist or the gardener, operating within the natural order – helping nature along in her work, coaxing her, nurturing her, gently bringing her own latent potentialities to fruition. To quote Paracelsus again, 'the Alchemist . . . brings forth what is latent in nature . . .'[1] Or, to quote Giambattista Della Porta, writing a few years after Paracelsus' death: 'The works of Magick are nothing else but the works of Nature, whose dutiful hand-maid Magick is . . . as in Husbandry, it is Nature that brings forth corn and herbs, but it is Art that prepares and makes way for them.'[2]

How do these metaphorical parallels translate themselves into more familiar psychological terms? The answer to that question, at least in part, can be illustrated by the concept of what we call personal 'growth' or 'maturation'. But what, precisely, do we mean by 'growth' and 'maturation'? In reality, one can 'grow' or develop in two basic ways.

In accordance with what has been defined here as profane magic, one can grow, as it were, by accumulation. In other words, one's ego, so to speak, remains essentially unchanged, retains essentially the same configuration. It simply takes more and more into itself – so many sexual conquests, so many cities or countries visited, so many adventures experienced, so many possessions acquired. By virtue of such accumulation, the ego becomes, metaphorically speaking, progressively larger, progressively more inflated; but it preserves its original configuration, in accordance with which experience is made to conform. On the other hand, one can attempt not to absorb experience, but to be absorbed by it. Instead of 'collecting' sexual conquests or places visited, one can allow oneself to be modified or transformed by each of them. Each new experience or adventure is internalized, so that the ego's basic configuration is constantly mutating, constantly changing shape, constantly adapting to the circumstances or context in which it is embedded. Size and quantity become less important than transformation. The tourist, for example, becomes the pilgrim.

By these distinctions, the profane magician can be seen as a species of storage cell – accumulating more and more power, more and more energy within himself until, finally, something must give way. Such a process is exemplified by an individual like Adolf Hitler. The sacred magician, on the other hand, functions as a conduit or a lens, reflecting or refracting power *through* himself to something beyond. Such would be the case of individuals undergoing a traditional mystical conversion – St Francis, for example, or the Buddha. Such would also be the case, perhaps, of a figure like Gandhi, or Martin Luther King. Such would be the case of any genuine healer.

If the metaphorical distinction between sacred and profane magic can have psychological implications, it can have profound theological implications as well. For Hermetically oriented Christians, it can define the underlying premise of the Incarnation. Thus was it regarded by Charles Williams, the novelist and theologian whose friends included C. S. Lewis and J. R. R. Tolkien, and who is credited with the conversion to Anglicanism of T. S. Eliot and W. H. Auden.

For Williams, as well as for other Hermetic thinkers, the God of the Old Testament can be perceived as a kind of profane magician, or profane alchemist. In this capacity, he precipitates the world as a form of alchemical experiment from which he himself stands aloof, remote, detached and immune. From his transcendent position, he orchestrates events like a puppet master or stage-manager, intervening quite literally as a *deus ex machina* when the fancy seizes him – to part the Red Sea, for example, or to impose an arbitrary test on Job, or to invoke a flood when he loses patience. He traffics in majesty and power, in

Cecil B. DeMille spectaculars, and commands obedience in often whimsical ways, for whimsical reasons. Like the profane magician, he manipulates his experiment from without, handling his creation as if with tongs.

In Christian tradition, the God of the Old Testament incarnates himself as man. He is thus, according to Williams, like the alchemist entering his own work, becoming the subject, object and, if necessary, victim of his own experiment. Instead of controlling from without, he endeavours to guide from within – while, at the same time, experiencing at firsthand, in his own corporeal being, the human condition he has created. In effect, he participates in his creation in order that that creation may have a soul of its own – may cease to be merely the toy of an omnipotent creator and assume for itself the responsibility of free will and ethical choice. In order thus to endow his creation, he must even allow himself to be martyred by that creation, should this be the course the creation dictates for him. Thus does the alchemical experiment come to fruition and fulfilment, even though it may entail the transformation, and immolation, of the alchemist himself.

From this theological point of view, then, the purpose of the Incarnation is to endow creation with a soul of its own – in other words, with the free will which manifests itself through the sacrifice of its creator. Herein lies the New Covenant and the possibility of redemption. Creation is no longer the puppet theatre of the Old Testament, in which the puppet master can meddle as he wishes, orchestrate events or impose arbitrary rules. On the contrary, creation is now endowed with the freedom, and the attendant responsibility, to account for itself.

But whether one accepts this theological position or not, there is scant evidence to suggest that humanity has made much constructive use of the free will, the redemption or the possibility for redemption conferred upon it. Some two thousand years after the events that marked the advent of the supposed New Dispensation, humanity does not appear to be significantly more redeemed than it was before. Instead of aspiring to Thomas à Kempis' *Imitation of Christ*, Western man – from the dawn of the Christian era, as much as before – has aspired to an imitation of Simon Magus; and he has used Hermetic thought in a fashion that makes not Jesus, but Faust, his 'role model'. The history of Western civilization is, ultimately, the history of humanity's aspiration to Fausthood. Faust is the supreme archetype and avatar of Western man. But the Faust of the sixteenth century, as already noted, sought knowledge beyond the constraints of Christian morality. The Faust of the twentieth century seeks knowledge – and power – beyond the constraints of all morality, all human hierarchies of value. If the forces unleashed by the sixteenth-century Faust could damn him by Christian standards, the forces unleashed by his modern equivalents threaten much more terrifying, and much more tangible, forms of damnation.

Metaphorically and often literally, the medieval and Renaissance magician would draw a magic circle around himself. From within this protective perimeter, he would then, as he believed, proceed to conjure up, channel and control powers or forces from celestial or infernal sources. Such forces were regarded as potentially dangerous. There are numerous folk-tales and legends of an over-ambitious magician invoking powers he cannot effectively control – powers which breach his protective circle and destroy him. But even if the magician does retain control over the forces he has invoked, the very circle that affords him protection also imposes on him a restriction. He cannot step outside his circle without risking some harm from the energy he has loosed. And the magic circle thus becomes a prison, insulating but also isolating the magician from the reality that lies beyond it – a reality in which newly unleashed and potent principles now move unpredictably at large.

Is this not a metaphor for our civilization as a whole? For our culture, technology and its products constitute a form of magic circle. From within the supposed safety of this circle, we invoke powers with apocalyptically destructive potential. We pollute our world with plastics and radiation, with toxic chemicals and industrial waste. From within the supposed safety of our circle, we arrogate to ourselves the power of godhood and perpetrate experiments which nature herself does not – in genetic engineering, in nuclear fission and fusion, in the development of biological and chemical weaponry. Like Dr Frankenstein, we create monstrosities. And like the careless magician of those seemingly quaint and irrelevant fables, we all too easily lose control of the forces we conjure up – as happened, for example, at Chernobyl. We then cease to be magicians of any kind, sacred or profane. We all become victims.

But even if we retain control, the magic circle of technology, which is supposed to shield us, constrains us. Technology extends the strength and reach of our arm, but not the wisdom with which we exercise it. Thus we delude ourselves into thinking we enjoy greater freedom when, in fact, we voluntarily submit to an ever-greater subjugation. We place ourselves, with ever-increasing helplessness, at the mercy of increasingly autonomous mechanical 'systems', from air-conditioning and artificially regulated environments to computerized networks of global scope. And in our dependence on technology, we become more and more impotent, surrendering more and more power, more and more responsibility. A modern city is less equipped to deal with an unexpected heavy snowfall than eighteenth-century Petersburg or Berlin. A glitch or a virus in a computer can create havoc in individual lives, can shake banks and multi-national corporations, can come close to precipitating a nuclear conflict. Already serious warnings have gone out concerning computer terrorism: a team of hackers could bring an entire country to a halt, or to ransom.

In the process, of course, we become, as already noted, progressively divorced and dissociated from the reality around us. We become over-cozened, overprotected, and less disposed or equipped to accept responsibility for our own lives. We incessantly blame others and rush to the courts for compensation when the vicissitudes of reality intrude incommodiously on our cocooned existence. We take umbrage at the slightest friction and sandpaper the edges of social interaction with the grotesque language of 'political correctness'. We entrust more and more authority to dark-suited 'specialists', who hover incessantly around us, waiting for something to go wrong in our lives, waiting to prey on our misfortunes. And in so doing, we become ever more vulnerable to manipulation.

Such manipulation constitutes a means of 'making things happen', and thus a form of magic. But the magic involved is something very different from the sacred magic of the Renaissance's Hermetic practitioners. It amounts, rather, to what Agrippa condemned as mere petty sorcery, practised by a multitude of petty Faust figures in their own circumscribed and fragmented domains. But if such magic is petty and profane, it is none the less dangerous, and certainly widespread. And we are all, potentially, if not already, its victims.

15

MUSIC AND MAGIC

In January 1965, Richard Nixon was inaugurated president of a country more dangerously divided than at any time since the Civil War of just over a century before. In April of that year, the number of American combat deaths in Vietnam exceeded those suffered in Korea. On the weekend of 15–17 August, a congregation of nearly half a million hippies, yippies, music devotees, students and professors from scores of colleges and universities, adherents of the so-called 'counter-culture' and a multitude of others converged for a highly publicized music festival at Woodstock, New York. The gathering assembled in the name of a plethora of causes, but its dominant theme was opposition to the conflict in Vietnam. At the time, it seemed to herald, even for the most dour pundits, some species of 'revolution' in American society and culture. For self-proclaimedly 'patriotic' defenders of truth, justice and the American way, it engendered alarm verging on panic, ostensibly signifying the eruption of anarchy, chaos and sinister 'dark forces'. For the more gullibly optimistic, it portended a new dawn for civilization. The dire and roseate expectations at both extremes were, needless to say, doomed to be thwarted. But even today, Woodstock stands as one of the landmark events of the 1960s – one of the defining moments of the era, perhaps indeed the era's apotheosis.

The repercussions of Woodstock reverberated around the world. In California, previously the vanguard of so much social and political protest and change, people felt upstaged. With the intention of giving America's west coast a 'Woodstock of its own', a music festival of comparably massive scale was organized. Attempts to stage it at a site within San Francisco – in Golden Gate Park, for instance – were frustrated, and the event was eventually fixed for 6 December at Altamont Speedway, a desolate and denuded auto racetrack in the bleak countryside on the city's outskirts. A number of west-coast bands were assembled, including the Jefferson Airplane and the Grateful Dead. The star attractions, however, were to be Mick Jagger and the Rolling Stones, who had just completed a tour of the United States. The Stones announced their preparedness to participate in a free concert because, as they said, 'that was the spirit of the times'.[1] Mick Jagger declared their objective of 'creating a kind of microcosmic society which sets an example for the rest of America as how one can behave in large gatherings'.[2]

For some time previously, there had been recurring friction between California students, bohemians, hippies and yippies, all opposed to the war in Vietnam, and the Hell's Angels – who, insofar as they were political at all, cultivated a rabidly right-wing, even neo-Nazi or pseudo-Nazi image. Subsequent to the event, at least one of the Stones, Keith Richards, denied that his group ever invited the Angels to the festival. He attributed their presence to an invitation from the California-based 'acid-rock' band, the Grateful Dead.[3] Ultimately, however, the source of the invitation is academic. What matters is that the Angels were invited. They were invited in the unlikely capacity of marshals, charged with establishing and maintaining order over the vast throng. And according to the pre-festival 'hype' and rumour circulating across America, it was the Stones who were credited, whether erroneously or not, with the declared intention of healing the rifts between the Angels and their former adversaries – of using music as a form of therapeutic magic which might 'exorcise' the 'negative energy' suffusing the California air like ozone, and of ushering in a new dispensation of social harmony.

Since the 'summer of love' at Woodstock, the atmosphere in America had indeed changed. When Nixon ordered the illicit invasion of Cambodia, the war in Vietnam assumed a new dimension. Attitudes towards the conflict hardened and became more polarized. In November, a quarter of a million protesters marched on Washington, and the demonstration was markedly angrier, markedly more militant, markedly less disposed to 'universal love' and 'flower power' than those in the past. Across the United States, the atmosphere had become more sombre, more potentially explosive. And in California particularly, the atmosphere was not just edgy and volatile, but charged with an added element of paranoid terror.

On the night of 9–10 August, a week before Woodstock, seven people – including Roman Polanski's wife, the pregnant young actress Sharon Tate – had been gruesomely slaughtered in Beverly Hills. But while there were suggestions of some sort of 'ritual killing', there was no reason at first to associate this atrocity with the 'counter-culture'. In any case, California was three thousand miles away from Woodstock. The murders, therefore, had had little effect on the mood of the festival in New York. In October, however, after a prolonged investigation, Charles Manson and his entourage of disciples had been arrested for the crime. For the duration of the autumn, the media had been filled with lurid stories about Manson's so-called 'family' and their bizarre alternative lifestyle. On 5 December, the day before the festival at Altamont, a California grand jury had begun to hear its first evidence on the Manson case. The proceedings were supposed to be secret; but prominent headlines that evening reported the 'Tate killers' to have been 'wild on LSD'. A link had thus been established with the 'counter-culture', whose impending festival at Altamont was the other leading story of the day. In the public mind, the two stories immediately became conflated; and the festival, by association, began with the shadow of the Manson case casting an ominous pall over it.

The mere presence of the Rolling Stones reinforced the sinister association. In October, when Manson's name first broke in the headlines, the Stones had been in Los Angeles to record the album *Let It Bleed*. This album quickly established them as the 'hardest-edged' rock group on the musical scene. Their song, 'Street Fighting Man', had become what one commentator described as 'an anthem for the era'. The Stones themselves were described in the media as 'an intimidating brooding coven'.[4] The mere use of the word 'coven' had encouraged association, in popular consciousness, with the likes of Manson's 'family'. So, too, of course, had such songs as 'Sympathy for the Devil'.

The Stones seemed wilfully oblivious to the change in America's atmosphere and to the impact of the image they projected. So, too, did their fans. But in expectation that the Altamont festival would be as memorable and 'historic' an event as Woodstock, film-makers were already busy. Cameras recorded the prelude and preparation for the occasion – the gradual assembly of the crowd of some 300,000 people, the bustle behind the scenes, the rehearsals, the chat and banter in the caravans which served as dressing-rooms – as well as the performances of the participating bands. The 1970 documentary *Gimme Shelter* constitutes a visual chronicle of what ensued.

To this day, it remains unclear what the role assigned to

the Hell's Angels was actually supposed to entail. The film shows them doing nothing more than forming a slack protective cordon around the stage – to prevent fans from swarming over the performers – and getting systematically drunk. And from the very beginning of the concert, long before the Stones themselves appear, there is violence. Angels are seen flailing at people with weighted pool cues. Pathetic calls are issued, with increasing frequency, over the PA system for fans to 'stop hurting each other'. Other calls are issued for a doctor. Scuffles continue to erupt around the stage and the music is constantly interrupted. At one point, there are nearly two hundred people on the stage simultaneously. Fighting around the stage spills on to the stage itself. A member of the Jefferson Airplane is punched in the face by an Angel and knocked unconscious.

The Stones do not make their appearance until nightfall. When they do, Mick Jagger looks distinctly apprehensive. His first words are to exhort the crowd to 'just keep cool down the front there . . .' In a somewhat less than inspired choice of material, the group then launch into 'Sympathy for the Devil'.

At this point, fighting erupts in the front ranks of the crowd and Jagger stops singing. The other members of the group continue to play almost desperately, as if not knowing what else to do, while the fighting turns into a massive brawl and Angels invade the stage. Jagger then asks Keith Richards to stop playing. Richards abruptly strangles his guitar and Jagger appeals frantically for calm:

'Hey! Hey! People, sisters, brothers and sisters, brothers and sisters, come on now, that means everybody, just cool out! Will you cool out, everybody! I know! I'm here! Everybody be cool now, come on, all right . . . Are we cool?'

And as the tumult gradually subsides, he adds, with a

nervous little laugh, that 'something very funny happens when we start that number'.

The Stones embark on 'Sympathy for the Devil' again from the beginning. This time, they manage to get several verses into it before a roar occurs off camera. Jagger and the band continue, but Keith Richards turns in the direction of the sound, looking seriously worried. A mêlée develops in the crowd. Jagger continues to sing and cavort around the stage for a moment longer, but is then stopped in his tracks by an Angel hurriedly approaching him and saying something into his ear. His face drops, looking suddenly haunted and haggard. Half-heartedly, he begins to dance again, then stops abruptly, looking out over the crowd with an expression of helplessness. It is clear that he has utterly lost control of his audience and has no idea what to do. The other Stones tentatively embark on another number while Jagger mutters calming words to the beat of the music. Then everything comes to a halt as an unconscious man is carried off by a party of Angels.

'Ah, people!' Jagger appeals. 'Who's fighting and what for? Why are we fighting? Why are we fighting? We don't want to fight. Come on! Who wants to fight? Every other scene has been cool!'

At this point, Keith Richards has manifestly had enough. He can see that philosophical exhortations to brotherhood are not going to be sufficient. Snatching the microphone from Jagger, he points angrily at a figure in the crowd and snaps:

'Look! That guy there! If he doesn't stop it, man . . . ! Listen! Either those cats cool it, man, or we don't play!'

A journalist describing the scene subsequently wrote: 'As Jagger sensed his loss of control and made requests for calm, Richards knew that if they hesitated or tried to reason with a rock and roll crowd they were lost. He strode to the microphone, pointed directly at a Hell's Angel in the crowd, who was beating an innocent bystander and shouted . . .'[5]

As more calls are issued for doctors, Jagger reclaims the microphone and issues another desperate plea:

'I don't know what's going on, who's doing what, it's just a scuffle. All I can ask you, San Francisco, is like, the whole thing, this could be the most beautiful evening we have for this winter, you know, and we're really . . . Don't let's fuck it up, let's get it together. I can't do any more than to just ask you, to beg you, to just keep it together. You can do it! It's within your power! Everyone! Everyone! Hell's Angels! Everybody! Let's just keep ourselves together. You know, if we are all one. Let's show we are all one!'

As a semblance of order is re-established, the Stones embark on 'Under My Thumb'. They get a few verses into it. Looking nervously to his left, Jagger has just sung and repeated the words, 'I pray that it's all right,' when a surge runs through the crowd. A space suddenly opens around a black youth in a light olive-green suit, on whom the hand of a Hell's Angel appears to descend twice, in a swift flashing arc. The youth's girlfriend – blonde, in a white crochet top and black miniskirt – screams. Other Angels swoop upon the youth and drag him quickly off to the left, out of camera. Most of the surrounding spectators remain motionless, either oblivious to what has just happened or paralysed by it. To the Stones on stage, the incident has only appeared to be another scuffle. Jagger loses patience, stops singing and barks:

'We are splitting, man, if those cats don't stop beating everyone up . . . I want them out of the way . . . !'

There is loud talk of someone having a gun. Here, however, the film cuts abruptly to an editing room, where close-ups are being run repeatedly of what has occurred. In these close-ups, the hand of the Hell's Angel, descending in its swift arc, is clearly seen to be wielding a knife.

Unaware that a murder had been committed, the Stones continued to perform, launching – with another tactful choice of material – into 'Street Fighting Man'. While they remained on stage, the other rock groups, in a military-style operation, were evacuated by helicopter. The Stones played for nearly another hour. Only later did they learn what had happened. In addition to the victim knifed on camera, there were, in fact, three other deaths at Altamont. There were also four births.

In the aftermath, of course, recriminations flew, and the Stones received more than their fair share. As Keith Richards subsequently said, 'We just walked into a situation. It happened to be 1969 in America.' But there was nevertheless more to it than that. According to *Newsweek*: 'After that bloodstained tour the Stones' music seemed to become a mythic force unto itself – ecstatic, ironic, all-powerful, an erotic exorcism for a doomed decade.'[6]

Perhaps the most revealing summation was offered by the late Jerry Garcia, guitarist with the Grateful Dead: 'it was the music that generated it . . . I realized when the Rolling Stones were playing at the crowd, and the fighting was going on and the Rolling Stones were playing "Sympathy for the Devil", then I knew that I should have known. You know, you can't put that out there without it turning up on you somewhere.'[7]

With an eloquence typical of the San Francisco 'scene' at the time, Garcia has put his finger on something important. *Gimme Shelter* offers more than just the lurid spectacle of a murder on camera. It also constitutes an illuminating parable. According to his biography, Keith Richards, at Altamont, was high on LSD, cocaine, opium and cannabis.[8] Whether this is true or not, he and the other members of the group were unquestionably high on adrenalin. In their 'psyched-up' state, they were all flagrantly performing an act of ritual shamanistic magic, with the stage serving as the equivalent of the sorcerer's magic circle – the perimeter from within which he performs his invocation. *Gimme Shelter* thus depicts a modern-dress variation of the medieval and Renaissance story, in which the magician loses control of the forces he has conjured up.

Voodoo and Rock Music

This book has already charted the association, dating from the earliest recorded history, if not before, of magic with music. The oldest music, it will be recalled, was associated with 'primitive', shamanistic and pre-Hermetic magic. Hermetic magic is reflected by the tradition extending from immediately pre-classical times – the Pythagorean 'music of the spheres' – through such figures as Bach and Mozart, Wagner, Mahler and Arnold Schönberg. This tradition has, of course, been exhaustively studied by musicologists. Its Hermetic underpinnings have been explored by other writers as well – by the Cuban novelist and musicologist Alejo Carpentier, for example, and, perhaps most profoundly of all, by Thomas Mann in *Doktor Faustus*.

Popular music, however, is an altogether different matter. Indeed, prior to the twentieth century, popular music is difficult to define. There are, of course, many folk-songs – the so-called Border Ballads, the Child ballads and those associated with Thomas the Rhymer – which are steeped in a pre-Hermetic pagan magic. As recently as the nineteenth century, the melody of 'Danny Boy', also known as 'Londonderry Air', was, according to legend, entrusted in a dream to a sleeping fiddler or harpist by the Sidhe, the faery people. *The Doubleman*, by the Australian novelist C.J. Koch, deals extensively with such so-called 'faery music' and its impact on the 'occult revival' of the 1960s.

For the most part, however, popular music, prior to the twentieth century, meant other things, at least in Britain and the United States. There were, for example, the ditties, shanties, anthems and marching songs of specific periods – 'The British Grenadiers', for example, David Garrick's 'Hearts of Oak', 'Yankee Doodle', 'The Girl I Left Behind Me'. In America during the mid nineteenth century, there were the ballads of the West, such as 'Red River Valley', and the perennially popular songs of Stephen Foster. There was the music – sometimes jaunty, sometimes powerfully majestic, sometimes poignantly haunting – of the American Civil War. Finally, of course, there was the ever more popular music of the operetta – Gilbert and Sullivan, for instance – and the music-hall. Apart from whatever happened to make it 'catchy', however, there was nothing deliberately or intentionally magical about any of this music. Certainly there was no self-consciously magical objective on the part of its composers.

With the invention and dissemination first of the phonograph, then of radio or wireless, popular music as we understand it today began to come of age. Except for jazz, however, most of it, until the 1950s, continued to derive, directly or indirectly, from the music-halls. Such music was exemplified by so-called 'crooners' like Bing Crosby and Frank Sinatra, and incorporated few, if any, magical elements. Jazz, on the other hand, did incorporate such elements, and was duly regarded, in certain quarters, as incipiently 'subversive'. But it remained in many respects rarefied, an 'acquired taste', and its magical elements were often counterbalanced by its intellectual demands. Although popular, therefore, its magic did not exercise the spell over successive generations of youth that the magic of rock and roll was soon to do. With rock and roll, the ancient association of magic with music was to be re-established with a vengeance, was to generate a massive industry and to play a decisive role in the evolution of modern Western culture.

It has long been recognized that rock derives ultimately from the black music of the American South – from spirituals and gospel music, from jazz, blues, rhythm and blues. Less widely recognized is the fact that these forms of music derive in turn from the system of religious beliefs generally known as voodoo. If black music is the father of rock, voodoo is its grandfather.

'In 1517, the Spanish missionary Bartolomé de las Casas, taking great pity on the Indians who were languishing in the hellish workpits of Antillean gold-mines, suggested to Charles V, king of Spain, a scheme for importing blacks, so that they might languish in the hellish workpits of Antillean gold-mines.'[9] Thus, according to Jorge Luis Borges, did Christian charity and compassion inspire the inauguration of the slave trade between Africa and the recently discovered Americas. In 1518, the first three slaves from West Africa were brought to the newly colonized Spanish possessions in the Caribbean. The slave trade – the traffic in so-called 'black ivory' – quickly became a business of staggeringly lucrative proportions and spread across the mainlands of North and South America. In 1526, the first slaves were imported into what subsequently became the continental United States.

The people abducted from their villages on the African coast and forcibly transported across the Atlantic were bereft of everything, except, in some cases, members of their family; and they were generally separated from these soon after arrival in the New World. Of their former lives, most slaves retained nothing save their religious faith. This faith was largely animistic, revolving around the shamanistic invocation of a multitude of nature deities not unlike those of pre-Christian pagan Europe. Drums, dance, rhythmic incantation and sometimes drugs would be employed to induce a state of trance, or 'possession' by spiritual entities. In the language of the Fon tribe of what used to be Dahomey, the term signifying 'natural god' was *Vodu*.[10]

The religion of the Fon took deeper root in the Americas than that of any other African people. As it spread westwards from the Caribbean, it absorbed, depending on the specific region, a greater or lesser admixture of Roman Catholicism. Thus hybridized, it became known in Cuba – where the influence of Catholicism was greatest – as Santeria. In Jamaica, it was called Obeah, in Trinidad Shango, in Brazil Macumba. In Barbados and then in Haiti, it acquired the name of Voudou or Voodoo.

Whatever the influence of the Church, voodoo and its variants retained a number of key elements of its African origin. These included music, chanting, dance, the sacrifice of domestic animals such as chickens, the eating of the sacrificed creature's flesh and the ritual use (sometimes for drinking) of its blood. Most important of all, however, was the induced state of trance or 'possession'.

> Perhaps the most dramatic of religious experiences in voodoo is the phenomenon of 'possession', those moments when a god enters the head of one of the faithful and the worshipper becomes the god in spirit, in action, and in speech. This phenomenon is as integral to African practices as it is to voodoo rites in the Western hemisphere.[11]

To be 'possessed' by a god or spirit is the ultimate objective of the voodoo ceremony. It is a mark of great favour, indicating that the god or spirit deems an individual a worthy receptacle or vessel for divine immanence.

European slave masters and slave owners were justifiably nervous about voodoo. They recognized it as perhaps the single principle capable of unifying the slave population of a given region and fomenting rebellion. And indeed, such rebellions were not long in coming. The first occurred in 1522, a mere four years after the arrival of the first slaves. For the next three centuries, further rebellions were to erupt at sporadic intervals, sometimes requiring suppression by substantial numbers of European troops. In 1804, while Napoleon was preoccupied with war in Europe and denied access to the West Indies by the British fleet, the slave population of Haiti revolted successfully against their French overlords and established their own kingdom.

Haiti, of course, was to become the place most generally associated with voodoo. Under its different names, however, it took equally strong root elsewhere. Even when revolts were unsuccessful, many slaves would seek refuge in the impenetrable, thickly forested hills and mountains, where their white masters could not pursue them. Between revolts, they would be joined by other slaves, escaping singly or in small groups from the sugar-cane, tobacco and other plantations. At night, Europeans in settled regions would hear the incessant, unnerving and hypnotic drum beats pounding out African rhythms in the distance. Secure in their remote fastnesses, refugee slaves kept alive not only their freedom, but also their religion. They became custodians of collective tribal memory, preserving the recollection of the gods and rituals of their African forefathers.

By the eighteenth century, British administrations in the West Indies and North America had come to recognize the potential threat. Most members of the Fon tribe were deported from Barbados and other British possessions and sold elsewhere. In British colonies, drums were prohibited to slaves. This impeded the performance of ritual; but many of the essential rhythms were kept alive by means of other instruments, often improvised, and through song. Yet if voodoo was prevented from establishing itself in the British territories of North America, it encountered no such obstacles in the French possession of Louisiana. New Orleans was soon to become a major centre not only for the North American slave trade, but also for voodoo. By 1800, it was firmly entrenched. In that year, the French administration made a feeble attempt to suppress it by banning the purchase of slaves from the more voodoo-ridden islands of the Caribbean. In 1803, however, Louisiana was purchased from Napoleon by the American government and incorporated into the United States. New Orleans was promptly swamped by refugees from Haiti and other islands. By 1817, voodoo had become so prevalent that the New Orleans city council felt compelled to promulgate a ban against black participation in public meetings.[12]

As a direct consequence of this prohibition, the bonds connecting the music of voodoo with the cult itself became progressively more tenuous – and, with increasing frequency, severed. Although it never really lost sight of its religious origins, the music began to evolve independently. African rhythms began to be played on the instruments of Western Europe and the United States, and there ensued the advent of the New Orleans brass bands. Thus, according to one commentator, 'the century-long gestation began that would ultimately produce the dominant popular musical styles of the twentieth century – jazz, the blues, rhythm and blues, and rock and roll.'[13]

In the aftermath of the Emancipation Proclamation and the Civil War, immense numbers of newly freed slaves migrated north. The majority made their way from New Orleans and the Mississippi Delta up the Mississippi River to Memphis and St Louis. Many continued further north, to Chicago and Detroit. It was in these cities that, towards the end of the nineteenth century, 'the birth of the blues' occurred. The same cities still midwife blues music today.

More, probably, than any other genre of black music, the blues was the immediate progenitor of rock. And more, probably, than any other genre of black music, the blues retained links with the voodoo in which it originated. Blues music is suffused with voodoo imagery and allusions – sometimes explicit, sometimes in the seemingly innocent guises evolved during the years of slavery to slip undetected past the ears of unsuspecting whites. Such images and allusions constitute a lexicon of their own – the kind of 'coded' lexicon devised by any oppressed or persecuted people to communicate freely without incurring the wrath of those who wield power over them. Thus, for example, blues music will allude frequently, in a sexually raunchy but otherwise ostensibly innocent context, to the 'mojo', a talismanic voodoo fetish. There are also references to 'John the Conqueror', a plant talisman used by the 'root doctor', a voodoo priest or shaman who became known as the 'hoochie-coochie man'. In consequence, Muddy Waters is referring to more than just amorous conquest when he sings of making a foray to Louisiana in quest of a mojo that works.[14]

This is even more apparent in another of Muddy Waters' most famous songs, the lyrics of which were composed by Willie Dixon:

> I got a black cat's bone
> I got a mojo too
> I'm John, the Conqueror
> I'm gonna mess with you
> I'm gonna make you girls
> Lead me by the hand
> Then the world will know
> That I'm the Hoochie Cooche [*sic*] man.[15]

One of the most significantly resonant and portentously evocative of voodoo images is that of the crossroads. In voodoo, the crossroads symbolizes the gate which affords access to the invisible world, the world of the gods and spirits. This gate must be approached with the appropriate prayers and requests for supernatural aid. In consequence, all voodoo rituals and ceremonies commence with a salutation to the god who guards the crossroads; and to pass the crossroads is to enter into voodoo initiation.

The crossroads figures prominently in the music of the most mysterious and sinister of blues singers, Robert Johnson. A profound influence on Muddy Waters and numerous others, Johnson recorded twenty-nine songs in a series of sessions between 1936 and 1937, and then vanished at the age of twenty-eight. He was subsequently discovered to have died in 1938 from a bottle of poisoned whiskey given him by his girlfriend. Among those familiar with his imagery, he was generally regarded as a voodoo initiate endowed with an awesome and infernal magical power, whose dexterity on the guitar was ascribed to a Faustian pact ratified 'at a crossroads'. His 'Crossroad Blues' is in fact a species of voodoo hymn. 'I went to the crossroads,' it begins, 'bent down on my knees . . .' Each of the ensuing verses invokes imagery used in voodoo ceremonies. Johnson's other songs reek similarly of demonic magic and damnation. The very title of 'Hell-hound on My Trail' is indicative. 'Me and the Devil Blues' begins: 'Good morning, Satan, I believe it's time to go . . .' Even Muddy Waters found Johnson frightening, with something ominously 'dark' about him. On seeing him perform, Waters reported that 'he was a *dangerous* man . . . and he really was *using* that git-tar . . . I crawled away and pulled out, because it was too heavy for me . . .'[16]

The whiff of sulphur clinging to Johnson may have been particularly redolent, but it clung to many others as well. It has been noted that most of the early blues singers had a 'Faustian atmosphere about them'. One, Peetie Wheatstraw, called himself 'the Devil's Son-in-Law and the High Sheriff of Hell'. The devil and demonic magic remain central motifs in blues music to this day. Songs such as 'Sympathy for the Devil' are quite deliberately in the same thematic tradition. So, for example, is 'Low Down Rounder Blues':

> I cannot shun the devil, he stays right by my side.
> There's no way to cheat, I'm so dissatisfied.[17]

It is hardly coincidental that the Rolling Stones have performed a number of Robert Johnson's songs, and derived their name from one of Muddy Waters'.

Like the Stones and other rock figures, blues singers regularly performed a species of shamanistic ritual calculated to induce a state of ecstatic hysteria in their audiences. Bessie Smith, for example, who began making records in 1923, would regularly elicit from her listeners, both black and white, what one commentator described as 'religious frenzy'.

> Walking slowly to the footlights, to the accompaniment of the wailing, muted brasses, the monotonous African pounding of the drum . . . she began her strange rhythmic rites in a voice full of shouting and moaning and praying and suffering . . . [the crowd] burst into hysterical, semi-religious shrieks of sorrow and lamentation. Amens rent the air.[18]

In this account, one can already see at work the elements which, some thirty-five years later, would come to characterize the rock concert. For Elvis Presley, for Jerry Lee Lewis, for the Everly Brothers, for the Beatles, the Rolling Stones and those who followed, it was only necessary to add an increasingly explicit sexual suggestiveness. This,

combined with the intrinsic dynamic power of the shamanistic performance, sufficed to wring solid sheets of scream
from ecstatic teeny-boppers and tremors of profound alarm
from their elders – elders who, having confronted the
potency of the irrational in Nazi Germany and Imperial
Japan, were appalled by eruptions of a seemingly similar
energy amid the supposed safety of rationalistic postwar
society.

But if the frenzy of the rock concert evoked eerily disqui-
eting reminders of the Nuremberg rallies, it is doubtful how
many commentators recognized the principles of shamanistic magic which governed both. The performers themselves, however, understood well enough – understood the
psychological and even neurological effects of sound, of
chant, of rhythm, of light, of mesmerizing ritual. According
to Keith Richards, 'They are just scared of that rhythm.
That disturbs them. Every sound's vibration has a certain
effect on you. You can make certain noises that automati-
cally make you throw up. Certainly every sound has an effect
on the body and the effects of a good backbeat make these
people shiver in their boots.'[19] According to Mickey Hart,
a drummer with the Grateful Dead, 'Looking back on the
early years of rock and roll now, I can see why the adults
were scared. The screams, the ecstatic states, the hysteria –
this music had a power that adults didn't understand.'[20]

Speaking of the impact of rock, R. F. Taylor observes, 'It
was as if the old shamans had cast away the last vestige of
disguise to stand openly on stage at last.'[21] He sees in rock
a specifically and consciously magical reaction to scientific
rationalism and its potentially destructive technology:

The general suspicion of modern technology's improvidence
seemed undeniably confirmed in the face of such weaponry.
Perhaps the old discredited magicians had been right after all

to insist on the necessity of learning wisdom before receiving power. Large numbers of people felt they wanted a lot more magic and a lot less science.[22]

And:

It was the young who led the way. The generation who woke up to find that one war was over but frantic preparations were already in process for the next, instinctively reached for an alternative to the new 'black arts'. What they discovered and developed over the following decades was a very shamanistic response. They turned to *healing magic*. It was not a religious movement in the usual sense . . . they wanted inspired magic in *this* world. They were, consequently, looking for shamans.[23]

It was precisely to this quest for shamans that the rock musician responded. Altamont can thus be seen as the shamanistic ritual which it was – or, rather, which it aspired to be. But if Altamont was unique in the bloodshed it provoked, it was certainly not so in its shamanistic power. And as they became increasingly aware of the energy they could manipulate, rock performers began to sound more and more like traditional sorcerers. John Lennon, for example, was acutely aware of the 'sacred and magical context' in which, during a performance, the Beatles and their audience were mutually embedded. 'We don't seem to play for them,' he said. 'They play *us*.' Neither had he any compunction about arrogating to himself a sacred, religious, even messianic status. In 1981, when asked why the Beatles did not come together again, he replied:

If they didn't understand the Beatles and the sixties, then, what the fuck could we do for them now? Do we have to divide the fishes and the loaves for the multitudes again? Do

we have to walk on water again because a whole pile of
dummies didn't see it the first time, or didn't believe it when
they saw?[24]

And like a traditional shaman, he spoke of himself as merely
a conduit or a vessel for an energy emanating from elsewhere:

> The most enjoyable thing for me . . . is the inspirational, the
> spirit . . . my joy is when you're like possessed, like a medium.
> I'll be sitting around, it will come in the middle of the night
> . . . this thing comes as a whole piece, you know, words and
> music. I think, can I say I wrote it? I don't know who the hell
> wrote it. I'm just sitting here and the whole damn song comes
> out.[25]

Nor, of course, were the Beatles alone in this respect. At
the age of four, Jim Morrison of the Doors reported, he and
his parents had driven past the scene of an auto accident in
which an elderly Indian had died. Morrison believed himself
to be 'possessed' by the Indian's soul. On stage, according
to a member of Morrison's group:

> It was like Jim was an electric shaman and we were the elec-
> tric shaman's band, pounding away behind him. Sometimes
> he wouldn't feel like getting into the state, but the band would
> keep on pounding and pounding, and little by little it would
> take him over. God, I could send an electric shock through
> him with the organ. John [Densmore] could do it with his
> drum beats. You could see every once in a while – twitch – I
> could hit a chord and make him twitch. And he'd be off again.[26]

The Doors, by their own admission, 'didn't represent the
attitude of the festival: peace and love and flower power. We

represented the shadow side of it.'[27] John Densmore, the drummer, reported that the 'concerts had evolved into ritual-like performances' in which Morrison was 'the medicine man leading us all through the ceremony'.[28] Morrison himself described the Doors' performance as being 'like a purification ritual in the alchemical sense'.[29]

If the literary artist, during the nineteenth and twentieth centuries, was the direct heir of the true Renaissance magus, the rock singer conformed to the more popular and conventional conceptions of the Faust figure. Elvis Presley, Jim Morrison, Jimi Hendrix, Janis Joplin and many lesser luminaries all exemplify the characteristics – the obsessive energy, the insatiable compulsion to experiment and explore, the ultimately self-destructive impetus – associated with traditional portrayals of Faust. So, too, for that matter, do those who survived, who pursued the Faustian quest to one or another brink, but then returned, as it were, to tell the tale – Bob Dylan, for example, Eric Clapton, Kris Kristofferson, Mick Jagger and in particular, and most famously, Keith Richards.

The magic originally embraced and practised by rock musicians – the magic derived, via the blues, from voodoo – was essentially shamanistic magic. Like voodoo, and like the pagan magic of Europe in the Dark Ages, it was ultimately 'primitive'. It can be seen, in effect, as a species of 'pre-Hermetic' magic. It did not foster the kind of integration and synthesis that characterized Hermeticism. It did not foster transcendence or refinement of self so much as it did immersion of self in a form of 'herd mentality'. It did not foster intensification of consciousness so much as it did eclipse of consciousness. To that extent, it did indeed have elements in common with the dynamic at work in such phenomena as the Nuremberg rallies.

But even as they pursued their Faustian quests, many rock

musicians were becoming more erudite, more sophisticated, more akin to such '*poets maudits*' as Baudelaire and Rimbaud. In the process, they began to grope their way towards one or another kind of Hermetic synthesis. Bob Dylan, for instance, fused a number of musical genres, such as rock and the 'faery music' of folk tradition. In such songs as 'A Hard Rain's A-Gonna Fall', hypnotic rhythmic incantation is combined with dazzling surreal imagery and an intellectual content designed to provoke intensified awareness, rather than mindless euphoria. The Beatles, too, as they moved from the stage to the studio, dispensed with infantile lyrics and began to synthesize musical genres so as to induce something more than mere hysteria in teeny-boppers – began to think in terms of 'cosmic magic' and 'cosmic harmony'. In the footsteps of blues singers like Robert Johnson, Kristofferson confronted 'the Devil'. But Kristofferson's 'Devil' was an altogether more complex, more sophisticated figure than Johnson's, a figure closer to Blake's Lucifer or Goethe's Mephistopheles. And when the confrontation ends, he says that although he did not succeed in beating the Devil, nevertheless he drank his whiskey and stole his song.[30] Jimi Hendrix may have lived a life reminiscent of the Faust story; and being part Cherokee, he felt a natural inclination to 'primitive' shamanism. His ideas about music, however, were essentially Hermetic. 'He imagined a music that would have a similar impact on the mind as psychedelic drugs, a sound that would actually alter consciousness and "open people's eyes to cosmic powers" . . . He openly wondered about the possibility of transmitting guitar sounds over incredible distances to affect everyone in their path . . .'[31] According to Monika Dennemann, his last companion, Hendrix sought 'to create clear, positive music which produced a harmonizing effect. Through the power of his music he tried to bring about fundamental changes in people's minds.'[32] And, further, 'Jimi believed that music is magic . . . a supernatural power . . . he saw his music work as a magical science . . . rhythm could become hypnotic – putting the hearer in a trance-like condition . . .'[33]

Hendrix endeavoured to devise a music capable of 'healing people's minds and enabling them to change the world into a better place'. He speculated about how one might 'produce music so perfect that it would filter through you like rays and absolutely cure'. According to Hendrix himself: 'It's more than music. It's like a church, like a fountain for the potentially lost. We are making music into a new kind of Bible, a Bible you can carry in your heart.'[34] Just before his death, he declared himself to be 'working on music to be completely, utterly magic science where it's all pure positive . . .'[35]

The transition from shamanistic to Hermetic magic was never clearly demarcated. In consequence, it was not always apparent or definable as such even to the singers and musicians themselves, still less to their fans. The distinction today remains blurred – the more so in that current pop music encompasses both the shamanistic and the Hermetic, and both are frequently practised by the same performers. Certain commentators, however, have noted the development:

> The idea that music could bring about states of altered consciousness needed no extra evidence for rock'n'roll musicians. They were all familiar with the trance-like states that some of their most ardent fans could get themselves into. Yet could this effect be extended to introduce states of peace, moments of insight or flashes of transcendence? Could rock-'n'roll bring healing and harmony if the right notes were found?[36]

The same commentator answers these questions by citing Hermeticism in everything but name:

> More important for musicians was the theory that sound contained healing qualities. In ancient times, it was said, musical formulae were known that could bring ecstasy, physical healing or universal harmony. Musicians in those times didn't need to *sing* about solutions, they could *create* them. They could be doctors, surgeons, priests, therapists and politicians, all through their instruments.[37]

It is in this essentially Hermetic direction that certain trends, at least, in popular music are moving today. In response to twenty-five years of 'Troubles', for example, a number of Irish groups are combining the pagan magic of the old 'faery music' with a mystical Hermeticism intended to foster peace and reconciliation. And Van Morrison, to cite another example, regards music as a form of healing magic in the traditional Hermetic sense. Imbued with his own profound sense of spirituality, Morrison declares the objective of his music as being 'ideally, to induce states of meditation and ecstasy as well as to make people think'.[38]

16

THE REDISCOVERY OF MEANING

Popular music aside, the story recounted in the second part of this book has come a long way from Hermeticism. And whatever the illusions of certain adherents and practitioners, most of us recognize that popular music will neither transform nor save the world. Despite the best efforts of popular music, we still inhabit a reality fractured into a jigsaw puzzle by the fragmentation of knowledge. We are still confronted by a gaggle of rival and conflicting absolutes, each jostling for supremacy, each promulgating its claim to hold the answers to all the relevant questions. We still distrust most, if not all, of these claims. And in our mistrust, we still yearn for some unifying principle, some evidence of underlying coherence, some pattern which will make sense of our existence, will impart meaning, purpose and direction to our lives.

If only intellectually, most of us recognize that synthesis is preferable to analysis, organism to mechanism, integration to fragmentation. For most of us, however, the preferable alternative seems unattainable because the logic governing our situation appears both inexorable and autonomous. We feel trapped by that logic, subservient to it, helpless in its thrall. And as the psychological shibboleth of the millennium approaches, the temptation intensifies to embrace even a facile solution to the dilemma – to seek refuge in the supposed safety of one or another self-arrogated authority. We are appalled by the possibility that our lives might be meaningless and devoid of significance. If suffering can justify our lives, can endow them with meaning and significance, we are even prepared to suffer.

And yet, as popular music indicates, the prospect is not unrelentingly bleak. The headlines that daily assail us bear, admittedly, scant testimony to enlightenment on the part of humanity as a whole. Despite these headlines, however, increasing numbers of people are nevertheless coming awake, are recognizing the nature of the cul-de-sac facing them and are actively looking for alternatives. Where might such alternatives lie? How might we attempt to reassemble, reintegrate and restore the fractured Humpty-Dumpty's egg of our world? By drawing an analogy with individual psychology, we might perhaps begin to glimpse an answer.

One of Freud's chief mistakes was to assume that imbalances or maladjustments in the psyche could simply be 'removed', exorcised or reversed. He assumed, for example, that certain tendencies, such as the 'death wish', could be 'cured' merely by diagnosing them, by forcing the patient to confront them and experience the attendant 'shock of recognition'. Jung, in contrast, realized that the imbalances or maladjustments of the individual psyche were intrinsically part of that psyche. Short of the psychic equivalent of a lobotomy, they could not just be eliminated. They could, however, be neutralized, counterbalanced, reduced to manageable proportions and even made productive if they could be embedded in an appropriate context. Instead of attempting to exorcise or reverse a potentially destructive propensity, Jung endeavoured therefore to contain it by incorporating it in a new equilibrium. Instead of trying to 'excise' a 'death wish', Jung would seek to offset it by imbuing the patient with an equally strong, or stronger, will to live.

The result would be a new totality, greater than the one which had existed before. This, for Jung, amounted to genuine growth. It can be visualized as a process of creating ever wider concentric circles, like those radiating out from a pebble dropped into a pool. Each new circle constitutes the psychic equivalent of 'scar tissue' over the imbalance or maladjustment it serves to heal. And when changing circumstances engender a new imbalance or maladjustment, it is time to create a new and wider circle. Thus does the individual continue to grow, to become ever more mature. The psyche, for Jung, was not static, as it was for Freud. On the contrary, the psyche, for Jung, was constantly in movement, in process – constantly engaged in a spontaneous and dynamic evolution towards equilibrium.

The same principles can be applied on a collective level, to society as a whole. Society as a whole is no more capable than the individual of returning to a vanished Eden, or reclaiming a lost virginity and innocence. Unlike our more naïve predecessors, we cannot aspire to a new 'Golden Age'. Indeed, unlike our more naïve predecessors, we recognize that such an age probably never existed at all. In consequence, society cannot simply jettison, disown or repudiate what it has acquired. Unless some global catastrophe compels us to do so, we will not voluntarily relinquish our cars, our aeroplanes, our television and telecommunications, our central heating, our fast foods and all the other technological developments which have become for us essential components of our everyday lives. We will not voluntarily revert to a 'lower standard of living', even if we must be enslaved to the things which ensure us a 'higher' standard. But it *is* possible to create, so to speak, a wider circle around those things – a circle which deprives them of their autonomy and their tyranny over us, which establishes for them a moral context and framework and thereby reduces them to manageable proportions, which denies them the power to be laws unto themselves and renders them subservient to human values. By reconnecting and reintegrating our fragmented spheres of knowledge and activity, we can create a new and unified matrix for our culture and civilization – a matrix which restores to us a sense of meaning, purpose and direction. Whatever the terminology we choose to confer on such a process, it will be essentially Hermetic.

The Unifying Vision of Art

Once again, the arts, and especially literature, have sign-posted the directions in which we must move to re-establish a collective balance and equilibrium. Major poets and novelists of the early to mid twentieth century had embraced Hermetic thought as a means of reintegrating a reality in which the old pillars of certainty – time, space, causality and personality – had become disconcertingly shaky. During the 1960s, there began to coalesce what amounted, in effect, to an entirely new aesthetic, which reflected an entirely new *Weltanschauung*. Although it drew upon – and was sometimes paralleled by – techniques from across the globe, this aesthetic has now come to be associated primarily with the countries and literature of Latin America. Its 'godfathers' are generally held to be a handful of figures born around the turn of the century – Jorge Luis Borges, Alejo Carpentier, Miguel Angel Asturias. It was subsequently exemplified by Gabriel García Márquez, Carlos Fuentes, José Donoso, Mario Vargas Llosa, Julio Cortázar and other names credited with the so-called 'boom' in Latin American fiction.

The 'boom', as José Donoso described it, is generally associated with the now familiar label of 'magical realism'. In fact, however, that term conveys very little. It is also misleading and not particularly accurate. One would do better to examine the central premise underlying recent Latin American literature – the premise which constitutes a unifying principle, a shared aesthetic underpinning, between the diverse contributors to the 'boom'. This premise implicitly or explicitly posits the work of art – and, by extension, reality itself – as a form of Hermetic phantasmagoria.

In other words, there is – as in traditional Hermeticism – only one everything, and the demarcation lines between different 'orders' or 'levels' of reality are effectively eradicated. According to Jung, psychological or spiritual 'facts' were every bit as 'real', every bit as valid, as the 'facts' of the phenomenal world. In the aesthetic underlying recent Latin American literature, all 'facts', psychological, phenomenal or of any other kind, are interwoven in a single seamless fabric, a single intricate, interconnected and undifferentiated tapestry which is all-inclusive, all-encompassing. Internal and external spheres flow into each other, mutate into each other, nourish each other. So do dreams or fantasies and so-called 'waking consciousness'. So do past, present and future. So do myth, legend and history. So do magic and science. So do the creative imagination and the material to which it addresses itself. So do the godlike artist and the worlds or characters he conjures into existence – the 'miracle of life out of ink'.

According to these tenets, the history of a people, a country or a culture does not consist solely of battles fought, treaties signed, frontiers established, governments installed or deposed, legislation passed. It also consists of what Jung called 'psychological facts', the 'facts' of psychic life – dreams, aspirations, superstitions, legends, fairy tales, the exaggeration and hyperbole of myth, the miracles people yearned to believe in and thereby convinced themselves they have witnessed. By according a legitimate status to these things, works such as García Márquez' *One Hundred Years of Solitude* and Carlos Fuentes' *Terra Nostra* perform a characteristically Hermetic synthesis, enabling Latin American readers to reintegrate their individual and collective fantasies, their individual and collective folklore, their individual and collective childhoods – all the elements which had originally stimulated psychological and spiritual growth, but were then disowned and repudiated by Western rationalism and materialism. Through the reincorporation of these elements, a lost sense of completeness is restored. Latin American readers are thus prompted to confront their origins and, in Carlos Fuentes' words, 'to create their origins anew'. Herein lies the real magic of so-called 'magical realism'. It is a typically and specifically Hermetic form of magic.

Not surprisingly, perhaps, the influence of this magic, from the 1960s on, spread rapidly across the globe. The impact was greater than that of anything produced since the writings of Joyce, Proust, Kafka, Eliot and Rilke during the 1920s. Writers working elsewhere in a similar vein of Hermetic phantasmagoria – Italo Calvino in Italy, for example – ceased to be marginalized oddities and acquired, at a stroke, a new 'legitimacy' and 'respectability'. Younger figures, as far afield as Eastern Europe, South Africa and the Indian subcontinent, found in Hermetic phantasmagoria a new source of artistic inspiration. Through the techniques developed and refined by the Latin Americans, writers from other cultures and ethnic groups – American Indians, for example, American blacks, Asians and Africans in Britain and France – found a means of reclaiming and reintegrating their personal and collective heritages, their personal and collective identities. Works which perform a similar function are now issuing from Britain, from Western Europe and from the United States.

But the Hermetic phantasmagoria of Latin American literature is more than just a fresh literary technique, more than a mere artistic fashion or trend. Above and beyond its purely aesthetic application, it offers a new and more complete way of coming to terms with reality, *a new and more complete way of seeing and understanding*. Through this device of Hermetic phantasmagoria, Western culture as a whole is attaining to a new comprehension of its own myth-making processes, its own collective identity, its own collective psychological history. We are all undergoing, to one degree or another, a subtle – and sometimes not so subtle – reorientation of consciousness. We are beginning to make vital and dynamic connections between our internal and external lives which would have been unthinkable some thirty-five or forty years ago.

This process has been facilitated by the extent to which the other arts are catching up with literature and promulgating an essentially Hermetic vision of their own. In recent years, for example, a new recognition and appreciation has been accorded to the Hermetic painters of the early twentieth century – Wassily Kandinsky, Franz Marc, Nicholas Roerich, Alfred Kubin. Sidney Nolan has been recognized as a visionary equivalent in painting of Patrick White in literature. The highly Jungian art of Cecil Collins is now placed in a species of neo-Blakean tradition. In the United States, Ernest Fuchs has established himself as a specifically Kabbalistic painter. Of particular significance is the German Joseph Beuys, who, as a Luftwaffe pilot, was shot down in 1943 over the Crimea. Rescued by local Tartar tribesmen, he acquired from them a profound understanding of shamanism, which he was later to fuse with his own highly mystical Christianity.

Beuys explicitly equated the artist with a characteristically Hermetic shaman, 'the healer and wise man of primitive tribes'.[1] The creative process entailed for him an act of ritual magic, involving specific tools and specific procedures calculated to enhance and deepen 'the life within'. In a world 'increasingly shaped by the sciences', Beuys felt, 'art . . . was the only really revolutionary force'.[2] According to one commentator, he believed that

> only art can again reactivate all of man's senses in the face of the exclusive *diktat* of rationality. All of Beuys' artistic actions and provocations were thus directed towards regenerating man's creativity, submerged beneath constant use of reason. Beuys hoped that the man whose creativity was thus revitalized . . . would then no longer comprehend himself as an individual . . . but rather as a creative element within an all-embracing organism . . . as a microcosm of a universal macrocosm.[3]

Many of Beuys' works bear titles such as *Communication with Powers beyond the Human*, *Healing Plants*, *Shaman's House* and *Shaman in Ecstasy*. At the same time, he 'always paid attention to the deep ancestral roots of Europe',[4] which he saw as being particularly manifest in Celtic culture. Not surprisingly, therefore, he regarded James Joyce with a special admiration. Although he never met Joyce personally, he would often jokingly claim to have added, 'at Joyce's request', two chapters to *Ulysses*. He hoped to exhibit six sketchbooks based on *Ulysses* in Dublin.[5] One of his contemporaries deemed him the artist most worthy of illustrating the works of Arno Schmidt, the postwar novelist who, in German, pursued into new dimensions the technical and linguistic innovations Joyce had introduced in English.

If Hermeticism in postwar painting is beginning to catch up with Hermeticism in literature, there is another artistic medium in which Hermeticism has effectively kept pace. This medium is film. Rooted respectively in German Expressionism and French Surrealism, Fritz Lang and Jean Cocteau, to take but two examples, began to experiment with Hermetic magic on celluloid. Even before the Latin Americans introduced their aesthetic of Hermetic phantasmagoria, directors like Federico Fellini, Andrei Tarkovsky and Luis Buñuel were adapting it to the cinema. Buñuel in particular was a major influence on, and sometimes collaborator with, the postwar luminaries of Latin American literature. The techniques they pioneered have more recently been embraced by such directors as Werner Herzog in Germany and Peter Weir in Australia. Through film, the work of art as Hermetically magical phantasmagoria has been able to attain new dimensions, and to reach an audience considerably greater than that which reads 'literary' novels. Through film, indeed, Hermeticism is beginning, if only subtly and very gradually, to transform our way of seeing. In the diluted form exemplified by such series as *Twin Peaks*, it is even beginning to infiltrate the cruder world of television.

If film impinges on the twentieth-century psyche more obviously than any other artistic medium, architecture, if only subliminally, impinges more pervasively, more inescapably. However oblivious one may be to the other arts, one remains surrounded by architecture. As this book has chronicled, architecture, for centuries, was deemed among the highest of arts, and a primary conduit and repository for Hermetic magic. Then, with the advent of the Age of Reason, it ceased to be so. The architecture of our own century has, until recently, existed at one of two extremes. There has been embellishment for embellishment's sake, novelty for novelty's sake, innovation for innovation's sake, with no status accorded the traditional Hermetic principles of harmony and proportion. At the opposite end of the spectrum, there has been a brutalistic utilitarianism, equally indifferent to harmony and proportion. Especially in the years following the Second World War, architecture tended to dismiss both its human and its natural context, to ignore its relationship to the community in which it existed. The result was a mere agglomeration of free-standing fragments which reflected the psychological and philosophical confusion of a fragmented society. Such architecture, familiar enough to all of us, is characterized by 'the spread of technology, the destruction of natural landscape and the repetitive nature of modern urban design'.[6] According to its critics, this so-called 'modernist' orientation has produced structures built not for the people who actually occupy them, but for other architects. As the Norwegian professor of architecture, Christian Norberg-Schulz, wrote in 1988:

> During the last decades our environment has not only been subject to pollution and urban sprawl, but also to a loss of those qualities which allow for man's sense of belonging and participation. As a result many feel that their life is 'meaningless' and become 'alienated'.[7]

'Alienation', in Norberg-Schulz's opinion, is primarily 'due to man's loss of identification with nature and man-made things which constitute his environment'.[8] It is exacerbated by most modern buildings, which 'exist in a "nowhere" . . . not related to a landscape and not to a coherent, urban whole'.[9]

Norberg-Schulz, having accurately diagnosed the problem, proposed his own alternative, which he called 'post-modernism': 'The many tendencies and currents which make up "post-modern" architecture have one thing in common: the demand for *meaning*.'[10] The urgency of conveying meaning is stressed as well by the British academic, Jonathan Sime:

The importance of *preserving* landscapes, historical sites or public urban settings which contribute to people's self-identity is . . . an important message to planners . . . The danger in being preoccupied with a grand architectural or planning scheme is in forgetting the life history of a locale and a myriad of past physically situated life events its local inhabitants have experience of.[11]

Norberg-Schulz elaborates further on the matter, emphasizing that 'man cannot gain a foothold through scientific understanding alone. He needs *symbols*, that is, works of art which "represent life-situations" . . . the purpose of the work of art is to "keep" and transmit meanings.'[12] Thus, for Norberg-Schulz, architecture is ultimately an adjunct, or a form, of poetry. 'Only poetry in all its forms . . . makes human existence meaningful, and *meaning* is the fundamental human need.' And: 'Architecture belongs to poetry, and its purpose is to help man to dwell.'[13]

According to Norberg-Schulz, his declared objective is 'to investigate the *psychic* implications of architecture rather than its practical side'.[14] In order to do this, he invokes an essentially Hermetic concept of the ancient Greco-Roman world, the *genius loci*, or 'spirit of place'[15] – a concept restored to twentieth-century culture initially by D. H. Lawrence and echoed subsequently by Lawrence Durrell. The *genius loci* (or *deus loci*) is the intangible 'spiritual' quality or character which suffuses and animates a particular site, imparting to it its unique identity and establishing its specific place in the overall scheme of things. Ancient man, Norberg-Schulz stresses, knew the 'importance to come to terms with the *genius* of the locality where his life takes place'. For ancient man, 'the environment is experienced as meaningful'. And: 'Human identity presupposes the identity of place.'[16]

The objective of architecture, for Norberg-Schulz, is 'to

concretize the *genius loci*'. This is accomplished, he concludes, 'by means of buildings which gather the properties of the place and bring them close to man. The basic act of architecture is therefore to understand the "vocation" of the place. In this way we protect the earth and become ourselves part of a comprehensive totality.'[17]

For Norberg-Schulz, as for the architects of antiquity and of the Renaissance, an architectural edifice reflects a spiritual and Hermetic process – an act of artistic or poetic creation rather than of scientific construction and assembly. He himself enunciates the Hermetic premise of the relationship between microcosm and macrocosm: 'To be able to dwell between heaven and earth, man has to "understand" these two elements, as well as their interaction.' And by 'understanding', Norberg-Schulz explains that he means not scientific knowledge, but a form of cognition which 'denotes the experience of *meanings*'. To be meaningful, a structure must be harmonious and in proportion – harmonious and in proportion with itself, and with its surroundings. 'When the environment is meaningful, man feels "at home".'[18] Ultimately, 'meaning is a *psychic* function. It depends on identification, and implies a sense of "belonging". It therefore constitutes the basis of dwelling. We ought to repeat that man's most fundamental need is to experience his existence as meaningful.'[19]

By Norberg-Schulz's own admission, his architectural principles were most effectively implemented by the Estonian-born Louis Kahn (1901–74), who emigrated to the United States and became perhaps the most acclaimed American architect of the postwar epoch. Kahn's orientation is reflected by the question he would invariably ask before designing a building: 'What does the building want to be?' According to one commentator:

First of all Kahn understood architecture in terms of place. A 'room' is for him a place with its particular character, its 'spiritual aura', and a building is a 'society of rooms'. A city is 'an assembly of place vested with the care to uphold the sense of a way of life'.[20]

Thus did Kahn formulate in his own terms the concept of the *genius loci* advocated by Norberg-Schulz. He was particularly influenced by works on Renaissance thought, art and architecture which began to appear during the 1950s and 1960s. These works, by such scholars as Edgar Wind and Frances Yates, stressed the contribution of Hermeticism to the Renaissance, while reducing to its true proportions the role played by secular humanism. And it was from the architecture of Renaissance Hermeticism that Kahn was to draw his inspiration. As one commentator observes, 'the Renaissance architects of centralized churches had in fact set up a decidedly spiritual sympathy between the microcosm of man and the macrocosm of God. Significantly, Kahn himself took happily to the task of designing proper sanctuaries, Jewish or Christian.'[21]

Until quite recently, debates about modern architecture were confined to a rarefied sphere, seemingly inaccessible to the general public. It is to his credit – a credit too often ignored by media intent on more luridly sensational issues – that the Prince of Wales, during the last decade, has dragged such debates from their previously remote ivory tower and placed them in the public domain. Some of the prince's criticisms – the description of the extension to the National Gallery as a 'giant carbuncle on the face of a friend', of the new British Library as a species of training academy for secret police – have passed by now into popular consciousness. So, too, has his assertion that postwar British architects have contrived to disfigure London more grievously than the bombers of the Luftwaffe. Less familiar are some of his more positive assertions, proffered in his book, *A Vision of Britain*. In this volume, he echoes the essentially Hermetic principles of Norberg-Schulz and Kahn: 'I believe that when a man loses contact with the past he loses his soul. Likewise, if we deny the architectural past . . . then our buildings lose *their* souls.'[22]

The prince observes that, when building on a fresh site, 'the trick, it seems to me, is to find ways of enhancing the natural environment'.[23] He articulates his own version of the *genius loci* extolled by Norberg-Schulz: 'Rather than planning from a drawing-board or plotting road routes on a map, we should feel the lie of the land and its contours and respect them as a result.'[24] The prince endorses the Hermetic architecture of Palladio. He speaks repeatedly of the importance of harmony and proportion. And in a passage which might have come almost verbatim from the manual of a Renaissance Hermeticist, he states: 'Man is the measure of all things. Buildings must relate first of all to human proportions and then respect the scale of the buildings around them.'[25]

Through his intervention in the architectural debate, the prince has had a very real and genuinely beneficial effect. He has prompted the public at large to become increasingly cognizant of their surroundings, increasingly aware, increasingly sensitized. Even more significantly perhaps, he has encouraged them to surmount the apathy and passivity fostered by a sense of helplessness. He has encouraged them to recognize that they have a voice, and a role to play, in the shaping of their environment.

Rebuilding the Fragments

In one of his early works, the verse drama *Sappho*, Lawrence Durrell asserts that humanity will come of age and mature 'when the mob becomes an artist'. To date, alas, 'the mob' has displayed little evidence of any such progressive development. But if the 'mob' remains recalcitrant, an increasing number of what the media calls 'ordinary people' are indeed beginning to venture into territory previously deemed the preserve of the artist, the philosopher, the psychologist and the mystic. More significantly still, perhaps, they are being encouraged to do so by individuals in positions of influence and authority.

In 1982, the Revd Michael Mann, then Dean of Windsor, was asked by the Duke of Edinburgh to convene an ongoing series of conferences. Although hardly secret, these conferences were never publicized. Running for the next three or four years, they brought together eminent representatives of the religious, scientific, business and educational establishments, with prominent Jungian psychologists acting as 'liaisons' or 'interpreters' between the diverse interests involved. Dialogues were stimulated, bridges were constructed between disciplines, a cross-fertilization of knowledge was inspired. Philosophical issues were confronted in a manner which compelled participants to learn something of each other's points of view. In the years that followed, the repercussions of the informal Windsor Conferences were to radiate out like ripples in a pool.

In 1986, on the twenty-fifth anniversary of the World Wildlife Fund, the Duke of Edinburgh convened a highly publicized conference in Italy, at Assisi. More than any other figure in Christian history, St Francis displayed a mystical sense of man's Hermetic interconnection with the natural world. At the Assisi Conference, under the symbolic patronage of St Francis, representatives of the world's major faiths were brought together to explore the spiritual relationship between man and nature. Here and there, of course, bigoted voices fulminated in protest. The Revd Tony

Higton, for example, an Anglican clergyman, waxed fulsome with prim, prissy and indignant disapprobation, finding it deplorable that other creeds should be accorded a status comparable to his own dogmatic version of Christianity. To judge from his fulminations in print, he seems to have feared the Church of England might incur, by contagion, some species of spiritual infection. But while the Revd Mr Higton blustered his outrage, the Assisi Conference emerged as a landmark in inter-faith rapprochement, and a blueprint for the kind of role religion might play in the twenty-first century. It also engendered a number of dynamic offshoots. Arts for Nature, to cite but one example, sponsors creative works in various mediums which convey to the public an essentially pantheistic vision, a sense of humanity's spiritual kinship with the natural order and the need to establish a harmonious relationship with the environment. The International Sacred Literature Trust ushers into print translations of important texts from across the globe, some from recognized faiths, some addressing the numinous from perspectives independent of any organized religion.

The initiatives of the British monarchy have been matched by a burgeoning number of other organizations and institutions. It is not feasible here, of course, to offer even a partial or selective list of these. But it is worth calling attention to the University of London's Warburg Institute, which, founded in the 1930s, remains one of the world's most active and prestigious centres for studies in Hermetic thought. It is worth calling attention to the Westminster Pastoral Foundation, which unites Christian and Jungian teaching in a training programme for psychological counsellors. And it is worth calling attention to 'The Scientific and Medical Network', a loose association of physicians, psychologists and scientists who endeavour to forge links between their disciplines and the moral and spiritual concerns of religion and philosophy. In the United States, there are such bodies as the Institute of Noetic Sciences in Sausalito and the California Institute for Integral Studies, where scientists, philosophers and psychologists emphasize an integrative approach to science and the arts. The Institute for Integral Studies maintains an affiliation with Schumacher College in Devon.

Through such conduits as these, as well as through small informal study and discussion groups, numerous individuals are using essentially Hermetic principles to reintegrate fragmented elements of reality. In the process, they are rediscovering a sense of meaning, purpose and direction – as well, frequently, as a sense of the sacred. Very often, they are learning that organized religion enjoys no exclusive proprietorship over the sacred, and are finding their way to it through other paths – through the arts, through psychology, through philosophy, even through the sciences. They are discovering that such figures as Blake or Rilke may indeed be 'more spiritual' than the Pope or than other conventional religious leaders – may have a more intense and profound understanding of 'spirituality', and may convey it more effectively, more immediately, in more personally comprehensible and relevant terms.

Increasing numbers of people are also coming to recognize that the functions governed by the 'masculine' left hemisphere of the brain – logical thinking, for example, ratiocination and rational analysis – are not in themselves sufficient or even necessarily reliable. New attention is being accorded the functions governed by the 'feminine' right hemisphere – so-called 'lateral thinking', intuition, an apprehension not just of facts but of the more elusive relationships between facts. From the prospect of the two hemispheres of the brain working in tandem, in balance, and complementing each other's activities, there has arisen the prospect of a new individual wholeness, a new psychic harmony, a new equilibrium.

At the same time, too, increasing numbers of people are beginning to learn a new language – the language of symbol and paradox, which resonates to levels of the psyche beyond the reach of the merely literal and of the rational intellect alone. Through the language of symbol and paradox, individuals are coming to terms with ambiguities, ambivalences and contradictions in their own natures, and finding therein an untapped reservoir of creative energy. Through symbol and paradox, they are obtaining access to an inner world of previously unsuspected richness and vitality.

Perhaps most important of all, increasing numbers of people are coming to adopt a new attitude towards that characteristically Anglo-Saxon accusation of having 'too much imagination'. They are learning that one can never ultimately have 'too much imagination', and that to believe otherwise betokens a paltriness of inner resources and a smallness of mind. Without necessarily knowing Coleridge, they are making his distinction between fancy or fantasy on the one hand and, on the other, the creative imagination. They are recognizing that even fancy or fantasy can be valid, and should not be repudiated or spurned. And they are coming to acknowledge the creative imagination as perhaps the most important of all man's mental faculties.

It need not be the unique preserve of the artist. On the contrary, it can – and, ideally, should – be an integral adjunct to all our mental activity, a species of dynamo which adds its power to all our other functions and faculties. It can contribute as much in the boardroom, in the classroom, in a relationship, in a job, around the negotiating table, as it can in the execution of a work of art. It can create meaning as well as beauty. It can constitute, as Paracelsus said, our magical link with the sacred or the numinous. It can enable us to see, perhaps for the first time, the repercussions, the implications, the ramifications of our actions; and in doing so, it can help us to establish a moral context for our lives. To use imagination is the ultimate act of magic, whereby we incessantly create the world anew. To use imagination is to come awake.

POSTSCRIPT

There is, needless to say, a great deal of silliness in the air nowadays, a great deal of gullibility and wishful thinking, a great deal of absurd jargon which might indeed warrant the sobriquet of 'psychobabble'. As we have noted, there is a plethora of cults, sects, disciplines and therapies which offer spurious solutions to the crisis of meaning resulting from the fragmentation of knowledge. There is much cynical exploitation of humanity's increasingly urgent desire to find something in which to trust and believe. And, however well-intentioned, there is much muddle-headedness.

But some measure of discrimination is required, some measure of insight, erudition and thoughtful assessment, to distinguish between the valid and the meretricious – and to avoid discarding the proverbial baby with the bath-water. Not many of the arbiters of public opinion possess these prerequisites. And before those who lack them swoop to the attack with gleeful bellows of 'Tally-ho!', it would be instructive to look at one dimension of the Faustian pact which has not hitherto been considered.

When Mephistopheles, in Goethe's dramatic poem, first appears and introduces himself to Faust, he does so with the words: '*Ich bin der Geist der stets verneint.*' *Geist* in German generally means 'spirit', although in this instance it also means 'principle'. *Verneint* is from the infinitive *verneinen*, which means 'to negate' or 'to deny'. The devil's statement might therefore be translated as: 'I am the spirit, or the principle, which negates or denies everything.' In other words, Mephistopheles is placing himself in the diabolical tradition of 'perpetual nay-saying'. But *verneinen* has much more sinister, and much more devastating, connotations than do its English equivalents. As Mephistopheles makes clear from his subsequent words and actions, his 'nay-saying' is more than just repudiation or refusal. It entails an active power which causes things to wither, to shrivel up, under a wintry gust of icy demoniac laughter.

Ultimately, of course, Mephistopheles embodies the 'sin' of 'intellectual pride' which Christian tradition has consistently ascribed to him under one of his other names, Lucifer. But 'intellectual pride' implies more for Goethe than those words might at first suggest. It implies an abyss of nihilism in which one believes in nothing save one's own cleverness. It implies a lofty detachment from everything human, from everything warm and vibrant – and a concurrent cold aloofness, a remoteness as frigid and sterile as the wastes of interstellar space. And it implies a complacently supercilious, cynical, sneering and mocking laughter, a laughter of scorn, which transmits the spiritual equivalent of frostbite to everything it touches with its breath. Nothing is proof against such laughter. Love, honour, beauty, sincerity, integrity, dignity, nobility – everything we hold most dear and most triumphantly, most uniquely human can be reduced by such laughter to the status of a joke. If one establishes a sufficiently inhuman distance from it, one can laugh at anything. One can even diminish something as atrocious as, say, Auschwitz to the level of a farce. This is something beyond so-called 'black humour', which attempts to provoke a reaction of outrage and often contains an element of valid satire. On the contrary, this is the laughter of utter and hopeless indifference, of spiritual and moral bankruptcy and despair.

It is in just such a spirit of supercilious, sneering mockery that terms like 'New Age psychobabble' are generally bandied about – usually by commentators who themselves believe only in pseudo-certainties accepted at second-hand, or in nothing at all save their own cleverness. It is in just such a spirit that any serious attempt at self-confrontation, self-recognition and self-knowledge is held up to ridicule. It is in just such a spirit that any effort to probe beneath the surface of things is considered a 'legitimate target', and sacrificed on the altar of mere egocentric wit.

However silly, however gullible, however credulous the 'New Age seeker' may often be, the very process of 'seeking' at least attests to something positive, something laudable. If nothing else, it bears witness to a desire to learn, a desire to know, a desire to improve, a desire to change. At the very least, it reflects an aspiration to 'something better'. Facile, simplistic, even misguided though such aspirations may sometimes be, they are surely preferable to the smug, self-satisfied complacency which shrinks from all such aspirations, which entrenches itself behind preconceived assumptions and does nothing more creative than sneer.

It is true, of course, that, according to the hoary cliché, 'everyone is entitled to an opinion'. But to have a valid opinion, one must be adequately informed. One must at least know something about what one has presumed to criticize. Few of those who sneer possess any such knowledge. And if one is inadequately informed, one's purported opinion is not really an opinion at all. It is merely a prejudice.

NOTES AND REFERENCES

NOTE The full bibliographical details, when not cited here, are to be found in the Bibliography.

1 Hermes, the Thrice Greatest

1 Philostratus, *Life of Appollonius*, p. 149 (vi, 11).

2 Butler, *The Myth of the Magus*, p. 73.

3 Epiphanius, *Contra Haereses*, ii, 4, quoted in Mead, *Simon Magus*, p. 27.

4 Jonas, *The Gnostic Religion*, p. 109.

5 *Acts of Peter*, xxxi–xxxii.

6 Jonas, op. cit., p. 111.

7 For a basic account of the Jamesian and Pauline factions in early messianic Judaism – out of which came Christianity – see Baigent and Leigh, *The Dead Sea Scrolls Deception*, pp. 180ff.

8 For the Library see: Fraser, *Ptolemaic Alexandria*, I, pp. 311ff.; Parsons, *The Alexandrian Library*, pp. 29ff.; Pfeiffer, *History of Classical Scholarship . . .*, pp. 96ff.; Blum, *Kallimachos . . .*, pp. 95ff.

9 The papyrus Scroll fragments found in Qumran Cave No. 7 were all in Greek. They comprised part of Exodus, part of Jeremiah, four unidentified biblical fragments and eighteen non-biblical fragments. See: Baillet, M., Milik, J.T., and de Vaux, R., *Discoveries in the Judaean Desert*, vol. III, Oxford, 1962.

10 Josephus, *The Jewish War*, p. 392.

11 Ammianus Marcellinus, *The Roman History*, Book XXII, 16.20 (p. 315).

12 ibid., 16.17 (p. 315).

13 ibid., 16.19 (p. 315).

14 Milne, 'Graeco-Egyptian Religion', *Encyclopaedia of Religion and Ethics*, 6, p. 376.

15 For a comprehensive review of religions operating in Alexandria see Fraser, op. cit., pp. 189ff.

16 Dodds, *Pagan and Christian in an Age of Anxiety*, p. 106.

17 Joyce, *Portrait of the Artist as a Young Man*, pp. 224–5.

18 Fowden, *The Egyptian Hermes*, p. 28.

19 ibid.

20 *Hermetica*, Copenhaver trans., p. xiv.

21 Bernal, *Black Athena*, p. 139.

22 Fowden, op. cit., p. 25.

23 *Hermetica*, op. cit., p. 58.

24 See Stoyanov, *The Hidden Tradition in Europe*; Runciman, *The Medieval Manichee*.

25 Trans. Robert Powell, *The Hermetic Journal*, 15, Spring 1981, 'Historical Note concerning the Emerald Tablet', p. 38.

26 Holmyard, *Alchemy*, pp. 97–8, quoting Steele, R., and Singer, D., in *Proceedings of the Royal Society of Medicine*, XXI (1928), p. 42.

27 Trans. Powell, op. cit.

28 Kingsley, *Ancient Philosophy, Mystery, and Magic*, p. 301.

29 ibid., p. 326.

30 Lindsay, *The Origins of Alchemy in Graeco-Roman Egypt*, p. 254.

31 For Maria the Jew see Lindsay, op. cit., pp. 240ff.; Patai, *The Jewish Alchemists*, pp. 60ff. She seems to have invented the water-bath or *bain Marie*, which is a double vessel; the outer section contains water, the inner contain the substance to be heated. She is also responsible for the oldest description of a still. See Patai, op. cit., p. 61.

32 Fowden, op. cit., p. 121.
33 ibid., p. 123.

2 Hermetic Magic, Alchemy and Islam

1 For a survey of the astrological magical cults of Harran see Baigent, *From the Omens of Babylon*, pp. 184ff.
2 Drijvers, 'Bardaisan of Edessa and the Hermetica', p. 209.
3 For Proclus see Siorvanes, *Proclus. Neo-Platonic Philosophy and Science*.
4 Tardieu, 'Sabiens Coraniques et "Sabiens" de Harran', pp. 13–18, 22–3.
5 Burnett, 'The Astrologer's Assay of the Alchemist', p. 103.
6 This story is given in *Hermetica*, trans. Scott, I, 97–101.
7 J. Wood Brown in 1897, quoted by Thorndike, *History of Magic and Experimental Science*, II, p. 814.
8 Garin, *Astrology in the Renaissance*, p. 49.
9 Pingree, 'Some of the Sources of the *Ghayat Al-Hakim*', p. 4.
10 Garin, op. cit., p. 51.
11 ibid.
12 Nasr, *Islamic Studies*, p. 76.
13 ibid., p. 69.
14 Affifi, 'The Influence of Hermetic Literature on Moslem Thought', p. 854.
15 Nasr, op. cit., p. 77.
16 Nasr, *Islamic Science*, p. 203.
17 ibid., p. 204.
18 Shah, *The Sufis*, p. 15.
19 Plessner, 'Geber and Jabir ibn Hayyan: An Authentic Sixteenth-century Quotation from Jabir', p. 115. Plessner is commenting upon a passage from Agrippa, who has had access to some work by Jabir which is no longer extant.

3 Dark Age Magic

1 Tacitus, *The Annals of Imperial Rome*, p. 327.

2 ibid.

3 Tolstoy, *The Quest for Merlin*, p. 29.

4 Gregory of Tours, *The History of the Franks*, VI, 35 (p. 365).

5 Augustine, *Letters of St Augustin*, no. 47, p. 293.

6 Bede, *A History of the English Church and People*, I, 30 (pp. 86–7).

7 For a detailed discussion of this process see Begg, *The Cult of the Black Virgin*.

8 Frazer, *The Golden Bough* (abridged edition), p. 162. Spelling modernized.

9 ibid.

10 MacRitchie, *Scottish Gypsies under the Stuarts*, pp. 57–8.

11 Chadwick, *Priscillian of Avila*, p. 2.

12 Kieckhefer, *Magic in the Middle Ages*, p. 54.

13 Brown, *The Cult of the Saints*, p. 4.

14 Le Mée, *Chant*, pp. 123–7.

15 Tyack, *A Book about Bells*, p. 59.

16 Morris, *Legends o' the Bells*, p. 30.

17 ibid.

4 Three Routes to Europe

1 Makki, M., 'The Political History of Al-Andalus', p. 40; in Jayyusi, *The Legacy of Muslim Spain*, vol. I.

2 See Hillenbrand, R., '"The Ornament of the World", Medieval Córdoba as a Cultural Centre', in Jayyusi, op. cit., pp. 112–35.

3 ibid., p. 115.

4 Ronay, *The Tartar Khan's Englishman*, pp. 29–30; quoting Matthew Paris.

5 ibid., p. 30.

6 ibid., p. 31.

7 ibid., p. 31.

8 See Fletcher, *The Quest for El Cid*, pp. 107ff.

9 Lomax, *The Reconquest of Spain*, p. 108.

10 Chadwick, *Priscillian of Avila*, p. 21; quoting Isidore of Seville.

11 ibid., p. 233.

12 Affifi, *The Mystical Philosophy of Muhyid Din-Ibnul Arabi*, p. 20.

13 Burnett, 'The Translating Activity in Medieval Spain', p. 1044; in Jayyusi, op. cit., vol. II, pp. 1,036–58. See also: Burnett, 'A Group of Arabic–Latin Translators Working in Northern Spain in the Mid-12th Century'; Thorndike, *A History of Magic and Experimental Science*, vol. II, pp. 66ff.

14 Burnett, 'The Translating Activity in Medieval Spain', p. 1,044; in Jayyusi, op. cit.

15 Socarras, *Alfonso X of Castile*, p. 121, n. 25.

16 For a comprehensive look at the Druse, see Abu-Izzeddin, *The Druzes*, 1984.

17 Masson, *Frederick II of Hohenstaufen*, p. 237.

18 ibid., p. 231.

5 Medieval Magi

1 Geoffrey of Monmouth, *History of the Kings of Britain*, p. 245.

2 Einhard, *The Life of Charlemagne*, iii, 25 (p. 79).

3 Augustine, *City of God*, p. 188.

4 Thorndike, *History of Magic and Experimental Science*, pp. 673, 689.

5 Smoller, summarizing Aquinas, in *History, Prophecy, and the Stars*, p. 31.

6 Smoller, op. cit., p. 32.

7 Boase, R., 'Arab Influences on European Love-poetry', pp. 461–2, in Jayyusi, *The Legacy of Muslim Spain*, I, pp. 457–82.

8 *Perlesvaus*, p. 25.

9 ibid.

10 ibid., p. 360.

11 Wolfram von Eschenbach, *Parzival*, ix, 469 (pp. 251–2).

12 ibid., p. 251, n. 11.

13 Sermoise, *Joan of Arc*, p. 13.

14 ibid., p. 39.

15 Thorndike, op. cit., II, p. 554–5.

16 ibid., p. 567.

17 ibid., p. 555.

18 Flamel, *His Exposition of the Hieroglyphical Figures*, p. 8.

19 ibid., p. 13.

20 ibid., pp. 15–16.

6 The Renaissance

1 Woodhouse, *George Gemistos Plethon*, p. 168.

2 Garin, *Astrology in the Renaissance*, p. 58.

3 Hankins, 'Cosimo de' Medici and the "Platonic Academy"', p. 150.

4 Ficino, *Letters*, I, p. 32 (no. 1).

5 ibid., p. 40 (no. 5).

6 Fowden, *The Egyptian Hermes*, p. 32.

7 Athanassakis, *The Orphic Hymns*, pp. 13–15 (no. 8).

8 Ficino, *The Book of Life*, p. 90.

9 ibid., p. 131.

10 ibid., p. 167.

7 The Spread of Hermetic Wisdom

1 Yates, *Ideas and Ideals in the North European Renaissance*, p. 185.

2 ibid., p. 187.

3 Yates, *Renaissance and Reform: the Italian Contribution*, p. 11.

4 ibid., p. 26.

5 Wirszubski, *Pico della Mirandola's Encounter with Jewish Mysticism*, pp. 5 and 11.

6 Idel, 'Hermeticism and Judaism', p. 67.

7 ibid., p. 66.

8 Pico della Mirandola, 'Oration on the Dignity of Man', p. 250.

9 ibid., p. 225.

10 Yates, *Giordano Bruno and the Hermetic Tradition*, p. 88.

11 Pico della Mirandola, op. cit., p. 249.
12 Yates, *Giordano Bruno and the Hermetic Tradition*, p. 107.
13 ibid., p. 111.
14 ibid., p. 116.
15 Lowry, *The World of Aldus Manutius*, p. 200.
16 Yates, *The Occult Philosophy in the Elizabethan Age*, pp. 24–5.
17 Lowry, op. cit., p. 264.
18 Yates, *The Occult Philosophy in the Elizabethan Age*, p. 30.
19 ibid.
20 ibid., p. 31.
21 Evans, *Rudolph II and His World*, p. 230.
22 ibid., p. 237.
23 *Fama Fraternitatis*, p. 28.
24 Churton, *The Golden Builders*, p. 92. In December 1611, the Paracelsian Adam Haslmayr sent a copy to Prince Augustus von Anhalt, who lived near Magdeburg in Schloss Plötzkau. He became an enthusiastic supporter of the Rosicrucian message.

8 Faustus

1 Baron, *Doctor Faustus from History to Legend*, p. 27.
2 ibid., p. 41.
3 ibid., p. 42.
4 ibid., pp. 13 and 48.
5 ibid., p. 13.
6 ibid., pp. 14–17.
7 ibid., p. 49.
8 ibid., p. 59.
9 Palmer and More, *The Sources of the Faust Tradition*, p. 91.
10 Baron, op. cit., p. 70.
11 Palmer and More, op. cit., p. 99.
12 Thorndike, *History of Magic and Experimental Science*, IV, pp. 524–5.
13 Yates, *Giordano Bruno and the Hermetic Tradition*, p. 145.
14 Thorndike, op. cit., V, p. 127.

15 Agrippa, *The Commendation of Matrimony*, pp. 33–4.

16 Agrippa, *Female Pre-eminence*, p. 79.

17 ibid., p. 78.

18 ibid., p. 82.

19 Agrippa, *Three Books of Occult Philosophy*, p. 460.

20 ibid., p. 329.

21 ibid., p. 354.

22 ibid., p. 3.

23 ibid., p. 48.

24 ibid., pp. 168–9.

25 Walker, *Spiritual and Demonic Magic*, p. 96.

26 Yates, *Ideas and Ideals in the North European Renaissance*, p. 262.

27 Yates, *Giordano Bruno and the Hermetic Tradition*, p. 141.

28 Quoted in Spence, *An Encyclopaedia of Occultism*, p. 315.

29 Paracelsus, *Hermetic and Alchemical Writings*, I, 'Tincture of the Philosophers', p. 21.

30 ibid., p. 19.

31 Pachter, *Paracelsus: Magic into Science*, pp. 152–3.

32 Paracelsus, *Hermetic and Alchemical Writings*, II, 'Alchemy: the Third Column of Medicine', p. 156.

33 ibid., 'The End of the Birth', p. 300.

34 ibid., p. 301.

35 Debus, *The English Paracelsians*, p. 14.

36 ibid., p. 20.

37 Paracelsus, op. cit., I, 'The Economy of Minerals', p. 99.

38 ibid., 'Concerning the Nature of Things', p. 189.

39 Quoted in Spence, op. cit., p. 315.

40 ibid.

41 *The Chemical Wedding of Christian Rosenkreutz*, p. 16.

42 Yates, *Theatre of the World*, p. 12.

43 French, *John Dee*, p. 63.

44 ibid., p. 179.

45 ibid., p. 180.

46 Yates, *The Occult Philosophy in the Elizabethan Age*, p. 156; see

also pp. 84–5.

47 ibid., pp. 88–9, 169–72.

48 Deacon, *John Dee*, p. 231.

49 Yates, *Theatre of the World*, p. 18.

50 French, op. cit., p. 19.

51 ibid., p. 56.

52 Yates, *Theatre of the World*, Appendix A, p. 194 (spelling modernized).

53 ibid., p. 196 (spelling modernized).

54 French, op. cit., p. 58.

55 ibid.

56 Yates, *Theatre of the World*, p. 18.

57 Yates, *Giordano Bruno and the Hermetic Tradition*, p. 197.

58 ibid., p. 211.

59 ibid., p. 214.

60 ibid., p. 213.

61 ibid., pp. 231–2.

62 ibid., pp. 312, 313, 320–21, 324.

63 ibid., p. 312, nn. 5 and 6.

64 ibid., pp. 273–4.

65 Yates, *Theatre of the World*, p. 46.

66 Fludd, *Essential Readings*, pp. 45ff.

67 ibid., p. 47.

68 ibid., p. 56.

69 Now held in the National Library of Scotland.

70 Yates, *The Art of Memory*, pp. 328–54.

71 Yates, *Theatre of the World*, pp. 51–2.

72 Inigo Jones, as a young man, may have studied under John Dee; he may also have travelled overseas, for a time, with Robert Fludd. Both returned to England in 1605. See Yates, *Theatre of the World*, pp. 82–3.

9 *Hermetic Thought and the Arts: the Talisman*

1 For a detailed exploration of this subject see Storr, *Music and*

the Mind, 1992; Robertson, *Music and the Mind*, 1996. The latter is a book published to accompany a Channel 4 Television series of the same name.

2 Walker, *Spiritual and Demonic Magic from Ficino to Campanella*, p. 14.

3 ibid.

4 Michell, *The Dimensions of Paradise*, p. 89.

5 Plato, *The Republic*, VII, vi; see also II, xvii.

6 *Hermetica*, XVIII; Copenhaver trans., p. 64.

7 *Asclepius*, 13; trans. by Fowden, *The Egyptian Hermes*, p. 102.

8 *Asclepius*, 38; in *Hermetica*, Copenhaver trans., p. 90.

9 Fowden, op. cit., pp. 118–19.

10 Walker, 'Musical Humanism in the 16th and Early 17th Centuries', p. 8.

11 See discussion in Donington, *The Rise of Opera*, pp. 34ff. He stresses the importance not only of the French poets of the Pléiade but also the rise of 'pastoral' dramas which were accompanied by music.

12 Ficino, *Letters*, 2, p. 66.

13 Walker, *Spiritual and Demonic Magic from Ficino to Campanella*, pp. 16–17.

14 ibid., p. 25.

15 Agrippa, *Three Books of Occult Philosophy*, I, lxxi (p. 156).

16 Ammann, 'The Musical Theory and Philosophy of Robert Fludd', p. 220.

17 ibid.

18 Agrippa, op. cit., II, xxviii (p. 278).

19 Read, *Prelude to Chemistry*, p. 250 (language modernized).

20 Khunrath, *Amphitheatrum sapientae aeternae*, ff. 15v–16r.

21 Ammann, op cit., p. 212.

22 ibid., pp. 198–9.

23 ibid., p. 212.

24 This is a central concept expounded in his *Utriusque cosmi historia*, 1617–18.

25 Elders, *Symbolic Scores*, p. 99.

26 See ibid., pp. 151–79.

27 Walker, *Spiritual and Demonic Magic from Ficino to Campanella*, p. 207.

28 Wittkower, *Architectural Principles in the Age of Humanism*, p. 103.

29 ibid., p. 100.

30 ibid., p. 103.

31 As put succinctly by Wittkower, ibid., pp. 103–4.

32 See the detailed analysis in Michell, op. cit., pp. 82–9.

33 For a comprehensive analysis of this painting see Wind, *Pagan Mysteries in the Renaissance*, pp. 125ff.; Yates, *Giordano Bruno and the Hermetic Tradition*, pp. 77–8; Snow-Smith, *The 'Primavera' of Sandro Botticelli*.

34 Wind, op. cit., p. 114.

35 Vitruvius, *On Architecture*, I, i, 3 (p. 9).

36 Wittkower, op. cit., p. 8.

37 Vitruvius, op. cit., I, ii, 4 (p. 27).

38 ibid., III, i, 1–4 (pp. 159–61).

39 Wittkower, op. cit., pp. 89 and 91.

40 ibid., p. 97.

41 Plato, *Timaeus*, 33 (p. 63).

42 Wittkower, op. cit., pp. 6–7.

43 ibid., p. 27.

44 ibid., pp. 27–8.

45 ibid., pp. 90–93.

46 ibid., p. 20.

47 ibid., p. 21.

48 ibid.

49 Taylor, 'Architecture and Magic', p. 85.

50 ibid., p. 81.

51 ibid., p. 90, n. 89.

52 Comito, *The Idea of the Garden in the Renaissance*, p. 78.

53 ibid., p. 162.

54 Strong, *The Renaissance Garden in England*, pp. 47–9; see also Yates, *Astraea*, pp. 59ff.; Yates (p. 79) quotes a couplet written after Elizabeth's death which 'seems to imply that the defunct Queen Elizabeth is now a second Blessed Virgin in heaven'. McLure and Wells in 'Elizabeth I as a Second Virgin Mary', p. 40, do not shrink from concluding that 'a mystical kinship between the Virgin Elizabeth and the Virgin Mary was central . . . to the cult of the English monarch . . .'

55 See the many illustrations of his automata in Caus, *Les Raisons des forces mouvantes*, 1623.

56 Strong, op. cit., p. 74.

57 Yates, *The Rosicrucian Enlightenment*, pp. 38–40.

58 Prest, *Garden of Eden*, p. 55.

59 Donington, *The Rise of Opera*, p. 36.

60 ibid.

61 Yates, *Ideas and Ideals in the North European Renaissance*, p. 125.

62 Yates, *Astraea*, p. 154.

63 ibid., p. 160.

64 ibid. The Guise family were the leaders of the Catholic League, which was opposed to the French King Henri III.

65 Yates, *The Occult Philosophy in the Elizabethan Age*, p. 107.

66 Donington, op. cit., p. 72.

67 Yates, *Theatre of the World*, p. 86.

68 Orgel, *The Illusion of Power*, p. 56.

69 ibid., p. 42.

70 Harris, Orgel and Strong, *The Kings Arcadia*, p. 35.

71 Orgel and Strong, *Inigo Jones*, p. 50.

72 Yates, *Theatre of the World*, p. 32.

73 ibid., p. 128.

74 ibid., pp. 134–5.

75 ibid., p. 189.

76 Quote from Yates, ibid., p. 172.

77 *Doctor Faustus*, I, i.

78 Frances Yates, in her *The Occult Philosophy in the Elizabethan*

Age, argues that both Shakespeare's King Lear (pp. 156–7) and Prospero (pp. 160–61) were portraits of John Dee.

79 The connection of Shakespeare with the John Dee/Sir Philip Sidney circle might be much closer than previously considered. A book published in 1665 stated that Fulke Greville, close friend of Sidney, was the patron of both Shakespeare and Ben Jonson. Fulke Greville had been with Sidney and Giordano Bruno when the latter visited England. Greville's family base was near Stratford-upon-Avon. Frances Yates speculates that when Shakespeare came to London as a young man 'he might have had access to Greville's house and circle . . .' See Yates, *The Art of Memory*, p. 309.

80 *As You Like It*, V, vii.

81 *The Tempest*, IV, i.

10 The Rise of Secret Societies

1 Godwin, *Athanasius Kircher*, p. 18.

2 Initiated 20 May 1641 into Scottish Lodge of Edinburgh, No. 1. See: Pick and Knight, *The Pocket History of Freemasonry*, p. 44.

3 See Yates, *The Rosicrucian Englightenment*, pp. 179–96.

4 ibid., p. 194. Yates points out that Leibniz's rules for his projected Order of Charity 'are practically a quotation from the *Fama*', one of the original Rosicrucian works.

5 Yates, *The Art of Memory*, p. 372.

6 Yates, *The Rosicrucian Enlightenment*, pp. 223–4.

7 Yates, *Ideas and Ideals in the North European Renaissance*, p. 64.

8 Eamon, *Science and the Secrets of Nature*, p. 324.

9 *Hermetica*, trans. Scott, p. 43.

10 Descartes, *Discourse on Method*, p. 29.

11 Naudé, *Instruction à la France sur la vérité de l'histoire des Frères de la Roze–Croix*, pp. 26–7.

12 Descartes, op. cit., pp. 32–3.

13 See Birch, *The History of the Royal Society of London*, Hartley,

ed., *The Royal Society*, and Purver and Bowen, *The Beginning of the Royal Society*.

14 See discussion in Baigent, 'Freemasonry, Hermetic Thought and the Royal Society of London'.

15 Dobbs, *The Foundations of Newton's Alchemy*, p. 6.

16 ibid., p. 12.

17 Dobbs gives a list of entries in the sale catalogue, ibid., pp. 235–48.

18 Keynes, 'Newton, the Man', pp. 27–9.

19 Dobbs, op. cit., p. 230.

20 Blake, 'Mock on, Mock on, Voltaire, Rousseau'.

21 Blake, 'Auguries of Innocence'.

11 The Fragmentation of Reality

1 *A Dictionary of Philosophy*, ed. A. Flew, London, 1984, p. 106.

2 Hooykaas, *Religion and the Rise of Science*, p. 66.

3 *Genesis*, i, 28.

4 Hooykaas, op. cit., p. 67.

5 See Goodricke-Clarke, N., *The Occult Roots of Nazism*, Wellingborough, 1985; Baigent, M., and Leigh, R., *Secret Germany*, London, 1994, pp. 240–50.

6 In 1934 the Curies voiced their alarm over this possibility; at a meeting in 1942 Edward Teller warned of the same danger; Robert Oppenheimer then agonized, 'Was there really any chance that an atomic bomb would trigger the explosion of the nitrogen in the atmosphere or the hydrogen in the ocean? This would be the ultimate catastrophe. Better to accept the slavery of the Nazis than to run a chance of drawing the final curtain on mankind.' See Rhodes, *The Making of the Atomic Bomb*, pp. 202–3, 418, 419.

7 *Bhagavad Gita*, 11, 12.

8 ibid., 11, 24.

9 Powers, *Heisenberg's War*, p. 464.

10 Wolpert, *The Unnatural Nature of Science*, p. 169.

11 ibid., p. 167.

12 ibid., p. 138.

12 *The Return to Unity*

1 Buranelli, *The Wizard from Vienna*, p. 119.

2 ibid.

3 Jung, *Psychological Reflections*, p. 350.

4 Jung, *Memories, Dreams, Reflections*, p. 114.

5 ibid., p. 87.

6 ibid., p. 232.

7 ibid., p. 154.

13 *The Rediscovery of Hermetic Thought*

1 Coleridge, *Biographia Literaria*, p. 141.

2 Flaubert, *Selected Letters of Gustave Flaubert*, p. 249.

3 ibid., p. 194.

4 Baudelaire, 'Correspondances' (translated under the title of 'Affinities').

5 Baudelaire, 'Alchemy of Sorrow'.

6 Rimbaud, *'Illuminations' and Other Prose Poems*, pp. xxx–xxxi.

7 Rimbaud, *A Season in Hell*, p. 51.

8 Yeats, 'Sailing to Byzantium'.

9 ibid.

10 ibid.

11 Joyce, *Portrait of the Artist as a Young Man*, p. 215.

12 ibid., p. 224–5.

13 Mann, *Confessions of Felix Krull, Confidence Man*, p. 227.

14 García Márquez, *One Hundred Years of Solitude*, pp. 421–2.

15 García Márquez, 'Blacamán the Good, Vendor of Miracles', *Leaf Storm*, pp. 119–20.

16 Eliot, 'Burnt Norton', in *Four Quartets*.

14 *The Magic Circle*

1 Paracelsus, *Hermetic and Alchemical Writings*, II, 'Alchemy: the

Third Column of Medicine', p. 156.

2 Eamon, *Science and the Secrets of Nature*, pp. 217–18.

15 *Music and Magic*

1 Booth, *Keith*, p. 152.

2 This and subsequent quotes from the concert at Altamont – unless otherwise attributed – come from the film *Gimme Shelter*, (c) by Maysles Films Inc., 1970, 1993.

3 Booth, op. cit., p. 152.

4 Bockris, *Keith Richards*, p. 163.

5 ibid., p. 165.

6 *Newsweek*, quoted in Bockris, op. cit., p. 167.

7 *Garcia*, p. 94.

8 Bockris, op. cit., p. 164.

9 Borges, *A Universal History of Infamy*, p. 19.

10 Gilfond, *Voodoo*, p. 3.

11 ibid., p. 5.

12 Hart, *Drumming at the Edge of Magic*, p. 224.

13 ibid., p. 225.

14 'Got My Mojo Working' by McKinley Morganfield (Muddy Waters).

15 'I'm Your Hoochie Coochie Man' by Willie Dixon.

16 Murray, *Crosstown Traffic*, p. 109.

17 'Low Down Rounder Blues' by Peg Leg Howell, see Taylor, *The Death and Ressurection Show*, p. 161.

18 Albertson, *Bessie*, pp. 106–7, quoting Carl Van Vechten, 'Memories of Bessie Smith' in *Jazz Records*, September 1947, p. 6.

19 Booth, op. cit., p. 189.

20 Hart, op. cit., p. 228.

21 Taylor, op. cit., p. 169.

22 ibid., p. 170.

23 ibid.

24 Taylor, op. cit., p. 202, quoting an interview in *Playboy*,

January 1981.

25 ibid., p. 205.

26 Densmore, *Riders of the Storm*, p. 144.

27 ibid., p. 114.

28 ibid., p. 208.

29 Turner, op. cit., p. 95.

30 'To Beat the Devil' by Kris Kristofferson.

31 Turner, op. cit., p. 120.

32 Danneman, *The Inner World of Jimi Hendrix*, p. 96.

33 ibid., p. 112.

34 ibid., p. 96.

35 ibid., p. 101, quoting Sue Clark, December 1969.

36 Turner, op. cit., p. 120.

37 ibid., p. 119.

38 ibid., p. 126.

16 The Rediscovery of Meaning

1 Beuys, *Joseph Beuys. Drawings*, p. 11.

2 Beuys, *In Memoriam Joseph Beuys*, p. 12.

3 ibid., p. 19.

4 Beuys, *Joseph Beuys. The Revolution is Us*, p. 9.

5 ibid.

6 Sime, 'Creating Places or Designing Spaces', in Groat, *Giving Places Meaning*, p. 30.

7 Norberg-Schulz, *Architecture: Meaning and Place*, p. 181.

8 Norberg-Schulz, *Genius Loci*, p. 168.

9 ibid., p. 190.

10 Norberg-Schulz, *Architecture: Meaning and Place*, p. 181.

11 Sime, op. cit., p. 32.

12 Norberg-Schulz, *Genius Loci*, p. 5.

13 ibid., p. 23.

14 ibid., p. 5.

15 ibid., p. 16.

16 ibid.

17 ibid., p. 23.
18 ibid.
19 ibid., p. 166.
20 ibid., pp. 197–8.
21 Masheck, *Building-Art*, p. 123.
22 HRH The Prince of Wales, *A Vision of Britain*, p. 10.
23 ibid., p. 103.
24 ibid., p. 78.
25 ibid., p. 82.

BIBLIOGRAPHY

Abu-Izzeddin, N. M., *The Druzes*, Leiden, 1984.

Acts of Peter, in *The Apocryphal New Testament*, trans. M. R. James, Oxford, 1986.

Addas, C., *Quest for the Red Sulpher. The Life of Ibn Arabi*, trans. P. Kingsley, Cambridge, 1993.

Affifi, A. E., *The Mystical Philosophy of Muhyid Din-Ibnul Arabi*, Cambridge, 1939.

Affifi, A. E., 'The Influence of Hermetic Literature on Moslem Thought', *Bulletin of the School of Oriental and African Studies*, XIII, 1951, pp. 840–55.

Agrippa, H. C., *The Commendation of Matrimony*, trans. D. Clapam, London, 1534.

Agrippa, H. C., *Three Books of Occult Philosophy*, trans. J.F., London, 1651 (Chthonios reprint 1986).

Agrippa, H. C., *Female Pre-eminence or the Dignity and Excellency of that Sex, above the Male*, trans. H. Care, London, 1670.

Albertson, C., *Bessie*, London, 1972.

Ammann, P.J., 'The Musical Theory and Philosophy of Robert Fludd', *Journal of the Warburg and Courtauld Institutes*, 30, 1967, pp. 198–227.

Ammianus Marcellinus, *The Roman History*, trans. C. D. Yonge, London, 1887.

Anastos, M. V., 'Pletho's Calendar and Liturgy', *Dumbarton Oaks Papers*, IV, 1948, pp. 183–305.

Anderson, W., *Green Man. The Archetype of Our Oneness with the Earth*, London, 1990.

Andreae, J. V., *The Chemical Wedding of Christian Rosenkreutz*, trans. J. Godwin, Grand Rapids, 1991.

Asclepius, see *Hermetica*.

Ashmole, E., *Theatrum Chemicum Britannicum*, London, 1652.

Ashmole, E., *The Diary and Will of Elias Ashmole*, ed. R. T. Gunther, Oxford, 1927.

Athanassakis, A. N., *The Orphic Hymns*, Atlanta, 1988.

Augustine, St, *Letters of St Augustin*, trans. J. G. Cunningham, in *A Select Library of the Nicene and Post-Nicene Fathers of the Christian Church*, vol. I, ed. P. Schaff, New York, 1892.

Augustine, St, *The City of God*, trans. Henry Bettenson, London, 1984.

Austin, R. W. J., *Sufis of Andalusia*, Sherborne, 1988.

Bacon, F., *The Advancement of Learning*, London, 1973.

Baigent, M., *From the Omens of Babylon*, London, 1994.

Baigent, M., 'Freemasonry, Hermetic Thought and the Royal Society of London', *Ars Quatuor Coronatorum*, 109, 1996.

Baigent, M., and Leigh, R., *The Dead Sea Scrolls Deception*, London, 1991.

Barber, R., *King Arthur in Legend and History*, Ipswich, 1974.

Baron, F., *Doctor Faustus from History to Legend*, Munich, 1978.

Bede, *A History of the English Church and People*, trans. Leo Shirley-Price, Harmondsworth, 1979.

Begg, E., *The Cult of the Black Virgin*, London, 1985.

Bernal, M., *Black Athena*, London, 1987.

Beuys, J., *Joseph Beuys. Drawings*, London, 1983.

Beuys, J., *In Memoriam Joseph Beuys*, Bonn, 1986.

Beuys, J., *Joseph Beuys. The Revolution is Us*, Liverpool, 1993.

The Bhagavad Gita, trans. J. Mascaró, Harmondsworth, 1985.

Biderman, A. D., *March to Calumny: the Story of American POWs in the Korean War*, New York, 1963.

Birch, T., *The History of the Royal Society of London*, 4 vols., London, 1756.

Blum, R., *Kallimachos. The Alexandrian Library and the Origins of Bibliography*, Madison, 1991.

Bockris, V., *Keith Richards*, Harmondsworth, 1993.

Bonwick, J., *Irish Druids and Old Irish Religions*, facsimile reprint, Dorset Press, 1986.

Booth, S., *Keith. Till I Roll Over Dead*, London, 1994.

Borges, J. L., *A Universal History of Infamy*, trans. N. T. Di Giovanni, London, 1973.

Bossy, J., *Giordano Bruno and the Embassy Affair*, New Haven, 1991.

Bowart, W., *Operation Mind Control*, London, 1978.

Bowman, A. K., *Egypt after the Pharaohs*, London, 1986.

Boyle, R., *The Sceptical Chymist*, London, 1911.

Broek, R. van den, and Vermaseren, M. J., *Studies in Gnosticism and Hellenistic Religions*, Leiden, 1981.

Brogan, H., *The Penguin History of the United States of America*, London, 1985.

Brown, P., *The Cult of the Saints*, London, 1981.

Browne, C. A., 'Rhetorical and Religious Aspects of Greek Alchemy', *Ambix*, 2, 1938, pp. 129–37.

Buranelli, V., *The Wizard from Vienna*, New York, 1975.

Burnett, C. S. F., 'The Legend of the Three Hermes and Abu Ma'Shar's *Kitab Al-Uluf* in the Latin Middle Ages', *Journal of the Warburg and Courtauld Institutes*, 39, 1976, pp. 231–4.

Burnett, C. S. F., 'A Group of Arabic–Latin Translators Working in Northern Spain in the Mid-12th Century', *Journal of the Royal Asiatic Society*, 1977, pp. 62–76.

Burnett, C. S. F., 'Herman of Carinthia and the *Kitab Al-Istamatis*: Further Evidence for the Transmission of Hermetic Magic', *Journal of the Warburg and Courtauld Institutes*, 44, 1981, pp. 167–9.

Burnett, C. S. F., 'The Astrologer's Assay of the Alchemist: Early References to Alchemy in Arabic and Latin Texts', *Ambix*, 39, 1992, pp. 103–9.

Burns, R. I., *The Worlds of Alfonso the Learned and James the Conqueror*, Princeton, 1985.

Butler, E. M., *The Myth of the Magus*, Cambridge, 1979.

Butterfield, H., *The Origins of Modern Science 1300–1800*, London, 1949.

The Cambridge History of Later Greek and Early Medieval Philosophy, ed. A. H. Armstrong, Cambridge, 1967.

Campion, N., *An Introduction to the History of Astrology*, London, 1982.

Campion, N., *The Great Year. Astrology, Millenarianism and History in the Western Tradition*, London, 1994.

Cassirer, E., Kristeller, P. O., and Randall, J. H., *The Renaissance Philosophy of Man*, Chicago, 1948.

Caus, S. de, *Les Raisons des forces mouvantes*, Paris, 1623.

Chadwick, H., *Priscillian of Avila*, Oxford, 1976.

The Chemical Wedding of Christian Rosenkreutz, trans. J. Godwin, Grand Rapids, 1991.

Chopra, D., *Quantum Healing*, New York, 1990.

Churton, Tobias, *The Golden Builders*, Lichfield, 2002.

Coleridge, S. T., *Biographia Literaria*, New York, 1967.

Comito, T., *The Idea of the Garden in the Renaissance*, Hassocks, 1979.

'Confessio Fraternitatis', see 'Fama Fraternitatis'.

Cornell, K., *The Symbolist Movement*, New Haven, 1951.

Corpus Hermeticum, see *Hermetica*.

Curran, J., and Gurevitch, M., *Mass Media and Society*, 2nd edn, London, 1996.

Deacon, R., *John Dee*, London, 1968.

Debus, A. G., *The English Paracelsians*, London, 1965.

Dee, J., *A True and Faithful Relation of What Passed for Many Years between Dr John Dee and Some Spirits*, ed. Meric Casaubon, London, 1659.

Dee, J., *The Private Diary of Dr John Dee*, ed. J. O. Halliwell, London, 1842.

Dee, J., *Essential Readings*, ed. G. Suster, London, 1986.

Dee, J., *The Heptarchia Mystica of John Dee*, ed. R. Turner, Wellingborough, 1986.

Densmore, J., *Riders on the Storm*, London, 1991.

Deren, M., *Divine Horsemen. The Living Gods of Haiti*, New York, 1953.

Descartes, R., *Discourse on Method*, trans. F. E. Sutcliffe, London, 1968.

Dichter, E., *The Strategy of Desire*, London, 1960.

Diogenes Laertius, *Lives of Eminent Philosophers*, trans. R. D. Hicks, 2 vols., London, 1925.

Dobbs, B. J. T., *The Foundations of Newton's Alchemy*, Cambridge, 1975.

Dodds, E. R., *Pagan and Christian in an Age of Anxiety*, Cambridge, 1990.

Donington, R., *The Rise of Opera*, London, 1981.

Drake-Brockman, H., *Voyage to Disaster*, London, 1964.

Drijvers, H., 'Bardaisan of Edessa and the Hermetica', *Jaarbericht van het Vooraziatisch-Egyptisch Genootschap Ex Oriente Lux*, XXI, 1970, pp. 190–210.

Durken, J., 'Alexander Dickson and S.T.C. 6823', *The Bibliotheck*, 3, 1952, no. 5, pp. 183–7.

Duveen, D. I., *Bibliotheca Alchemica et Chemica*, London, 1949.

Eamon, W., *Science and the Secrets of Nature*, Princeton, 1994.

Einhard, *The Life of Charlemagne*, Harmondsworth, 1979.

Eisenman, R. H., *James the Just in the Habbakkuk 'Pesher'*, Leiden, 1986.

Elders, W., *Symbolic Scores. Studies in the Music of the Renaissance*, Leiden, 1994.

Eliot, T. S., *Four Quartets*, New York, 1943.

Encyclopaedia of Islam, new edition, 8 vols., Leiden, 1954–95.

Encyclopaedia of Religion and Ethics, ed. J. Hastings, 13 vols., Edinburgh, 1908–26.

Evans, J., *The Ancient Stone Implements, Weapons and Ornaments of Great Britain*, 2nd rev. edn, 2 vols, London, 1897.

Evans, R. J. W., *Rudolph II and His World*, Oxford, 1984.

'Fama Fraternitatis' and 'Confessio Fraternitatis': The Fame and Confession of the Fraternity of R: C: Commonly of the Rosie Cross. Trans. Eugenius Philalethes, London, 1652. Facsimile edn, Margate, 1923.

Ficino, M., *The Letters of Marsilio Ficino*, 5 vols., London, 1975–95.

Finn, J., *The Bluesman*, London, 1986.

Flamel, N., *His Exposition of the Hieroglyphicall Figures*, ed. L. Dixon, New York, 1994.

Flaubert, G., *Selected Letters of Gustave Flaubert*, ed. F. Steegmuller, New York, 1953.

Fletcher, R., *The Quest for El Cid*, London, 1989.

Flint, V. I. J., *The Rise of Magic in Early Medieval Europe*, Oxford, 1991.

Fludd, R., *Essential Readings*, ed. W. H. Huffman, London, 1992.

Forey, A. J., *The Templars in the 'Corona de Aragón'*, London, 1973.

Fowden, G., *The Egyptian Hermes*, Cambridge, 1986.

Fraser, P. M., *Ptolemaic Alexandria*, Oxford, 1972.

Frazer, J. G., *The Golden Bough*, abridged edn, London, 1976.

French, P., *John Dee*, London, 1972.

Galbraith, J. K., *The Affluent Society*, 4th edn, London, 1985.

Garcia, by the Editors of *Rolling Stone*, London, 1996.

García Márquez, G., *One Hundred Years of Solitude*, trans. G. Rabassa, New York, 1970.

García Márquez, G., *Leaf Storm*, trans. G. Rabassa, New York, 1972.

Garin, E., *Astrology in the Renaissance*, London, 1983.

Geoffrey of Monmouth, *The History of the Kings of Britain*, trans.

L. Thorpe, London, 1969.

Geoghegan, D., 'A Licence of Henry VI to Practise Alchemy', *Ambix*, VI, 1957, pp. 10–17.

Gilfond, H., *Voodoo: Its Origins and Practices*, New York, 1976.

Gill, J., *The Council of Florence*, Cambridge, 1959.

Gill, J. S., 'How Hermes Trismegistus was Introduced to Renaissance England: The Influences of Caxton and Ficino's "Argumentum" on Baldwin and Palfreyman', *Journal of the Warburg and Courtauld Institutes*, 47, 1984, pp. 222–5.

Godwin, J., *Athanasius Kircher. A Renaissance Man and the Quest for Lost Knowledge*, London, 1979.

Godwin, J., *Harmonies of Heaven and Earth*, London, 1987.

Good, D. J., *Reconstructing the Tradition of Sophia in Gnostic Literature*, Atlanta, 1987.

Green, T. M., *The City of the Moon God. Religious Traditions of Harran*, Leiden, 1992.

Gregory of Tours, *The History of the Franks*, trans. Lewis Thorpe, Harmondsworth, 1977.

Grese, W. C., *Corpus Hermeticum XIII and Early Christian Literature*, Leiden, 1979.

Groat, L., ed., *Giving Places Meaning*, London, 1995.

Guinsburg, A. M., 'Henry More, Thomas Vaughan and the Late Renaissance Magical Tradition', *Ambix*, 27, 1980, pp. 36–58.

Haddow, A. J., 'Sir Robert Moray's Mark', *Year Book of the Grand Lodge of Scotland*, Edinburgh, 1970, pp. 76–80.

Hale, J., *The Civilization of Europe in the Renaissance*, London, 1993.

Hamarneh, S. K., 'Arabic–Islamic Alchemy – Three Intertwined Stages', *Ambix*, 29, 1982, pp. 74–87.

Hankins, J., 'Cosimo de' Medici and the "Platonic Academy"', *Journal of the Warburg and Courtauld Institutes*, 53, 1990, pp. 144–59.

Harris, J., Orgel, S., and Strong, R., *The Kings Arcadia: Inigo Jones and the Stuart Court*, London, 1973.

Hart, M., *Drumming at the Edge of Magic*, New York, 1990.

Hartley, H., ed., *The Royal Society. Its Origins and Founders*, London, 1960.

Haschmi, M. Y., 'The Beginning of Arab Alchemy', *Ambix*, 9, 1961, pp. 155–61.

Haskins, J., *Voodoo & Hoodoo*, Lanham (MD), 1990.

Haynes, A., *Invisible Power: The Elizabethan Secret Services*, Stroud, 1992.

Hermetica, ed. and trans. W. Scott, reprint, Boulder, 1982.

Hermetica, ed. and trans. B. P. Copenhaver, Cambridge, 1992.

Herodotus, *The Histories*, trans. A. de Sélincourt, Harmondsworth, 1981.

Hershbell, J. P., 'Democritus and the Beginnings of Greek Alchemy', *Ambix*, 34, 1987, pp. 5–20.

Heym, G., 'Al-Razi and Alchemy', *Ambix*, 1, 1937, pp. 184–91.

Hillgarth, J. N., *The Spanish Kingdoms, 1250–1516*, 2 vols., Oxford, 1976.

Holmyard, E. J., *Alchemy*, Harmondsworth, 1968.

Hooykaas, R., *Religion and the Rise of Modern Science*, Edinburgh, 1972.

Horkheimer, M., and Adorno, T. W., *Dialectic of Enlightenment*, trans. J. Cumming, London, 1973.

Huffman, W. H., *Robert Fludd and the End of the Renaissance*, London, 1988.

Hutin, S., *Les Disciples anglais de Jacob Boehme*, Paris, 1960.

The Hypnerotomachia, or The Dream of Poliphilus, ed. A. McLean, Edinburgh, 1986.

Iamblicus of Apamea, *On the Mysteries*, trans. Alexander Wilder, London, 1911, reissued by Chthonios Books, 1989.

Idel, M., *Kabbalah. New Perspectives*, New Haven, 1988.

Idel, M., 'Hermeticism and Judaism', in Merkel and Debus, *Hermeticism and the Renaissance*, 1988, pp. 59–76.

Irenaeus, *Against Heresies*, in *The Ante-Nicene Fathers*, vol. I, reprint, Grand Rapids, 1985.

Iversen, E., *Egyptian and Hermetic Doctrine*, Copenhagen, 1984.

Jacob, M. C., 'John Toland and the Newtonian Ideology', *Journal of the Warburg and Courtauld Institutes*, 32, 1969, pp. 307–31.

Jacob, M. C., *The Radical Enlightenment*, London, 1981.

James, M. R., ed., *The Apocryphal New Testament*, Oxford, 1986.

Jayyusi, S. K., ed., *The Legacy of Muslim Spain*, 2 vols. Leiden, 1994.

Jonas, H., *The Gnostic Religion*, Boston, 1963.

Josephus, *The Jewish War*, trans. G. A. Williamson, Harmondsworth, 1978.

Josten, C. H., 'William Backhouse of Swallowfield', *Ambix*, 4, 1949–51, pp. 1–33.

Joyce, J., *A Portrait of the Artist as a Young Man*, New York, 1961.

Jung, C. G., *Psychology and Alchemy*, trans. R. F. C. Hull, London, 1974.

Jung, C. G., *Memories, Dreams, Reflections*, trans. R. and C. Winston, London, 1979.

Jung, C. G., ed., *Man and His Symbols*, London, 1980.

Jungk, R., *Brighter than a Thousand Suns*, trans. J. Cleugh, London, 1958.

Justin Martyr, *The First Apology*, in *The Ante-Nicene Fathers*, vol. I, reprint, Grand Rapids, 1985.

Karpenko, V., 'Coins and Medals Made of Alchemical Metal', *Ambix*, 35, 1988, pp. 65–76.

Kepel, G., *The Revenge of God*, trans. Alan Braley, Cambridge, 1994.

Key, W. B., *Subliminal Ad-Ventures in Erotic Art*, Boston, 1992.

Keynes, J. M., 'Newton, the Man', in *The Royal Society Newton Tercentenary Celebrations*, Cambridge, 1947, pp. 27–34.

Khunrath, H., *Amphitheatrum sapientae aeternae*, Hanover, 1609.

Kieckhefer, R., *Magic in the Middle Ages*, Cambridge, 1989.

Kingsley, P., 'Poimandres: The Etymology of the Name and the Origins of the Hermetica', *Journal of the Warburg and Courtauld*

Institutes, 56, 1993, pp. 1–24.

Kingsley, P., 'From Pythagoras to the *Turba Philosophorum*: Egypt and the Pythagorean tradition', *Journal of the Warburg and Courtauld Institutes*, 57, 1994, pp. 1–13.

Kingsley, P., *Ancient Philosophy, Mystery and Magic*, Oxford, 1995.

Kinsey, J., 'The Use of Children in Advertising and the Impact of Advertising Aimed at Children', *International Journal of Advertising*, 6, 1987, pp. 169–77.

Klein-Franke, F., 'The Geomancy of Ahmad b.'Ali Zunbul. A Study of the Arabic Corpus Hermeticum', *Ambix*, 20, 1973, pp. 26–35.

Klibansky, R., *The Continuity of the Platonic Tradition during the Middle Ages*, London, 1939.

Kraemer, J. L., *Humanism in the Renaissance of Islam*, Leiden, 1986.

Kristeller, P. O., *Renaissance Concepts of Man*, New York, 1972.

Lawlor, R., *Sacred Geometry*, London, 1987.

Le Mée, K., *Chant*, London, 1994.

Lloyd, G. E. R., *Magic, Reason and Experience*, Cambridge, 1979.

Lindsay, J., *The Origins of Alchemy in Graeco-Roman Egypt*, London, 1970.

Lippmann, E. O. von, 'Some Remarks on Hermes and Hermetica', *Ambix*, 2, 1938, pp. 21–5.

Lomax, D. W., *The Reconquest of Spain*, London, 1978.

Lowry, M., *The World of Aldus Manutius*, Oxford, 1979.

Luhrmann, T. M., 'An Interpretation of the *Fama Fraternitatis* with Respect to Dee's *Monas Hieroglyphica*', *Ambix*, 33, 1986, pp. 1–10.

Lyon, D. M., *History of the Lodge of Edinburgh*, Edinburgh, 1873.

McClure, P., and Wells, R. H., 'Elizabeth I as a Second Virgin Mary', *Renaissance Studies*, 4, 1990, pp. 38–70.

McKie, D., 'The Origins and Foundation of the Royal Society of London', in Hartley, H., *The Royal Society. Its Origins and Founders*, London, 1960, pp. 1–37.

McLean, A., 'A Rosicrucian/Alchemical Mystery Centre in

Scotland', in *The Hermetic Journal*, 4, 1979, pp. 10–13.

MacKay, A., *Spain in the Middle Ages*, London, 1977.

MacRitchie, D., *Scottish Gypsies under the Stuarts*, Edinburgh, 19 84.

Mahdihassan, S., 'Early Terms for Elixir hitherto Unrecognized in Greek Alchemy', *Ambix*, 23, 1976, pp. 129–33.

Mann, T., *Confessions of Felix Krull, Confidence Man*, trans. H. T. Lowe-Porter, New York, 1955.

Marks, J., *The Search for the 'Manchurian Candidate'*, London, 1979.

Marquet, Y., 'Quelles furent les relations entre "Jabir Ibn Hayyan" et les Ihwan As-safa?', *Studia Islamica*, 64, 1984, pp. 39–51.

Masheck, J., *Building-Art: Modern Architecture under Cultural Construction*, Cambridge, 1993.

Masson, G., *Frederick II of Hohenstaufen*, London, 1973.

Matthews, J., *Robin Hood. Green Lord of the Wildwood*, Glastonbury, 1993.

Mead, G. R. S., *Simon Magus*, London, 1892.

Merkel, I., and Debus, A. G., *Hermeticism and the Renaissance*, Cranbury (NJ), 1988.

Merkur, D., 'The Study of Spiritual Alchemy: Mysticism, Gold-making, and Esoteric Hermeneutics', *Ambix*, 37, 1990, pp. 35–45.

Merrifield, R., *The Archaeology of Ritual and Magic*, London, 1987.

Michell, J., *The Dimensions of Paradise*, London, 1988.

Milne, J. G., 'Graeco-Egyptian Religion', in *Encyclopaedia of Religion and Ethics*, vol. 6, 1913, pp. 374–84.

Mookerji, R., *Asoka*, London, 1928.

Morley, H., *The Life of Henry Cornelius Agrippa von Nettesheim*, 2 vols., London, 1856.

Morris, E., *Legends o' the Bells*, London, 1935.

Morse, A. A., 'Commercial Speech as a Basic Freedom', *International Journal of Advertising*, 9, 1990, pp. 271–6.

Müller-Jahncke, W. D., 'The Attitude of Agrippe von Nettesheim (1486–1535) towards Alchemy', *Ambix*, 22, 1975, pp. 134–50.

Murray, C. S., *Crosstown Traffic: Jimi Hendrix and Post-war Pop*, London, 1990.

The Nag Hammadi Library in English, ed. James M. Robinson, Leiden, 1977.

Nakra, P., 'Zapping Nonsense: Should Television Media Planners Lose Sleep over It?', *International Journal of Advertising*, 10, 1991, pp. 217–22.

Nasr, S. H., *Islamic Studies*, Beirut, 1967.

Nasr, S. H., *Islamic Science*, London, 1976.

Nasr, S. H., *An Introduction to Islamic Cosmological Doctrines*, rev. edn, London, 1978.

Naudé, G., *Instruction à la France sur la vérité de l'histoire des Frères de la Roze-Croix*, Paris, 1623.

Netton, I. R., *Muslim Neoplatonists*, Edinburgh, 1991.

Newman, W., 'Prophecy and Alchemy: The Origin of Eirenaeus Philalethes', *Ambix*, 37, 1990, pp. 97–115.

Nicholl, C., *The Reckoning: The Murder of Christopher Marlowe*, London, 1992.

Norberg-Schulz, C., *Genius Loci. Towards a Phenomenology of Architecture*, London, 1980.

Norberg-Schulz, C., *Architecture: Meaning and Place*, New York, 1988.

Norwich, J. J., *The Normans in the South*, London, 1981.

Orgel, S., and Strong, R., *Inigo Jones. The Theatre of the Stuart Court*, 2 vols., Berkeley, 1973.

Orgel, S., *The Illusion of Power: Political Theatre in the English Renaissance*, Berkeley, 1975.

Oulton, J. E. L., and Chadwick, H., *Alexandrian Christianity*, London, 1954.

Outram, D., *The Enlightenment*, Cambridge, 1995.

Pachter, H. M., *Paracelsus: Magic into Science*, New York, 1951.

Packard, V., *The Hidden Persuaders*, Harmondsworth, 1991.

Palmer, P. M., and More, R. P., *The Sources of the Faust Tradition*, New York, 1936.

Palmer, R., *Dancing in the Street*, London, 1996.

Papathanassiou, M., 'Stephanus of Alexandria: Pharmaceutical Notions and Cosmology in His Alchemical Work', *Ambix*, 37, 1990, pp. 121–33.

Paracelsus, A. P. T. B., *Hermetic and Alchemical Writings*, ed. Arthur Edward Waite, 2 vols., London, 1894.

Parsons, E. A., *The Alexandrian Library*, London, 1952.

Patai, R., *The Jewish Alchemists*, Princeton, 1994.

Peacock, J., 'The Stuart Court Masque and the Theatre of the Greeks', *Journal of the Warburg and Courtauld Institutes*, 56, 1993, pp. 183–208.

Pearson, B. A., *Gnosticism, Judaism, and Egyptian Christianity*, Minneapolis, 1990.

Pennick, N., *The Ancient Science of Geomancy*, London, 1979.

The Perlesvaus, trans. S. Evans as *The High History of the Holy Grail*, Cambridge, 1969.

Pétrement, S., *A Separate God. The Christian Origins of Gnosticism*, trans. C. Harrison, London, 1991.

Pfeiffer, R., *History of Classical Scholarship from the Beginnings to the End of the Hellenistic Age*, Oxford, 1968.

Philo Judaeus, *On The Contemplative Life*, London, 1967.

Philostratus, *Life of Apollonius*, trans. C. P. Jones, Harmondsworth, 1970.

Pick, F. L., and Knight, G. N., *The Pocket History of Freemasonry*, 8th edn, 1991.

Pico della Mirandola, G., 'Oration on the Dignity of Man', trans. E. L. Forbes, in Cassirer, Kristeller and Randall, *The Renaissance Philosophy of Man*, Chicago, 1948, pp. 223–54.

Piggott, S., *The Druids*, Harmondsworth, 1977.

Pingree, D., 'Some of the Sources of the *Ghayat Al-Hakim*', *Journal of the Warburg and Courtauld Institutes*, 43, 1980, pp. 1–15.

Pingree, D., 'Between the *Ghaya* and *Picatrix*', *Journal of the Warburg and Courtauld Institutes*, 44, 1981, pp. 27–56.

Plato, *Timaeus*, trans. R. G. Bury, London, 1981.

Plato, *The Republic*, trans. P. Shorey, 2 vols., London, 1982.

Plessner, M., 'Hermes Trismegistus and Arab Science', *Studia Islamica*, 2, 1954, pp. 45–59.

Plessner, M., 'Geber and Jabir Ibn Hayyan: An Authentic Sixteenth-century Quotation from Jabir', *Ambix*, 16, 1969, pp. 113–18.

Plotinus, *Enneads*, trans. A. H. Armstrong, 7 vols., Cambridge (Mass.), 1966–88.

Porter, E., *Cambridgeshire Customs and Folklore*, London, 1969.

Powers, T., *Heisenberg's War: The Secret History of the German Bomb*, London, 1994.

Prest, J., *The Garden of Eden*, New Haven, 1981.

Preston, I. L., *The Tangled Web They Weave. Truth, Falsity and Advertisers*, Madison, 1994.

HRH The Prince of Wales, *A Vision of Britain*, London, 1989.

Principe, L. M., 'Robert Boyle's Alchemical Secrecy: Codes, Ciphers and Concealments', *Ambix*, 39, 1992, pp. 63–74.

Pritchard, A., 'Thomas Charnock's Book Dedicated to Queen Elizabeth', *Ambix*, 26, 1979, pp. 56–73.

Purver, M., and Bowen, E. J., *The Beginning of the Royal Society*, Oxford, 1960.

Radford, P. R., *Subliminal Persuasion: The Theoretical Possibilities of Persuasion without Awareness*, Dissertation, Sheffield City Polytechnic, 1983.

Radhakrishnan, S., ed., *History of Philosophy Eastern and Western*, London, 1952.

Ramsay, I., *Consumer Protection*, London, 1989.

Ranelagh, J., *The Agency: The Rise and Decline of the CIA*, London, 1986.

Read, J., *Prelude to Chemistry*, London, 1936.

Read, J., 'Alchemy under James IV of Scotland', *Ambix*, 2, 1938, pp. 60–7.

Reid, R. W., *Tongues of Conscience: War and the Scientist's Dilemma*, London, 1969.

Rimbaud, A., *'Illuminations' and Other Prose Poems*, trans. L. Varèse, New York, 1946.

Rimbaud, A., *A Season in Hell*, trans. L. Varèse, New York, 1961.

Robertson, A., *The Life of Sir Robert Moray*, London, 1922.

Robertson, P., *Music and the Mind*, London, 1996.

Ronay, G., *The Tartar Khan's Englishman*, London, 1978.

Rostovtzeff, M., *The Social and Economic History of the Hellenistic World*, 3 vols., Oxford, 1941.

Runciman, S., *A History of the Crusades*, 3 vols., Harmondsworth, 1971.

Runciman, S., *The Medieval Manichee*, Cambridge, 1984.

Schudson, M., *Advertising, the Uneasy Persuasion*, London, 1993.

Schuler, R. M., 'William Blomfild, Elizabethan Alchemist', *Ambix*, 20, 1973, pp. 77–87.

Segal, J. B., 'Pagan Syriac Monuments in the Vilayet of Urfa', *Anatolian Studies*, 3, 1953, pp. 97–119.

Segal, J. B., 'Some Syriac Inscriptions of the 2nd-3rd Century A.D.', *Bulletin of the School of Oriental and African Studies*, 16, 1954, pp. 13–36.

Sermoise, P. de, *Joan of Arc and her Secret Missions*, trans. J. Taylor, London, 1973.

Sheppard, H. J., 'Gnosticism and Alchemy', *Ambix*, 6, 1957, pp. 86–101.

Sheppard, H. J., 'The Redemption Theme and Hellenistic Alchemy', *Ambix*, 7, 1959, pp. 42–6.

Sheppard, H. J., 'Alchemy: Origin or Origins?', *Ambix*, 17, 1970, pp. 69–84.

Shirley, J. W., 'The Scientific Experiments of Sir Walter Ralegh, the Wizard Earl, and the Three Magi in the Tower 1603–1617', *Ambix*, 4, 1949–51, pp. 52–66.

Siorvanes, L., *Proclus. Neo-Platonic Philosophy and Science*, Edinburgh, 1996.

Smoller, L. A., *History Prophecy and the Stars*, Princeton, 1994.

Snow, C. P., *The Two Cultures and the Scientific Revolution*, Cambridge, 1959.

Snow-Smith, J., *The 'Primavera' of Sandro Botticelli: A Neoplatonic Interpretation*, New York, 1993.

Socarras, C. J., *Alfonso X of Castile: A Study on Imperialistic Frustration*, Barcelona, 1975.

Spence, L., *An Encyclopaedia of Occultism*, New York, 1960.

Stapleton, H. E., Lewis, G. L., and Taylor, F. S., 'The Sayings of Hermes Quoted in the *Ma' Al-Waraqi* of Ibn Umail', *Ambix*, 3, 1949, pp. 69–90.

Stevenson, D., *The Origins of Freemasonry*, Cambridge, 1988.

Storr, A., *Music and the Mind*, London, 1993.

Stoyanov, Y., *The Hidden Tradition in Europe*, London, 1994.

Strabo, *Geography*, trans. H. C. Hamilton and W. Falconer, 3 vols., London, 1854–57.

Strong, R., *The Renaissance Garden in England*, London, 1979.

Summerson, H., *Inigo Jones*, Harmondsworth, 1983.

Szulakowska, U., 'The Tree of Aristotle: Images of the Philosopher's Stone and Their Transference in Alchemy from the Fifteenth to the Twentieth Century', *Ambix*, 33, 1986, pp. 53–77.

Tacitus, *The Annals of Imperial Rome*, trans. Michael Grant, rev. edn, Harmondsworth, 1979.

Tardieu, M., 'Sabiens Coraniques et "Sabiens" de Harran', *Journal Asiatique*, 274, 1986, pp. 1–44.

Tarn, W. W., *Hellenistic Civilisation*, 3rd edn, London, 1952.

Taylor, F. S., 'The Origins of Greek Alchemy', *Ambix*, 1, 1937, pp. 30–47.

Taylor, F. S., 'Thomas Charnock', *Ambix*, 2, 1938, pp. 148–76.

Taylor, R., 'Architecture and Magic', in *Essays in the History of Architecture Presented to Rudolph Wittkower*, 2 vols., London, 1967.

Taylor, R. P., *The Death and Resurrection Show*, London, 1985.

Theissen, W. R., 'John Dastin's Letter on the Philosophers' Stone', *Ambix*, 33, 1986, pp. 81–7.

Theissen, W. R., 'John Dastin: The Alchemist as Co-creator', *Ambix*, 38, 1991, pp. 73–8.

Thomann, J., 'The Name Picatrix. Transcription or Translation?' in *Journal of the Warburg and Courtauld Institutes*, 53, 1990, pp. 289–96.

Thomas, G., *Journey into Madness. Medical Torture and the Mind Controllers*, London, 1988.

Thorndike, L., *A History of Magic and Experimental Science*, 8 vols., New York, 1923–58.

Thorndike, L., *Michael Scot*, London, 1965.

Thune, N., *The Behmenists and the Philadelphians*, Uppsala, 1948.

Tolstoy, N., *The Quest for Merlin*, London, 1985.

Turnbull, G. H., *Samuel Hartlib*, Oxford, 1920.

Turnbull, G. H., *Hartlib, Dury and Comenius*, London, 1947.

Turner, S., *Hungry for Heaven. Rock and Roll and the Search for Redemption*, rev. edn, London, 1995.

Tyack, G. S., *A Book about Bells*, London, 1898.

Vasari, G., *Lives of the Artists*, trans. George Bull, 2 vols., London, 1988.

Verbeke, W., 'Advertisers Do Not Persuade Consumers; They Create Societies around Their Brands to Maintain Power in the Marketplace', *International Journal of Advertising*, 11, 1992, pp. 1–13.

Vitruvius, *On Architecture*, trans. F. Granger, 2 vols., London, 1970.

Vleeschauwer, H.J. de, 'The Hellenistic Library', *Mousaion*, 71, 1963, pp. 50–99.

Wallis, R. T., ed., *Neoplatonism and Gnosticism*, Albany, 1992.

Walker, D. P., 'Musical Humanism in the 16th and Early 17th Centuries', *The Music Review*, 2–3, 1941–2, pp. 1–13, 111–21, 220–27, 288–308, 55–71.

Walker, D. P., *The Ancient Theology*, London, 1972.

Walker, D. P., *Spiritual and Demonic Magic from Ficino to Campanella*, London, 1975.

Walker, D. P., *Studies in Musical Science in the Late Renaissance*, London and Leiden, 1978.

Waterson, M.J., 'Advertising Facts and Advertising Illusions', *International Journal of Advertising*, 3, 1984, pp. 207–21.

Watt, W. M., and Cachia, P., *A History of Islamic Spain*, Edinburgh, 1977.

Webb, J., *The Flight from Reason*, London, 1971.

Welles, E. B., 'The Unpublished Alchemical Sonnets of Felice Feliciano: An Episode in Science and Humanism in 15th Century Italy', *Ambix*, 29, 1982, pp. 1–16.

Wellesz, E., 'Music in the Treatises of Greek Gnostics and Alchemists', *Ambix*, 4, 1949–51, pp. 145–58.

Westra, J. H., *From Athens to Chartres. Neoplatonism and Medieval Thought*, Leiden, 1992.

Wilkinson, R. H., *Symbol and Magic in Egyptian Art*, London, 1994.

Wilson, R. McL., *Nag Hammadi and Gnosis*, Leiden, 1978.

Wind, E., *Pagan Mysteries in the Renaissance*, rev. edn, London, 1980.

Wirszubski, C., *Pico della Mirandola's Encounter with Jewish Mysticism*, Cambridge (Mass.), 1989.

Wittkower, R., *Architectural Principles in the Age of Humanism*, London, 1949.

Wolfram von Eschenbach, *Parzival*, trans. H. M. Mustard and C. E. Passage, New York, 1961.

Wolpert, L., *The Unnatural Nature of Science*, London, 1992.

Woodhouse, C. M., *George Gemistos Plethon: The Last of the Hellenes*, Oxford, 1986.

Yamauchi, E. M., *Pre-Christian Gnosticism*, London, 1973.

Yates, F. A., *The Rosicrucian Enlightenment*, St Albans, 1973.

Yates, F. A., *The Art of Memory*, Harmondsworth, 1978.

Yates, F. A., *Giordano Bruno and the Hermetic Tradition*, London, 1978.

Yates, F. A., *The Occult Philosophy in the Elizabethan Age*, London, 1979.

Yates, F. A., *Lull & Bruno*, London, 1982.

Yates, F. A., *Renaissance and Reform: The Italian Contribution*, London, 1983.

Yates, F. A., *Ideas and Ideals in the North European Renaissance*, London, 1984.

Yates, F. A., *The Theatre of the World*, London, 1987.

Yeats, W. B., *The Poems*, Dublin, 1983.

Zabughin, V., *Giulio Pomponio Leto*, 2 vols., Rome, 1909–10.

INDEX